THE METROPOLIS

THE METROPOLIS
Its People, Politics, and Economic Life

FOURTH EDITION

John C. Bollens
University of California, Los Angeles

Henry J. Schmandt
Saint Louis University

HARPER & ROW, PUBLISHERS, New York
Cambridge, Philadelphia, San Francisco,
London, Mexico City, São Paulo, Sydney

1817

Photograph Credits

Cover: Howard Sochureck, Woodfin Camp; Chapter 1–3: John L. Michel; Chapter 4: Forsyth, Monkmeyer; Chapter 5: Skytta, Jeroboam; Chapter 6: American Airlines; Chapter 7: Shelton, Monkmeyer; Chapter 8: Johnson, DeWys; Chapter 9: Kiroual, Monkmeyer; Chapter 10: Beame, DPI; Chapter 11: Cron, Monkmeyer; Chapter 12: Johnson, DeWys; Chapter 13: Shelton, Monkmeyer; Chapter 14: Hoops, DeWys.

Sponsoring editor: John L. Michel
Project editor: Jo-Ann Goldfarb
Cover and text designer: Gayle Jaeger
Production manager: William Lane
Photo researcher: Mira Schachne
Compositor: David Seham Associates, Inc.
Printer and binder: Halliday Lithograph Corporation
Art studio: Vantage Art Inc.

THE METROPOLIS: Its People, Politics, and Economic Life, Fourth Edition
Copyright © 1982 by John C. Bollens and Henry J. Schmandt

Library of Congress Cataloging in Publication Data
Bollens, John Constantinus, Date-
   The metropolis, its people, politics, and economic life.

   Bibliography: p.
   Includes indexes.
   1. Metropolitan areas—United States. 2. Metropolitan government—United States.
I. Schmandt, Henry J., joint author. II. Title.
JS422.B6 1982   307.7'6'0973   80-27877
ISBN 0-06-040794-8

Contents

Preface

At the time the second edition of *The Metropolis* was written in the late 1960s the tranquility of many American cities had been shattered by militant activism and civil strife. The quest for human rights had moved from the legislative chambers and courts to the streets where it had been joined by the bitter opposition to the nation's military involvement in Southeast Asia. By the time the third edition appeared in 1975 the cities and campuses had become relatively peaceful, the Great Society programs adopted in response to the violence had been largely dismantled, and the country was not engaged in combat anywhere across the globe. National concerns had turned to the economy, inflation, energy, women's liberation, the environment, and Watergate.

As the nation proceeds into the 1980s many of the trends of the last decade have become more pronounced. Energy costs continue to escalate, industrial productivity shows little improvement, and the fiscal woes of the cities offer no signs of abatement. Contributing to the "urban predicament" are the tax rebellion, economic recession, regional population shifts, and the swing toward political conservatism so dramatically evidenced in the 1980 presidential and senatorial elections. Symbolic of the current era are Proposition 13 and other tax limitation measures, double-digit inflation, record interest rates, the Moral Majority, the near nuclear disaster at Three Mile Island, the Chrysler bailout by government, the revival of the Ku Klux Klan, acts of random violence, and single-issue politics. Developments abroad—the seizure of American hostages in Iran, the Iraq–Iran war, the invasion of Afghanistan by the Soviet Union and its opposition to the independent labor movement in Poland, the breakdown of détente—have dangerously heightened international tensions and are causing a greater share of the country's resources to be diverted to national defense. It is within this troubled setting that cities and metropolitan areas operate.

We have extensively revised *The Metropolis* to take account of the new developments and their impact on urban institutions and life-styles. As in the three previous editions our objective is to provide a comprehensive overview and analysis of American communities. We are concerned with their social and economic characteristics, their physical features, the manner in which they are organized and governed, the roles they play, the resources they have at their disposal, and the problems they face. Attention is focused primarily on the metropolitan community (the socioeconomic city) rather than on the municipality alone (the legally defined city). The incorporated entities and other local jurisdictions within individual SMSAs do not function in social, economic, or political isolation from one another. To portray them realistically requires that they be treated as interacting parts of the territorially more inclusive community.

No single conceptual theme dominates the book. Urban communities are the product of many forces that shape their behavior and affect the fortunes of their residents. They are far too complex to be subsumed under any one theory or thesis. Attempts to do so have the appeal of simplicity and ingenuity but run the inevitable risk of ending with questionable generalizations and dubious explanations. We have chosen to avoid such an approach—given the still early state of urban research—by examining American metropolises from varying analytical perspectives without trying to fit the subject onto some Procrustean bed.

This edition contains a number of substantive changes in addition to the updated material. The treatment of intergovernmental relations is substantially enlarged to reflect the growing dependence of local communities on higher levels of public authority. Added attention is paid to the revitalization of the older and distressed cities, a matter of increasing importance in an era calling for the conservation and efficient use of national resources. More consideration is given to the role of the courts as urban policymakers and to the position of women and other minorities in metropolitan society. And greater emphasis is placed on the differences (as well as similarities) that exist among SMSAs.

We are greatly indebted to the many scholars who have written so perceptively on various aspects of community life and to the public officials, professional administrators, civic leaders, and neighborhood organization workers who have shared with us their insights into urban reality. We are particularly grateful to Professors Dennis Judd, Albert R. Karnig, Thomas M. Scott, G. Ross Stephens, and Joseph Zimmerman, who provided us with detailed suggestions for improving this edition; and to our colleagues Frank Avesing, John T. Manns, George Otte, and George D. Wendel, who gave us invaluable advice and assistance at many stages in the revision.

We hope that this comprehensive analysis of urban America, drawing as it does on the work of many researchers, will contribute to a better understanding of cities and suburbs and will be of use to students in the social sciences and to government practitioners and concerned citizens in general.

John C. Bollens
Henry J. Schmandt

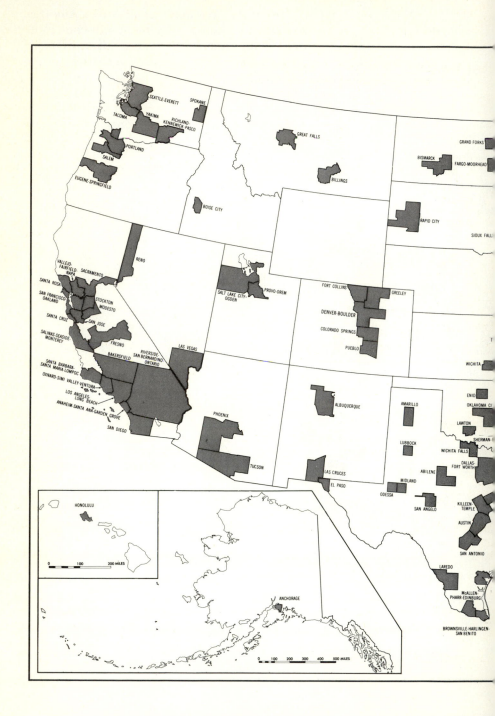

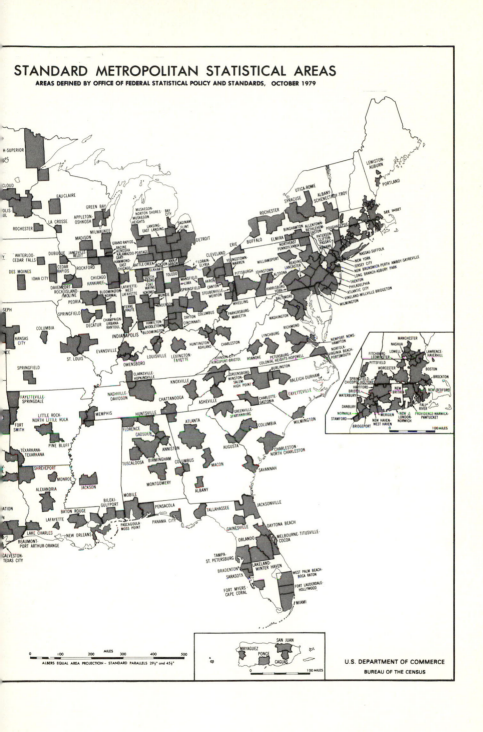

STANDARD METROPOLITAN STATISTICAL AREAS

AREAS DEFINED BY OFFICE OF FEDERAL STATISTICAL POLICY AND STANDARDS, OCTOBER 1979

U.S. DEPARTMENT OF COMMERCE
BUREAU OF THE CENSUS

ALBERS EQUAL AREA PROJECTION – STANDARD PARALLELS 29½° and 45½°

THE METROPOLIS

Chapter 1
Metropolitan America

The United States is a predominantly urbanized nation. Its farm population has shrunk to less than 8 million, whereas the number of its residents living in areas of 50,000 or more inhabitants is now in excess of 160 million. This transformation from a rural and agricultural people to an urban and industrialized society has created great centers of economic, social, and cultural activity and enabled Americans to achieve a standard of living equaled by few countries. But the metamorphosis has also brought problems—congestion, blight, environmental pollution, and rising crime rates among others—that sorely tax the capacity of governmental and private institutions to cope with them.

Urbanization, or the concentration of people in dense settlements, is not peculiar to the United States but is a worldwide phenomenon. In 1800 only 2 percent of the earth's inhabitants lived in cities of 20,000 or more; now the proportion is over one-third. Intensive urbanization is of relatively recent origin, beginning only after the Industrial Revolution. Before 1850 no country could be described as predominantly urban, and by 1900 only Great Britain could be referred to as such. Since then all the industrial powers have achieved this status and many of the developing nations are moving steadily in this direction (Figure 1.1).[1]

The most spectacular manifestations of urban growth are seen in the large human settlements scattered across the globe. A century ago there were only five urban areas with more than a million residents; today the number is approximately 150. Behind this phenomenal expansion is the "population explosion" that the world has experienced during the current century. From 1900 to the end of the 1970s, the number of global inhabitants almost tripled to an estimated total of 4.4 billion. During this period the fastest growth

[1]Kingsley Davis, "The Urbanization of the Human Population," *Scientific American* 213 (September 1965): 41–54. Davis distinguishes between urbanization (the proportion of the total population concentrated in human settlements) and urban growth (the increase in the number of city or town residents).

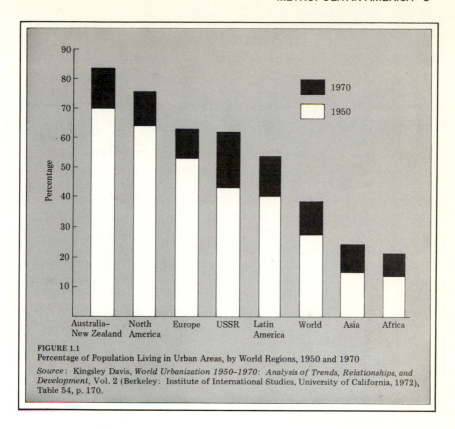

FIGURE 1.1
Percentage of Population Living in Urban Areas, by World Regions, 1950 and 1970
Source: Kingsley Davis, *World Urbanization 1950–1970: Analysis of Trends, Relationships, and Development*, Vol. 2 (Berkeley: Institute of International Studies, University of California, 1972), Table 54, p. 170.

shifted from the economically advanced countries of Europe and North America to the developing nations of Africa, Asia, and Latin America where three-fourths of the earth's populace now lives. Only recently, for the first time in history, has the world rate of increase shown a decline, dropping from a peak of 2.0 percent in 1966 to 1.9 percent in 1976. The principal reason for the slowdown is the declining birthrate, first evidenced in the industrially mature regions and now in the developing countries.

Population trends in the United States have followed the common pattern. In 1850 the number of inhabitants was only 23 million; by the turn of the century the total had more than tripled, and by 1980 it had exceeded 225 million. In recent years growth has dropped sharply because of a declining birth rate. During the "baby boom" of the 1950s, over 25 infants per 1000 people were born each year; presently the figure is about 15 per 1000. When deaths are taken into account, the natural increase in population plummeted from a high of 1.6 percent annually in the 1950s to an average of 0.7 percent during the last decade. This demographic change signaled the end of rampant population growth in this country and introduced a new dimension to the study of urban America.

FROM CITY TO METROPOLIS

The *Census of Governments* in 1977 listed nearly 19,000 incorporated places (cities, towns, and villages established as legal entities under general state enabling legislation or, in earlier cases, by special laws). As Table 1.1 shows, these municipalities range widely in size, with six having a population of over one million and the preponderant majority less than 2500 inhabitants. Further, more people live in incorporated places of between 10,000 and 50,000 than in cities of over one-half million. In fact, almost 50 percent of all municipal dwellers live in places of less than 50,000.

These statistics can be misleading unless put in proper perspective. Although they show that the majority of Americans are not big city dwellers, they fail to indicate that many of the smaller municipalities—and many unincorporated places as well—are parts of more extensive urban complexes. It is unrealistic, for instance, to refer to suburbanites in the New York or Chicago area as small-town dwellers even though they may reside in a community of 5,000 or 10,000. For the same reason it is a mistake to approach the study of cities without reference to the larger urban setting in which they function.

During the nation's first century of existence individual municipalities constituted the prevalent form of urban organization. Situated in relative isolation from each other, they accommodated increases in population and economic activity simply by enlarging

Table 1.1 MUNICIPALITIES BY POPULATION SIZE, 1977

POPULATION SIZE	NUMBER OF MUNICIPALITIES	POPULATION (IN MILLIONS)	PERCENTAGE OF TOTAL
1 million or more	6	17.9	13.1
500,000–1,000,000	17	11.4	8.3
250,000–500,000	35	12.3	9.0
100,000–250,000	105	14.9	10.9
50,000–100,000	230	16.1	11.8
10,000–50,000	1,726	37.0	27.1
2,500–10,000	3,465	17.3	12.6
Less than 2,500	13,278	9.8	7.2
Total	18,862	136.7	100.0

SOURCE: U.S. Bureau of the Census, "Governmental Organization," *Census of Governments: 1977*, Vol. 1 (Washington, D.C., 1978), p. 2.

their corporate boundaries whenever the need arose. The early growth of communities such as Chicago, Philadelphia, and Pittsburgh took place in this way. As a consequence, the spatial limits of the "socioeconomic city" (the area of day-to-day interaction) and the "political city" (the legally defined entity for governmental purposes) remained essentially coterminous. By the early 1900s, however, the single city area had begun to give way to the multicentered metropolis, as increasing numbers of people and businesses settled beyond the boundaries of the central municipality.

The Bureau of the Census gave recognition to this new development in 1910 when it introduced the category "metropolitan district" to its classification system.[2] The action was prompted by the need to develop a uniform means of collecting and reporting data for both large cities and their growing environs. At about the same time pioneers in the study of municipal government began to refer to "metropolises" in their writings, pointing out that the political boundaries of many of the larger municipalities no longer corresponded to the arena of shared activities and institutions.[3] This early attention to the changing character of urban areas helped to popularize the "metropolitan" concept and set the stage for the later (but largely unsuccessful) efforts to restructure the pattern of local government.

The Definition of Metropolitan

Three census-related terms are common to the discussion of cities and metropolitan areas: urban places, standard metropolitan statistical areas (SMSAs), and urbanized areas.[4] As defined by the Bureau of the Census, an *urban place* is a population concentration—either incorporated or unincorporated—of 2500 or more residents. Persons who live in such settlements are classified as urban dwellers; those who reside outside of them are categorized as rural. Under the census definition, three of every four people in the United States are now urbanites.

[2] A metropolitan district consisted of a central city and its suburbs with a combined population of at least 100,000.
[3] See, for example, Chester C. Maxey, *An Outline of Municipal Government* (Garden City, N.Y.: Doubleday, 1924), p. 120.
[4] A fourth commonly used term *suburban* or *suburbia* is not officially defined but is loosely employed for statistical purposes to include all portions of an SMSA that lie outside the central city. Thus when Census Bureau publications refer to the suburban population, they mean all persons in SMSAs living outside the core municipalities. Under this meaning, sparsely settled areas are included which we do not normally think of as suburban.

The term *standard metropolitan statistical area* was officially employed for the first time in the 1960 census, replacing earlier versions of metropolitan status.[5] Responsibility for establishing the qualifying criteria and designating the eligible areas now rests with the Office of Federal Statistical Policy and Standards in the Department of Commerce.[6] The requirements are detailed and technical, but basically an SMSA consists of a county containing a city of at least 50,000 inhabitants (or a population of this magnitude with a city of no less than 25,000 persons). It also includes neighboring counties that are closely linked to the central county by daily commuting and social and economic ties. (In New England, cities and towns rather than counties are the units used in defining SMSAs.) The definition provides for the inclusion of only entire counties so that federal agencies can use common political boundaries of a stable nature for collecting and publishing data. In this way comparable information can be made available from census to census.[7]

Not all metropolitan dwellers are classified as urban; those who live in sparsely settled sections (nonurban places) of SMSAs fall into the rural category. Incongruous as it may appear, almost one-third of the rural population in the United States resides in metropolitan areas, and only one-tenth of the total territory within these areas is urban in character. To take account of this anomaly, the Census Bureau established the category *urbanized areas* as units for data collection. These units comprise a city of at least 50,000 population plus contiguous, closely settled territory sometimes referred to as the "urban fringe." County lines and other governmental boundaries are ignored in defining urbanized areas.

Unlike SMSAs, urbanized areas exclude the rural portions of metropolitan counties. Thus they reflect more accurately the degree and extent of urban settlement but are less satisfactory for sta-

[5]The 1950 census replaced the metropolitan district category with the standard metropolitan area (SMA) definition that included entire counties. In 1960 the term was changed to standard metropolitan statistical area (SMSA) to give a better indication of the nature and purpose of the designation.
[6]This responsibility was formerly exercised by the Office of Management and Budget (OMB) in the Executive Office of the President but was transferred to the Department of Commerce in late 1977.
[7]A contiguous county is included in an SMSA if at least 70 percent of its resident labor force are engaged in nonagricultural work and at least 30 percent are employed in the central city. If a county does not meet the second of these requirements it may still be included, provided it falls within certain other criteria pertaining to both metropolitan character (degree of urbanization) and integration (worker commuting patterns). For a detailed description of the criteria see Office of Management and Budget, Statistical Policy Division, *Standard Metropolitan Statistical Areas, 1975,* rev. ed. (Washington, D.C., 1976).

tistical purposes, because their fluid boundaries do not readily permit comparisons from one point in time to another. (SMSA boundaries also change but only by the addition or subtraction of entire counties.) Largely for this reason the urbanized area category has not achieved the extensive use or popularity of the SMSA designation.

Criticism of the SMSA Definition

Although widely accepted and employed for many official and private purposes, the SMSA definition is not without its critics.[8] One of the more serious complaints is that the inclusion of entire counties distorts the concept of a metropolitan area as an urban community. San Bernardino, California, the central county of an SMSA, is an extreme example of this problem. Stretching some 180 miles east from Los Angeles County to the Nevada and Arizona state lines, it encompasses vast sections of sparsely populated and uninhabited desert land. In fact, one can drive from Los Angeles to the gambling and entertainment mecca of Las Vegas over many miles of open desert without ever leaving a metropolitan area. A similar example is the Reno, Nevada, SMSA which has a population of less than 150,000 but a land area (Washoe County) of 6,366 square miles, five times as large as the state of Rhode Island.

A second objection relates to the population size requirement which some observers say is too low. William A. Robson, a British political scientist, argues that the 50,000 minimum robs the word *metropolitan* of any political or sociological significance. He believes that only areas with a central city of at least 300,000 and a total population of not less than 400,000 should be included. Any smaller size, he contends, fails to take into account the functions to be performed by a metropolitan area worthy of the name, such as serving as a great governmental, commercial, or cultural center.[9]

Another criticism of the SMSA definition questions the validity of using precise spatial limits to identify metropolitan complexes. Planners John Friedmann and John Miller, for example, believe that current developments are producing a new ecological unit in

[8]Technical limitations of the SMSA definition are discussed in U.S. Bureau of the Census, "Metropolitan Area Definition: A Re-Evaluation of Concept and Statistical Practice," Working Paper No. 28 (Washington, D.C., 1969). See also Ira Rosenwaike, "A Critical Examination of the Designation of Standard Metropolitan Statistical Areas," *Social Forces* 48 (March 1972): 322–333.

[9]William A. Robson and D. E. Regan (eds.), *Great Cities of the World*, 3d ed. (London: Allen & Unwin, 1972), vol. 1, pp. 29–30.

the United States which they call an "urban field."[10] This unit contains a core area of at least 300,000 people plus all of the surrounding territory within a radius equivalent to a two-hour drive (approximately 100 miles) over modern expressways. As defined, about 90 percent of the nation's population and 35 percent of its land area would fall within such fields. This diffusion of the functioning urban community, according to Friedmann and Miller, is a natural continuation of the outward expansion from the nineteenth-century central city. The development of these fields, they say, will result in more extensive life space, broader choice of living environments, a wider community of interests, and a geographical spread of activities that will help revitalize the peripheral rural areas.

Melvin Webber, another planning theorist, goes a step beyond the urban field concept. He maintains that we are entering a post-city age in which urban society is replacing the geographic community and the nation, not the metropolis or even the region, is the new turf.[11] Underlying this transformation to a national city is the creation of a new social class which trades information and ideas across territorial and political boundaries and whose arena of interests and commitments is no longer the local or metropolitan community. Webber's concept of a city that transcends space is intellectually stimulating but too abstract to be of value in charting public policy or finding solutions to the problems associated with our population aggregations. Moreover, it downplays the fact that only a relatively minor portion of the citizenry fits into the category of the new social or cosmopolitan class to which it refers. For most Americans their turf—the place with which they most closely relate and identify—remains the neighborhood or local community.

Despite their abstractness, however, both the urban field and national city concepts reflect a certain reality. Metropolitan areas continue to expand territorially and in some instances to link up with each other, forming a continuous chain of urban development. Geographer Jean Gottmann speaks of "megalopolis," the vast urbanized area stretching along the northeastern seaboard from New Hampshire to Virginia.[12] Similar aggregations, although of lesser magnitude, are also forming along the Pacific coast from San Francisco to San Diego, around the Great Lakes, and from Jacksonville to Miami, Florida. In acknowledgment that metropolitan areas in

[10]"The Urban Field," *Journal of the American Institute of Planners* 31 (November 1965): 312–319.
[11]Melvin M. Webber et al., *Explorations in Urban Structure* (Philadelphia: University of Pennsylvania Press, 1964).
[12]Jean Gottmann, *Megalopolis: The Urbanized Northeastern Seaboard of the United States* (New York: Twentieth Century Fund, 1961).

many sections of the country are themselves becoming closely linked to each other socially and economically, the national government in 1975 added a new classification—standard consolidated statistical area (SCSA)—to the urban list. Such an area includes two or more contiguous SMSAs, one of which has a population of at least one million, that meet certain criteria relating to worker commuting patterns and overlapping or adjacent urbanized sections. By the end of the 1970s 13 areas, including those around Boston, Chicago, Detroit, Houston–Galveston, New York, and Seattle–Tacoma, had been designated SCSAs.[13]

SMSAs, it should be emphasized, are not legal entities (as municipalities and counties are) but statistical artifacts designed to provide common units for the collection and presentation of data. Yet it is well to recognize that they have taken on a meaning far beyond their statistical role. They represent the dominant form of urban organization in this country: the enlarged community that embraces the central city and the surrounding settlements. Even though they cannot be equated with bigness (their number includes places of relatively minor size such as La Crosse, Wisconsin, and Owensboro, Kentucky), they symbolize growth and vitality. Smaller areas eagerly welcome the SMSA designation because of the prestige it entails and the value it has for promotional and marketing purposes.

Beyond 1980

The 1980 census introduced a new set of terms and categories for the collection and aggregation of metropolitan area data. On the basis of criteria established by the Office of Federal Statistical Policy and Standards in the late 1970s, the familiar SMSA label and the less known SCSA classification have been replaced by three new designations: (1) metropolitan statistical area (MSA); (2) primary metropolitan statistical area (PMSA); and (3) consolidated metropolitan statistical area (CMSA).

MSAs include those relatively "freestanding" metropolises that are not contiguous to others and are typically surrounded by rural counties. More than two-thirds of the total number of existing SMSAs fall within this category. PMSAs consist of neighboring metropolitan areas that are closely linked to each other by economic and social ties, such as Dallas and Fort Worth. CMSAs are composed of two or more sets of adjoining PMSAs that form "mega-

---

[13]Previously two metropolitan concentrations—New York–Northeastern New Jersey, and Chicago–Northwestern Indiana—had been designated standard consolidated areas. This designation was superseded by the SCSA title.

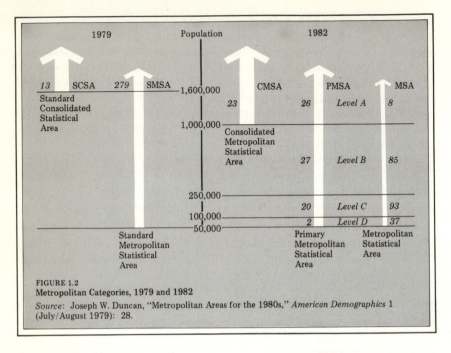

FIGURE 1.2
Metropolitan Categories, 1979 and 1982
Source: Joseph W. Duncan, "Metropolitan Areas for the 1980s," *American Demographics* 1 (July/August 1979): 28.

lopolitan" complexes. This category is the equivalent of the former SCSA classification.[14]

Although the Federal Committee on Standard Metropolitan Statistical Areas (which developed the criteria for the Commerce Department) gave some consideration to the criticism that the minimum population requirement for metropolitan status is unreasonably low, it rejected a higher threshold figure so as not to disqualify any existing SMSA. The new regulations instead introduce four levels of metropolitan areas—A, B, C, and D—based on population size (Figure 1.2). The establishment of these levels was prompted largely by feedback from census material users that it is desirable for some purposes to look at data for urban areas in relation to specific size categories.[15]

The changes in the criteria and regulations leave the fundamental concept of metropolitan areas untouched. They are de-

[14]We continue to employ the SMSA designation in this book because existing data are aggregated on this basis and the new terminology will not come into general use for at least several years.

[15]For a description of the new terms and definitions by the director of the Office of Federal Statistical Policy and Standards, see Joseph Duncan, "Metropolitan Areas for the 1980s," *American Demographics* 1 (July/August 1979): 25–32. The new criteria are summarized by Joseph Zimmerman in *National Civic Review* 69 (March 1980): 157–158.

signed primarily to make federal statistical data available in forms that will be more helpful for research, marketing, and policy-making purposes. However, the undue sensitivity to political factors shown by those responsible for formulating the new rules has resulted in unnecessary refinements and additional complexity. Labeling the size classifications by letters because of fear that pejorative connotations might be attached to descriptive designations is one example of this sensitivity; refusing to raise the size requirements for eligibility is another.

METROPOLITAN ATTRIBUTES

Metropolitan areas are communities in the sense that they constitute settlements of people living within a specified geographical space and interacting with each other in terms of daily needs. Few, if any, of them are communities in the classical meaning that their residents identify with the overall area, take pride in its features and accomplishments, and have strong feelings of commitment to it. The civic loyalties of metropolitan dwellers are more likely to run to the subcommunities—neighborhood, city, suburb—than to the larger complex.

Although SMSAs differ widely in population size, territorial extent, and economic base, they possess certain common attributes that distinguish them as a form of community. The most important of these qualities are decentralization, specialization, and interdependence. (A fourth major characteristic, governmental fragmentation, is discussed in Chapter 4.)

Decentralization

The first great expansion of civilization occurred when large numbers of people came together to form the preindustrial cities of the past. In this movement the city served as a container or magnet attracting people of the hinterlands into a centralized urban culture. Security, religious worship, and greater economic and social opportunities were among the factors that drew the isolated villager within the protective walls of the town. Until well into the nineteenth century most urban areas were territorially small, highly compact, and largely self-contained. They stood in visible relation and in stark contrast to their surrounding rural environs. Residents of even the largest community could travel on foot from one section or neighborhood to any other within a relatively short time. Marketplace, temple, work, and kinsfolk were within easy walking distance. Industry was confined to the home or small workshop around which revolved family, religious, and economic activities—all localized in a definable residential district.

In modern times the movement to the urban centers greatly accelerated, but unlike the compact container of the past the city, in Lewis Mumford's words, "burst open and scattered its complex organs and organizations over the entire landscape." This combination of centralization and deconcentration—the movement of people into the urban centers and the continuous dispersal within these areas—has resulted largely from the scientific and technological advances of the past century. Mechanization sparked the shift from farm to city and freed the nation from reliance on a predominantly agricultural economy. Since the early days of the Republic, American cities have grown faster than rural areas as surplus agricultural populations have been joined by migrants from foreign countries in the larger centers. The transformation that began in the nineteenth century was truly an "urban" revolution. It heralded the concentration of a large proportion of the population into areas of relatively limited territorial size. This change could not have occurred without the fantastic developments in public health, engineering, transportation, communication, and, most important, the rise of productive activity made possible by the power-operated factory.

The new modes of transportation and communication that emerged from the Industrial Revolution have permitted urban dwellers to settle far beyond the walls of the citadel. First the interurban railway and the horse-drawn tram, later the electric streetcar, and still later the private automobile eliminated the necessity of having home and place of work in close proximity. The advances in transportation and technology have also influenced factory location. Originally, industry was tied to the waterways and later to the railroads for its access to supplies and markets. (As late as 1910 there were more miles of railroads than highways in the United States.) This dependence has been lessened as the development of motor truck transportation, the national highway system, and the greater mobility of the labor force have opened up new locational opportunities.

Specialization

A second characteristic of the metropolitan community is the high degree of specialization found within its boundaries. This feature is reflected in land use as well as in commercial and industrial pursuits. Sections of every metropolis are devoted to various purposes—shopping centers, office sites, industrial parks, residential neighborhoods, and many other activities. Some suburbs, similar to sections of the central city, are entirely residential; a much smaller but still significant number are predominantly industrial; and still others contain varied combinations of factories, shops, and homes.

The division of labor that formerly characterized the compact city has now been extended to include a wide range of outlying settlement. New subcenters, closely linked to the core municipality and dependent on it for the more specialized and integrating functions, have multiplied in recent decades. In addition, long-established communities on the periphery have been drawn into the orbit of the central city and its sphere of economic influence. These include settlements that formerly served as local trading posts for the adjacent farm areas; industrial satellites that had been established on railroads and waterways some distance from the central municipality; and wealthy dormitory suburbs peopled by the railroad commuters at the turn of the present century.

Interdependence

One of the consequences of specialization is interdependence. Just as occupational diversity increases the number of individuals and firms on which urbanites must depend for their needs, so the spatial separation of activities enlarges the reliance of metropolitan subcommunities on each other. Most suburbs look to other sections of the area for at least a portion of such basic requirements as food, clothing, newspapers, entertainment, and hospitalization. They must also depend on other sections of the area, some of them as far distant as 30 or 40 miles, for the employment opportunities necessary to support many of their inhabitants. Conversely, the central city must rely on the outlying suburbs for a substantial portion of its labor force, including middle and top management. The people of the metropolis, in short, share a common spatial area for their daily activities. Within this arena an intricate web of business and social interrelationships exists and a high degree of communication and interchange continually takes place.

The close interrelations within a metropolitan area are reflected in many ways other than the work–residence pattern and the territorial division of labor. They are evidenced by the numerous private and semipublic organizations crossing local governmental boundaries: the community chest, professional and trade organizations, labor unions, social clubs, and the many other groups that are established and operate on an areawide basis. They are demonstrated by the privately owned utilities—telephone, electric, gas—organized to serve the total metropolis. They are manifested in the social and cultural fabric of the larger community: the symphony that is supported by central city dwellers and suburbanites alike; the urban university that provides educational opportunities for area residents; the medical facility that ministers to the specialized health needs of the metropolis; the professional sports team that elicits the loyalty of fans throughout the area. Despite the obviousness of this interdependence, it is difficult for individuals to identify their primary self-interests with a mosaic of diverse units covering many square miles. To most urbanites the concept of "metropolitan" citizenship has little concrete meaning.[16]

PATTERN OF GROWTH

Until well into the nineteenth century the United States was predominantly a rural nation. At the time of the first federal census in 1790, only 24 urban places of 2500 or more inhabitants existed (the total now exceeds 7000) and they contained less than 5 percent of the population (Figure 1.3). Not before the second decade of the present century did the number of Americans living in urban places surpass the rural total, and not until the 1930s did metropolitan dwellers become a majority.

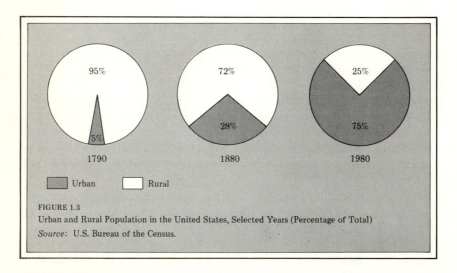

FIGURE 1.3
Urban and Rural Population in the United States, Selected Years (Percentage of Total)
Source: U.S. Bureau of the Census.

---

[16]One of the major objectives of the Metropolitan Fund, a prominent civic organization in Detroit, has been the promotion of the "metropolitan citizenship" concept. See Kent Mathewson, "A Regional Ethic," in Kent Mathewson (ed.), *The Regionalist Papers*, 2d ed. (Southfield, Mich.: Metropolitan Fund, 1978), pp. 5–15.

Table 1.2   METROPOLITAN AREA POPULATION, 1940–1977

YEAR	NUMBER OF SMSAs	POPULATION (IN THOUSANDS)	PERCENT CHANGE	SMSA POPULATION AS PERCENTAGE OF U.S. POPULATION	SMSA LAND AREA AS PERCENTAGE OF U.S. TOTAL
1940	168	69,279*	—	52.6	7.0
1950	168	84,501†	22.0	56.1	7.0
1960	209	112,885†	33.6	63.0	8.7
1970	243	137,058†	21.4	68.6	11.0
1977	264	153,087‡	11.7	72.0	13.8

*Contained in SMSAs as defined in 1950
†As defined in year shown
‡As defined in 1974
(Because of continuing changes in the number and territorial extent of SMSAs, Census Bureau reports presenting aggregate metropolitan area data employ different bases for computational purposes. This fact should be kept in mind when making comparisons between two points in time.)
SOURCE: U.S. Bureau of the Census, "Social and Economic Characteristics of the Metropolitan and Nonmetropolitan Population, 1977 and 1970," *Current Population Reports,* Special Studies P-23, No. 75 (Washington, D.C., 1978), p. 2.

The original 168 standard metropolitan areas designated in 1950 contained 56 percent of the country's population. Twenty years later the proportion had risen to almost 69 percent and by 1977 to 72 percent. We should note in citing these figures that changes in the percentage of inhabitants characterized as metropolitan depend not only on natural increase (excess of births over deaths) and net inmigration (persons moving into such areas less those leaving) but also on additions to the territory defined as metropolitan. When this territory is excluded from the computation, the ratio of SMSA dwellers to the total population declined slightly from 1970 to 1977. In other words, the rise of 3.4 percent shown in Table 1.2 for this period was not due to population growth within SMSAs as they were delineated in 1970 but to the designation of new metropolitan entities and the addition of counties to already established areas (almost 10 million people were added in this way).[17]

The 279 SMSAs existing in 1978 (an increase of 36 since the beginning of the decade) range in size from Meriden, Connecticut, with 55,000 inhabitants to New York with over 9 million. Thirty-six of the SMSAs have in excess of one million residents, and 25 are below 100,000. Two-thirds of the metropolitan complexes have populations of between 100,000 and 500,000. The seven with over 3

[17]Most population statistics cited for years after 1970 represent Census Bureau estimates based on sampling.

Table 1.3 NUMBER OF SMSAs BY POPULATION SIZE, 1970 AND 1978

SIZE CATEGORY	NUMBER OF SMSAs 1970*	PERCENTAGE OF SMSA POPULATION 1970	NUMBER OF SMSAs 1978†	PERCENTAGE OF SMSA POPULATION 1978
3 million or more	6	27.0	7‡	24.6
1 to 3 million	27	30.9	29	31.2
500,000 to 1 million	32	15.7	36	16.1
250,000 to 500,000	60	14.2	72	15.8
100,000 to 250,000	92	10.7	110	11.0
Less than 100,000	26	1.5	25	1.3
Total	243	100.0	279	100.0

*As defined in 1970.
†As defined in 1978.
‡Since 1978, an eighth SMSA has surpassed the 3 million mark.
SOURCE: U.S. Bureau of the Census, *Statistical Abstract of the United States 1979* (Washington, D.C., 1979), p. 17.

million inhabitants contain 18 percent of the nation's people and one-fourth of its metropolitan dwellers. Those over one million are the places of residence for 40 percent of all Americans and well over one-half of the SMSA population (Table 1.3).

The land area included within metropolitan boundaries has also expanded substantially during the last quarter century. This growth is due to both the emergence of new SMSAs and the territorial enlargement of existing complexes. Even with this gain, however, SMSAs collectively occupy only about 14 percent of the land area in the United States. Their density is more than six times that of the nonmetropolitan sections of the country. The central cities are by far the most compactly settled, the average number of inhabitants per square mile being 22 times that of the suburbs.

Despite the large increase in the metropolitan population, density in most SMSAs has been materially reduced. With people leaving the core municipality and spreading out over the suburban landscape, the overall ratio in urbanized areas has dropped during recent decades in both the SMSAs as a whole and the central cities, the decline in the latter being particularly great. The borough of Manhattan, the most crowded section of real estate in America, provides one of the more dramatic examples of this development. In 1910 over 100,000 persons per square mile lived within its boundaries; today the number is less than 65,000.

Regional and State Variations

Although metropolitanism is a national phenomenon, its magnitude and extent vary among regions and states. The Northeast is the most highly urbanized with 83 percent of its population living in SMSAs.

The proportion in the West is 80 percent, the North Central region (also referred to as the Midwest) 68 percent, and the South 63 percent (Figure 1.4). During the last several decades the South has shown the greatest growth in its metropolitan population. As late as 1960, less than half of its inhabitants resided in SMSAs; now the proportion is approaching two-thirds.

Census reports graphically document the direction of growth. From 1970 to 1977 the number of metropolitan dwellers in the South rose by one-fourth and in the West by one-seventh. These gains contrast to the less than 5 percent growth recorded in the other two regions (Table 1.4). The magnitude of the increases in the South and West is due principally to the large-scale migration of people and economic enterprises to the "Sunbelt" (the southern perimeter of states that extends from North Carolina to California). Since 1970 approximately 40 percent of the total population expansion in the United States has taken place in three of these states: Florida, California, and Texas. The full economic and political implications of this development are yet to be felt.

SMSAs exist in all states (and the District of Columbia) with the exception of Vermont and Wyoming. Slightly over 100 of them consist of a single county: the remainder contain from 2 to as many as 15. Thirty-nine also cross state lines—the Cincinnati SMSA, for example, includes counties in Ohio, Kentucky, and Indiana. A number of others that border state lines are interstate in impact although not in formal designation. Five SMSAs, moreover, have an international character because they adjoin substantial urban settlements in other countries. They include the Detroit SMSA which borders Windsor, Canada; Buffalo which is adjacent to Niagara Falls, Canada; and three areas that lie across from Mexican cities: San Diego

Table 1.4 METROPOLITAN POPULATION CHANGE BY REGION, 1970 TO 1977

REGION	POPULATION 1970* (IN THOUSANDS)	POPULATION 1977† (IN THOUSANDS)	PERCENT CHANGE 1970 TO 1977
Northeast	38,675	40,443	4.6
North Central	37,173	38,970	4.8
South	34,416	43,066	25.1
West	26,794	30,608	14.2
U.S. total	137,058	153,087	11.7

*Based on 243 SMSAs as defined in 1970. Totals adjusted to exclude institutional inmates and members of armed forces for comparability with 1977 data.
†Based on 264 SMSAs as defined in 1974.
SOURCE: U.S. Bureau of the Census, "Social and Economic Characteristics of the Metropolitan and Nonmetropolitan Population, 1977 and 1970," *Current Population Reports,* Special Studies, P-23, No. 75 (Washington, D.C. 1978), pp. 30, 31.

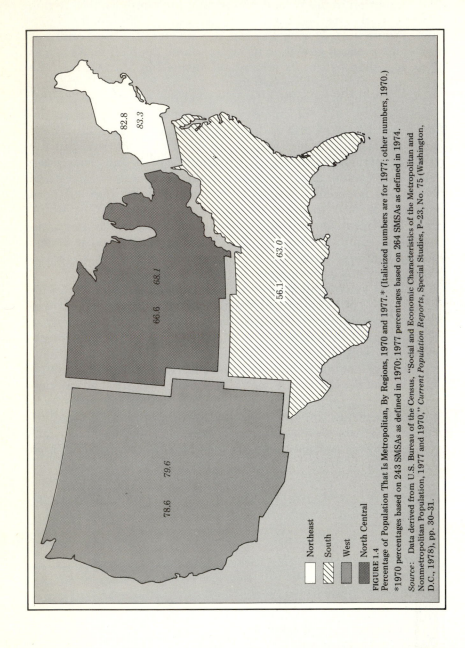

FIGURE 1.4

Percentage of Population That Is Metropolitan, By Regions, 1970 and 1977.* (Italicized numbers are for 1977; other numbers, 1970.)

*1970 percentages based on 243 SMSAs as defined in 1970; 1977 percentages based on 264 SMSAs as defined in 1974.

Source: Data derived from U.S. Bureau of the Census, "Social and Economic Characteristics of the Metropolitan and Nonmetropolitan Population, 1977 and 1970," *Current Population Reports,* Special Studies, P-23, No. 75 (Washington, D.C., 1978), pp. 30–31.

Northeast

South

West

North Central

82.8
83.3

56.1
63.0

66.6 68.1

78.6
79.6

from Tijuana, El Paso from Ciudad Juarez, and Laredo from Nuevo Laredo.

The Central City Exodus

The suburban movement in the United States began around a few large cities in the late nineteenth century but its extent remained relatively small for several more decades. As late as 1920, two-thirds of the metropolitan population lived in central cities. In 1960 the distribution was nearly equal between city and fringe area; by 1980 the suburban proportion had risen to almost 60 percent. Related to the national scene, this means that two of every five Americans are now suburbanites. It also means that central city dwellers presently constitute only 28 percent of the total number of residents in the United States (Figure 1.5).

The degree of suburbanization, like other aspects of the metropolitan scene, varies widely among individual areas. In San Antonio, for example, less than one-third of the SMSA population lives outside the central city, whereas in Johnstown, Pennsylvania, more than four-fifths reside in the outlying communities. The core municipalities remain the most populous sections in about half of the SMSAs, mainly those of smaller size. Among the 20 largest metropolises, all of more than 1.5 million population, the distribution of

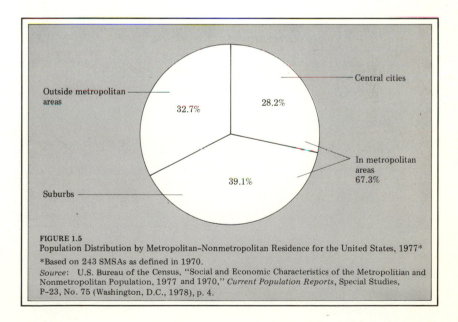

FIGURE 1.5
Population Distribution by Metropolitan–Nonmetropolitan Residence for the United States, 1977*
*Based on 243 SMSAs as defined in 1970.
Source: U.S. Bureau of the Census, "Social and Economic Characteristics of the Metropolitian and Nonmetropolitan Population, 1977 and 1970," *Current Population Reports*, Special Studies, P–23, No. 75 (Washington, D.C., 1978), p. 4.

residents predominantly favors the suburbs. Only in two instances where special circumstances prevail do central city dwellers outnumber their fringe area counterparts—in New York with its huge concentration of households in the five boroughs, and Houston where the major municipality through annexation has more than tripled its territorial size since 1950 (Figure 1.6).

The flight from the central cities continued throughout the 1970s despite sharply rising energy and housing costs and a shortage of gasoline. The big cities were the hardest hit, particularly the older manufacturing centers founded during the nineteenth cen-

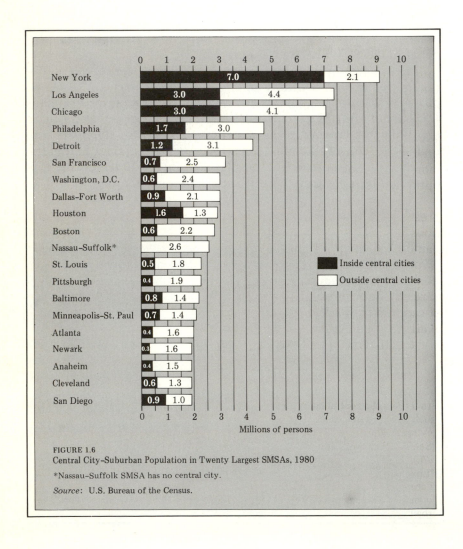

FIGURE 1.6
Central City–Suburban Population in Twenty Largest SMSAs, 1980

*Nassau–Suffolk SMSA has no central city.

Source: U.S. Bureau of the Census.

tury. Of the 30 largest municipalities, 18 lost population during the last decennial period. According to the 1980 census tabulations, St. Louis, Cleveland, and Detroit suffered declines of more than 20 percent, and Pittsburgh and Washington, D.C. over 15 percent. Although all but two of the gainers are located in the South and West, the pattern of central city loss was also evident in these regions.[18] Atlanta, for example, was down by almost 15 percent and Seattle, San Francisco, New Orleans, and Denver by more than 5 percent. Outmigration in the South and West, however, represents primarily a relocation to the suburbs; in other sections of the country a significant number of the moves are across regional boundaries or to nonmetropolitan areas.[19]

Back-to-the-City Movement

Pertinent to the question of flight from the core municipalities is the so-called "back-to-the-city" movement that has been the subject of considerable publicity in recent years. Pointing to the rehabilitation of various inner-city neighborhoods as proof of this inward trend, some of the more enthusiastic commentators have hailed the development as the beginning of central city revival. A more sober look at the evidence, however, fails to substantiate this optimistic appraisal.

The movement back to the core cities, such as it is, finds expression in three sets of activities: the efforts of locality organizations to stabilize their residential environs, gentrification, and urban homesteading.[20] Under the first category a substantial number of neighborhood groups have established not-for-profit corporations to purchase and rehabilitate deteriorating dwelling units and to resell them to responsible families. Because of the large amounts of capital required for this purpose, the quantity of housing made available by neighborhood initiative has been relatively small.

Gentrification, a term borrowed from the British, refers to the

[18]In most of the central cities that continue to show substantial population increases, much (and in some cases all) of the gain is due to the annexation of suburban territory rather than internal growth.

[19]See Thomas Muller, "Urban Growth and Decline," *Challenge* 19 (May/June 1976): 10–13.

[20]Luxury apartments in and around central business districts also constitute a source of attraction for the more affluent retirees and young professionals who work in the downtown area. Many of these units were constructed on land made available by urban renewal projects.

return of affluent householders to the inner city where they buy and restore old residences. (The process at times arouses the opposition of neighborhood organizations but in a majority of cases it proceeds with their blessing and encouragement.) Most targets of gentrification are the formerly prestigious or architecturally significant neighborhoods of the city, such as Philadelphia's Queen Village, St. Louis' Soulard Market, Washington's Capitol Hill, and Baltimore's Charles Village. One of the charges leveled against this practice is that it displaces poor and elderly residents for the benefit of the wealthy. Supporters maintain, however, that the housing, if left unrestored, would soon be lost to the private market because of lack of maintenance and continued deterioration.

Urban homesteading is based on the historical analogy of the Homestead Act of 1862 which authorized the sale of 160 acres of the public domain for a nominal sum to each household that would establish residence on the land and bring it under cultivation. Under the modern version of homesteading, the city sells abandoned dwelling units (taken over for tax delinquency or acquired by the Department of Housing and Urban Development [HUD] through mortgage foreclosures) for a nominal payment (usually $1) on condition that the purchaser occupy the premises for a specific period of time and bring it up to code standards. Unlike gentrification, urban homesteading is confined mainly to the less desirable sections of the city that enjoy no particular historic distinction and where families of modest means lived in the past. The new "pioneers," moreover, are mostly enterprising young people with present incomes substantially less than the gentry.[21]

Although gentrification and urban homesteading have been widely lauded, neither has involved large numbers of people. Survey findings indicate that the movement back to the blighted and abandoned areas of the city is more potential than real and the amount of renovation is insignificant when compared to total new residential production in the remainder of the SMSA. The population figures previously cited lend little support to the contention that the outward flow of urbanites has been reversed. Contrary to popular impression also, scattered evidence shows that many of the households moving into old neighborhoods come from other parts

[21]See in this connection James W. Hughes and Kenneth D. Bleakly, *Urban Homesteading* (New Brunswick, N.J.: Center for Urban Policy Research, Rutgers University, 1975); and Ann Clark and Zelma Rivin, *Homesteading in Urban U.S.A.* (New York: Praeger, 1977).

of the central city and not from the suburbs.[22] In final analysis, the important question is whether the quality of the housing stock (and its environs) in the older core municipalities can be improved enough at reasonable costs to attract large numbers of middle-class residents back to the central city. Many observers doubt that it can.

"REBIRTH" OF NONMETROPOLITAN AMERICA

Urban growth in the United States followed a common pattern for more than 175 years. Population concentrations increased in number and size as rural dwellers left the farms and hamlets for the economic and social attractions of the city. Later, as the large central municipalities became overcrowded, people and business enterprises began to move outward to the suburbs, creating in the process metropolitan complexes. Population in the rural or nonmetropolitan areas also rose as the nation expanded, but heavy outmigration to the urban settlements kept the rate of increase well below the national average. This general pattern continued to prevail until the late 1960s. Since then several unprecedented trends in the territorial distribution of people have become apparent. Metropolitan growth has leveled out, a number of SMSAs are losing inhabitants, and nonmetropolitan areas collectively are showing higher rates of population increase than SMSAs.[23]

Many central cities have been experiencing population losses for several decades even though the metropolitan areas in which they are located have been recording gains. Prior to 1970 the sole major SMSA to suffer a decline was Pittsburgh (2 percent during the 1960s). Since then at least 25 SMSAs, including 10 of the 50 largest, have lost residents. Of those areas with over 3 million peo-

---

[22]Dennis E. Gale, "Middle Class Resettlement in Older Urban Neighborhoods," *Journal of the American Planning Association* 45 (July 1979): 293–301. Also see George Sternlieb and Kristine Ford, "Some Aspects of the Return to the Central City," in Herrington Bryce (ed.), *Revitalizing Cities: Policies and Prospects* (Lexington, Mass.: Heath, 1979); and Pierre de Vise, "The Expanding Singles Housing Market in Chicago: Implications for Reviving City Neighborhoods," *Urbanism Past and Present*, No. 9 (Winter 1979-1980): 30–39. More favorable findings are discussed in S. Gregory Lipton, "Evidence of Central City Revival," *Journal of the American Institute of Planners* 43 (April 1977): 136–147.

[23]A discussion of recent trends in metropolitan growth is contained in Vincent P. Barabba, "The National Setting: Regional Shifts, Metropolitan Decline, and Urban Decay," in George Sternlieb and James Hughes (eds.), *Post-Industrial America: Metropolitan Decline and Inter-Regional Job Shifts* (New Brunswick, N.J.: Center for Urban Policy Research, Rutgers University, 1975), pp. 39–76.

ple, New York, Detroit, and Philadelphia registered declines; and the others in this size category showed only moderate increases.

Metropolitan areas collectively continue to record population gains but their upward growth has diminished substantially. The slowdown is obscured by the rise in the SMSA total resulting from the designation of new metropolitan territory. A more accurate picture is obtained by comparing the increases that occurred within the 1970 boundaries of SMSAs in each of the last two decades. Such a comparison clearly points up the sizable drop that has taken place in the rate of metropolitan expansion. From 1960 to 1970 the number of residents inside these areas rose by 17 million and in the subsequent years by well under half this amount.

The principal factor in the decline in metropolitan growth is the extraordinary change in the domestic migration pattern that has long prevailed in the United States. For the first time since the founding of the Republic, more people are leaving metropolitan areas than are moving into them from small towns and rural places. As recently as the 1960s, nonmetropolitan areas were experiencing a net loss of 300,000 persons each year to SMSAs.[24] In a surprising reversal of this trend, such areas are now showing a net inflow of more than one-third million persons annually. Largely because of this turnaround, the nonmetropolitan population increased by almost 11 percent from 1970 to 1977 compared to less than 5 percent for the SMSAs (Table 1.5). This trend is not confined to any one section of the nation; many nonmetropolitan counties in all regions are showing population gains.[25] The movement is not sparked by agricultural opportunities but by the availability of manufacturing, service, and mining jobs (new technology and interstate highways have permitted the wide dispersal of industry), the desire of retirees to escape the problems of the large cities, and the general yearning of many Americans for the open countryside.[26]

Although no uniformity exists among individual SMSAs as to growth rates, two clear trends can be observed, one relating to re-

[24]The Census Bureau uses the term "nonmetropolitan areas" to refer to all territory in the United States that is not included in SMSAs. These areas encompass both urban and rural dwellers; in fact, nearly one-fifth of the nation's urban population lives in nonmetropolitan areas.

[25]See Calvin Beale, "A Further Look at Nonmetropolitan Population Growth," *American Journal of Agricultural Economics* 58 (December 1976): 953–958; also Leonard F. Wheat, *Urban Growth in the Nonmetropolitan South* (Lexington, Mass.: Heath, 1976).

[26]The increased rate of growth in nonmetropolitan areas does not, in other words, represent a return to the farm. The farm population continues to decline, dropping from 9.7 million in 1970 to 8 million in 1978.

Table 1.5 POPULATION BY TYPE OF RESIDENCE, 1970 AND 1977
(numbers in thousands)

TYPE OF RESIDENCE	1970	1977	PERCENT CHANGE 1970 TO 1977
Metropolitan areas*	137,058	143,107	4.4
Central cities	62,876	59,993	−4.6
Suburban areas	74,182	83,114	12.0
Metropolitan areas of 1 million or more	79,489	82,367	3.6
Central cities	34,322	31,898	−7.1
Suburban areas	45,167	50,469	11.7
Metropolitan areas of less than 1 million	57,570	60,739	5.5
Central cities	28,554	28,095	−1.6
Suburban areas	29,016	32,644	12.5
Nonmetropolitan areas	62,761	69,459	10.7

*Based on 243 SMSAs as defined in 1970.
SOURCE: U.S. Bureau of the Census, "Social and Economic Characteristics of the Metropolitan and Nonmetropolitan Population, 1977 and 1970," *Current Population Reports*, Special Studies P-23, No. 75 (Washington, D.C., 1978), p. 4.

gional location and the other to size. The first is closely associated with the age of metropolitan areas. With some exceptions outmigration and population losses are more prevalent among the older SMSAs of the Northeast and North Central regions. In the South and West, where the urban concentrations are of more recent vintage, the net inflow continues to favor the metropolises. This difference is evident from Table 1.6. Since 1970, northeastern and north central SMSAs have shown an average net outmigration of one-half of one percent yearly, whereas southern and western areas have experienced a net inflow approaching one percent. As Table 1.6 also indicates, growth in the northeastern sector has been further impeded by a rate of natural increase only one-half that of the other regions.

The smaller metropolitan areas are now faring better than their larger counterparts in terms of population growth. All size categories below 500,000 have been able to maintain a level of increase close to that of the 1960s. Most areas in these groups continue to enjoy a migration advantage in contrast to the net outflow being experienced by many of the super metropolises. This pattern holds true for each region, indicating that the shift from the large SMSAs to the smaller metropolitan areas and nonmetropolitan places is occurring nationwide. In the Northeast only areas of less than 250,000 show any net migratory inflow since 1970. In the North Central region, all size categories have suffered net outmigration during the past decade, with the rates substantially lower for the smaller areas.

Table 1.6 AVERAGE ANNUAL RATE OF CHANGE IN NATURAL
INCREASE AND NET MIGRATION, SMSAs* BY REGION, 1970 TO 1977

REGION	NATURAL INCREASE (%)	NET MIGRATION (%)
Northeast	0.4	−0.5
North Central	0.7	−0.5
South	0.8	0.8
West	0.8	0.7
U.S. Total	0.7	0.1

*Based on 243 SMSAs as defined in 1970.
SOURCE: U.S. Bureau of the Census, "Population Profile of the United States, 1978,"
Current Population Reports, Series P-20, No. 336 (Washington, D.C., 1979), p. 33.

And in the South and West, SMSAs of all sizes are experiencing net
inflows but the rates for those over one million have dropped
sharply.

A DEMOGRAPHIC RECAP

As the various trends described in this chapter indicate, the nation
is witnessing a series of demographic changes that challenge some
of the common assumptions about the urban universe.

1. Metropolitan population growth has slowed significantly,
   with the gains now due primarily to natural increase and
   immigration from abroad. The large increases that formerly
   resulted from the net inflow of rural and nonmetropolitan
   residents have in many cases changed to losses.
2. The drop in the birth rate is impacting most heavily on the
   SMSAs, particularly the larger complexes, because natural
   increase has been their major source of population gain in
   recent years.
3. Present growth trends favor the smaller SMSAs over the
   larger regardless of regional location. They also favor metropolitan areas of all size categories in the South and West
   over those in the Northeast and North Central sections of
   the country.
4. The proportion of Americans living in central cities continues to drop while the suburban share increases.
5. Nonmetropolitan areas generally are demonstrating greater
   vitality than they have at any time since the turn of this century. Not only are they attracting more people than they are
   losing to the metropolises but they are also forming new urban concentrations of moderate size, some of which are

achieving SMSA status.[27] This phenomenon, moreover, is not confined to places on the periphery of existing SMSAs. Some counties situated well beyond any metropolitan field are also, for the first time within recent memory, experiencing net inmigration. President Carter emphasized the change when he announced a small community and rural development program in December 1979, noting that since 1970 "the population of the rural areas has increased 40 percent more than the population in our urban centers." Demographers, however, caution that the rural turnaround may be temporary. There are indications, they say, that the rate of outmigration from SMSAs is now beginning to decline.[28] Even if this should be the case, the nonmetropolitan areas collectively will continue to grow, although at a slower pace than at present.

6. Some movement of urban dwellers back to the central city is now evident among young households and older couples who have passed the child-rearing stage. The number involved, however, is insignificant compared to the total of those leaving.

IMPLICATIONS OF CHANGE

Robert Ardrey, author of the widely read *The Territorial Imperative*, once remarked that we cannot struggle with today as though it were yesterday. To paraphrase him, neither can we hope to ameliorate the current problems of our cities if we ignore the fundamental changes that have taken place in the nation as a whole. Municipalities and metropolitan areas no longer function in an arena of unlimited growth, abundant natural resources, and an ever rising standard of living. They now operate within a context of soaring energy costs, an environment threatened by human excesses, and a growing need to modify wasteful life-styles. Although the critical problems that have long plagued urban communities remain basically unchanged, efforts to cope with them must now take place within a setting that is unfamiliar to American experience.

---

[27]For a discussion of development in these areas see Luther Tweeten and G. L. Brinkman, *Micropolitan Development* (Ames: Iowa State University Press, 1976); also James Zurcher, "The Changing Character of Nonmetropolitan Population, 1950–1975," in Thomas Ford (ed.), *Rural Society in the United States* (Ames: Iowa State University Press, 1978).

[28]See in this connection Richard Engels and Mary K. Healy, "Rural Renaissance Reconsidered," *American Demographics* 1 (May 1979): 16–19.

As this chapter has shown, demographic changes of import to the problems and prospects of metropolitan areas are taking place. The nation continues to become increasingly urban but the rate of population growth has slowed and the distributional pattern has become more dispersed, favoring the South and West and the smaller areas. These changes have obvious political implications. One of the most important relates to the decennial reapportionment of congressional seats. On the basis of the 1980 census a total of 17 seats will switch states, with the Sunbelt gaining at the expense of the Northeast and Midwest. New York is the biggest loser with 5, followed by Pennsylvania, Ohio, and Illinois with 2 each. Florida, the largest gainer, will receive an additional 4 seats; and 3 will go to Texas and 2 to California.[29] A second, but less apparent, implication is the increased political strength that the smaller SMSAs and non-metropolitan areas will acquire at both the national and state levels as their populations and economies continue to grow.[30]

Neither of these developments—the political gains of the sun-belt metropolises and the increasing influence of smaller urban concentrations—are welcome news to the large SMSAs of the Northeast and Midwest. It is in the central cities of these complexes that problems are most severe and the need for federal aid greatest. For these areas to lose political strength, especially at a time when government is retrenching in response to the taxpayer revolt, seri-ously disadvantages them in the competitive struggle for scarce public resources.

Whatever interests the large SMSAs have in common, they are overshadowed by the differences that exist between the newer and more affluent metropolises of the South and West and the older and more "distressed" central cities of the Northeast and North Central

[29]The 1980 census came under heavy attack from a number of large municipalities. New York City, for example, charged that 800,000 of its residents, mostly black and Hispanic, were missed in the count. Philadelphia, Cleveland, Chicago, Detroit, and St. Louis, among others, made similar claims. Several of these cities instituted suits, which are still pending, against the Census Bureau to require adjustment of the figures. The bureau director defended the count as the best in history, saying that local officials who claimed undercounts were unwilling to face up to the fact of declining population.

[30]As one urbanologist points out, the fact that one of every 12 Americans lived in New York City or Chicago in the 1930s and fewer than one in 20 in the 1970s is more than a statistical curiosity. It is an index of political reality in the big central cities, revealing their loss of political strength and dependence on "outsiders" to take up their cause (Thomas Muller, "Urban Growth and Decline"). Equally significant is the regional shift in population. Of the approximately 156 million eligible voters in the nation, over 50 percent reside in an area that stretches from Florida across the Sunbelt and into the Pacific Northwest.

regions. These differences have already surfaced in congressional debates over federal aid policies, particularly in regard to distribution formulas. Given the direction of political power as reinforced by current population trends, proposals favoring the distressed communities, such as channeling the bulk of federal urban aid into cities most in need, stand little chance of adoption.

Metropolitan areas are not masters of their fate. They are affected in many ways by events and forces over which they have no control and by actions—state, national, and even international—taken outside their borders. It is not enough therefore to focus attention on the internal politics and operations of SMSAs and the tensions between their central cities and suburbs. Nor is it sufficient to examine the differences between SMSAs, important as these are in view of the intensifying economic competition among regions. Both intra- and intermetropolitan affairs must be placed within the context of national politics, economic developments, and social trends. Failure to do so is to ignore the realities of urban America.

Chapter 2
Social Topography

Metropolitan communities can be viewed in many ways—as aggregations of people and institutions interacting with one another, as economic units of production and consumption, as loosely linked sets of neighborhoods and local governments, as arenas of competing interests, as places that house the bulk of the nation's population. To the more cosmopolitan they are centers of enlightenment and culture; to those who extol the virtues of small towns and rural areas they represent the least desirable features of American life. Social scientists tend to regard them as systems but disagree widely as to their nature or how they are to be studied. Some place greater emphasis on the social components of such entities, others on the economic, and still others on the political and governmental. From this welter of views one clear conclusion emerges: there is no simple set of concepts, no comprehensive or overarching theory to explain the urban world.

No matter how they are perceived, metropolitan communities involve a network of social relationships that exist within a given geographical area. This web or structure presents a mosaic of social worlds arranged territorially in an often confused and seemingly incompatible pattern. "The other side of the tracks" is an expression well known to many small-town dwellers. But in the large population centers there are many "sides of the track." Numerous neighborhoods and suburban groupings of varying social, ethnic, and economic characteristics are scattered throughout the metropolitan complex. The black ghetto is ringed by a wall of white neighborhoods. The industrial suburb lies adjacent to the village enclave of the wealthy. Luxury apartments border a slum section in the inner city. Young couples renovate dilapidated homes in an area populated by elderly poor.

Critical to an understanding of urban communities is a knowledge of the social geography or pattern in which individuals and families of different socioeconomic rank, life-style, and ethnic background are distributed in territorial space. Just as sections of a metropolis are identified with particular industrial and commercial

activities, so also are entire neighborhoods and suburban settlements given over to socially differentiated groups. As the social scientist would put it, people who identify with a particular status
level tend to congregate in areas or neighborhoods possessing an
identification with that status. Or as the nonprofessional observer
would say, people desire to live with their "own kind." The
result—whether due to individual choice, enforced segregation, or
simply economic circumstances—is a pattern familiar to all urban
dwellers: small subcommunities of homogeneity distinguished
from one another by differences in social class, race, or life-style.

In seeking to explain this pattern, sociologist Robert Park and
his colleagues at the University of Chicago turned to ecological
principles borrowed from biology. Drawing on the knowledge in
this field they conceptualized the spatial distribution of people in
cities as a natural response, an adaptation, of human beings and
activities to their environment. There are forces at work in an urban
community, Park said, that tend to bring about an orderly grouping
of its institutions and population.[1] Business and industry seek ad-
vantageous locations and people settle in neighborhoods where
their circumstances permit and they can best cope with their needs
and problems. Ethnic immigrants, for example, group together in
subcommunities of their own nationality for social and psychological support; the wealthy establish enclaves to separate themselves
physically from the poor; and racial minorities form ghettos because they have little other choice.

Park's natural adaptation theory pays scant attention to governmental institutions and how they influence the spatial pattern of
city dwellers through such policies as zoning and the location of
public facilities. It does, however, stress the relationship—and this
is probably its most important contribution—between the territorial distribution of people and resources and the social and cultural
effects (to which we would add political) of such geographical differentiation. The racially imbalanced schools in the North, the
product in large part of the residential segregation of black and
white families, provide a telling example of this relationship.

The present chapter examines six developments of a demographic and sociological nature that are bringing about changes in
the social structure and ecological geography of metropolitan areas.
These developments relate primarily to central city–suburban differences, immigration from abroad, racial distribution patterns, the
new status of women, family composition, and the age structure of

[1]Robert E. Park, "The City: Suggestions for the Investigation of Human Behavior in
the Urban Environment," *American Journal of Sociology* 20 (March 1916): 577–612.

the population. The trends now manifest in these various categories have important policy implications for government and necessitate a rethinking of some of the long-held notions about urban
communities and their future.

CITY AND SUBURB

Discussions of metropolitan areas are often premised on a simple
dichotomous pattern of social geography in which disparities between the central city and suburbs are overemphasized and variations among SMSAs largely ignored. The population of core cities
is commonly characterized as nonwhite, ethnic, poor, undereduca-
ted, unskilled, and Democratic; and that of suburbia as white, nonethnic, affluent, high occupational status, and Republican. This
widely accepted stereotype is substantiated in part when metropolitan areas are considered as a whole. In the aggregate, central municipalities do contain a greater proportion of racial minorities, ethnic groups, low-skilled workers, poverty families, and Democratic
voters than the outlying areas. The median family income of their
residents is about $3000 less than that of suburbanites and they
house 37 percent of the nation's poor compared to 23 percent in the
fringe areas (Figure 2.1).

Statistics of this nature, however, must be viewed in proper
context. They deal with aggregates, and not with individual SMSAs
and their populations. The common tendency to speak of urban
areas as though they were all cut from the same cloth obscures the
obvious. No two of these agglomerations are identical in their social

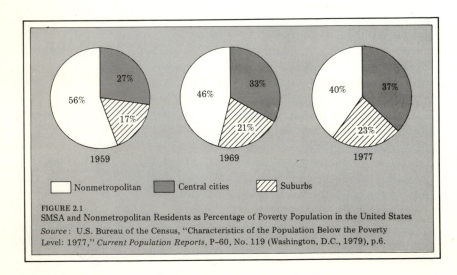

FIGURE 2.1
SMSA and Nonmetropolitan Residents as Percentage of Poverty Population in the United States
Source: U.S. Bureau of the Census, "Characteristics of the Population Below the Poverty
Level: 1977," *Current Population Reports,* P–60, No. 119 (Washington, D.C., 1979), p.6.

geography. Each has its own distinctive features and its own con-
tour of settlement. Each is composed of a set of neighborhoods or
subcommunities of different values, life-styles, and social attributes. In some metropolitan areas the divergencies between the
central city and suburbs approach the popular image; in others they
are far less intense or virtually nonexistent; and in a number the
social map favors the major municipality. Whatever the case, wide
variances in socioeconomic and life-style characteristics are likely
to be found among the neighborhoods of both the central city and
its surrounding suburbs.[2]

City–Suburban Differences

Sociologist Leo Schnore's examination of 200 metropolitan areas
demonstrated that the popular view of city–suburban disparities
holds true mainly for the larger and older urban complexes.[3] The
national Advisory Commission on Intergovernmental Relations
(ACIR) also found that only the largest SMSAs—principally those
in the Northeast where most of the long-established metropolises
are located—fit the stereotype.[4] In a more recent statistical study of
urban complexes Richard Nathan and his associates reached similar
conclusions. They found that the central municipalities most disadvantaged relative to their suburbs are those of large size in the
Northeast and North Central regions of the country. The data they
assembled show that the big cities in the South and West exhibit
less disparity and in some cases are better off than their outlying
sections. The findings also underscore the fact that even in instances where the suburbs collectively exceed the core city on socioeconomic measures, the advantage is seldom enjoyed by all the
fringe area communities individually.[5]

[2]For a study of disparities among metropolitan suburbs see Richard C. Hill, "Separate and Unequal: Governmental Equality in the Metropolis," *American Political
Science Review* 68 (December 1974): 1557–1568.
[3]Leo F. Schnore, "The Socioeconomic Status of Cities and Suburbs," *American Sociological Review* 28 (February 1963): 76–85. An overview of the literature on this
subject is contained in James R. Pinkerton, "City-Suburban Residential Patterns by
Social Class: A Review of the Literature," *Urban Affairs Quarterly* 4 (June 1969):
499–515.
[4]Advisory Commission on Intergovernmental Relations, *Metropolitan Social and
Economic Disparities: Implications for Intergovernmental Relations in Central
Cities and Suburbs* (Washington, D.C., January 1965), p. 23.
[5]Richard P. Nathan and Charles Adams, "Understanding Central City Hardship,"
Political Science Quarterly 91 (Spring 1976): 47–61, and Richard P. Nathan and
Paul R. Dommel, "The Cities," in Joseph A. Pechman (ed.), *Setting National Priorities: The 1978 Budget* (Washington, D.C.: The Brookings Institution, 1977), pp. 283–
292.

The Nathan study emphasizes the importance of viewing disparities in relation to the condition of both the city and its suburban ring. Two cases illustrate this point. In the first, the core municipality ranks substantially below its outlying area in social status yet is relatively well off compared to other cities nationally. The disadvantage appears not because the city is impoverished but because its suburbs are extremely affluent.[6] In the second situation, both the central municipality and the rest of the metropolitan area are characterized by hardship conditions and show little difference between them on socioeconomic measures. If policymakers were to look only at the extent of disparity as the test for granting aid, they would adopt provisions to assist the city in the first case but would ignore the more serious need in the second.

To set the question of disparities in a context that takes account of city and suburban well-being or hardship, Nathan and his colleagues utilized two indexes, one referred to as "urban conditions," the other as "city–suburban disparities." The former compares central cities with each other; the latter compares each core municipality with its surrounding area. The indexes are based on various socioeconomic and demographic factors such as income, education, and population change.[7]

Table 2.1 shows how the central cities in 20 of the largest SMSAs rank on the two indexes. Various groupings of these municipalities can be identified from the table. One, for example, consists of cities that are highly disadvantaged in relation to their suburbs as well as to their counterparts nationally. St. Louis, Newark, Cleveland, Boston, Baltimore, and Philadelphia—all old industrial communities in the Northeast and North Central regions—fall into this category, ranking poorly on both the urban conditions and disparity indexes. Another group includes cities that are better off than both the national average and their suburbs. Dallas, Houston, and Phoenix—all sunbelt localities—are examples of this type. A third is composed of central cities with poor scores on the urban conditions index and more favorable ratings on the disparities scale, an indication that their suburbs are also relatively disadvantaged. New Orleans and Jersey City are representative of this category.[8] These

---

[6]The city of Atlanta, for example, is reasonably well off compared to other large core municipalities but it rates poorly in relation to its affluent suburbs.

[7]The urban conditions index is based on three measures: population decline, age of city, and degree of poverty. The disparities index utilizes six factors: unemployment, dependency, education, income, crowded housing, and poverty.

[8]A third index formulated by the Nathan group for comparing the suburban portions of SMSAs with each other shows that the suburbs in both Jersey City and New Orleans rank extremely poorly in relation to the national average.

Table 2.1 RANKING OF CENTRAL CITIES IN 20 SELECTED SMSAs OF OVER ONE MILLION POPULATION ON URBAN CONDITIONS AND CITY–SUBURBAN DISPARITY INDEXES

CITY	REGION	URBAN CONDITIONS INDEX*	RANK ON URBAN CONDITIONS INDEX	CENTRAL CITY– SUBURBAN DISPARITY INDEX†	RANK ON DISPARITY INDEX
St. Louis	NC	351	1	231	5
Newark	NE	321	2	422	1
Buffalo	NE	292	3	189	11
Cleveland	NC	291	4	331	2
New Orleans	S	274	5	168	12
Pittsburgh	NE	260	6	146	13
Boston	NE	257	7	198	10
Jersey City	NE	226	8	129	15
Baltimore	NE	224	9	256	3
Philadelphia	NE	216	10	205	9
Chicago	NC	201	11	245	4
Detroit	NC	201	12	210	8
San Francisco	W	188	13	105	16
New York	NE	180	14	211	7
Minneapolis	NC	174	15	131	14
Atlanta	S	118	16	226	6
Los Angeles	W	74	17	105	16
Dallas	S	38	18	97	18
Houston	S	36	19	93	19
Phoenix	W	19	20	85	20

*A score of 100 on the urban conditions index represents the average of the composite measurements. A rating above 100 indicates worse than average conditions. Cities scoring below 100 are better off than the average city in the sample.

†Cities scoring 100 have essentially the same socioeconomic conditions as their suburbs. Those rating above 100 have poorer conditions whereas those below are better off.

SOURCE: Richard P. Nathan and Paul R. Dommel, "The Cities," in Joseph Pechman (ed.), *Setting National Priorities: The 1978 Budget* (Washington, D.C.: The Brookings Institution, 1977), pp. 290–291, and Richard P. Nathan and Charles Adams, "Understanding Central City Hardship," *Political Science Quarterly* 91 (Spring 1976): 47–61.

distinctions are important to bear in mind when examining national urban policies and programs.

The Suburban Myth

Although the large cities have been roundly condemned as impersonal, congested, polluted, crime ridden, and unfit places to raise a family, the suburbs have also been the targets of criticism. They have been ridiculed for their mediocrity and cultural barrenness, charged with "freeloading" on the core city, and chastised for failing to meet their social responsibility to racial minorities and the poor. Conversely, just as the cities have been extolled as centers of culture, rich diversity, cosmopolitan life-styles, and broad opportunities, the suburbs have been lauded as the fulfillment of the middle-class dream: small communities of good schools, clean streets, well-maintained homes, low crime rates, friendly and responsible neighbors, and plenty of open space. Both the criticism and the praise contain elements of truth, but the stereotypes they present distort reality.[9]

Suburbs, as we previously noted, are not undifferentiated aggregates; they vary from one another in terms of their housing quality, educational and occupational levels, the social origins of their residents, and the life-styles they reflect. Park Forest may be representative of the fringe area community populated by the professional and managerial elite, and Levittown typical of the mass-produced tract developments of young middle-class families, but neither is a microcosm of suburbia itself. In fact, as Leo Schnore has shown, the common notion of the suburbs as bedroom communities specializing in the provision of residential amenities is true for only about one-third of the urban-fringe settlements. The remainder are characterized by various levels of industrial and trade activity, with a substantial proportion of them drawing at least part of their labor supply from other communities, including the central city.[10]

Contrary to popular impression, suburbs are not a recent innovation. As early as 1850 Chicago had more than 60 fringe settlements, and by the turn of the century outlying communities in many urban areas were seeking to lure families away from the central city. Typical was an advertisement in a Milwaukee paper in 1893 picturing Wauwatosa as "the most attractive suburb of Milwaukee with fine churches, street lights, transit facilities, and freedom from saloons and heavy industry." First the commuter railroad, then the trolley car, and finally the automobile made land beyond the built-up center increasingly accessible for development. The real push, however, did not come until after World War II when the shortage of housing (and federal mortgage guarantee practices that favored suburban locations) sparked an unprecedented movement outward—an "implosion" as Lewis Mumford

---

[9]A Louis Harris poll conducted in 1978 found that the overwhelming majority of respondents had negative images of the large city as a place to live yet many regarded it as an economic, cultural, and recreational center.

[10]Leo Schnore, *The Urban Scene: Human Ecology and Demography* (New York: Free Press, 1965).

called it. Today there are over 85 million suburban Americans, and the number is likely to exceed 100 million before the end of the century.

The Levittowns and Park Forests that came to symbolize the new movement prompted a spate of satirical novels and critical commentary, such as John Keats' *The Crack in the Picture Window,* A. C. Spectorsky's *The Exurbanites,* and William H. Whyte's *The Organization Man.* It became fashionable in this context for journalists and academicians alike to speak of the sterility of suburban life, its homogenized character, and its "barbecue pit" culture, marked by child rearing, lawn mowing, and a hyperactive social life. Popularized by the media these pronouncements gave rise to the stereotypes and imagery that have represented much of the conventional wisdom about American suburbs.

One of the more common myths about suburbia is that central city dwellers who move to the urbanized ring tend to change their value orientations as they become immersed in the social and political culture of their new environment. Supposedly they become more conservative, identify more closely with their local community and its ethos, and (if previously Democrats) switch to the Republican party. Research findings, however, give little support to this "conversion" theory. Herbert Gans' detailed analysis of Levittown, a tract development near Philadelphia, found that the lives of the former city dwellers were not significantly altered after their move.[11] His conclusion that urban and suburban environs largely reflect the class differences and life-styles of their populations is consistent with the results of other research. A nationwide survey, for example, showed that the attitudinal patterns and political behavior of metropolitan dwellers are correlates of social class and race, and not of place of residence within the urban complex. What these findings indicate, in short, is that the values of individuals differ because of the kind of people they are and not because of where they live. As one exasperated suburban housewife expressed

---

[11]*The Levittowners* (New York: Pantheon, 1959). See also Bennet M. Berger, *Working Class Suburb: A Study of Auto Workers in Suburbia* (Berkeley and Los Angeles: University of California Press, 1960), where it was found that a group of auto workers moving to suburbia maintained their working-class attitudes and life-style in their new setting. Later studies have also reached similar conclusions. See Harvey Marshall, "Suburban Life Styles: A Contribution to the Debate," in Louis H. Masotti and Jeffrey Hadden (eds.), *The Urbanization of the Suburbs* (Beverly Hills, Calif.: Sage, 1973), pp. 243–249, and Mark Baldassare and Claude Fischer, "Suburban Life: Powerlessness and Need for Affiliation," *Urban Affairs Quarterly* 10 (March 1975): 314–326.

it, "Just because I moved here doesn't mean that I've changed my values."

Much of the satirical literature on suburbia has now given way to analyses that depict the fringe area communities in a more sympathetic and objective light.[12] Instead of the facile assumptions marking the earlier discourses, the new commentary recognizes the suburbs as a need-fulfilling component of contemporary metropolitan society. It also regards the outward push as in part a quiet revolt against the bigness and impersonalism of the large city; in part a reflection of the deep-seated preferences of many for an environment more conducive to familistic life-styles; and in part the availability (until recently) of satisfactory housing within the economic means of moderate income families. This more favorable view of the suburbs was strengthened by the emergence of the neighborhood control movement in the latter half of the 1960s with its emphasis on decentralization and citizen input into the local decision-making process. The rationale for the new cause added legitimacy to the "grass-roots government" philosophy long invoked by defenders of suburbia.

Although the reality remained unrecognized for several decades, Americans are finally beginning to realize that the suburbs, whatever their advantages, offer no escape from urban problems. Like the central cities, the fringe area communities find themselves confronted with rising crime rates, wide use of drugs among their youth, traffic congestion, environmental pollution, and high taxes. They are being hard hit by energy costs and gas shortages, and the price of their housing has escalated to the point where it is beyond the means of many families.

Some of the older suburbs in the inner ring are experiencing population losses, physical blight, economic decline, and racial tensions. A number of them are in the process of transition to poor and minority communities, much like the familiar pattern in inner-city neighborhoods. As one urbanologist aptly puts it, suburbs in older and larger SMSAs have collectively become de facto big cities with big city problems, such as decaying neighborhoods, racial segregation, inadequate housing for low- and moderate-income

[12]Representative writings in this vein include Bryan T. Downs (ed.), *Cities and Suburbs* (Belmont, Calif.: Wadsworth, 1971); Charles M. Haar (ed.), *The End of Innocence: A Suburban Reader* (Glenview, Ill.: Scott, Foresman, 1972); Frederick M. Wirt, Benjamin Walter, Francine Rabinovitz, and Deborah Hensler, *On the City's Rim: Politics and Policy in Suburbia* (Lexington, Mass.: Heath, 1972); and Thomas P. Murphy and John Rehfuss, *Urban Politics in the Suburban Era* (Homewood, Ill.: Dorsey, 1976).

families, and deteriorating physical plants.[13] The magnitude of the problems may be greater in the core municipality and the resources to meet them less adequate, but in looking at the central city of today we may be seeing the suburbs of tomorrow.

FOREIGN-BORN URBANITES

No nation has been so generous with its citizenship as the United States but, in the words of one writer, no other country has benefited so much from its immigrants.[14] During the 150-year period from 1820 to 1970, over 45 million immigrants—almost 9 million alone during the first decade of this century—came to the United States. The early arrivals had been mostly from northern and western Europe, but in the several decades before World War I, newcomers of Italian, Polish, and other southern and eastern European stock predominated. The vast majority of the latter migrants settled in the large industrial cities of the Northeast and Midwest where they added a distinctive ethnic flavor to the urban populace and provided the main basis of support for the political machines. Later the cities again served as ports of entry for the great internal migration of blacks and displaced farm workers.

The number of foreign born in the United States grew continuously until 1930 when the total exceeded 14 million. By 1970 the figure had declined to 9.6 million. Since then, however, it has risen to more than 10 million. In addition to the immigrants there are approximately 25 million second-generation Americans, identified in the census as "of foreign or mixed parentage" (one or both parents born abroad). The importance of immigration to the subject of urban communities is underscored by two facts: (1) foreign immigration now accounts for almost one-fourth of the nation's population growth; and (2) nearly 90 percent of the foreign born are urban dwellers, as are most second-generation Americans (the latter are more likely than their parents to live in suburbia).

Immigration policies have determined the nationality pattern of the newcomers. In 1921 Congress placed a numerical ceiling on admissions for the first time in the country's history. Prior to this action only particular categories of persons, such as the mentally defective and those likely to become welfare dependents, were denied entry. From the 1920s to the mid-1960s admissions were

---

[13]George D. Wendel, in *St. Louis Post Dispatch,* June 10, 1979.
[14]Richard E. Kipling, "Illegal Aliens," *Skeptic: The Magazine of Great Debates,* No. 20 (July/August 1977): 43.

based on quotas determined by a "national origins" formula that was heavily weighted in favor of Western Hemisphere nations.[15]

In 1965 Congress abolished the quota system and set numerical limitations on immigration from the two hemispheres (170,000 annually for the eastern and 120,000 for the western), thus giving persons from both sections of the world an equal chance for entry. Special acts passed by Congress also provide for the admission of refugees from Communist dominated countries without regard to the numerical ceilings. (The Refugee Act of 1980 extended such status to persons outside their native country who would face persecution upon their return.) By virtue of these acts hundreds of thousands of individuals, including Cubans, Haitians, and natives of Southeast Asia (the latest from Vietnam and Cambodia), have gained entry in recent years.

The number of foreign born in the United States is considerably higher than the official figures show. Along with the approximately 500,000 persons admitted legally each year, a large but unknown number of aliens (commonly referred to as "undocumented workers") enter the country unlawfully.[16] In one recent year alone, the Immigration and Naturalization Service apprehended almost 900,000 such persons attempting to come in illegally. Estimates of the number of undocumented workers now in the United States range from several million to 12 million, the predominant majority of them being Mexican nationals.[17] They are concentrated mainly in the Southwest where they constitute a "clandestine population" that is undercounted in the census and not credited to local governments for federal and state aid purposes.[18]

[15]The annual quota for each country was determined by the proportion of each nationality living in the United States in 1920 to the total population. The formula grossly discriminated against Asians because relatively few of them resided in the United States in 1920. Discrimination against Asian immigration occurred as early as 1882 when Congress passed the Chinese Exclusion Law, an act not repealed until 1943. For an overview of present policy see Elliott Abrams and Franklin Abrams, "Immigration Policy—Who Gets in and Why, *The Public Interest*, No. 38 (Winter 1975): 3–29.

[16]The term "undocumented worker" has come into general use (replacing the more pejorative "illegal alien" designation) at the urging of Hispanic leaders and others who point out that it is a more appropriate description in many cases.

[17]Professor Dudley Poston of the Population Research Center at the University of Texas estimates that 400,000 undocumented workers entered the United States each year between 1970 and 1975. He also estimates that a total of about 4 million such individuals are now living in this country (*Los Angeles Times*, February 2, 1978). These figures are probably closer to reality than the more extreme estimates.

[18]For a treatment of various aspects of Mexican migration to this country see Thomas Weaver and Theodore Downing (eds.), *Mexican Migration* (Tucson: University of Arizona Press, 1976).

The abolishment of the quota system has significantly altered the character of current immigration, shifting the emphasis from Europe to Asia and Latin America. During the 1950s 1.5 million immigrants came from Europe and only 157,000 from Asia. From 1971 to 1978, in contrast, newcomers from Asia outnumbered those from Europe by a margin of more than three to two. In the earlier period, for example, 346,000 Germans and 17,000 Philippine nationals were admitted; and in the later the totals were reversed with 240,000 entering from the Philippines and 46,000 from Germany (Table 2.2).

The changed character of the immigration is resulting in a pattern of settlement different from that associated with the earlier newcomers. Unlike the European entrants who have historically gravitated to the eastern and midwestern states, those from Asia and Latin America tend to establish their homes in the western and southern regions of the country. As a consequence, the West increased its share of the nation's foreign born from 18 percent in 1960 to 25 percent at the end of the decade, and the South from 10 percent to 14 percent. Since then these proportions have risen further according to all estimates. Various metropolitan areas in these regions thus find themselves faced with the task of assimilating a sizable number of newcomers whose culture differs in many respects from that of the majoritarian society.

The statistics on immigration serve to remind us of the continued significance of ethnicity in American society. About one-sixth of the population, a segment predominantly urban, is either foreign

Table 2.2 IMMIGRATION TO UNITED STATES FROM SELECTED COUNTRIES, 1951 to 1978 (in thousands)

COUNTRY OF BIRTH	1951–1960	1961–1970	1971–1978
Germany	345.5	200.0	46.4
Italy	188.0	206.7	111.1
Poland	128.0	73.3	29.2
United Kingdom	208.9	230.5	79.9
China*	32.7	96.7	129.4
India	3.1	31.2	113.6
Korea	7.0	35.8	181.1
Philippines	17.2	101.5	239.5
Vietnam	2.0	4.6	25.0
Canada	274.9	286.7	70.5
Mexico	319.3	443.3	436.1
Cuba	78.3	256.8	216.4

*Principally from Taiwan.
SOURCE: U.S. Bureau of the Census, *Statistical Abstract 1979*, p. 90.

born or of "foreign or mixed parentage." Assimilation has reduced the number and diluted the character of many of the old ethnic neighborhoods that served the earlier groups, but the "melting pot" process has by no means destroyed the cultural pluralism long characteristic of the large metropolitan communities. The 1960s and 1970s witnessed a renewed interest in ethnicity as pride in one's national lineage and identification with one's ethnic subcommunity reemerged as important forces in urban life.[19] It would be a mistake, however, to assume that this development heralds a revival of the old ethnic neighborhoods as some writers like to romanticize.

INTERNAL MIGRATION

Migration from one section of the country to another has always been a major characteristic of American society. The westward thrust of the pioneers, the trek of displaced farm workers and Appalachian miners to the industrial centers, and the exodus of blacks from the South all represent efforts to find new homes and new opportunities. The most significant of these movements, at least in terms of size, has been the black migration into the urban areas of the Northeast and Midwest. This phenomenon did not begin on a large scale until after 1920. By that time the entry of large numbers of foreign immigrants into the country had ceased, thus easing the competition for the older housing stock of the large cities.

Contrary to the impression held by some, the scale of black migration has been relatively small compared to the earlier waves of European immigrants. From 1910 to 1970 the net outmigration of blacks from the South was less than 6.5 million. Even during the 1960s the 1.5 million who left the South (a figure also recorded in each of the two prior decades) were outnumbered more than two to one by newcomers from abroad. The shift northward, however, has radically changed the geographical distribution of the black population. As late as 1940, 77 percent of the blacks were concentrated in the South; by 1978 this proportion had declined to 53 percent. During the same period blacks living in the Northeast increased from 11 to 18 percent and in the North Central region from 11 to 20

---

[19]This phenomenon has received considerable attention in recent years. See, for example, Richard J. Krickus, "The White Ethnics: Who Are They and Where Are They Going?" *City*, (May–June 1971): 23–31; Michael Novak, *The Rise of the Unmeltable Ethnics: Politics and Culture in the Seventies* (New York: Macmillan, 1972); Andrew M. Greeley, *Why Can't They Be Like Us: America's White Ethnic Groups* (New York: Dutton, 1971); and Mark R. Levy and Michael S. Kramer, *The Ethnic Factor: How America's Minorities Decide Elections* (New York: Simon & Schuster, 1972).

Table 2.3 BLACK POPULATION BY REGION, 1940 TO 1978

	PERCENT DISTRIBUTION				
REGION	1940	1950	1960	1970	1978
Northeast	11	13	16	19	18
North Central	11	15	18	20	20
South	77	68	60	53	53
West	1	4	6	8	9
U.S. Total	100	100	100	100	100

SOURCE: U.S. Bureau of the Census, "The Social and Economic Status of the Black Population," *Current Population Reports,* Special Studies, Series P-23, No. 80 (Washington, D.C., 1979), pp. 13, 167.

percent. The West, which had few black residents in 1940, recorded 9 percent in 1978 (Table 2.3). The states with the largest black populations are in fact outside the South, New York heading the list with 2.4 million, followed by California and Illinois with 1.6 million each.[20]

Black Urbanization

The new migration radically altered the racial composition of urban areas. In 1978 blacks totaled approximately 25 million or almost 12 percent of the nation's residents. A largely rural people prior to World War I, they have become a predominantly urban population, three-fourths of them living in SMSAs (Figure 2.2). From 1960 to 1978 the number of black metropolitan dwellers rose by nearly 50 percent to a total of 18.4 million. Not all of this growth, however, was due to inmigration. Natural increase accounted for about one-half of it outside the South and virtually all in southern SMSAs.

Within metropolitan areas the black population is heavily concentrated in the central cities. These have served as ports of entry for the black migrants as they had earlier for immigrants from abroad. During the past quarter century the proportion of blacks in the core municipalities almost doubled. The greatest gains have been taking place in SMSAs of one million or more inhabitants where collectively central city blacks now constitute around 28 percent of the area residents (Table 2.4). Changes in the individual SMSAs have even been greater. From 1950 to 1970 blacks as a percentage of the central city population almost tripled in Cleveland and Detroit and more than doubled in New York, Chicago, San

[20]The problem of undercounting blacks and Hispanics in recent decennial censuses should be kept in mind in examining population statistics.

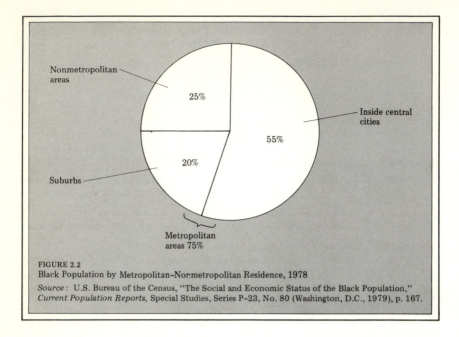

FIGURE 2.2
Black Population by Metropolitan–Nonmetropolitan Residence, 1978
Source: U.S. Bureau of the Census, "The Social and Economic Status of the Black Population," *Current Population Reports,* Special Studies, Series P-23, No. 80 (Washington, D.C., 1979), p. 167.

Francisco, Boston, and St. Louis (Table 2.5). The increases continued through the 1970s although at a substantially reduced rate. At
the end of the decade blacks comprised a majority of the population
in large cities, including Baltimore, Detroit, New Orleans, and
Washington, D.C.

Black migration patterns, however, have begun to undergo sig-

Table 2.4   BLACKS AS A PERCENT OF TOTAL POPULATION IN SMSAs
AND NONMETROPOLITAN AREAS, 1960, 1970, AND 1975

TYPE OF RESIDENCE	1960 (%)	1970 (%)	1975 (%)
SMSAs*	10.7	11.9	12.5
Central cities in areas of 1 million or more	18.8	25.2	27.6
Central cities in areas of less than 1 million	13.2	14.9	16.8
Suburbs	4.8	4.6	5.0
Nonmetropolitan areas	10.3	9.1	8.8

*As defined in 1970.
SOURCE: U.S. Bureau of the Census, "The Social and Economic Status of the Black Population," *Current Population Reports,* Special Studies, Series P-23, No. 80, (Washington, D.C., 1979), p. 15.

Table 2.5 PERCENTAGE OF BLACKS IN CENTRAL CITIES OF
SELECTED LARGE SMSAs, 1950 TO 1980

CITY	1950	1960	1970	1980
New York	10	14	21	24
Chicago	14	23	33	40
Philadelphia	18	26	34	38
Detroit	16	29	44	63
San Francisco	6	10	12	12
Washington, D.C.	35	54	71	75
Boston	5	9	13	21
St. Louis	18	29	41	46
Baltimore	24	35	38	54
Cleveland	16	29	41	44
New Orleans	32	37	45	53
Atlanta	36	38	51	66

SOURCE: U.S. Bureau of the Census, *Census of Population: 1960 and 1970* (Washington, D.C., 1961 and 1973), and Census Bureau releases (1981).

nificant change, calling for a reassessment of predictions about the future racial composition of cities and suburbs. Most importantly, the historical exodus from the South has come to a halt. For the first time since the Reconstruction Period, more blacks are migrating to the South than leaving it.[21] Although the net outflow from the Northeast and Midwest is relatively small, the effect is substantial because at least one-half the black population growth in the SMSAs of these regions during the last several decades has been due to inmigration. Assuming the continuation of present trends, future gains in the number of black residents in the core cities will therefore depend on natural increase. This does not mean that the proportion of blacks in these municipalities will necessarily decline or remain stable. The percentage is more likely to go on rising in many of them because of the continued outmigration of white families.

The impact of the reversed migration can already be seen in the population statistics. From 1970 to 1978 the number of black dwellers in the central cities of SMSAs increased by only 6 percent compared to 39 percent in the prior decade. Since 1974, moreover, the black population in these municipalities has registered no growth and in some individual cases, such as St. Louis, has even declined.[22]

[21]A study as to why people move is Larry H. Long and Kristen A. Hansen, "Reasons for Interstate Migration," U.S. Bureau of the Census, *Current Population Reports*, Special Studies, Series P-23, No. 81 (March 1979).
[22]Census tabulations indicate that 14 of the 15 congressional districts represented by blacks have lost population since 1970, a development that might well jeopardize some of the "safe" seats for blacks after the decennial reapportionment.

This shift in interregional migration patterns is being paralleled by a developing trend in the spatial location of black households within SMSAs: the movement to suburbia. Although the total involved is not overwhelming, black families, mostly upper- and middle-class, have been leaving the core municipalities of the large metropolitan areas in increasing numbers since the late 1960s.[23] Like their white counterparts, they are seeking better schools, more desirable dwelling units, and safer neighborhoods.[24] Some also are leaving because of displacement by innercity revitalization projects.

The inroads into predominantly white suburbia, modest as they now are, may well portend a change in the long-familiar pattern of black confinement to the central city. During the 1960s the black population in the suburbs increased by less than one million, whereas the number of white residents rose by 15.5 million. In the following eight years the black suburban population grew by more than 4 percent annually compared to the white rate of slightly over 1 percent (Figure 2.3).[25] The absolute numbers are less impressive because of the small base from which the blacks start (white residents increased by 7 million and blacks by 1.3 million), but the gains are now more proportionate to the racial composition of metropolitan areas.

The growing suburbanization of blacks, however, is not to be equated with racial integration; it represents for the most part an extension of the segregated housing patterns long typical of the central city. Although a small percentage of black families locate on scattered sites in white communities, the outmigration tends to follow well-defined corridors. For most of the new entrants the pattern is a familiar one. As they move into the inner ring of suburbs whites begin to leave, ultimately resulting in segregated clusters of black households.[26] In St. Louis, to cite one example, where "black flight" has been evident for some time, most of the suburban in-

---

[23]Not all SMSAs are experiencing black suburbanization. A study of 19 of the largest metropolitan areas showed that in about half of them the rate of black movement to suburbia has approached that of the whites since 1970, but in the other half the rate increased little. Kathryn P. Nelson, "Recent Suburbanization of Blacks," *Journal of the American Planning Association* 46 (July 1980): 287–300.

[24]The suburban movement has caused some black leaders to complain that middle-class blacks are becoming too engrossed in their own concerns and not active in the cause of those they are leaving behind (*Los Angeles Times*, December 6, 1976).

[25]The number of blacks in nonmetropolitan areas is also rising in marked contrast to the trend of the last four decades. This growth, however, is not farm related but is occurring principally in urban places that are moving toward metropolitan status.

[26]Much of the entry of blacks into suburbia is the result of spillover from the adjacent ghettos of the central city. In a minority of instances the movement is being accommodated by the expansion of already existing black communities some distance from the city limits; New Rochelle near New York City and Harvey in the Chicago area are examples.

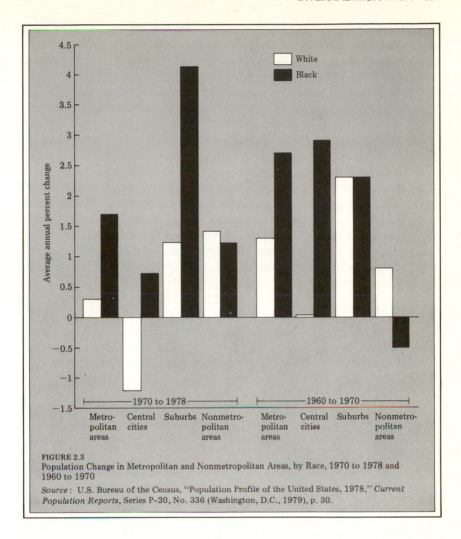

FIGURE 2.3
Population Change in Metropolitan and Nonmetropolitan Areas, by Race, 1970 to 1978 and 1960 to 1970

Source: U.S. Bureau of the Census, "Population Profile of the United States, 1978," *Current Population Reports*, Series P–20, No. 336 (Washington, D.C., 1979), p. 30.

crease is taking place in a corridor that extends outward from the black neighborhoods within the city. In the process one suburban municipality has become almost totally black and at least ten others, all of small size, are in various stages of transition.[27] The

[27]A statistical study of the Chicago area indicates that the movement of blacks there has been along the path of least resistance, avoiding the lower-class districts of well-entrenched white ethnics and spreading into middle-class neighborhoods occupied by white residents with sufficient means to move in the face of racial penetration. The West Side ghetto, for example, expanded into middle-class Austin but not into Cicero, a working-class community of Slavic background. Philip H. Rees, "The Factorial Ecology of Chicago: A Case Study," in Brian J. Berry and Frank Horton (eds.), *Geographic Perspectives in Urban Systems* (Englewood Cliffs, N.J.: Prentice-Hall, 1970), pp. 319–394.

new exodus to suburbia is a further blow to the big cities, especially those in the Northeast and Midwest, that have already lost a large portion of their middle-class white constituency and can ill afford to see their higher status blacks also leave.

The National Advisory Commission on Civil Disorders warned in 1968 that "our nation is moving toward two societies, one black, one white—separate and unequal." Although gains have been made since then in curtailing discriminatory practices in employment and education, virtually no progress has been achieved in altering segregated housing patterns. As far as place of dwelling is concerned, the nation remains two societies. The rigid pattern of residential segregation that accompanied the growth of the black population in urban areas continues within the central city and is now being extended to suburbia.[28] As a long line of research shows, Americans are less willing to desegregate their residential environs than almost any other public realm of life.[29]

Hispanic Origin Urbanites

The second largest minority in the United States, those now classified by the Census Bureau as "persons of Hispanic origin," numbered nearly 12 million in 1978 (not counting "undocumented workers"), a gain of almost one-third since 1970 (Table 2.6). This

Table 2.6   POPULATION CHANGES IN SMSAs* BY HISPANIC ORIGIN, 1970 TO 1978 (numbers in thousands)

RESIDENCE	1970	1978	PERCENT CHANGES 1970–1978
Metropolitan areas	7409	9961	34.4
In central cities	4646	5886	26.7
Outside central cities	2763	4075	47.4
Nonmetropolitan areas	1578	1829	15.9
U.S. total	8987	11,790	31.2

*As defined in 1970.
SOURCE: U.S. Bureau of the Census, "Population Profile of the United States, 1978," *Current Population Reports,* Series P-20, No. 336 (Washington, D.C., 1979), p. 34.

[28]Karl E. Taeuber and Alma Taeuber, *Negroes in Cities* (Chicago: Aldine, 1965), p. 68. Also Annemette Sorenson, Karl Taeuber, and L. J. Hollingsworth, "Indexes of Racial Residential Segregation for 109 Cities in the United States, 1940 to 1970," Institute for Research in Poverty Discussion Papers (Madison, Wis., 1974). The growing apartheid in metropolitan communities is documented in a series of articles "Race and Residence in American Cities," *Annals of the American Academy of Political and Social Science* 441 (January 1979).
[29]See in this connection Gerald D. Suttles, *The Social Construction of Communities* (Chicago: University of Chicago Press, 1972).

segment of the nation's population is predominantly urban. Eighty-four percent of the Hispanics live in SMSAs, a proportion higher than that of both blacks and whites. Within the metropolitan areas, the percentage who reside outside central cities (41 percent) is much greater than the corresponding ratio for blacks (26 percent). They are also a young population, 42 percent being under 18 years of age and only 4 percent 65 years and over; the comparable proportions for non-Hispanics are 29 and 11 percent, respectively.

Six of every ten persons of Hispanic origin are either Mexican born or descendants of Mexican families. Puerto Ricans comprise the second largest group, followed by Cubans and those of Central and South America origin (Figure 2.4). The highest proportions are found in California, Texas, and New York, with secondary concentrations in Arizona, Colorado, Florida, Illinois, and New Mexico. The first wave of Hispanic immigrants came from Mexico during the 1920s, but many returned to their homeland during the Great

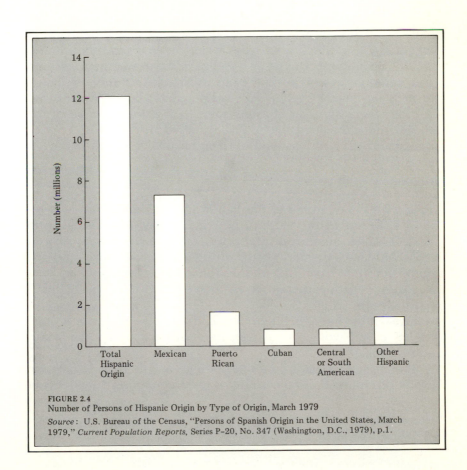

FIGURE 2.4
Number of Persons of Hispanic Origin by Type of Origin, March 1979

Source: U.S. Bureau of the Census, "Persons of Spanish Origin in the United States, March 1979," Current Population Reports, Series P-20, No. 347 (Washington, D.C., 1979), p.1.

Depression of the following decade. The influx resumed in the 1950s and has continued to the present. Large households are still characteristic of the Hispanics but the family as an institution is no longer the bulwark of tradition it once was.

Other Ethnic Minorities

A third segment of the population, native American Indians, is the least urban of the minority groups. Of the 750,000 in this category, only about 200,000 reside in metropolitan areas, congregated largely in the poorer neighborhoods, and the remainder live on reservations. The Los Angeles–Long Beach area contains the highest number of the urban dwellers, about 50,000. Other concentrations of 10,000 or more are found in Chicago, Oklahoma City, Phoenix, and Tulsa. The American Indian Movement (AIM) began to play an activist role during the late 1960s in behalf of the urban Indians but now focuses its attention mainly on the reservations.

A fourth minority, persons of Asian origin, is relatively small in numbers but growing significantly because of changed immigration policies and the influx of refugees from Vietnam and other Southeast Asian countries. A large percentage of the newcomers settle in urban communities in the West. In Los Angeles County, for example, only one census tract in 1950 was populated by an Asian majority; today there are over 50 such tracts. It is estimated that of the 200,000 Indochinese refugees that resettled in the United States prior to mid-1979, at least half of them located in California.

WOMEN: A NEW MINORITY

Along with the elderly and the handicapped, women are now referred to as one of the nation's new minorities. This designation does not reflect numerical inferiority—women outnumber men in the United States by more than 6 million—but symbolizes the discrimination they have long endured in a male-dominated or "sexist" society.[30] Although there have been earlier campaigns by feminists to secure women's rights—the efforts of the suffragettes, for instance—it has been the liberation (Lib) movement of recent years that has raised women's consciousness of their individual worth and potential.

Pressure from feminist organizations and federal legislation barring discrimination on account of sex are opening new doors to

[30]Women outnumber men only in the urban areas. The nonmetropolitan population is almost equally divided between the two sexes.

women. Gains in achieving greater equality with men have been slow in coming, however. Lending agencies, credit bureaus, social and religious institutions, employers, labor unions, and society in general have found it difficult to adjust to the changed status of women. Disparities between the sexes in wages and promotion policies continue, equal opportunity laws receive only token compliance in many cases, and ratification of the Equal Rights Amendment (ERA) to the Constitution remains stalled.

Women are making their most prominent advances in the public sector. A 1976 survey found that they held from 4 to 7 percent of all elective offices in the United States, a proportion that has undoubtedly increased since then.[31] At the national level they presently (1981) occupy 18 seats in the House of Representatives and two in the Senate (Nancy Landon Kassebaum of Kansas and Paula Hawkins of Florida). They also hold one cabinet level post (the number was two in the previous Administration) and 42 federal judgeships. The preponderant majority of them serving on the national bench are appointees of President Carter. Congressional authorization for over 125 new judgeships early in his term of office gave him opportunity to make an unprecedented number of judicial appointments.

At the state level women hold from 8 to 10 percent of the elective offices in the executive and lawmaking branches of government (a record total of women, over 1400, ran for legislative seats in 1980). Two of their number were serving as state governors at the end of the decade: the late Ella Grasso of Connecticut and Dixy Lee Ray of Washington who was defeated for reelection in 1980. Locally, although the figures are not impressive—women occupy only about 4 percent of all mayoralty and council posts—they have achieved some notable victories in recent years. At the close of the 1970s they held the office of mayor in such large cities as Chicago, Cincinnati, Oklahoma City, Phoenix, San Francisco, San Jose, and St. Petersburg. The public, moreover, is now generally receptive to their candidacies at all levels of the political system. According to a recent Gallup poll, three of every four Americans believe that the country would be as well, if not better, governed if more women held office. About the same proportion also say that they would vote for a quali-

---

[31]Marilyn Johnson and Kathy Stanwick, *Profile of Women Holding Office* (Rutgers, N.J.: Eagleton Institute of Politics, Center for the American Woman and Politics, 1976). See also R. Darcy and Sarah Schramm, "When Women Run Against Men," *Public Opinion Quarterly* 41 (Spring 1977): 1–12; and Marilyn Johnson, "Women and Elective Office," *Society* (May/June 1980), 63–69. For a discussion of the feminist movement see Barbara Deckard, *The Women's Movement*, 2d ed. (New York: Harper & Row, 1979).

fied female candidate for president (in a 1937 poll only one-third answered similarly).

As women become more numerous and established in responsible governmental and private positions they are likely to bring about changes in the long-standing mores and practices of business and the professions and in the conduct of public office. Based on fragmentary data it appears that women officials as a whole are more supportive of human needs, more open in their dealings, and far less prone to corruption than men officeholders.[32] A study in 1977 by the Center for the American Woman and Politics at Rutgers University found that women officials—regardless of their party affiliation or ideological predispositions—are more concerned than their male counterparts with such issues as child care, abortion, family violence, drug abuse, and social security for homemakers. Aside from the question of equity, it is a failure on the part of society not to draw more heavily on the perspectives and talents that women can bring to the governance of urban communities and the nation in general. To paraphrase one feminist, women are America's unrecognized political resource.

URBAN HOUSEHOLDS

The social structure of metropolitan areas reflects not only current population movements and racial settlement patterns but also the changes that are taking place in the size and composition of urban households. (Household is a broader term than family and includes persons whom the census refers to as "unrelated individuals," those living alone or with nonrelatives.) There are over 50 million households in the nation's SMSAs, three-fourths of which are maintained by families. In recent years their average size has dropped sharply, from 3.33 in 1960 to 2.86 in 1977.

The decline in size is attributable in part to the lower birthrate of recent years and in part to the huge increase in the number of households composed of adults only, many of a single person. This increase is due to several factors: (1) the high divorce rate (one for every two marriages); (2) the growing proportion of women in their early twenties who remain unmarried; (3) the entrance of more women into the work force; (4) the large rise in the number of unmarried couples living together; and (5) the trend among the elderly to maintain their own homes.

The most important development relative to household compo-

---

[32]See John C. Bollens and Henry J. Schmandt, *Political Corruption: Power, Money, and Sex* (Pacific Palisades, Calif.: Palisades Publishers, 1979).

Table 2.7 FAMILIES MAINTAINED BY WOMEN, BY TYPE OF
RESIDENCE, 1977 AND 1970 (numbers in thousands—1970
metropolitan area definition)

TYPE OF RESIDENCE	1977	1970	PERCENT CHANGE 1970 TO 1977
United States	*7713*	*5629*	*37.0*
Metropolitan areas	5655	4088	38.3
Central cities	3221	2480	29.9
Suburban areas	2434	1608	51.4
Metropolitan areas of 1 million or more	3388	2487	36.2
Central cities	1850	1477	25.2
Suburban areas	1538	1010	52.2
Metropolitan areas of less than 1 million	2267	1601	41.6
Central cities	1,371	1003	36.7
Suburban areas	896	598	49.8
Nonmetropolitan areas	2058	1541	33.5

SOURCE: U.S. Bureau of the Census, "Social and Economic Characteristics of the
Metropolitan and Nonmetropolitan Population, 1977 and 1970," *Current Population
Reports,* Special Studies, Series P-23, No. 75 (Washington, D.C., 1978), p. 10.

sition is the rapid increase of female-headed families (those maintained by women with no husband present).[33] From 1970 to 1977
the number of such families in metropolitan areas rose by over 1.5
million, about one and one-half times the increase during the entire
1960s (Table 2.7). The central cities, although containing only 40
percent of all SMSA households, have 57 percent of those maintained by women. About one of every four central city children
compared to one of eight suburban youngsters are members of such
households. This disproportion is due principally to the racial geography of the SMSAs. Blacks are heavily concentrated in the core
municipalities and the incidence of one-parent families among
them is twice as high as among whites.

    Families living in central municipalities and their urban rings
are in the aggregate more similar in composition than the popular
image of each area would lead one to believe. Little difference exists between the two sections in the average size of families and in
the proportion of them with no children under 18 years of age living

[33]Starting with the 1980 census the terms "head of family" and "head of household"
have been dropped because, as the Census Bureau explains, "recent social changes
have resulted in a trend toward more nearly equal status for adult members of a
household."

at home. Where the two vary sharply is in the percentage of single-individual households. One of every three such households in the city is now maintained by a person living alone or with nonrelatives, compared to one of five in the fringe area. The suburbs, in other words, are more familistic than the central municipalities but do not differ appreciably on other factors relating to households. These similarities and variances have obvious implications for the kind of services that local governments are called on to provide. The single person and the childless couple, for example, are more likely to be interested in recreational and cultural amenities (which the central city offers) than in the quality of the schools (which the suburbs offer).

AGE STRUCTURE

Along with class, race, and household composition, the age structure of a community comprises an important facet of its social profile. This structure is more than an object of sociological interest. It reflects the kinds of needs that residents have as well as trends in fertility, mortality, and migration. Each age group has its own set of public service requirements. Young families want good schools and recreational areas for their children; the middle-aged are more interested in neighborhood maintenance and a quiet environment; and the elderly are particularly concerned with health facilities, personal safety, and means of transportation. Each group also has certain behavior characteristics associated with it. Crime, for example, is highest among youths between the ages of 14 and 21; young people under 25 are less likely to belong to organizations and to vote than those between the ages of 25 to 55; and the elderly change their place of residence less often than the rest of the population.

A wide range of age patterns is found among urban communities. At one extreme are the retirement settlements, such as Sun City, Florida, where children are barred and at least one of the spouses must be over 55 years of age. At the other end of the spectrum are the suburban tract developments, such as Irvine, California, composed predominantly of younger families in the child-rearing stage of life.

Two-thirds of Americans 65 and over reside in SMSAs, almost equally divided between central cities and suburbs (Figure 2.5). However, a great proportion of the elderly poor are located in the core municipalities, reflecting the socioeconomic and racial composition of these units. Black and Hispanic persons in the 65 and over category, a majority of whom live in the central cities, are dispro-

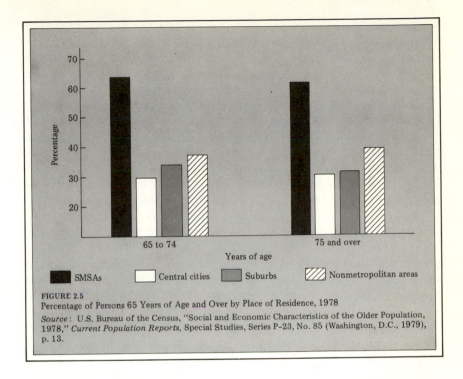

FIGURE 2.5
Percentage of Persons 65 Years of Age and Over by Place of Residence, 1978

Source: U.S. Bureau of the Census, "Social and Economic Characteristics of the Older Population, 1978," *Current Population Reports*, Special Studies, Series P–23, No. 85 (Washington, D.C., 1979), p. 13.

portionately represented among the poor. In 1977, for example, 36 percent of the black and 22 percent of the Hispanic elderly had incomes below the poverty level in contrast to the white ratio of 12 percent.

Age Trends

Four demographic trends of recent years are changing the age structure of urban areas: increasing life expectancy, expansion of the senior citizen group, rise in the median age, and decrease in the school age population. The first two are related primarily to the drop in the mortality rate; the third to both lower mortality and a declining birthrate; and the fourth to the decrease in births.

The life expectancy of Americans at time of birth is now 69 years for males and 76.7 for females, the highest in the nation's history (the corresponding figures in 1960 were 66.6 and 73.1). Although the gap between the two sexes has lengthened by more than one year during the last two decades, experts predict that it will narrow in the future as more women become subjected to the same job stresses as men. A gap also exists between the life expectancy of whites and blacks. A newly born white child is expected to live approximately 74 years and a black child 69. The difference has decreased markedly over the last several decades—it was 11 years in 1940—as economic conditions have improved for many blacks and better health services have become available to them.

With the increase in life expectancies the proportion of elderly in the society has risen. Since the turn of the century the number of persons 65 and over has increased nearly eight times, whereas the total population tripled. By the end of the 1970s the elderly constituted over 11 percent (25 million) of the total population. The rise in the number of older residents has led to a growing national awareness of their needs and contributions. Congressional action in 1978 barring mandatory retirement at age 65 is but one indication of the increasing political impact of senior citizens. At the local level the expansion of the upper-age categories is bolstering support for public action in such functional areas as mass transit, police protection, emergency ambulance service, and subsidized housing for the elderly poor. It is also causing suburban governments, which have generally ignored the special needs of their older residents, to give more attention to this segment of their constituencies.

Because of fewer births and greater longevity, the population of the United States is becoming older. At the end of the 1970s the median age nationally was slightly over 30 compared to 28 at the beginning of the decade. Both of the large minority populations are considerably younger than the white average of 31, the median age of metropolitan area blacks being 24 and Hispanics 22. The disparity is somewhat greater in the central cities of the large SMSAs (those over one million) where the median age for whites is 33; blacks, 25; and Hispanics, 23. As the ratios indicate, persons of Hispanic origin constitute the youngest age group in the society.

Related to the lower birthrate is the precipitous drop in the number of school age children. Both city and suburb are experiencing the decline which began in the late 1960s.[34] Enrollment in elementary and high schools is down by more than 11 percent since 1970 and is expected to fall by another 10 percent during the next decade. Hundreds of schools have already been closed in suburban communities as well as in the central cities, setting off at times almost as much controversy as the desegregation issue. The full impact of this change in age structure is yet to be felt. It will have a major effect on the size of the labor force, military recruitment, col-

---

[34]Enrollment in kindergarten through eighth grade peaked at about 37 million in 1969. The total has dropped each year since then.

lege enrollment, local public services, the housing market, and perhaps even crime rates (criminologists predict that they will drop as
the number of youths decline). The decreased birthrate, moreover,
does not appear to be a temporary phenomenon that will soon pass
but a fundamental social change reflecting the new role and status
of women in society.

NEW DIRECTIONS

The urban scene is one of long-standing features and new trends, of
anticipated changes and unexpected developments. Continuity can
be observed in the persistent pattern of residential segregation by
class and race and discontinuities in the revolutionary changes in
the concept of the family and the status of women. These and other
trends discussed in this chapter give us some sense of the direction
in which metropolitan America is moving.

1. Wide disparities continue to exist (and in some cases are
   increasing) between the large and aging cities of the Northeast and North Central regions and their suburbs, whereas
   near parity prevails between the two segments in the South
   and West.
2. Unanticipated reversal of the black migration pattern (along
   with lower birthrates and the stepped-up movement of nonwhites to suburbia) has brought black population growth to
   a virtual halt in the large core cities of the Northeast and
   North Central states. It is too early to say whether this development will lead to more racially balanced core cities.
3. Blacks who are leaving the central cities to either go south
   or enter suburbia are typically younger, more educated, and
   economically better off than those who remain, a trend
   highly disadvantageous to the core municipalities.
4. One of every four blacks and two-thirds of the whites in
   SMSAs live outside the central municipality. The number of
   black suburbanites—approximately 5 million in 1980—is
   showing substantial gains although the proportion relative
   to the total outlying population has risen by less than one
   percentage point over the last two decades. This share will
   expand as the slower growth of the suburban white population, first evidenced in the 1970s, continues.
5. An increasing number of older and formerly all-white suburban communities adjacent to the large central cities are
   undergoing racial transition.

6. The Hispanic segment of the urban populace is increasing at a faster rate than other minority groups. About 10 million persons of Hispanic origin (as compared to 18.5 million blacks) now reside in SMSAs, a rise of more than one-third since 1970. Unlike the black population that is widely dispersed throughout the United States, the Hispanics are highly concentrated, more than one-half their number residing in California and Texas. In several SMSAs, principally Los Angeles, San Antonio, Denver, and Miami, they constitute the predominant minority.

7. The decreasing size of urban households is a factor that is contributing to the population losses in many large cities and some suburbs. (As noted in Chapter 1, the 1980 census figures brought frantic charges of miscounting from officials in these areas.) The matter is of great importance to them because population provides the basis for much federal funding under the grant programs as well as for the reapportionment of congressional seats.

The social topography of urban areas is obviously not a static configuration of territorially situated groups and life-styles. Although the basic features of the social map persist, developments are occurring that carry the potential for reshaping the urban pattern in important ways. It is still not clear as to how changing population characteristics, energy shortages, resource limitations, and slower growth will impact on metropolitan communities and their component parts. There is, however, increasing recognition of the import of these developments for economic strategies, social programs, and political actions at all levels of government.[35]

[35]See in this connection Reid Reynolds, Bryant Robey, and Cheryl Russell, "Demographics of the 1980s," *American Demographics* 2 (January 1980): 11–19.

Chapter 3
Economic Structure

SMSAs collectively represent an impressive aggregation of wealth and power. They contain almost 75 percent of the nation's people, more than three-fourths of its labor force, and in excess of 75 percent of its taxable property. They serve as headquarters for most of its large corporate organizations, house most of its financial institutions, and produce (and consume) the preponderant share of its goods and services. Not all SMSAs, however, are dynamic centers of commerce and finance. Some face serious economic decline, and some resemble small towns more than cosmopolitan cities. All have certain economic similarities but they differ widely in the content and extent of their specialization.

The economic structure of urban communities is a legacy of the Industrial Revolution. The transformation brought about by industrialization, such as mass production of goods and intense specialization, is familiar to all Americans. What often remains unrecognized is that economic forces are prime determinants of the physical and ecological structure of cities. Directly or indirectly these forces influence the pattern of living as well as the social and governmental institutions of urban complexes. Changes in the mode of production or economic organization are inevitably reflected in the urban scene. Technological advances can revolutionize even the social geography of communities. The automobile is a prime example; in less than half a century it transformed closely textured cities into sprawling metropolises and changed the life styles of millions of families.

Urban economics is a relatively new field. The first textbook on the subject did not make its appearance until 1965 and few economists concerned themselves with urban-related research before then.[1] What knowledge there was of the economies of cities and SMSAs came mostly from the works of geographers and planners. This situation, however, changed over the last two decades as an

---

[1]Wilbur R. Thompson, *A Preface to Urban Economics* (Baltimore: Johns Hopkins Press, 1965).

impressive number of economists turned their attention to the urban realm. At least a dozen textbooks in the field have been published in recent years and a professional periodical (*Journal of Urban Economics*) has been inaugurated.[2] Today the subject has increased in stature to the point where it has become a recognized specialty in the discipline.

Much of the research in this area involves the application of conventional economic principles, such as the law of supply and demand, to the problems of cities and metropolitan aggregations. To the economist the urban community is a dynamic system of interdependent markets: land, housing, labor, transportation, public services. As one representative text illustrates, these markets are the focal points around which urban economics as a subject of inquiry is organized.[3] Most economists specializing in the urban field direct their efforts primarily to analyses of the various markets and the problems associated with them. They deal with such concepts as economic base (the mix of income generating activities), externalities (the spillover of costs and benefits from one jurisdiction to another), economies of scale (the decrease in unit costs of public goods or services as production rises), and price (a mechanism for influencing consumer behavior).

ECONOMIC BASE

Urban areas differ widely in their economic characteristics, whether income levels, type and degree of specialization, or geographical sphere of influence.[4] A report by a national commission in 1937 emphasized the importance of distinguishing communities according to their economic features. As it noted,

> Whatever uniformities may be found in the life of urbanites, it will make some difference whether the city in which they live is an indus-

[2]Representative of such works are David W. Rasmussen, *Urban Economics* (New York: Harper & Row, 1973); Richard F. Muth, *Urban Economic Problems* (New York: Harper & Row, 1975); and Harry W. Richardson, *The New Urban Economics and Alternatives* (London: Pion, 1977). See also Harry W. Richardson, "A Guide to Urban Economic Texts: A Review Article," *Urban Studies* 10 (October 1973): 399–405.

[3]Werner Z. Hirsch, *Urban Economic Analysis* (New York: McGraw-Hill, 1973).

[4]Many different classifications of cities have been made. Among them are Jeffrey Hadden and Edgar Borgatta, *American Cities: Their Social Characteristics* (Chicago: Rand McNally, 1965); Richard L. Forstall, "A New Social and Economic Grouping of Cities," *Municipal Year Book, 1970*, pp. 102–152; and Beverly Duncan and Stanley Lieberson, *Metropolis and Region in Transition* (Beverly Hills, Calif.: Sage, 1970). For a treatment of classification methods see Brian J. L. Berry (ed.), *City Classification Handbook: Methods and Applications* (New York: Wiley, 1972).

trial, commercial, or residential city; a capital, an educational center, or a resort; whether it depends on mines, oil wells, timber, a port, river, or railroad; and whether its economic base is unitary or multiple, balanced or unbalanced.[5]

A community's economic base, in other words, influences the manner and style in which its residents live. To identify this base it is necessary to know what types of productive activity the community is engaged in and their magnitude relative to each other. The structure may be highly diversified, with many categories of business and industry operating; or it may be relatively narrow with a single industry, such as aircraft manufacturing, or a single group of businesses, such as those serving a tourist trade, dominating the economic life of the area.

Export and Local Industries

The economic base of an urban area may be thought of simply as the productive activities that enable the residents to earn their livelihood. Analyses of this base commonly distinguish between export and local industries. The first includes those that bring money into the community from outside; the second, those that produce goods and services for consumption by people residing within the area. Automobile and steel manufacturing are typical of the export industries because most of the output is destined for external markets. Conversely, the retail trade and service industries are representative of the locally oriented sector because their output is primarily for the satisfaction of internal demands.

The ascribed importance of specialized production for outside markets has prompted some writers to classify businesses engaged principally in this type of activity as basic or city-forming, implying that such industries provide the major source of urban growth and the prime reason for the existence of urban settlements as centers of economic enterprise. The local activities, on the other hand, are referred to as nonbasic or city-serving. The general assumption underlying the distinction is that most metropolitan areas are self-sufficient with respect to one set of industries and at the same time are specialized producers of certain types of output beyond their own needs. The revenues derived from the external sales of these latter commodities enable a community to finance the importation of goods and services it cannot produce for itself.

[5]National Resources Committee, *Our Cities: Their Role in the National Economy* (Washington, D.C., 1937), p. 8.

This depiction of an urban area as heavily dependent on external trade casts the export sector in the key role relative to the economic well-being and growth of metropolitan settlements. Not all economists, however, are willing to accept the proposition that export activities are more important to a community than those of a local character. Some even argue that the service sector is basic because its efficiency is critical to the operation of export firms. In their view the high development of business, personal, and governmental services, together with other ancillary activities, enables a metropolis to sustain, expand, and when necessary replace primary industries that may be lost to the uncertainties of the market. As planner Hans Blumenfeld puts the case, it is the nonbasic industries that "constitute the real and lasting strength of the metropolitan economy. As long as they continue to function efficiently, the metropolis will always be able to substitute new 'export' industries for any that may be destroyed by the vicissitudes of economic life."[6]

Whatever the merits of this position, several facts should be noted concerning the export-local pattern. First, a community improves its balance of payment ratio when it produces goods it previously imported. The effect of this production is the same as a corresponding increase in its exports. Second, as a community increases in size and becomes more metropolitan in character the percentage of persons employed in basic activities decreases, whereas the proportion furnishing goods and services needed locally rises. In short, the larger the community, the greater the variety and differentiation of its activities and the more its inhabitants live, to use Blumenfeld's expression, "by taking in each other's washing." Third, as local business services become more varied and improve in quality, they inevitably replace similar services previously imported from larger and more highly developed neighboring areas. The net effect is for the local economy to increase its degree of self-sufficiency in this sector also.

Virtually all large SMSAs now exhibit some activity in each major nonagricultural group of industries, and the overall trend is for them to produce more of their own requirements. Despite this enlargement of the local sector, however, the economic fortunes of urban areas remain tied in varying degrees to their chief export activities: automobiles in Detroit, cameras in Rochester, tourism in Miami, public administration in the nation's capital. Like countries, cities must trade with each other. They must reach out for raw ma-

[6]"The Economic Base of the Metropolis: Critical Remarks on the Basic-Nonbasic Concept," *Journal of the American Institute of Planners* 21 (Fall 1955): 131.

terials and semiprocessed goods for their manufacturing plants (and food products for their populations). To maximize their economic position, they must produce goods and services in which they enjoy comparative cost advantages over other areas (because of favorable location, skilled labor, or other factors) in order to trade for commodities in which they have comparative disadvantages. Here the local service sector is an important contributing factor because its efficiency will be reflected in the costs of the export industries.

Growth Determinants

Aside from such basic factors as geographical location and industry mix, the most important single determinant of economic well-being and growth in any metropolitan area or region is the level of production and expansion in the national economy. A rise or decline in the rate of production for the country as a whole will be reflected in varying degrees among its parts. When the nation surges ahead economically, most of the regions evidence substantial growth; when the nation lags, so do the regions. The reason is clear: The country in large measure has become a single, highly interdependent economic unit. Major industries produce for a national market; securities and money markets have become predominantly nationwide in scope; and psychological attitudes of both business decision makers and consumers are transmitted throughout the economy.

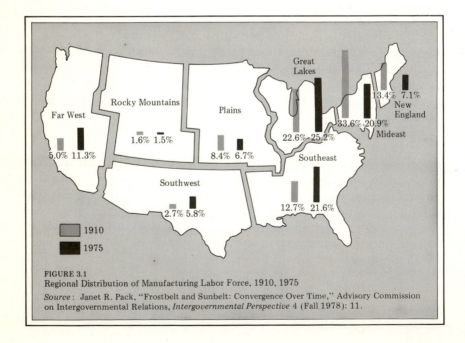

FIGURE 3.1
Regional Distribution of Manufacturing Labor Force, 1910, 1975

Source: Janet R. Pack, "Frostbelt and Sunbelt: Convergence Over Time," Advisory Commission on Intergovernmental Relations, *Intergovernmental Perspective* 4 (Fall 1978): 11.

Changes in the national picture, however, do not affect all areas in the same way. Some grow at a faster rate than others and some even decline. Technological advances, product substitutes, changes in merchandising practices, and the increased mobility of retired citizens are among the factors that have greater impact on one community than another. The most significant interregional development of recent years, noted previously in connection with population movement, is the shift of economic activity from the Northeast and Midwest to the new growth poles of what geographer Brian Berry calls the "amenity-rich locations of the western and southern rimland"(see Figure 3.1). On almost any measure—value added by manufacturing, retail and wholesale trade, or rate of income increase—the sunbelt metropolises are outpacing the rest of the nation. From 1970 to 1975 more than 85 percent of the new jobs in the United States were located in the South and West. The causes of this shift are many and varied. Those most frequently cited are a more favorable labor climate (right-to-work laws, less unionization, less worker activism), lower land values, better access to energy, lower living costs for employees, less congestion and industrial obsolescence, and lower taxes.[7]

Changes in personal income also affect the economies of metropolitan areas differently. Consumers with rising per capita incomes tend to increase their spending more on durable goods and luxuries such as automobiles and color televison sets than on staple items such as food and clothing. Economists refer to this phenomenon as "income elasticity of demand," or the ratio of the percent change in spending on a product to the percent change in disposable income. SMSAs specializing in the production of goods with an income-elastic demand are generally in the most favorable long-run position, although they may be hardest hit in times of recession.

The economic fate of an urban community, in brief, depends largely on what happens nationally. An individual metropolis can, at best, adapt itself to external forces and trends and provide some insulation against adverse effects of cyclical changes in the national economy. It can, for example, strengthen its competitive capabilities by upgrading the area's labor pool through education and training. Or it can vigorously recruit industries that would diversify its productive base and provide more stability to the local economy.[8]

---

[7]The development of air conditioning has also increased the attractiveness of the South to business and industry.

[8]Some communities endeavor to utilize local capital expenditures in ways that improve the investment climate for business, such as upgrading the physical infrastructure, developing industrial parks, and constructing plants for lease to private firms. Many of them are also using tax incentives to stimulate private investment. One popular method is not to tax the improvements on land for a given period of years.

To proceed effectively along these lines, a metropolitan community must have a sophisticated understanding of its economic structure, be able to identify its capabilities, and know what is needed to take advantage of technical progress—expertise too often lacking. Also important, an SMSA cannot permit internal competition among the local units for industry and resources to undermine its competitive position vis-à-vis other metropolitan areas.

THE LABOR MARKET

The metropolis can be viewed in economic terms as an instrument for the creation of wealth and the provision of want-satisfying goods and services. Essentially it is a local labor market, a fact emphasized by R. D. McKenzie and other social ecologists who define the territorial boundaries of the metropolitan community by place of residence—place of work criteria. In an advanced urban society the economic structure will be characterized by an extensive division of labor and a high degree of occupational differentiation. A great variety of job opportunities is required for large numbers of people to reside together at reasonable standards of living. In the sizable urban settlements these opportunities, similar to the social groupings we observed earlier, are widely distributed in space. No longer is the lion's share of jobs found within central cities as was formerly the case. The continued dispersion of industrial and commercial activities to suburban locations has brought about major revisions in the classic pattern.

Approximately 100 million Americans are now in the nation's civilian work force. This represents an increase of almost 30 million since 1960. The large majority of these workers (nearly 70 percent) are SMSA dwellers, three of every five living in suburbia. The number of employed central city residents has declined in most northern and midwestern metropolises, reflecting population losses. The work force in nonmetropolitan areas, on the other hand, showed substantial gains during the 1970s, increasing by almost 7 million.

The stereotypical image of employed suburbanites as mostly white-collar and core city workers as blue-collar is applicable to only some SMSAs. Nationally, the difference in the occupational distribution of the two residential groups is not great. As Table 3.1 shows, the only substantial variance occurs in the service category, where the proportion is higher in the central municipality. Greater differences are found when the occupational distribution of workers within and outside SMSAs is compared. The proportion of the nonmetropolitan labor force in white-collar employment (41

Table 3.1 PERCENT DISTRIBUTION OF EMPLOYED PERSONS BY MAJOR OCCUPATION GROUP WITHIN AND OUTSIDE SMSAs,* 1977

OCCUPATION GROUP	CENTRAL CITY (%)	SUBURBAN AREAS (%)	NON-METROPOLITAN AREAS (%)
White collar			
Professional and technical	15.8	17.5	12.5
Managerial	10.5	11.8	9.9
Sales workers	6.4	7.2	4.9
Clerical	20.9	19.1	13.8
Blue collar			
Craft workers	11.1	13.2	13.7
Operatives	14.5	13.3	19.0
Laborers	4.3	4.1	5.1
Service workers	16.3	12.5	14.1
Farmers and farm workers	0.2	1.3	7.0
Total	100.0	100.0	100.0

*1970 SMSA definition.
SOURCE: U.S. Bureau of the Census, "Social and Economic Characteristics of the Metropolitan and Nonmetropolitan Population, 1977 and 1970," *Current Population Reports,* Special Studies, P-23, No. 75 (Washington, D.C., 1978), p. 13.

percent) is substantially smaller than the corresponding ratio within metropolitan areas (54 percent). The percentage of blue-collar workers, on the other hand, is higher in nonmetropolitan counties (38 percent) than in SMSAs (30 percent), an indication of the extent to which rural America has become dependent on industrial jobs. In fact, only 7 percent of its labor force is now involved in agricultural pursuits.

During the past several decades the economy of the United States has been converted from one based predominantly on the manufacture of tangible goods to one strongly oriented toward the production and consumption of services.[9] Some economists refer to this transformation as the entrance into a "postindustrial society." The change, however one describes it, is evident in the employment statistics. In 1947 over one-half the nation's work force produced tangible goods and the rest, intangibles or services. By 1978 the picture had dramatically altered, with less than one of every three employed persons in the manufacture of tangible products.[10]

[9]The switch to a service-oriented economy was made possible by technological advances that greatly increased productivity in the manufacturing sector.
[10]See Chester A. Newland, "Future Images: Urban Diversity and Democracy," *Municipal Year Book, 1979,* p. 5.

The move to a service economy can also be seen in the distribution of workers among the occupational categories. Over the past quarter century the rate of increase of white-collar workers has been three times as great as that of blue-collar employees. The service-oriented sectors have experienced similar expansion. (These include the three categories designated by the Census Bureau as "service industries," "public administration," and "finance-insurance-real estate.")[11] During a recent six-year period (1972 to 1978), employment in these three groups increased by almost 6 million compared to 1.6 million in manufacturing.

Historically, the service sectors have not offered as many employment opportunities in urban areas as the goods-producing industries. Now the situation is reversed, with the preponderant majority of new jobs being generated by the service industries. This shift in the occupational pattern has opened up new work opportunities for women, young people, and part-time personnel. Conversely the switch to a "postindustrial society" has adversely affected the older cities of the Northeast and North Central regions whose economies have long revolved around manufacturing. Many now find themselves left with an industrial infrastructure that is becoming increasingly obsolete.

Employment Among Minorities

Despite affirmative action programs, employment opportunities and job mobility are not enjoyed equally by all segments of the population. Jobless rates in the poorer sections of the larger cities are more than double those of other neighborhoods and similar wide differences are found between central municipalities and suburbs. Unemployment among urban blacks is more than twice as high as among whites, a ratio that has remained virtually unchanged over the last two decades. Black teenagers are particularly disadvantaged in the labor market with a persistent jobless rate six to seven times that of the labor force in general. Unemployment among workers of Hispanic origin is also high, the percentage being more comparable to that of blacks than whites.

Blacks now constitute about one of every ten—and Hispanics one of every 25—persons in the civilian labor force. Their occupational pattern, however, differs from that of whites. Only one-third

---

[11]The service industries, as defined by the Census Bureau, include the fields of health, education, welfare, entertainment, recreation, business and personal services, and repairs.

Table 3.2   EMPLOYED WORKERS BY RACE AND HISPANIC ORIGIN, 1978 (in millions)

EMPLOYMENT CATEGORY	WHITE	BLACK	HISPANIC
White-collar workers	43.4 (52)*	3.0 (34)	1.4 (33)
Blue-collar workers	27.6 (33)	3.5 (39)	2.0 (47)
Service workers	10.3 (12)	2.2 (25)	0.7 (17)
Farm workers	2.5 (3)	0.2 (2)	0.1 (3)
Total	83.8 (100)	8.9 (100)	4.2 (100)

*Numbers in parentheses represent percent.
SOURCE: U.S. Bureau of the Census, "Population Profile of the United States, 1978," *Current Population Reports,* Series P-20, No. 336 (Washington, D.C., 1979), pp. 56–58.

of blacks are employed in white-collar jobs in contrast to the 52 percent of whites in this category (Table 3.2). Only about one in eight holds a professional or managerial position, a proportion less than half that in the case of white workers.[12] The long-established pattern of denying minorities access to jobs in the upper levels of the occupational scale has been legally and politically challenged in recent years with only a modicum of success. The greatest gains for blacks (and to a lesser extent for persons of Hispanic origin) have been in the public sector where the number who have achieved high-status positions exceeds that in private industry by a substantial margin.

Women in the Labor Force

The most striking change in the composition of the civilian labor force has been the rapid rise in the number of female employees.[13] Women now constitute more than 40 percent of the nation's work complement, and over the past two decades they have accounted for 60 percent of the increase in its size. Those employed come from suburban and nonmetropolitan areas as well as from the central city (Figure 3.2). They include not only single persons but also married women at all stages of the family cycle. Currently, 60 percent of women with school age children and 40 percent of those with preschool youngsters are in the work force. The proportion of

[12]The occupational distribution pattern differs among Hispanics according to origin. Only 17 percent of Mexican origin workers, for example, are in the white-collar classification, compared to 37 percent of Cuban origin employees.
[13]The impact of this change is discussed in Eli Ginzberg, "The Job Problem," *Scientific American* 237 (November 1977): 43–51.

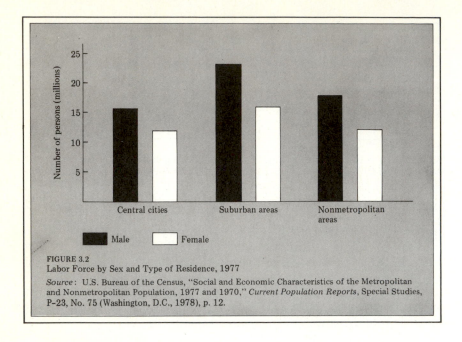

FIGURE 3.2
Labor Force by Sex and Type of Residence, 1977
Source: U.S. Bureau of the Census, "Social and Economic Characteristics of the Metropolitan and Nonmetropolitan Population, 1977 and 1970," *Current Population Reports*, Special Studies, P-23, No. 75 (Washington, D.C., 1978), p. 12.

employed among those with small children has more than tripled since 1950, an indication of the profound change in attitude on the part of many American families toward child rearing.[14]

Increases in the number of employed women are taking place in all industrial categories (Table 3.3). The largest growth is occurring in the service sector (particularly in health-related activities) and in wholesale and retail trade (principally the latter), with gains totaling more than 5 million from 1972 to 1978. In two of the groups (service industries and financial-insurance-real estate) women now outnumber men.

Similar to the case of blacks and Hispanics, women remain concentrated at the lower end of the occupational hierarchy. More than one of every two in the white-collar labor force, compared to less than one of six male workers, is employed in clerical positions (Table 3.4). The proportion in the managerial and administrative class (less than 10 percent) is only about one-fourth that of men who are in this group. The more favorable ratio in the professional and technical category (still 11 percentage points less than the corresponding figure for males) is due mainly to the large number of female teachers in elementary and secondary education. The record

[14]In over half the two-parent families in the United States both husband and wife are employed. In 1947 less than 20 percent of such families contained two earners.

Table 3.3 NUMBER OF EMPLOYED WORKERS BY INDUSTRY AND SEX, 1972 TO 1978 (in millions)

	MALE		FEMALE	
INDUSTRY CATEGORY	1972	1978	1972	1978
Agriculture and mining	3.5	3.5	0.8	0.8
Construction	5.0	5.6	0.3	0.4
Manufacturing	14.2	14.9	5.6	6.6
Transportation and communication	4.3	4.7	1.1	1.4
Wholesale and retail trade	9.6	10.5	6.9	8.8
Financial, insurance and real estate	2.2	2.4	2.1	3.0
Service industries	8.7	10.5	13.0	16.2
Public administration	3.1	3.4	1.3	1.7
Total	50.6	55.5	31.1	38.9

SOURCE: U.S. Bureau of the Census, "Population Profile of the United States, 1978," *Current Population Reports,* Series P-20, No. 336 (Washington, D.C., 1979), p. 45.

of women penetrating the upper ranks of the business world is poorer than in the public sector. A survey of 20 major corporations in 1975 revealed that female personnel represented less than 1 percent of all officials, managers, and professionals.[15]

INCOME

Closely related to the character of a metropolitan labor market and its occupational structure is the level of personal income enjoyed by residents of the area. Trends in per capita or family income are

Table 3.4 DISTRIBUTION OF WHITE-COLLAR WORKERS BY MAJOR OCCUPATION GROUP AND SEX, 1978 (numbers in millions)

	NUMBER OF WHITE-COLLAR WORKERS		PERCENTAGE OF TOTAL	
OCCUPATION GROUP	MALE	FEMALE	MALE	FEMALE
Professional and technical	8.2	6.0	36.1	24.8
Managers and administrators	7.7	2.4	34.2	9.6
Sales workers	3.3	2.7	14.5	10.8
Clerical workers	3.4	13.5	15.2	54.8
Total	22.6	24.6	100.0	100.0

SOURCE: Adapted from U.S. Bureau of the Census, "Population Profile of the United States, 1978," *Current Population Reports,* Series P-20, No. 336 (Washington, D.C., 1979), p. 44.

---

[15]For a general overview of this problem see Sandra Stencel, "Women in the Work Force," *Editorial Research Reports,* Vol. 1, No. 7 (February 18, 1977): 123–141.

constantly used as barometers for measuring the performance of an urban economy. Not only is income a sound indicator of purchasing power and productivity, but its local distributional pattern also reflects the social stratification of a community's population. Differences in this pattern occur in connection with population size, region, race, sex, and city–suburban location.

Income levels in the large SMSAs as a group are higher than in the less populous metropolitan areas (the gap, however, is narrowing). In 1976 both the median and mean family incomes in SMSAs of one million or more were approximately 10 percent higher than in the smaller metropolises (Table 3.5). Similarly, the income level in metropolitan communities as a whole exceeded that outside SMSAs by more than one-fifth. The importance of size—of aggregating a sufficient mass of people to permit broad specialization and thereby upgrading occupational opportunities—is evident even in the case of the nonmetropolitan areas. The 1976 median income of families living in nonmetropolitan counties having an urban place of at least 25,000 population was only 6 percent below the SMSA average; in the other less urbanized counties it was almost one-fourth less.

The variance in median family income is relatively small among all regions except the South where the average (in the late 1970s) was $2000 less than in other sections of the country. This gap, reflecting the lower degree of industrialization in the southern states, has been shrinking as their economies become more like those of the North. Bolstered by sharp employment gains during recent decades in such fields as textiles and apparels, chemicals,

Table 3.5 MEDIAN AND MEAN FAMILY INCOME BY PLACE OF RESIDENCE, 1976

PLACE OF RESIDENCE	MEDIAN INCOME (DOLLARS)	MEAN INCOME (DOLLARS)
SMSAs of 1 million or more	15,550	17,399
Central cities	12,937	14,890
Suburbs	17,156	18,959
SMSAs under 1 million	14,139	15,717
Central cities	13,031	14,980
Suburbs	14,859	16,336
All SMSAs	14,909	16,678
Nonmetropolitan areas	11,600	13,342

SOURCE: U.S. Bureau of the Census, "Money Income in 1976 of Families and Persons in the United States," *Current Population Reports*, Series P-60, No. 114 (Washington, D.C., 1978), p. 19.

machinery, printing, and fabricated metals, the South's per capita income rose from about two-thirds of the national average in 1940 to over 90 percent in 1980. Variations in this measure have been steadily declining among all the states since 1929 when per capita income ranged from 38 percent of the national average in South Carolina to 165 percent in New York. By 1969 the spread had narrowed, from 61 percent in Mississippi to 125 percent in Connecticut, a trend that continues to persist.[16]

Income Disparities Among Groups

Within SMSAs, wide income differentials exist between whites on the one hand and blacks and persons of Hispanic origin on the other. The median family income for whites in 1977 was $16,740; the corresponding figure for blacks was only $9,563 and for Hispanics $11,421. These proportions have changed little during the past decade, dispelling the belief that employment gains by minorities have significantly reduced income disparities between the races.[17]

The median for black families is somewhat misleading in that it is pulled down by the inordinate percentage of households, mainly those with no husband present, in low-income categories.[18] A significant number of black families have made economic gains and, as television documentaries like to point out, have moved into the middle class. In 1977, 30 percent of all black households had incomes of over $15,000 (in many cases only because both spouses worked). The corresponding ratio for white families was 57 percent and for those of Hispanic origin, 35 percent. Collectively, both blacks and Hispanics were worse off economically in 1977 than they were at the beginning of the decade. Increases in real income for all segments of the society were extremely sluggish during this period due to the rising rate of inflation. Yet, as Figure 3.3 shows,

[16]Advisory Commission on Intergovernmental Relations, *Improving Urban America: A Challenge to Federalism* (Washington, D.C., September 1976), p. 215.

[17]Black women, however, have fared better. In 1947 they earned only one-third as much as white women (primarily as domestics); in 1977 their salaries were nearly equal. They have benefited more than other groups from affirmative action programs because employers can meet both race and sex "quotas" by hiring black women.

[18]Thirty percent of the poverty population in the United States is black and 11 percent Hispanic. Almost one-third of all households with a female parent, no husband present, are below the poverty level compared to 5 percent of husband-wife families. Blacks are particularly disadvantaged in this respect because of the large number of female parent families among them (three-fifths of all black poor are members of such families).

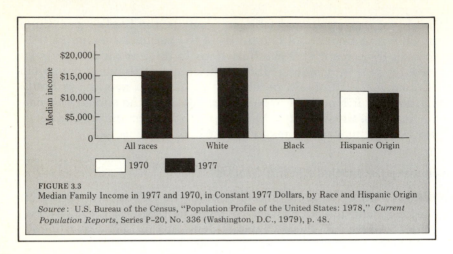

FIGURE 3.3
Median Family Income in 1977 and 1970, in Constant 1977 Dollars, by Race and Hispanic Origin
Source: U.S. Bureau of the Census, "Population Profile of the United States: 1978," *Current Population Reports*, Series P-20, No. 336 (Washington, D.C., 1979), p. 48.

median income for white families rose by 5 percent in constant dollars (adjusted for inflation) but dropped slightly for blacks and Hispanics—another indication that adverse economic conditions fall heaviest on minority groups. (Since 1977 real income for whites has also declined.)

Disparities also exist in the income structure between male and female workers. The median income of women who work full time is less than 60 percent that of fully employed men. Most of the difference is due to the occupational distribution pattern in which women are disproportionately represented in the lower-paying job categories. But a part of it is also attributable to the disparity in wages and salaries between male and female employees for comparable work. This inequity continues to persist, although not on the scale it once did, despite legislation barring discriminatory employment practices. The President's Council of Economic Advisors estimated in 1973 that women generally make less than men, "perhaps on the order of 20 percent less," on jobs calling for the same skill level, training, and experience.

Income disparities are also common (and in many cases increasing) between the older central cities and their suburbs. In 1960 core municipality families had median incomes 89 percent as large as those of suburban households; by 1978 the ratio had fallen to 79 percent. The variance between the two metropolitan segments, as discussed earlier, arises mainly from differences in their socioeconomic structure. Central cities in the aggregate contain a greater proportion of the poor, blue-collar workers, racial minorities, and families maintained by women than do the outlying areas.

However, it would be wrong to assume that the core communities are devoid of affluent residents. Over 5 million families with incomes above $20,000 live within their borders, a total that represents about one-third of all metropolitan households with comparably high incomes.

The total income of central city dwellers has been affected most by outmigration. Not only have the core municipalities lost population but they have also experienced an inflow of newcomers who are economically less well off than those who leave. During a recent two-year period over one million more families (and 54,000 unrelated individuals) left the cities than migrated to them. The average income of those families who entered was almost $1000 less (and for unrelated individuals $443 less) than that of the outmigrants. These changes represent an aggregate income loss (or drop in the buying power of central city residents) of $18 billion (Table 3.6).[19]

Approximately 25 million persons were members of households that had incomes below the poverty level in 1977.[20] Of this

Table 3.6 MEAN INCOME IN 1976 OF FAMILIES AND UNRELATED INDIVIDUALS WHO MIGRATED TO AND FROM CENTRAL CITIES, 1975 TO 1977

	MOVED OUT	MOVED INTO	NET LOSS 1975 TO 1977
Families (thousands)	2,003	985	−1,018
Mean income	$15,986	$14,992	−$994
Aggregate income (in billions)	$32.0	$14.8	−$17.2
Unrelated individuals (thousands)	994	940	−54
Mean income	$8,055	$7,612	−$443
Aggregate income (in billions)	$8.0	$7.2	−$.8

SOURCE: U.S. Bureau of the Census, "Social and Economic Characteristics of the Metropolitan and Nonmetropolitan Population, 1977 and 1970," *Current Population Reports,* Special Studies, Series P-23, No. 75 (Washington, D.C., 1978), p. 8

[19]See in this connection George Sternlieb and James Hughes, "New Regional and Metropolitan Realities of America," *Journal of the American Institute of Planners* 43 (July 1977): 227–241.

[20]The total number of individuals in the poverty category was almost 40 million in 1959. It dropped rapidly during the 1960s but has changed little since then. The International Labor Organization (ILO) has estimated that one of every four American families would be below the poverty line, as defined by federal agencies, if it were not for welfare programs such as aid for dependent children, Medicaid, and food stamps. (The poverty threshold in 1977 was $6191 for a nonfarm family of four. This threshold is updated every year to reflect changes in the annual average Consumer Price Index.)

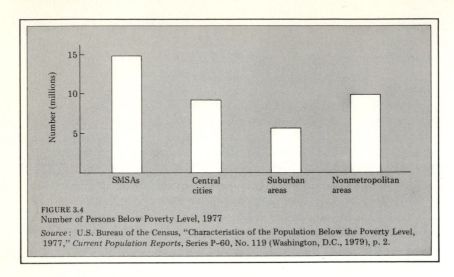

FIGURE 3.4
Number of Persons Below Poverty Level, 1977

Source: U.S. Bureau of the Census, "Characteristics of the Population Below the Poverty Level, 1977," *Current Population Reports*, Series P–60, No. 119 (Washington, D.C., 1979), p. 2.

number, 60 percent resided in SMSAs, disproportionately concentrated in the central cities (Figure 3.4). Nonmetropolitan areas, with only slightly more than one-fourth of the country's total population, contained 40 percent of its poor. This proportion, however, has dropped materially in recent decades (it was 56 percent in 1959 and 46 percent in 1969). The decline is due principally to the outmigration of low-income families and, more recently, to the economic advances being made in the nonmetropolitan counties. As a result of these trends, the percentage of the nation's poverty population residing in SMSAs has risen since 1959 by more than one-third in the central cities and two-fifths in the suburbs.[21]

CENTRAL CITY ECONOMY

The central city dominated urban life in the United States for a century and a half.[22] Only in the last several decades has the economic viability of the older core communities been called into question by the loss of industrial and commercial activities and the outmigration of the more affluent residents. The story is a familiar one. Transportation technology in the form of motor vehicles and improved highway networks enlarged the locational freedom of

[21]This increase occurred at the same time when the proportion of the population living in central cities dropped from 32 percent to 28 percent while increasing in suburbia from one-third to more than two-fifths.
[22]See Declan Kennedy and Margrit I. Kennedy (eds.), *The Inner City* (New York: Halsted Press, 1974).

manufacturing establishments and gave urban dwellers the mobility to settle beyond the congested center. At the same time new methods of production outmoded much of the city's industrial infrastructure, such as the old loft buildings and multistoried factories. Discouraged from expanding within the city by the high cost of land and the difficulty of assembling parcels large enough to meet the new space requirements, industry turned to the periphery where land was cheaper, congestion less, and general amenities better.

Manufacturing

The "suburbanization" of industry is most pronounced in the older and larger metropolitan areas. In Chicago a significant movement of manufacturing and warehousing facilities to the northwest suburbs has been under way for more than two decades. In Boston the electronics industries and other commercial firms along Route 128 form a circumferential arc around the core municipality. In St. Louis the city lost 6000 retail businesses and 869 manufacturing plants between 1948 and 1972. And in Detroit 248 manufacturing establishments moved from the city during the first half of the 1970s. Because of this exodus many central cities have been losing jobs to the suburbs and to the Sunbelt at a higher rate than they have been replaced.

The decline in manufacturing employment has been particularly heavy among the 15 largest metropolitan areas. Not only the core municipalities but the SMSAs as a whole experienced losses from 1967 to 1972, and the trend continued throughout the remainder of the 1970s (Table 3.7). Only the Houston, Dallas–Fort Worth, and Newark complexes recorded gains (the latter two registering only slight increases). A large portion of the decline took place in the central cities, all but Houston showing decreases.

Retail Trade

The retail trade pattern has undergone changes similar to those in manufacturing. As population moved outward, the vendors of goods and services followed. Huge shopping centers were established on the periphery, downtown department stores opened suburban branches, food chains were quick to tap the growing market, and discount houses emerged to offer competition to the merchandising traditionalists. Convenient to the suburban housewife and equipped with ample parking facilities, the new centers lure shoppers away not only from the downtown stores but also from the

Table 3.7 EMPLOYMENT IN MANUFACTURING SECTOR IN 15 LARGEST SMSAs AND THEIR CENTRAL CITIES,* 1967 AND 1972 (in thousands)

	1967		1972	
SMSA	SMSA TOTAL	CENTRAL CITY	SMSA TOTAL	CENTRAL CITY
New York	1,147	895	951	757
Los Angeles–Long Beach	855	310	780	281
Chicago	983	547	909	430
Philadelphia	574	264	498	203
Detroit	585	210	556	180
Boston	316	80	273	59
San Francisco–Oakland	198	52	181	44
Washington, D.C.	56	23	55	19
Dallas–Fort Worth	227	175	230	153
Houston	138	98	160	105
St. Louis	296	132	256	98
Pittsburgh	300	86	262	63
Baltimore	210	107	180	91
Minneapolis–St. Paul	204	124	199	109
Newark	264	69	271	47

*Excludes Nassau–Suffolk SMSA which has no central city.
SOURCE: Compiled from U.S. Bureau of the Census, *1972 Census of Manufacturers*, Vol. 3, Area Statistics, Parts 1 and 2 (Washington, D.C., 1976).

business districts of outlying neighborhoods and the older suburban communities. These latter concentrations are especially vulnerable, because they have neither the amenities of the new shopping centers nor the wide selection of merchandise of the central business district (CBD).

Before 1920 nearly 95 percent of all retail sales were made in the central city; today the proportion is less than one-half. As the *1977 Census of Retail Trade* revealed, the core municipality's share of SMSA sales is above 50 percent in only three of the 15 largest metropolitan areas. Two of these are in the South: Houston which has annexed much of the county in which it is situated, and the Dallas–Forth Worth combination which has experienced its greatest population and economic growth in recent decades. The third, New York City, is the center of fashion and as such has retained its retail predominance. Others in the large-size category have not fared as well. Boston, Detroit, Pittsburgh, St. Louis, and Washington, D.C. now have one-fifth or less of the area trade and Newark only 10 percent. Although retail sales in each of the 15 SMSAs increased substantially from 1972 to 1977, the central city's share declined in all of them (Table 3.8).

Table 3.8   RETAIL SALES IN 15 LARGEST SMSAs* AND PERCENTAGE IN CENTRAL CITIES, 1972 AND 1977

	1972		1977	
	SMSA TOTAL (IN BILLIONS	PERCENTAGE OF SALES IN CENTRAL	SMSA TOTAL (IN BILLIONS	PERCENTAGE OF SALES IN CENTRAL
SMSA	OF DOLLARS)	CITY	OF DOLLARS)	CITY
New York	20.4	74	24.8	69
Los Angeles–Long Beach	17.2	45	25.9	44
Chicago	17.2	44	25.2	36
Philadelphia	10.5	34	14.8	29
Detroit	10.5	26	15.8	19
Boston	7.1	24	9.6	20
San Francisco	7.7	38	12.1	33
Washington, D.C.	7.6	24	11.4	18
Dallas–Fort Worth	6.1	57	10.3	54
Houston	5.3	72	10.5	68
St. Louis	5.2	23	8.0	18
Pittsburgh	4.9	23	7.5	20
Baltimore	4.7	38	6.9	30
Minneapolis–St. Paul	4.6	39	7.5	29
Newark	4.6	13	6.3	10

*Excludes Nassau–Suffolk SMSA which has no central city.
SOURCE: Compiled from U.S. Bureau of the Census, *1972 Census of Retail Trade,* Vol. 2, Area Statistics, Parts 1, 2, and 3 (Washington, D.C., 1976), and *1977 Census of Retail Trade,* Geographic Area Series (Washington, D.C., 1979).

Central Business District

Disturbing as the plight of some central cities may be, the picture is not one of unmitigated bleakness. Even though the city is losing its hold on retail trade and manufacturing, it has advantages that no other section of the area can offer. The concentration of office buildings, financial institutions, department stores, governmental agencies, and related service facilities within its CBD provides a business environment that would be difficult to duplicate elsewhere in the metropolitan community. Because of these features certain activities continue to remain within the special province of the core municipality despite the changing character of urban society and the forces of obsolescence.

These seemingly contradictory trends are well illustrated in the case of Detroit. Like other major cities, it long served as the commercial and industrial center of the region, handling at one time 70 percent of all retail sales in southeastern Michigan (today its share is less than 20 percent). Its population has declined by more than 300,000 since 1970, and sections of the inner city have never recovered from the disastrous riots of the late 1960s. Yet looking only at its downtown area, one would hardly sense the deep-seated fiscal and social problems that the city faces. Large sections in and around the CBD have been rebuilt, new hotels and office buildings have been constructed, and the business community has invested over $350 million in Renaissance Center, a commercial and residential complex bordering the Detroit River. Similar revitalization projects have also been undertaken in the CBDs of other old central cities. Pittsburgh has its Golden Triangle, Atlanta, its Peachtree Center; Boston, its Faneuil Hall Marketplace; and Philadelphia, its Market Square East.

According to a study of 25 CBDs conducted for the Department of Housing and Urban Development (HUD) in 1977, service and office employment is rising in this area of the city, whereas retail sales (in constant dollars) are declining and the demand for residential space is weak.[23] The authors of this survey emphasize that central business districts are the single largest contributor to the cultural, recreational, and entertainment life of SMSAs, contain their largest concentration of retail activity, and constitute their major transportation hub. Not all observers are so sanguine. Many feel that the CBD is being artificially maintained through tax concessions and heavy public investments. Some even go as far as to suggest that the old CBDs be written off as obsolete and the nation's social investments redirected elsewhere.

The evidence of downtown viability is mixed. The dominant orientation of major office space users continues toward the CBD despite the inroads being made by suburban subcenters, but the future of retail trade appears far less promising. Until World War II the downtown area remained the key retail center of the SMSA for all but convenience goods, such as groceries and minor household items. Since then its role as metropolitan shopkeeper has been badly eroded by the territorial decentralization of retail trade. Whatever advantages the downtown area now retains in this sector rest largely with the opportunities it offers for comparative shopping. Its large aggregation of department stores and specialty shops enables it to provide a depth and variety of merchandise and a

[23]A study of the areas within two miles of the CBD in 20 of the largest SMSAs to determine whether the more affluent are returning to the inner city found the situation mixed. There was limited movement in this direction in some of the cities but not in others. When it did occur, it was mainly in areas where urban renewal projects had uprooted lower-income groups and subsidized the construction of luxury apartments. S. G. Lipton, "Evidence of Central City Renewal," *Journal of the American Institute of Planners* 43 (August 1977): 136–144.

range of choice in brand, style, and quality that are difficult to duplicate in the outlying shopping centers.[24]

The future of downtown obviously does not lie in retail trade, even though this sector will continue to play an important part in its economy. In the large and intermediate size metropolitan areas, the CBD is likely to become increasingly dependent on office employment, specialized services, entertainment and recreation, conventions, and government operations.[25] The downtowns of the small SMSAs are disadvantaged in most of these respects because their size does not permit the range and variety of activities that are the main attractions of large cities. Their future is therefore more problematic.

GOVERNMENT AND THE ECONOMY

The economic structure of metropolitan communities, like the social, bears an important relationship to their government and political systems. As scholars from classical times to the present have pointed out, politics and economics cannot be divorced. The urban community is a workshop and a producer of wealth. The activity it generates takes place within an institutional or governmental framework that is closely related to the economic side of urban existence.

Industry and business depend on local government for such essential services as water supply, sewage disposal, police and fire protection, roads, schools, and zoning. At the same time, the character and trend of economic activity affect and, in a sense, even determine the operations of the governmental system. No public body can intelligently plan its service expansion, capital improvement programs, or land use patterns without a knowledge of the community's economic structure and its potential. An area that is expanding in the direction of heavy industry will have a different set of service needs and land use requirements from one that is developing into an electronic research center. A static or declining community will require different governmental treatment from one experiencing explosive growth. Similarly a large, heterogeneous SMSA will have needs that vary from those of a smaller, homogeneous

[24]The potential of retail trade in the CBD is discussed in Al Smith, "The Future of Downtown Retailing," *Urban Land* 31 (December 1972): 3–10.

[25]Cities, both large and of intermediate size, are vigorously competing for the convention trade. Many of them—Indianapolis, St. Louis, and Gary, Indiana, among others—have constructed new convention centers in or near their downtown areas, hoping to capitalize on this elusive economic resource.

one. In short, the ability of a metropolitan governmental system to meet current requirements and anticipate the direction of change in its economic structure is vital to its well-being.

Many other interconnections can be cited. One that has important consequences for the administration and financing of government is the daily movement of people throughout the area, a result largely of the wide spatial distribution of jobs and economic activities. The population in some sections of the metropolis, the central business district in particular, swells during the daytime and then drops sharply at night as workers and shoppers disperse homeward over the countryside. To accommodate this movement, public services in the locations of daytime concentration must be greatly expanded over the requirements of the resident population. Changes in the territorial distribution of economic activity necessitate corresponding modifications in the transportation and utility networks. The movement of jobs from the inner city to the outlying areas, for instance, greatly increased intraurban commuting and made the road and transit systems of many SMSAs obsolete.

Contrary to the popular image of the bulk of suburban workers pouring into the central city each morning, census data show that those who both live and are employed in suburbia make up the largest group of commuters in SMSAs. For every fringe area dweller who travels into the core municipality to work, two commute to places of employment in suburbia. Most workers (80 percent) who reside within the central city are employed there, the remainder "reverse commuting" to suburban jobs.

Externalities, a pervasive aspect of metropolitan functioning, provides a further illustration of government's relation to the economic sector. SMSAs are places where large amounts of labor and capital are combined with relatively small amounts of land in the production of goods and services. This concentration of activities in limited geographical space results in numerous externalities or costs to third parties who are not involved in particular transactions.[26] As economists point out, everything affects everything else in urban communities. The automobile pollutes the air for the nonuser as well as the user; the traffic generated by a shopping center inconveniences nearby householders; the waste from an industrial plant makes a stream less desirable for recreational purposes—the list could go on indefinitely. How large a role local government

---

[26]Externalities also involve benefits as well as costs. Construction of an expressway enhances the value of adjacent property; the location of a factory increases the business of nearby taverns; and a public park in one muncipality may be used by residents of another.

should (or can) play in regulating and controlling these externalities is an unresolved issue.

One of the more critical relationships of government to the
economy is in the field of energy and environmental protection.
The role of the public sector in balancing economic demands with
environmental imperatives has assumed growing importance in recent years. The matter is of serious concern to urban areas, particularly the central cities. Conservation policies, as is widely admitted,
impact most heavily on low-income and working-class families.
They are the first to be adversely affected by production curtail-
ments caused by ecological safeguards and the scarcity of natural
resources. Although the major political battles over energy and conservation will continue to be fought in the national and state arenas,
local units will increasingly feel the effects of governmental decisions made at these levels. The issues have a great potential for
social conflict, as we have already seen in the demonstrations over
nuclear power.

Economics as a science is basically concerned with the process
by which scarce resources are allocated among competing interests
and goals. In urban communities, as in the nation as a whole, market forces and the pricing mechanism are the major allocators of
goods and services. Local government plays a part in this process
through its decisions on expenditures for education, recreation, and
other functions and through its action on urban revitalization projects, mass transit, planning and zoning, and capital improvement
programs. The economic structure and general development of
cities and metropolises are, in brief, determined by the cumulative
effect of a multitude of decisions made by individual households,
business and industry, institutions, and public agencies. The extent
to which this diffused system is capable of resolving urban problems and achieving socially desirable results in our cities without
more direct governmental intervention and control is a question of
continuing concern to metropolitan America.

Chapter 4
Governmental Pattern

Public services in a metropolitan area are provided through a complex system composed of many governmental units and agencies (and by private firms under government contract). These entities are of various types, with different powers and functional responsibilities. Each operates within specified territorial limits, its spatial jurisdiction frequently overlapping that of other agencies established for public purposes. The pattern varies from SMSA to SMSA and from state to state, although its essential features are similar throughout most of the nation.

The importance of organizational structure to governmental operations is a matter of dispute among political scientists. Some maintain that local political forms, such as mayor–council or council–manager (or a consolidated city–county government as against a multiunit system) have little influence on policy outputs. In their view social and economic factors are all-determinative of who gets what. Others, although recognizing the importance of the socioeconomic environment in which the polity operates, hold that structural features do make a difference in the way public bodies function and the policies they adopt.

The present chapter describes the formal pattern of government in metropolitan areas, looking at the abundance and types of local units, their historical development, and the management problems they face. It then examines the possible relationship between government structure and (1) environmental factors, such as population size, social status, and ethnicity; and (2) policy outcomes.

GOVERNMENTAL FRAGMENTATION

The governmental pattern of SMSAs resembles a horn of plenty filled to overflowing. In 1977 these complexes contained almost 26,000 local governments, one-third of the national total and an average of 95 for each metropolis. This number, moreover, consists only of units classified by the Bureau of the Census as "independent governments." It does not include public agencies that lack fiscal and administrative autonomy, such as municipal-owned utilities, regional planning commissions, councils of governments, and certain housing authorities. (To be considered a government according to the census definition, an entity must have "sufficient discretion in the management of its own affairs to distinguish it as separate from the administrative structure of any other governmental unit.")

Although wide variations exist, the "typical" SMSA, as described by the Advisory Commission on Intergovernmental Relations, has 2 counties, 13 townships, 21 municipalities, 18 school districts, and 30 special districts.[1] Some metropolitan areas have only a small number of local jurisdictions, as few as five. Located chiefly in the South, many in this category have undergone large-scale population growth in recent years that has brought them metropolitan status. At the other extreme, about one of every 12 areas has 250 or more local units. The most prolific is the Chicago SMSA with a total of 1214, followed by Philadelphia with 864 and Pittsburgh with 744.

Generalizing broadly, the greater the population of an urban area, the more local units it is likely to contain. As Table 4.1 shows, major differences in the number of governments exist in every succeeding population size group. The average in SMSAs of one million or more is 293 and in areas under 100,000 slightly less than 28. There are, however, many exceptions to the rule. The Madison, Wisconsin, SMSA, for example, with fewer than 300,000 inhabitants has 85 local governments, three times as many as Metropolitan

Table 4.1 SMSAs BY TOTAL AND AVERAGE NUMBER OF LOCAL GOVERNMENTS, 1977

SMSA SIZE GROUP (1970 POPULATION)	NUMBER OF SMSAs	NUMBER OF LOCAL GOVERNMENTS	AVERAGE NUMBER OF LOCAL GOVERNMENTS
All SMSAs	272	25,869	95.1
1,000,000 or more	35	10,266	293.3
500,000–1,000,000	37	4,349	117.5
300,000–500,000	43	3,805	88.5
200,000–300,000	48	2,924	60.9
100,000–200,000	84	3,826	45.5
50,000–100,000	25	699	27.9

SOURCE: U.S. Bureau of the Census, "Governmental Organization," *Census of Governments: 1977*, Vol. 1, No. 1 (Washington, D.C., 1978), p. 11.

---

[1]Advisory Commission on Intergovernmental Relations, *Improving Urban America: A Challenge to Federalism*, M-107 (Washington, D.C., September 1976), p. 147.

Baltimore, one of the nation's largest urban areas with a population exceeding 2 million.

Types and Numbers

The different types of local government—municipalities, counties, school districts, special districts, and townships—as well as their numerical growth, contribute to the organizational complexity of metropolitan areas (Figure 4.1). Of these types, special districts are the most numerous, comprising 37 percent of the total units in SMSAs. Most of these districts have been established to perform a single service or function, such as supplying water, operating a sewage disposal plant, or providing fire protection. For several decades their number has been increasing at a faster rate than the other categories of local governments.

Municipalities (variously called cities, villages, towns, or boroughs) constitute the second largest class of public units in metropolitan areas. Unlike special districts they are general purpose governments incorporated by the state to provide a broad range of

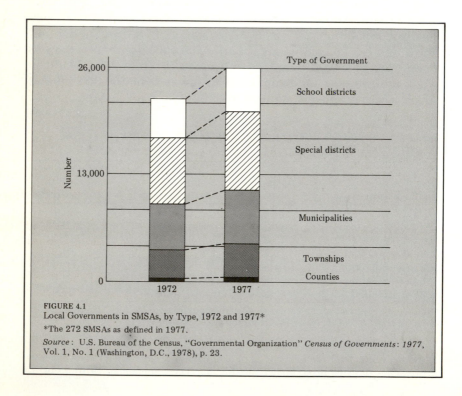

FIGURE 4.1
Local Governments in SMSAs, by Type, 1972 and 1977*

*The 272 SMSAs as defined in 1977.

Source: U.S. Bureau of the Census, "Governmental Organization" *Census of Governments: 1977*, Vol. 1, No. 1 (Washington, D.C., 1978), p. 23.

Table 4.2 NUMBER OF LOCAL GOVERNMENTS IN SMSAs, 1977, AND CHANGES IN NUMBER, 1972–1977

CLASS OF LOCAL GOVERNMENTS	NUMBER IN SMSAs 1977	PERCENTAGE IN SMSAs 1977	INCREASE IN NUMBER 1972–1977	PERCENT CHANGE IN NUMBER 1972–1977
All local governments	25,869	100.0	3,684	16.6
Special districts	9,580	37.0	1,526	19.0
Municipalities	6,444	24.9	977	17.9
School districts	5,220	20.2	462	9.7
Towns and townships	4,031	15.6	569	16.4
Counties	594	2.3	150	33.8

SOURCE: U.S. Bureau of the Census, "Governmental Organization," *Census of Governments: 1977*, Vol. 1, No. 1 (Washington, D.C., 1978), p. 11.

services to a specific population concentration within a defined territorial area. A great expansion in their number has occurred since World War II. A substantial portion of the overall gain, however, has resulted from the designation of new SMSAs rather than from the creation of new municipalities.

School districts rank third in quantity. In contrast to the other types, they have experienced a rapid decline in number since 1940 due to extensive consolidation. Although the *Census of Governments* shows an increase of such districts within metropolitan areas between 1972 and 1977 (see Table 4.2), this rise is attributable wholly to the addition of new SMSAs and the enlargement of already existing metropolitan areas. Excluding the new territory from the computation reveals an actual loss in the number of school districts during this period.

Organized townships or towns, the fourth largest set of governments in SMSAs, are presently operative in 20 states, mostly in the Northeast and North Central sections of the country. Not to be confused with incorporated towns (which are included in the municipality total), they differ widely in their powers, with most performing only a very limited range of functions for predominantly rural populations. However in several states, such as Wisconsin, they have relatively broad authority, administering services similar to those of municipalities. In 6 states they comprise all territory other than that included within incorporated areas. Their number has remained fairly constant in recent years, the increase in the metropolitan total resulting from the addition of new SMSAs.

Counties are the least numerous of the SMSA governments but generally the largest in terms of territory (only some special districts surpass them in this respect). They are found in all states except Connecticut and Rhode Island. (In Louisiana they are called "parishes" and in Alaska "boroughs.") Although their number has remained virtually unchanged for decades, an increasing proportion have achieved metropolitan status, the total rising by one-third since 1972. Currently about 600 of the 3042 county governments in the nation are within SMSAs.

A further contributor to the structural complexity of metropolitan areas is the public authority, usually an adjunct of a local or state government and therefore not classified as an independent unit. Each such authority operates in an area that may be part of the geographical territory of a local government or may cover the entire state (as does the New York Urban Development Corporation). Public authorities serve a variety of purposes, such as running government owned utilities and airports and administering housing assistance programs. They are commonly authorized to raise capital for their projects by issuing revenue bonds. Critics describe them as shadowy figures on the political landscape because of the secrecy with which many of them conduct their business. Political scientist Annmarie Hauck Walsh, for example, has strongly condemned them for insufficient public accountability and closed methods of operation.[2]

Size and Territorial Overlapping

People usually think of metropolitan areas as characterized by bigness: political, industrial, commercial, physical. There are SMSAs that match this description. Some contain counties that are larger in area than certain states, cities of more than a million people, annual public budgets of billions of dollars, school districts of more than a hundred thousand students, and special districts stretching over and beyond entire metropolitan complexes and even state and national boundaries. These huge local entities, however, comprise only a small fraction of the SMSA total.

Collectively, the governmental units of SMSAs present an awesome aggregation of public authority serving the local needs of almost three-fourths of the nation's population. Individually, many are far less impressive, performing few functions and having few constituents. About one-half of the municipalities in SMSAs have populations of less than 2500 (Figure 4.2). Only one-fourth have jurisdiction over more than four square miles of territory. The same

[2]Annmarie Hauck Walsh, *The Public's Business: The Politics and Practices of Government Corporations* (Cambridge, Mass.: The MIT Press, 1978), particularly chap. 12.

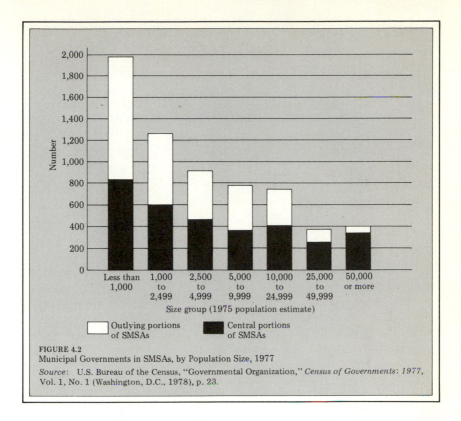

FIGURE 4.2
Municipal Governments in SMSAs, by Population Size, 1977
Source: U.S. Bureau of the Census, "Governmental Organization," *Census of Governments: 1977*, Vol. 1, No. 1 (Washington, D.C., 1978), p. 23.

is true of school districts despite the extensive consolidation that has taken place. About one of each ten has fewer than 300 students (Figure 4.3); and many cover relatively small areas. The situation is similar in the case of special districts. A large proportion have few residents (less than a hundred in some instances) and small service areas (as little as a fraction of a square mile).

The manner in which these units are organized in metropolitan areas also compounds the complexity of the governmental pattern. Overlapping jurisdictions and multiple layering of public agencies are common. Residents typically find themselves served by as many as five to ten local jurisdictions: municipality, school district, county, various special districts, and sometimes a township.[3] The

[3]For a discussion of indicators of public service capabilities relative to fragmentation and overlapping, see Alan K. Campbell, H. George Frederickson, and Frank Mauro, *Administrative and Political Indicators* (Syracuse: Syracuse University, Maxwell School Metropolitan Studies Program, 1971), chap. 3.

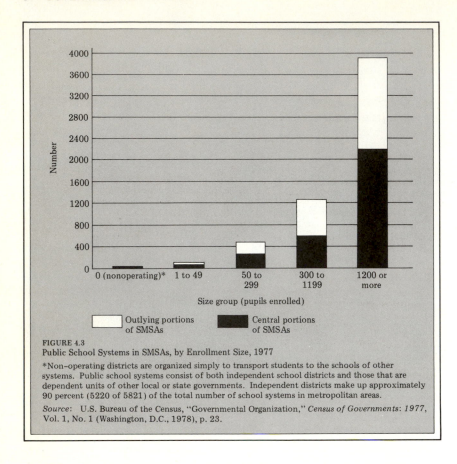

FIGURE 4.3
Public School Systems in SMSAs, by Enrollment Size, 1977

*Non–operating districts are organized simply to transport students to the schools of other systems. Public school systems consist of both independent school districts and those that are dependent units of other local or state governments. Independent districts make up approximately 90 percent (5220 of 5821) of the total number of school systems in metropolitan areas.

Source: U.S. Bureau of the Census, "Governmental Organization," *Census of Governments: 1977*, Vol. 1, No. 1 (Washington, D.C., 1978), p. 23.

boundaries of these units are usually not coterminous with each other, a source of confusion at times to metropolitan dwellers. Only about one-fifth of the school districts and one-fourth of the special districts coincide territorially with a general purpose government, either a municipality or a county. These overlapping layers of local government, moreover, are not accompanied by any mechanism to control their total combined demands on the taxpayers or coordinate their activities.

Because most local governments are small in territorial size, they individually occupy only a minor portion of a metropolitan area. Few of them, most often a county or a special district, encompass an entire SMSA. In fact, in many metropolitan communities no local government has areawide jurisdiction. As a result of this diffusion, the governmental pattern of a metropolis commonly consists of several or many uneven layers of overlapping units, with at most two or three local public agencies covering the whole area.

AN HISTORICAL PERSPECTIVE

It is useful in examining the contemporary system of local government in the United States to look back briefly at its origins and the manner in which it evolved over time. This perspective is helpful in understanding why the pattern developed as it did and why many of its characteristics continue to persist despite the social and economic transformation that the nation has undergone since its founding. Historically, the system has moved from relative simplicity to considerable complexity, but its basic features have changed little from those first designed by the political architects of the post-colonial period.

The trading companies and colonies laid out a system of local government that was adapted largely from seventeenth century England. After independence the states built upon this framework to develop an orderly and rational pattern, consisting essentially of counties and municipalities. Counties were created to fulfill two purposes: (1) to aid state government in carrying out certain functions required in all areas but not readily subject to administration at the higher level, such as conducting elections and recording legal documents, and (2) to provide essential services to rural sections, such as maintaining farm roads and keeping the peace. To assure the performance of these responsibilities, the entire state was divided into counties.

Municipalities were established only in areas of population concentration to supply urban-type services not available from the counties (fire protection, sanitation, and water supply are examples). As such they covered only a small portion of the state's territory. Contrary to the practice during the colonial period when public schools were under the jurisdiction of general local units, most states formed independent school districts, purportedly to free their financing and operations from political control. Such units were kept small in territorial size because youngsters of a "bus- and car-free" society had to travel to school on foot or by horse.

The two major exceptions to this commonly established pattern were towns and townships, the first confined largely to New England and the second to the North Central region. In the colonial era the New England towns were small and compact. They grew up around the church, the public meeting place, and the fort or stockade, and included the agricultural fields of their residents. The units were "natural" communities in the classical sense of the term, based on social groupings of people linked together by mutual interests and needs and by feelings of close identification with their individual settlements. Population increases were usually accommodated by dividing existing towns or organizing additional ones in new settlements. As these units became more densely inhabited, they took on many municipal-type functions. Only occasionally was a heavily populated center detached from its rural or agricultural portions and organized as a city, as in the cases of Providence and Worcester.

Townships followed a different and generally less successful course of development. From their creation they did not conform to any settlement pattern but were an artifact of the surveyor's measure. (All public lands in the United States were originally laid out in townships of six miles square by federal surveyors.) Many of the early townships attempted to imitate the New England towns as institutions of local self-government but with little success. Because of the artificial character of their boundaries and the practice of separating the expanding urban sections from their jurisdiction (thereby sharply diminishing their fiscal resources), they were doomed to failure as viable governments.

When the states formulated their original systems of local government, they made no provision for what is now a significant element of the structure: nonschool special districts. The types of local agencies they initially authorized appeared capable of supplying the whole range of public service needs as perceived at that time. The special district device was not unknown—one, for example, was organized in the Philadelphia area as early as 1790—but its use was extremely rare. It was not until the twentieth century, particularly the period since the 1930s, that special districts became an important part of the nationwide local governmental system.

Premetropolitan Period

Significant changes occurred in the governmental pattern of most urban areas as they proceeded from early urbanization to metropolitanization. For most of the nineteenth century they were composed of compact and largely self-contained communities. By the time they became metropolitan they were considerably larger in both territorial size and population. During this transitional span their governmental system changed from a simple arrangement of few units to a complicated and improvised hodgepodge of numerous and often overlapping agencies. The original concept of a system of local governments in which each would serve different purposes had been emasculated in the process.

An area that is now metropolitan contained in its early years a central municipality and in some cases a few outlying settlements, all separated from one another by large expanses of rural land. A county government overlaid both the rural and urban portions of the area, furnishing certain services to all residents within its boundaries and certain others only to the inhabitants of its rural sections. School districts were the most numerous units, as the drive got under way early to have a separate government for each school. And if the area was in certain sections of the North Central region, it also had townships performing a few functions, predominantly in the rural sections.

As urbanization intensified, the governmental pattern responded in various ways. Many municipalities enlarged their territorial size by annexing adjoining land to accommodate the growth. Some new incorporations occurred on the periphery, but they were not numerous. Also during this period many counties were divided to meet the demands for services at close range. California, for example, had 27 counties when it was admitted as a state in 1850; a little more than a half century later it had 58. Towns in New England continued to exhibit great durability, partly because they were firmly established in custom and tradition and partly because they played the functional role handled elsewhere by cities and counties.[4] In the North Central region many townships declined in importance as sections were annexed to existing municipalities or incorporated as new units.

The Metropolitan Age

By the time an area reached metropolitan stature in population size and in such social and economic characteristics as interdependence and specialization, its governmental pattern had become far more diffused than originally conceived. Although the structure demonstrated some ability to adjust to changing circumstances, it was not sufficiently flexible to meet the new demands made on it for expanded urban services. Jeffersonian democracy with its emphasis on keeping local government close to the people continued to hold a tenacious grip on popular attitudes, militating against any major restructuring of the system. As a consequence, odd-looking patches began to appear on the governmental quilt.

Both demographic and political decentralization accompanied the arrival of the metropolitan age. By the early decades of the twentieth century the outward movement of people started to outrun the ability of the central city to enlarge its corporate boundaries. Municipalities began to multiply on the periphery, many bor-

[4]Counties in New England play a much more limited role than elsewhere in the country. They are not units of general government as in the other states.

dering one another.[5] Already, as political scientist Norton Long and others have observed, the people of high socioeconomic status were walling themselves into suburbia as a move of residential segregation from other segments of society. The dramatic increase in the number of fringe area municipalities was largely the result of state laws adopted during the late nineteenth and early twentieth centuries. These enactments deliberately made annexation more difficult and incorporation outlandishly easy. Central cities were thus hindered severely in extending their territorial limits to encompass the growing urban population. (Through incorporation, an area can prevent its annexation by another municipality.)

Despite widespread incorporation not all the land within metropolitan areas became encompassed by municipalities. Freed from the fear of annexation by the stiffened laws for expanding municipal boundaries, residents of newly developed settlements frequently opted to remain unincorporated, usually because they found this alternative less costly in taxes. This situation continues to exist in many SMSAs. Currently about one-fourth of all metropolitan dwellers live in unincorporated territory, much of which is distinctly urbanized. They receive city-type services from special districts and from county governments which have expanded their functional capabilities. Officials and residents of the municipalities often complain, with some justification, that the inhabitants of these areas are enjoying the benefits of incorporation while avoiding its costs.

Although a considerable surge in annexation activity has taken place since World War II, use of the device (except in the newer SMSAs of the South and West) has been confined mainly to the acquisition of unincorporated fringe areas where serious service deficiencies have made the inhabitants more receptive to absorption. For most of the large cities in the Northeast and Midwest annexation is of little value since they are now substantially or completely hemmed in by other municipalities.

School districts represent the lone important simplification of the local governmental pattern. In contrast to the trend manifested by other types of local units their number has been sharply reduced over the last several decades. Many of those merged, however, continue to have boundaries that differ from the municipalities in

---

[5]For discussions of incorporation patterns during a recent decade, see Henry J. Schmandt, *The Municipal Incorporation Trend, 1950–1960* (Madison: University of Wisconsin, Bureau of Government, 1961) and Richard L. Stauber, *New Cities in America: A Census of Municipal Incorporations in the United States, 1950–1960* (Lawrence: University of Kansas, Governmental Research Center, 1965).

which they are located. In some instances this lack of congruence has resulted from the inclusion of unincorporated settlements on the city fringe in order to bring residents of these areas into the school system. In other cases it has occurred because of planned action by professional educators and school board members fearful that coterminous boundaries might lead to the eventual merger of municipal and school district governments.

Local units in SMSAs have responded to metropolitanization by expanding their functional responsibilities, intensifying the level of long-established services, and taking on new activities. Many counties, for example, have substantially enlarged their public health efforts and social programs. They have developed airports, built public hospitals, installed sewage disposal systems, and provided park and recreational facilities. According to a recent survey of county commissioners (governing board members) in Florida and Georgia, the preponderant majority believe that counties should increase their functions and wherever necessary furnish the full range of services normally associated with municipalities. They also believe that as rural counties experience urbanization, their own governments should adapt to the change by assuming more responsibilities.[6] County officials, in other words, prefer the strengthening of county government rather than the creation of new cities as a means of coping with population growth. This expansionist attitude differs from that of the past when counties were generally content to perform the traditional services and let other units take care of the new urban demands.

Local governments other than counties have similarly moved to accommodate present-day needs. Municipalities have developed extensive public works sytems, modernized law enforcement, added fire prevention to fire fighting, and initiated airport, hospital, and recreational projects. Some have taken over the operation of mass transit systems, constructed cultural facilities, and engaged in manpower training programs.[7] School districts have broadened their curricula, inaugurated adult education activities, and taken steps to equalize educational opportunities for all persons, including the handicapped and racial minorities. A large number of towns and some townships have undertaken specific urban-type func-

---

[6]Vincent Marando and Robert D. Thomas, *The Forgotten Governments: County Commissioners as Policy Makers* (Gainesville: The University Presses of Florida, 1977).

[7]Service expansion has not been the pattern of all municipalities in the metropolis. The public activities of many of these units that are small in both population and financial resources remain narrow in range.

tions, such as refuse and sewage disposal. Although special districts have seldom assumed new service responsibilities, preferring to remain with their original assignment, many new functional types have been created to deal with such urban needs as fire protection, water supply, and street lighting.

Many local units, in addition to improving and increasing their services to the public, have also enlarged their role by assuming various regulatory activities. Municipalities in particular, and counties to a lesser degree, have imposed land use controls affecting the subdivision of land and the purposes for which it may be utilized. They have also adopted building and housing codes that set standards for structural soundness and health and safety. A number of them have gone beyond these more conventional concerns to engage in urban redevelopment programs, provide housing for low-income residents, and promote affirmative action efforts. The contemporary governmental scene, in short, contrasts sharply with that portrayed by historian Blake McKelvey in describing public activities of the typical city in the 1860s.

> Some basic tasks, such as fire fighting, appealed to the lusty energies of volunteers: others often went by default... Nowhere did [water mains] reach half the residences.... Less obvious civic functions were little improved, if at all, over those of the colonial cities ... law enforcement generally retained the characteristics of the volunteer period. Boards of health and similar civic agencies, except in the case of a few school boards, were temporary bodies with at best a small emergency staff. Sanitation was loosely regulated by ordinances adopted impulsively from time to time, but the collection of garbage was [generally] left to the pigs, which were more numerous in some towns than the human residents. Horses and cows, dogs and cats, chickens and geese were accepted members of the urban community and contributed a bucolic aroma even to the largest [city].[8]

INTERNAL STRUCTURE

Urban communities in adjusting to the metropolitan age have made changes in their internal organization and procedures. These modifications have occurred most often in the cities where efforts have been made to achieve a more integrated structure by reducing the number of elected officials, decreasing the use of administrative boards, placing public employees under a merit system, and establishing a strong executive. The changes are a product largely of the

---

[8]Blake McKelvey, *The Urbanization of America (1860–1915)* (New Brunswick, N.J.: Rutgers University Press, 1963), p. 13.

municipal reform or "good government" movement that waxed strong during the early years of the current century.

Basically, there are three forms of municipal government: mayor–council (either weak or strong mayor), commission, and council–manager.[9] The first predominated up to the present century. In its weak form, now largely discredited but still in use in some cities, it represents an arrangement in which the mayor has limited appointive and removal powers over department heads and is circumscribed in his or her administrative role by semi-independent boards and commissions that exercise authority over certain functions such as parks, libraries, and even law enforcement in some cases.

The strong mayor–council plan, which resembles the national and state prototypes, provides for the separation of powers between a popularly elected chief executive and a legislative body. Under this form, a product mainly of the present century, the chief executive is endowed with a substantial measure of direction and control over the municipality's administrative machinery. Important budgetary and appointing powers are centralized in the position along with the right to veto legislative actions of the council. Unlike the weak mayor–council type, administrative authority is not shared with a bevy of other elected officials and independent boards and commissions. Occupants of the office are also in a strategic position to emerge as political leaders with significant influence over policy. This role is frequently enhanced by their stature in one of the national political parties (more often Democratic in the large cities). The strong mayor–council form now prevails in the major central cities, although there are notable exceptions, such as Los Angeles and Minneapolis.[10]

The commission type, espoused enthusiastically by some early reformers, combines both executive and legislative powers in a small (three- to seven-member) governing board elected at large. The members serve collectively as the policy-making council and individually as heads of the principal departments. Reformers hoped that the concentration of power in the hands of a few officials would make administration more effective and enhance public accountability. The plan, first inaugurated in Galveston, Texas, after a

[9]Form of government and related characteristics for individual cities are listed in "Municipal Profiles," *Municipal Year Book, 1978,* pp. 3–44.

[10]Some of the large cities have established the position of chief administrative officer (CAO) under the mayor to handle the day-to-day operations of the government, thus leaving the latter free to concentrate on policy formulation and ceremonial tasks. In this way professional management is combined with political leadership.

disastrous hurricane in 1900 almost destroyed the city, enjoyed considerable popularity for about two decades. Since 1920, however, it has steadily declined in use; only about 75 municipalities of over 10,000 population now operate under it (Portland, Maine, and Tulsa, Oklahoma, are two principal examples). Although offering more integration than the weak mayor–council form, commission government tends to provide inadequate coordination, insufficient internal control, and amateur direction of administration.

Council–Manager Form

One of the key elements in the reformist creed has been the creation of a strong and apolitical executive office as the centerpiece of the municipal structure. This concept has been translated into reality in a large number of cities by the adoption of the council–manager form of government. The structure parallels that of the private business corporation. Voters (stockholders) elect the council (board of directors) which in turn appoints the manager (president). Unlike the mayor–council form where the major emphasis is on political leadership, the predominant norms in the city manager type are efficiency and professional competence.

The manager is the chief administrative officer of the city. He or she supervises and coordinates the departments, appoints and removes their directors, prepares the budget for legislative consideration, and makes reports and recommendations to the council. The mayor in a manager community is the ceremonial head of the municipality and presides over council meetings. Beyond these duties the office seldom carries any additional formal powers other than those vested in all council members. The position is filled either by council selection from among its own membership or by popular election (the latter is slightly more prevalent).

The city manager plan, first used in Staunton, Virginia, in 1908, received nationwide attention six years later when Dayton, Ohio, became the first sizable city to put it into effect. Subsequently, the plan had a steady but not spectacular growth until after World War II. At that time many municipalities were confronted with a lengthy list of deferred services and improvements that had backlogged since the depression years of the 1930s. It became increasingly apparent to them that professional assistance was needed for the tasks at hand. The answer in many cases was adoption of the council-manager form of government. The plan has been especially attractive to small and medium-sized localities, many of them metropolitan suburbs, but it has not generally caught hold in the large cities—Cincinnati, Dallas, Kansas City (Missouri), Phoenix, and

San Diego are among the major exceptions. It operates in a majority of the municipalities with populations of 25,000 to 250,000 but is used in only about one-fourth of the cities containing more than 500,000 people. Most of the large council–manager municipalities, moreover, were medium sized at the time of adopting the plan.

The council–manager form is viewed by many middle- and upper-class whites as a businesslike replacement for the "political" mayor–council type. The role of the appointed chief executive in this system, however, is not a matter of universal agreement. Most of the city managers interviewed in a study of San Francisco Bay Area municipalities saw themselves as policy innovators and advocates, about half of them believing they should take public positions on controversial matters even in the face of important opposition. In contrast, most council members tended to regard the appointed executive as a staff administrator whose participation in the policy process should be limited to serving as advisor and political agent of the legislative body.[11] City managers are left to resolve this conflict in one of two ways: They can camouflage their political activities and confine their efforts to behind-the-scenes manipulation, or they can limit their involvement to "safe" policy areas. In any event this difference in role conceptions tends to circumscribe the extent to which managers can exercise innovative public leadership.

Elections

Two parallel reforms to the council–manager plan—at large election of council members and nonpartisan elections—have come under increasing criticism in recent years. Selecting members of the council at large rather than by districts was intended to eliminate parochialism and ward trade-offs and bring a citywide perspective to the deliberations and actions of the governing body. However, as municipalities grew in size and developed subcommunities or neighborhoods, especially of an ethnic or racial nature, many residents came to feel that their localized interests were being neglected. The need to be responsive to a particular area is considerably lessened if a council member has only to cultivate a citywide constituency to stay in office and if large campaign funds are obtainable from special interest groups such as business or labor organizations.

[11]Ronald O. Loveridge, "The City Manager in Legislative Politics: A Collision of Role Conceptions," *Polity* 1 (May 1968): 213–236. For additional details see Loveridge's book of the same general title (Indianapolis: Bobbs-Merrill, 1971).

More than half the municipalities of over 5000 population employ elections at large. These include Boston and Detroit as well as a number of big cities with council–manager governments. The desire on the part of residents in various at large communities to acquire better access to their local officials and the increased emphasis on neighborhood involvement have generated interest in converting to a ward or district system of elections. The courts also have started to question the constitutionality of at-large elections in cities where it can be shown that the method works to the disadvantage of minority group candidates. Many reformers, cognizant of the political and legal objections against this method of selection, support a combination of the two types with some members chosen by wards and others at large.[12] About one-fifth of the mayor–council cities, including Buffalo and Houston, now follow this arrangement, hoping to secure the advantages of both forms.

Under nonpartisan elections, the second feature common to council–manager communities, candidates for office appear on the ballot without party identification. The purported objective of this type of election is to eliminate partisan politics and permit the choice to be based on the qualifications of the individual candidates. Nonpartisan elections are utilized for municipal offices in two-thirds of the cities with over 5000 population and in most smaller communities. Partisan contests are more common in the large municipalities and counties although there are many exceptions, including Detroit and Los Angeles. Differences also occur even within the same SMSA. In Montgomery County, Ohio, to cite one instance, members of the Dayton city council are selected on nonpartisan ballots whereas county and township officials are chosen in partisan contests.

Political parties in cities with nonpartisan elections are generally not prohibited from working behind the scenes on behalf of candidates, although in many states they are barred from formally endorsing them or contributing to their campaigns. Some communities carefully observe nonpartisanship in practice and spirit as well as form; in others partisanship merely operates under a nonpartisan label. An extreme example of the latter is found in Chicago where the highly politicized board of aldermen is selected on nonpartisan tickets. Generally, however, nonpartisan elections impose restraints on the extent of party activity but do not prevent candidates from identifying with private organizations and receiving their endorsement and support. Business, labor, professional, and

[12]See Town Hall, John C. Bollens, director of study, *A Study of the Los Angeles City Charter* (Los Angeles: 1963).

other well-funded groups can participate effectively in elections without ballot identification.

What nonpartisanship does, in other words, is remove from the electoral process the one organizing mechanism through which persons not represented by the special interest groups can have a voice in the selection of candidates.[13] The absence of the party label also leaves voters without a ready guide as to the general orientation and stand of the contenders. And it works most often to the advantage of those contestants who are Republicans because they usually have more campaign money available to them in nonpartisan races than do Democrats.[14]

Where political parties are able to nominate and elect candidates to municipal and county offices, their involvement in local affairs will be greater than when they are excluded from these activities. As a study of nonpartisanship in California cities found, "removal of the party label tends to reduce the stake of the party organization and leaders in the outcome of the local races, and their interest and activity [are] correspondingly lessened."[15] Yet even in jurisdictions where partisanship prevails, the insignificant amount of patronage that remains at the local level diminishes the inducement for intensive involvement by the party leadership. When patronage jobs were available on a large scale, a party could readily utilize these rewards to recruit loyal workers and strengthen its organization for pursuing the more important stakes at the state and national levels. Now the widespread adoption of merit systems in municipal governments has greatly lessened these opportunities.[16]

Partisan elections are not to be equated with political machines as they existed in the past. The days of the big city bosses—Tweed, Pendergast, Curley, Daley, and others—have largely vanished from the American scene. Few observers would deny that the machines played important roles as mediators between conflicting interests and as mechanisms for concentrating sufficient power in the hands

[13]Howard D. Neighbor, "The Case Against Nonpartisanship: A Challenge from the Courts," National Civic Review 66 (October 1977): 447–451.

[14]See Stanley Scott and John C. Bollens, The San Francisco Bay Area: Governing the Metropolitan Region (Berkeley: Institute of Governmental Studies, University of California, 1968) and Willis D. Hawley, Nonpartisan Elections and the Case for Party Politics (New York: Wiley, 1973).

[15]Eugene Lee, The Politics of Nonpartisanship (Berkeley and Los Angeles: University of California Press, 1960), p. 176. See also Eugene Lee and Jonathan Rothman, "San Francisco's District System Alters Electoral Politics," National Civic Review 67 (April 1978): 173–178.

[16]Frank J. Sorauf, "The Silent Revolution in Patronage," Public Administration Review 20 (Winter 1960): 28–34.

of municipal officials to enable them to govern effectively. Yet to bemoan their demise or wax nostalgic about them, as some social scientists are inclined to do, is to overlook the dark side of their record: the tendency to graft and corruption, favoritism and the rewarding of mediocrity, and the avoidance of controversial social issues.

Municipal Councils

As late as 1900, approximately one-third of all municipalities over 25,000 population had bicameral or two-house legislative bodies. Since then, virtually all have abandoned this structure in favor of a single chamber. The councils vary widely in size, ranging from as few as 3 members to as many as 50, with no close relationship to the number of residents in a community. Boston, Detroit, and Pittsburgh, for example, have 9 members, whereas Dallas has 11; Los Angeles, 15; Philadelphia, 17; St. Louis, 29; New York, 43; and Chicago, 50. A relatively small number of the councils have professional staffs to conduct research and to evaluate policy proposals for them. Many others are moving toward such assistance in order to free themselves from dependence on the executive and administrative offices for their information input.

The legislative bodies in all forms of municipal government have tended to become more activist oriented in recent years. Members generally perceive their roles more broadly than in the past. They act more independently and seek a greater voice in the management of the community. One observer has identified four role types that are presently common among local lawmakers: the activist member who critically questions existing policies and practices and pushes for change; the political manager who is concerned principally with obtaining greater efficiency in the day-to-day operations of the government; the citizen legislator who is closely attuned to and reflects the concerns of community residents; and the special interest representative.[17]

The interplay of these various roles, combined with the tendency to reject mayoral or executive leadership, has complicated the legislative process, particularly in the larger and more heterogeneous municipalities. The increase in the number of young people, women, and racial minority representatives as council members, the decline in importance of national political parties in local elections and issues, and the increased involvement of community-

[17]Michael S. Deeb, "Municipal Council Members: Changing Roles and Functions," *National Civic Review* 68 (September 1979): 411–416.

based organizations have all contributed to the less-disciplined character of these bodies. Greater openness and responsiveness to a broader range of constituencies have resulted but decision making has become more prolonged and in many cases less decisive.

County Government

Metropolitan counties have also undergone internal change, although not to the same extent as municipalities. The merit system for employees has developed sporadically and the number of administrative posts filled by popular election remains large. Most counties still have a long list of elected officials who perform either duties calling for considerable training and skill (the coroner or medical examiner, for instance) or functions of a routine and clerical nature (such as the recorder of deeds). However, as new departments have been created to handle newly assumed responsibilities, the tendency has been to provide for the appointment of directors with professional qualifications. Although this practice does not reduce the large number of elected officeholders, it places important functions and a larger proportion of county activities under the immediate supervision of individuals with relevant training and experience.

County governments operate under one of three basic forms: commission, council-administrator, and council-elected executive, paralleling to a large extent the three types of municipal governments.[18] The first combines legislative and administrative authority in an elected body known variously as the county commission, board of supervisors, or county council. The second, initially adopted in Tredell County, North Carolina, in 1927, is the most rapidly growing form (now numbering almost 600), reflecting the need for professional management as counties take on more urban functions. The powers of the appointed administrator vary widely. In some counties the role is similar to that of the city manager and in others its formal authority is considerably weaker.

The third form, the elected executive, is analogous to the mayor–council type in municipalities. First established in the 1930s, it is currently operating in approximately 150 counties (half, however, are in Arkansas where the state legislature in 1977 mandated the shift from commission to elected executive for all its counties). The county executive, elected at large, is the chief administrative officer with responsibility for preparing the budget,

[18]For a profile of individual counties see *The County Year Book, 1978*, pp. 3–44.

appointing the heads of departments and coordinating their operations, formulating policy proposals for council consideration, and serving as the political and ceremonial head of the government. With one of every five counties now located within SMSAs, the need for centralized administration and executive leadership is becoming more imperative. This need is impelling moves toward the council-administrator and elected executive forms in an increasing number of urbanized counties.

MANAGEMENT

Until the middle of the nineteenth century cities did not have professional bureaucracies or well-organized administrative structures. The first full-time fire department in the nation, for example, was not established until 1853. Today, bureaucracies are well entrenched in the governmental systems of all major municipalities and other large units such as certain school districts, special districts, and counties. Professional management developed in response to the growing needs of the cities. It has brought great improvement to the service delivery system at the local level, but it has also given rise to certain problems. One of the most important involves the relationship of the bureaucracy to political officials and to the public generally.

Bureaucracies in the large local units are formal, impersonal, and highly resistant to change. They also tend to be inflexible, unwilling to make exceptions to the rules in the interest of justice and common sense, a trait that has subjected them to public ridicule on numerous occasions. Critics charge them with being high handed in their operations, insensitive to human feelings, and unresponsive to citizen needs. Schools, police departments, welfare agencies, and expressway commissions are frequently singled out as targets of popular dissatisfaction. Much of the criticism grows out of citizen frustration with government as a whole and its seeming inability to cope with such troublesome matters as inflation, energy shortages, and crime in the street; but some of the charges are well founded.

Part of the problem lies in the fact that professional bureaucrats are difficult to hold accountable because they are shrouded in a degree of expertness beyond the understanding of the lay public and most elected officials. The statement of political scientist Theodore Lowi that the bureaucratic machine has replaced the political machine may be stretching the point, but it reflects the dominant position now occupied by the professionalized agencies in the gov ernmental structure.[19] This specter of big government is one reason that small suburban units, despite the inefficiency of many of them, have retained a strong hold on the loyalty of their constituents.

Another management problem relates to the method of hiring and firing personnel. Replacing the old patronage system with appointment on the basis of merit marked a decided advance toward the goal of professional administration. However, the new method has in turn become a kind of spoils system.[20] Those appointed under it commonly enjoy permanent tenure after a short probationary period. Protected by civil service rules, they can be discharged only for wrongdoing or for what amounts to gross incompetence. Appointing officers, moreover, are reluctant to resort to the firing process because of its cumbersome nature and the extensive appeal procedures involved.

The merit system was designed to safeguard employees from dismissal for political reasons, but in the opinion of many observers and public officials it has outlived its usefulness. Some argue that patronage employees tend to be more sensitive to public feelings, well aware that their tenure depends on the continuance of their party in office. They say that the old system may have been inefficient but to some citizens it appeared more humane than the present-day bureaucracy. The civil service reform act passed by Congress in 1978 attempts to correct the weaknesses of the merit system with respect to discharge procedures in federal employment but little progress toward this end has been made at the state and local levels.

Public Employee Unions

The relationship of public management to its employees has also been altered in recent years by unionization. Government employee organizations, largely unknown at the local level before the 1950s, have experienced meteoric growth since then. The American Federation of State, County and Municipal Employees more than doubled its rolls from 1960 to 1977, and the American Federation of Teachers jumped from 110,000 members to 445,000 in the ten-year period from 1965 to 1975. Ironically, the enlargement of the governmental bureaucracy was a major factor prompting public

[18]Theodore J. Lowi, "Machine Politics—Old and New," *The Public Interest*, No. 9 (Fall 1967): 83–92.
[20]E. S. Savas and Sigmund G. Ginsburg, "The Civil Service: A Meritless System," *Public Interest*, No. 32 (Summer 1973): 72–85.

workers to turn to collective bargaining for a sense of control over their employment destiny.

Because of unionization, unilateral determination of working terms by management is no longer the accepted practice in the public sector. Municipal, county, and teachers unions are now bargaining not only over levels of compensation and fringe benefits; they are also demanding that such matters as working conditions, transfers and promotions, classroom size, and administrative procedures be negotiated.[21]

Despite the illegality of strikes by public employees in most states, government unions at the local level frequently resort to this strategy when negotiations fail. Originally the tactics tended to stop short of full-fledged strikes so as to circumvent the legal prohibition. Police personnel engaged in massive sickouts ("blue flu") and other functional groups took part in selective forms of work stoppage, such as firefighters doing nothing other than answering alarms or teachers failing to perform any extracurricular tasks. These strategies are still employed, but total walkouts and more militant action have now become commonplace. In 1975 more than 20 times the number of work stoppages by public employees occurred than a decade earlier and 3 million workdays were lost as against less than 200,000 in 1967.

Although some states still do not authorize collective bargaining with government workers, the practice is becoming increasingly widespread in urban jurisdictions, both in the central city and suburban municipalities and in some counties and school districts. Employee organizations usually enjoy considerable success in such negotiations. One important factor in their favor is the political power they wield. In the private sector strikes or work stoppages are designed to put economic pressure on management; in the public sector their sole purpose is to exert political pressure on officials.[22] Because there are no readily available alternatives to most of the functions performed by public employees—fire protection, garbage collection, and mass transit—the citizens are seriously inconvenienced by a disruption of the service. This fact places mayors and other officials in a position where their political interests dictate getting the workers back on the job quickly.

Employee–management relations in the public sector could

---

[21]Sam Zagoria (ed.), *Public Workers and Public Unions* (Englewood Cliffs, N.J.: Prentice-Hall, 1972), p. 2.
[22]See Harry Wellington and Ralph K. Winter, "The Limits of Collective Bargaining in Public Employment," in Alan Saltzstein (ed.), *Public Employees and Policymaking* (Pacific Palisades, Calif.: Palisades Publishers, 1979), pp. 102–117.

well deteriorate as the demands of the unions run up against the fiscal restraints imposed on government by the tax revolt. Personnel costs consume from two-thirds to three-fourths of the local operating budget. If economies are to be achieved, they must come largely at the expense of the payroll. Declining revenues and the resulting resistance by public officials to worker demands are likely to be accompanied by increased militancy on the part of the unions, particularly in view of the eroding effects of inflation. Added to the problems urban areas already face, this prospect is not a welcome one.

Affirmative Action

An additional area of management–employee relations involves programs aimed at eliminating discriminatory hiring and promotion practices based on race, ethnic origin, or sex and correcting the imbalance caused by past actions. Title 7 of the Civil Rights Act of 1964 prohibits private employers, labor unions, and state and local governments from discriminating against women and minorities in personnel matters.[23] It also established the Equal Employment Opportunity Commission to investigate complaints and institute legal action against violators. Executive orders by successive presidents since that time require all governmental agencies and all businesses and institutions holding federal contracts or receiving federal funds to take positive steps (affirmative action) to remedy the effects of past discrimination. Under the regulations employers must set up goals and timetables for hiring minorities and women.[24]

Affirmative action goes beyond the mandate that individuals be given equal opportunity, regardless of race, ethnic background, or sex, to enter governmental service (or private employment) through open competition. It requires all public agencies to extend preferential treatment in hiring and promotion to those classes of persons who are underrepresented in the work force because of prior discrimination. As supporters of affirmative action point out, simply providing equal opportunity is not the answer for those who have been victimized by centuries of discrimination and excluded from the cultural mainstream. Not all Americans, however, agree with this rationale. Many contend that all individuals should be

[23]The Equal Employment Opportunity Act of 1972 strengthened the laws against discrimination in personnel practices and added strong enforcement powers.

[24]Affirmative action programs in local governments are described in Horace G. Bussell, "Result-Oriented Affirmative Action," *Municipal Year Book, 1975,* pp. 163–170.

judged solely on their personal qualifications. As opinion polls reveal, there is considerable support for the principle of equal opportunity but stiff opposition to employment quotas and other favored treatment for women and minorities.[25]

Affirmative action programs have also been attacked in the courts as reverse discrimination, depriving male Caucasians of benefits they would otherwise obtain. In the first such suit to come to national attention (the highly publicized Bakke case), the Supreme Court invalidated the admissions program of the University of California (at Davis) medical school that set aside a specific number of places for minority students. In doing so, however, the court also stated that it was constitutionally permissible for schools to consider race (and presumably sex or ethnic background) as a factor in admissions decisions.[26] Because of this apparent "fence-straddling," the decision provides no clear guidelines as to what measures are constitutionally permissible. It therefore leaves uncertain the validity of lower court rulings in affirmative action suits brought against local governments. In a number of instances, for example, federal district courts have ordered city agencies to hire only minority applicants until the imbalances in their work forces are corrected. As is generally acknowledged, the percentage of blacks (and Hispanics) is disproportionately low in many police and fire departments.

STRUCTURE AND POLICY

Structure can refer either to the organizational features of local units (such as type of executive and size of council) or to the overall pattern of government in an urban area (such as a consolidated city–county). Our concern in this chapter has been mainly with the former. We have described the various kinds of public agencies that operate in SMSAs, the manner in which they are organized, and the functions they perform. This overview gives rise to two broad ques-

[25]See Seymour M. Lipset and William Schneider, "An Emerging National Consensus," *The New Republic* (October 15, 1977): 8–9.

[26]*Regents of University of California* v. *Bakke,* 98 Supreme Court 2733 (1978). A year after the *Bakke* decision, the Supreme Court upheld a racial quota system under which blacks and whites were admitted on a 50-50 basis into a special training program to eliminate racial imbalances in the defendant company's skilled work force. *Kaiser Aluminum and Chemical Corporation* v. *Weber,* 99 Supreme Court 2721 (1979). In a still later case the Court approved a congressional mandate that 10 percent of public works grants to localities go to minority contractors. *Fullilove* v. *Klutznick,* 40 CCH Supreme Court Bulletin B4276 (1980).

tions. (1) Are the variations in the formal structure of these governments related to differences in the socioeconomic and demographic
characteristics of a community? (Do working-class municipalities,
for instance, tend to have one form of government and upper-class
suburbs another?) (2) Are there linkages between structure and policy outcomes? (Is one type, for example, likely to be more responsive to certain community needs or interest group demands than
another?)

Political scientist Thomas Scott, in seeking an explanation for
the wide organizational differences among municipalities, found
scattered evidence suggesting that the governmental structure of a
particular unit is the product of the interplay among four factors: (1)
state constitutional and statutory provisions, (2) regional and local
customs and traditions, (3) unique local idiosyncracies, and (4) the
social and economic composition of the community. He concluded
that variations in these factors are largely responsible for the differences in structure that exist throughout the nation.[27] Because of
their complex nature, however, these linkages are not readily subject to empirical verification. Only the fourth relationship on his
list—between structure and socioeconomic variables—has been
the subject of systematic research.

Studies over the past two decades are in general agreement
that large cities with heavy proportions of blue-collar workers, low-
income families, and ethnic and racial minorities are likely to have
"unreformed" governmental structures (mayor–council, partisan
elections, district or ward constituencies). Conversely, middle-
sized, white-collar, and nonethnic communities tend to have "reformed" structures (council–manager, nonpartisan elections, at
large representation).[28] The assumption here is that the more socially heterogeneous a city, the greater and more disparate will be
the demands made on its government. Unreformed structures, so it
is reasoned, are retained in such communities because they are
more adept at managing conflict and accommodating differences.

[27]Thomas M. Scott, "Suburban Governmental Structures," In Louis H. Masotti and
Jeffrey H. Hadden (eds.), *The Urbanization of the Suburbs* (Beverly Hills, Calif.:
Sage, 1973), pp. 213–238.
[28]Thomas R. Dye and Susan MacManus, "Predicting City Government Structure,"
American Journal of Political Science 20 (May 1976): 257–271 and Richard M.
Bernard and Bradley R. Rice, "Political Environment and the Adoption of Progres-
sive Municipal Reform," *Journal of Urban History* 1 (February 1975): 149–174. For
a study questioning this relationship see Raymond E. Wolfinger and John Field,
"Political Ethos and the Structure of City Government," *American Political Science
Review* 60 (June 1966): 306–326.

The reformed or apolitical type, on the other hand, is assumed to be more compatible with smaller and relatively homogeneous populations whose needs and value orientations are similar.[29]

The second question, whether local political forms affect policy output, relates essentially to the allocation of public resources among the various services and functions and the extent to which this process may benefit some segments of the community more than others. Some analysts believe that governmental or structural factors make an important difference in determining the mix and level of services and their distribution (who gets what); others see little if any such connection. Research studies provide no clear answer to this question. A number of them report that unreformed governments tend to tax and spend more than the reformed types and are therefore more responsive to the needs of the poor and minority residents.[30] Other studies, however, reach different conclusions, some finding no significant relationship between form of government and taxing and spending patterns,[31] and at least one suggesting that cities with reformed political structures are likely to be more responsive to constituency demands.[32]

Most research dealing with the correlates of municipal output find a strong relationship between socioeconomic factors (commonly referred to as environmental variables) and the content of local public policy. This linkage should come as no surprise. It is obvious, for example, that a homogeneous community of stable families is likely to have a different set of service priorities and different attitudes toward government spending than a city of low-income residents. The findings in a widely cited survey of 200 mu-

[29]See, for example, Leo F. Schnore and Robert A. Alford, "Forms of Government and Socioeconomic Characteristics of Suburbs," *Administrative Science Quarterly* 8 (June 1963): 1–17.

[30]Thomas R. Dye and John A. Garcia, "Structure, Function, and Policy in American Cities," *Urban Affairs Quarterly* 14 (September 1978): 103–122. See also Albert K. Karnig, "Private Regarding and the Mediating Impact of Municipal Reforms," *American Journal of Political Science* 19 (February 1975): 91–106. This study found that civil rights groups were more successful in obtaining favored policy outputs from unreformed than reformed urban governments.

[31]Chester B. Rodgers, "Environment, System and Output," *Social Forces* 48 (September 1969): 72–87.

[32]See, for instance, Wayne Hoffman, "The Democratic Response of Urban Governments," in Terry N. Clark (ed.), *Citizen Preferences and Urban Public Policy* (Beverly Hills, Calif.: Sage, 1976): 51–74. See also Alana Northrop and William H. Dutton, "Municipal Reform and Group Influence," *American Journal of Political Science* 22 (August 1978): 691–711, where it was found that chief executives in unreformed governments are no more responsive to lower-income and minority groups than those in reformed systems.

nicipalities with populations of 50,000 or more are typical in this regard. They show that the higher the percentage of middle-class residents and the greater the proportion of homeowners, the lower are the community's tax and spending levels. Conversely, the larger the percentage of religious and ethnic minorities in the population, the higher are tax rates and expenditures.[33]

On the basis of these various findings, many social scientists tend to downplay the importance of governmental factors to urban policy, some rejecting them entirely as having little explanatory power.[34] Such assessment, however, is premature given the fact that the bulk of current research in this field either ignores political process variables or improperly measures them.[35] It is quite possible that political dimensions, such as governmental form, leadership structure, federal and state pressures, and the extent to which the community is organized (interest group pattern), play a greater role in the determination of local government output than existing studies acknowledge. The answer to this question awaits more definitive research. In the meantime, Brett Hawkins' reasoned observation seems most appropriate, that while environmental variables appear to have the greater impact, political system factors simultaneously help shape local public policy.[36]

[33]Robert L. Lineberry and Edmund P. Fowler, "Reformism and Public Policies in American Cities," *American Political Science Review* 61 (September 1967): 701–716.

[34]A study which places greater emphasis on governmental variables is Terry N. Clark, "Community Structure, Decisionmaking, Budget Expenditures, and Urban Renewal in 51 American Communities," in Charles M. Bonjean, Terry N. Clark, and Robert L. Lineberry (eds.), *Community Politics: A Behavioral Approach* (New York: Free Press, 1971): pp. 293–313.

[35]The measures of both governmental factors and policy outputs are grossly oversimplified. There are many kinds of mayor–council structures, many gradations of partisanship, and many policies, such as zoning, that are not reflected in the variables commonly employed.

[36]Brett W. Hawkins, *Politics and Urban Policy* (Indianapolis: Bobbs-Merrill, 1971), p. 87.

Chapter 5
The Dynamics of Power

Government and the private market are the two major institutions through which wealth and power are distributed in a society. David Easton's widely cited definition of politics as the authoritative allocation of values (resources) speaks to the role of the public sector in this process. So does Harold Lasswell's classic description of politics as "who gets what, when, and how." Government is engaged in the continuous process of determining what goods and services will be distributed by the public sector, who will receive them, and how they will be financed. In a democratic society these collective decisions are made by representatives of the people and, theoretically at least, they reflect the popular will. The important question, however, is who influences the determinations. To whom are the formal decision makers responding when they act: to the public generally, to an inner circle of social or economic leaders, to special interest groups? Where, in other words, does the power reside to control government policy or output?

The political process, whether at the national, state, or local level, involves the translation of demands into official (authoritative) policy and action. One need not be an expert in governmental affairs to appreciate the fact that influence and power are critical to the making and execution of law. Zoning ordinances, business licensing regulations, tax levies, park site selections, and urban redevelopment projects are among the many items on urban agendas. Decisions on these matters are not made in a political or social vacuum. Those who formally adopt and administer public policy—council members, mayors, county commissioners, school officials, department heads—are subject to various pressures from competing groups and interests in the community. This pressure may at times be overt, as when property owners protest a zoning change or the owners of a professional sports team threaten to move the franchise elsewhere unless the city provides a new stadium. Often it will not be so apparent as when a vacancy on an important public commission is to be filled or a tax concession is sought by a prospective downtown developer. Implicit in all these matters is the question, Who really runs the community?

ELITIST OR PLURALIST?

Two competing models of community power have dominated the study of public decision making at the local level. The first, or elitist, posits the existence of an oligarchy, a cohesive group of economic and institutional influentials (more popularly referred to as "the establishment") who make the key decisions for the community. The second, or pluralist, depicts local policymaking as the product of a competitive and democratic process that is open to all segments of the community. According to this conception multiple centers of power exist, with the participants varying according to the issue at hand. The name of Floyd Hunter, a sociologist, is most prominently associated with the elitist model and that of Robert Dahl, a political scientist, with the pluralist.[1]

Empirical support for the elitist conception of community power is derived mainly from studies that assess influence on the basis of reputation or position. Hunter, for example, identified the power holders in Atlanta by assembling the names of civic, governmental, and business leaders, and having them rated as to their influence by a panel of local informants.[2] The pluralist model, on the other hand, derives its support primarily from findings as to who the key decision makers are in specific issues. Dahl's seminal study of New Haven, Connecticut, laid the foundation for this approach. In it he sought to identify those individuals who controlled or influenced the decisional process in three major areas of local concern: urban renewal, public education, and party nominations.[3]

The results of the two studies differed sharply. In the case of Atlanta, Hunter found that a small group of high-echelon business executives possessed the real power in the city and were the "people to see" when one wanted things done. With their blessing projects moved ahead, without their express or tacit approval little of significance was accomplished. In the New Haven setting Dahl

[1]An annotated summary of important books and articles dealing with community power is found in Willis D. Hawley and James H. Svara, *The Study of Community Power: A Bibliographic Review* (Santa Barbara: American Bibliographic Center, 1972).

[2]Floyd Hunter, *Community Power Structure: A Study of Decision Makers* (Chapel Hill: University of North Carolina Press, 1953).

[3]A third approach, sometimes employed as an adjunct to the other two, is the "positional" study. This method searches for the likely power offices in the community's institutional structure such as mayor or president of the chamber of commerce. It rests on the assumption that formal position is directly related to influence. The most widely read work employing this technique is C. Wright Mills, *The Power Elite* (New York: Galaxy, 1959), which treats of influence at the national level. The three approaches are compared in James D. Preston, "Identification of Community Leaders," *Sociology and Social Research* 53 (June 1969): 204–216.

found a pluralistic system in which community power was widely dispersed, with different clusters of influentials exercising control in different issue areas. In matters involving urban renewal one set of participants dominated; in those dealing with school questions another coalition of leaders made the decisions; and in party nominations a third group of power holders called the signals.[4]

The two studies sparked a long controversy over the validity of their respective approaches. Pluralist partisans attacked the basic assumptions of the elitists that (1) each community possesses an ordered structure of power or network of stable influence relationships and (2) the reputation for influence (as systematically determined) reflects this pattern of power distribution.[5] Elitists in turn charged that the pluralist methodology offers no adequate way of assuring selection of the "key" issues. How, they asked, can one know that the real power holders are at all interested in the decisions chosen for examination?[6] Some critics also objected to the pluralist assumption that power is reflected solely in concrete and overt decisions. They pointed to the distinct possibility of nondecision making, or the existence of influentials in the community who are capable of preventing issues from being placed on the civic agenda. By this means such individuals can restrict public consideration to those matters they consider "safe." As a result, the demands or grievances of some segments of the community may never be heard.[7]

Who Does Rule?

The large volume of power structure studies conducted since the elitist–pluralist debate was first touched off by Hunter and Dahl in the 1950s has done little to settle the issue of who really rules. Conflicting evidence and strong disagreement over methodology and findings have generated more uncertainty than enlightenment. Po-

---

[4]Robert Dahl, *Who Governs?* (New Haven: Yale University Press, 1961).

[5]An extensive criticism of the reputational method and a defense of pluralism is Nelson W. Polsby, *Community Power and Political Theory,* 2d ed. (New Haven: Yale University Press, 1980). A recent defense of pluralism is William A. Kelso, *American Democratic Theory: Pluralism and its Critics* (Westport, Conn.: Greenwood Press, 1979).

[6]A critique of the decisional approach is found in Thomas Anton, "Power, Pluralism, and Local Politics," *Administrative Science Quarterly,* 7 (March 1963): 425–457.

[7]Peter Bachrach and Morton Baratz, "The Two Faces of Power," *American Political Science Review* 56 (December 1962): 947–952. For a critique of the nondecision position see Geoffrey Debnam, "The Two Faces of Bachrach and Baratz," *American Political Science Review* 69 (September 1975): 889–899.

litical scientist Kent Jennings' issue-oriented study of Atlanta, for example, contradicts Hunter's earlier findings of a monolithic influence structure in that city.[8] And G. William Domhoff's recent examination of New Haven, drawing on much of the same data collected by Dahl, concludes that power there is concentrated in the hands of the banks, chamber of commerce, and Yale University.[9] Which version of Atlanta or New Haven does one accept?

Case studies relying on interviews and personal observation have generally reached conclusions more compatible with the pluralist than elitist position. Edward Banfield's analysis of policymaking in Chicago during the late 1950s is an example in point. Its investigation of how a half-dozen major issues were resolved revealed that the ability to make binding decisions for the city was not in the hands of a privileged few but was dependent on the broker, either an elected official or other influential, who could bring the various interests and factions together.[10] Political scientist Robert Salisbury, on the basis of his analysis of big city politics, presents a somewhat similar picture. He suggests that the power structure of many large municipalities is typically composed of a coalition of locally oriented economic interests headed by the elected mayor, with much of the innovative force for problem identification and solution provided by the professional bureaucracy. This "convergence" of forces, as he depicts it, constitutes a power triumvirate for determining the course of the community.[11]

Different patterns of power clearly exist among urban communities but neither the Hunter nor Dahl model is adequate to describe the complexity of these configurations. The bulk of evidence tends to support the view that decision making in the large cities is influenced by a variety of competing groups operating in specific issue areas.[12] Whatever center of power exists with respect to local public issues is more apt to be found in the political offices than in the business sector. However, in the smaller municipalities—those

[8]Kent Jennings, *Community Influentials: The Elites of Atlanta* (New York: Free Press, 1964). Because this study was made ten years after Hunter's, it is possible, of course, that the pattern of influence changed during the interval.

[9]G. William Domhoff, *Who Really Rules? New Haven and Community Power Reexamined* (New Brunswick, N.J.: Transaction Books, 1978). Domhoff is a strong proponent of the elitist view of society. See his *The Powers That Be: The Processes of Ruling-Class Domination in America* (New York: Random House, 1979).

[10]Edward Banfield, *Political Influence* (New York: Free Press, 1961).

[11]Robert Salisbury, "The New Convergence of Power," *Journal of Politics* 26 (November 1964): 775–797.

[12]Linton Freeman, Warner Bloomberg, Jr., Stephen Koff, H. Morris, and Thomas Fararo, *Metropolitan Decision-Making* (Syracuse: University College, 1962).

under 50,000—the likelihood of business or elitist domination (by the Main Street merchants, for instance) appears greater.[13] The large SMSA as a whole represents still another case. It lacks any centralized governmental mechanism through which the "establishment," if one existed, could exercise power.

Government by the Few

Divergent as the findings of the power structure studies are, they agree on one very important point—most people have little or nothing to do with making the decisions that affect their communities. No matter what methodology is employed, and no matter what the size or type of city or town examined, the results invariably show that only a small minority of the citizen body, actually less than 1 percent, are active and direct participants in the community decision-making process. Pluralists and elitists place radically different interpretations on this phenomenon.

The pluralists do not dispute the contention that modern large-scale government is controlled by elites—those with better education, more income, and higher social rank than the population generally. What they maintain, however, is that those who exercise power do not form a cohesive group that acts in concert across a broad range of issues. Pluralism is manifested in the multiplicity of groups—occupational, racial, ethnic, religious, business, labor, among others—each with its own set of elites or leaders and each engaged in making claims on the political system. Government provides a neutral arena in which these factions battle for public policies, entering and leaving on the basis of the issue at hand. The political elites who manage the community are required to seek legitimation through fair and open competition for popular support. It is this contest for electoral endorsement and the resulting accountability of the leaders to the led that results in a high degree of congruence between the preferences of the citizens and the acts of the governors.

Elitists deny that the political system is responsive to the interests of all groups. Contrary to the pluralists, they hold that a small and cohesive clique of social and economic dominants controls the community, exercising power over a broad range of issues. These elites are not limited to specialized areas, as in the pluralist conception, nor are they responsible to any constituency. They are in

---

[13]Claire Gilbert, "Community Power and Decision-Making: A Quantitative Examination of Previous Research," in Terry N. Clark (ed.), *Community Structure and Decision-Making: Comparative Analyses* (San Francisco: Chandler, 1968), pp. 139–158.

nearly total agreement insofar as their own basic value systems are concerned and united on most of the important issues. Political officials and various organizations may exercise day-to-day control over the housekeeping functions of the community, but only the top elite possess the necessary power for determining major policy. Social scientists with a Marxist perspective go further in contending that government is only a front for the upper class or privileged few and that public officials serve as guardians of the interests of this group.

Some writers, even those who reject the notion of a monolithic power structure or upper-class domination of local public affairs, charge that pluralists overstate the extent to which access to political decision making is available throughout the population. They are highly dubious of the assumption that any segment of the community, no matter how lacking in resources, can have a significant impact on policy through organizing. Questioning that influence is broadly shared among countervailing groups, they point to the plight of minorities and the poor as evidence of the unequal distribution of power.[14]

Studies of community influence have apparently run their course, with few appearing in the last several years.[15] On the whole they suffered from two serious deficiencies. First, they gave little attention to the relationship between who governs and who benefits. Few made efforts to determine whether different configurations of influence lead to different policy outcomes that favor certain groups or segments of the population over others.[16] This is a far more important question than merely identifying the purported power wielders. Second, little attempt was made to assess the role and impact of external actors on local policymaking. Major decisions in urban areas are often shaped more by the policies and

[14]Michael Parenti, "Power and Pluralism: A View from the Bottom," *Journal of Politics* 32 (August 1970): 501–530.

[15]This cessation comes as no disappointment to urban officials and nonacademics interested in local politics. About all they have gained from the studies and the intellectual fray accompanying them is the ability to embellish their own rhetoric with such terms as economic dominants, power elite, and the establishment. Domhoff's New Haven study, however, has momentarily rekindled the pluralist-elitist debate. See the symposium "Community Power," A New Look at Some Old Issues," *Social Science Quarterly* 60 (June 1979): 134–156.

[16]An example of research efforts in this direction is sociologist Terry Clark's statistical study of 51 cities in which he explores the possible linkages between the decision-making structure and policy output. See his "Community Structure, Decision-Making, Budget Expenditures, and Urban Renewal in 51 American Communities," in Charles M. Bonjean, Terry N. Clark, and Robert L. Lineberry (eds.), *Community Politics: A Behavioral Approach* (New York: Free Press, 1971), pp. 293–313.

actions of higher levels of government and businesses headquartered elsewhere than by the distribution of power locally. Nearly all such decisions directly, or indirectly involve outside parties—officials of the Department of Housing and Urban Development, the Department of Justice, the state office of education, or national business firms, to name several. Studies of community power that ignore these nonlocal influentials provide only a partial picture of reality.[17]

CENTERS OF PUBLIC POWER

No matter who may be the real wielders of power in a community, decisions on public policy ultimately rest with those who occupy positions of formal authority in the governmental system. Only the city council, for example, can appropriate public funds for a new park or rezone a parcel of land. Only the school board can approve the site for a new school or let the contracts for its construction. (Some decisions require voter ratification by referenda, but the vast bulk of local government business is carried on by the elected and appointed officials.) Individuals or organizations seeking to influence governmental policy may enjoy high status in the locality, but they must depend on the appropriate authorities to act. Unless the formal decision makers are simply the agents of the privileged few, as elitist theory holds, their action will not be automatic but will be based on an assessment of various factors including the political impact of the proposed policy.

Local officials are subject to many pressures. A council member dependent for election on the support of the party committeeperson or on campaign funds provided by tavern operators will not be unsympathetic to their interests. Nor will the mayor of an industrial community be likely to slight the wishes of its working-class constituency. However, individuals and groups providing electoral support for public officials are normally concerned with only a limited number of issues that are of particular relevance to their own interests. They make no effort to influence the disposition of most items on the local public agenda, thus giving the official policymakers a greater area of freedom in directing the course of the community than is commonly assumed.

[17]The nationalization of many local issues is pointed out in the revised edition of *The Rulers and the Ruled* by Robert Agger, Daniel Goldrich, and Bert Swanson (Belmont, Calif.: Wadsworth, 1972). See also John Walton, "Vertical Axis and Community Power," *Southwestern Social Science Quarterly* 48 (December 1967): 353–368.

The central city mayor is the dominant political figure in most SMSAs. (This position is challenged only in areas where there is a strong county government and an elected county executive—St. Louis is an example.) The downfall of the political machine and the loss of patronage jobs to merit systems took away the mayor's traditional sources of power. These supports, however, have been replaced in a sense by federal aid programs, such as the Community Development Block Grant, that have given the chief executive a large measure of control over new resources. Even in the weak-mayor form of government, occupants of the post have generally been successful in gaining recognition as the key actors. In Milwaukee, for example, Mayor Henry Maier has been able to establish his primacy over the municipal structure despite the weak formal powers of his office.

The Bureaucracy

Political officials have received considerable attention as community influentials but the professional bureaucrats, those whom Max Weber referred to as "politicians for hire," have been largely overlooked as local policymakers. To regard them solely as administrators executing statutory mandates and ordinances or carrying out the directives of mayors and governing boards is a misconception. Many career executives, especially those serving autonomous agencies such as school districts or metropolitan transit authorities, exercise a substantial measure of influence over the policies of their units. Even within the municipal government structure itself, they play key roles in the decisional process. Elected officials find themselves increasingly dependent on their knowledge, specialized skills, and advice. Intuition, common sense, and native shrewdness, the stock-in-trade of the successful politician, are no longer sufficient to run local governments.

The central city mayor, the urban county executive, or the elected council of a large suburban government cannot afford, politically or otherwise, to formulate programs and to determine policies without the assistance of administrative technicians and specialists. Political judgment must feed on bureaucratic appraisal and know-how in the attack on such complex problems as traffic, air and water pollution, juvenile delinquency, crime, and governmental financing. Moreover, as amateurs in the many technical aspects of community functioning, political officials find it more and more difficult to challenge policy advice based on specialized knowledge. The experts may be on tap and not on top, but the demands of a technological society have increased their influence over political officials. Council–manager governments provide a readily observ-able illustration of this development. There the city manager, once looked on as the employee and servant of the elected council, is now—by virtue of expertise—frequently an influential policyma-ker guiding the chosen representatives of the people.

The Judiciary

We are not accustomed to think of members of the court as commu-nity decision makers. Judges are seldom among those listed as in-fluentials in local power structure studies. (C. Wright Mills was more perceptive in *The Power Elite;* he included supreme court justices among his national elite.) Most people are aware of court decisions that relate to local government operations—those prohib-iting certain police practices, ordering the busing of school chil-dren, or invalidating zoning ordinances are examples. Yet these actions are seldom conceptualized as policy output, even though they have significant impact on the way a community is run or de-veloped.[18]

The judiciary in American political doctrine serves as a check on arbitrary action by the executive and legislative arms of govern-ment. It has the power not only to restrict but also to mandate action when the other two branches fail to meet their constitutional re-sponsibilities. In recent years the courts, particularly the federal, have played an activist role in safeguarding the rights of the politi-cally less powerful (one might even say that they have been the major lawmakers in the field of human rights). They have fashioned desegregation plans for school districts, struck down zoning that excludes low-income families from suburban localities; compelled local governments to modify their electoral systems to give minori-ties opportunity for representation; and directed public personnel departments to revise their examination procedures and tests to eliminate racial or cultural bias.[19]

[18]Court decisions having major impact on local public policy are discussed at various points throughout this book.

[19]In Cleveland, for example, a federal district judge recently (July 1980) took control of desegregation from the school board and turned the responsibility over to a court-appointed administrator. And in Dallas a federal court mandated the city to abandon its at-large system of elections for the municipal council on the grounds that such a selection method discriminated against blacks. (The legal drive to open up local councils to minority group membership received a setback, however, in 1980 when the Supreme Court by a divided vote upheld the use of at-large elections in Mobile, Alabama. According to the majority opinion proof must be shown that the system was intentionally designed for the purpose of excluding blacks. *City of Mobile* v. *Bolden,* 48 Law Week 4436 [1980].)

The assumption of a major policymaking (and administrative) role by the judiciary in such sensitive issue areas as school desegregation, affirmative action, and low income housing poses an important question. Is the courtroom a good forum in which to resolve matters of this nature? These issues are highly complex, requiring both value judgments and extensive technical knowledge. School desegregation is a good example. A trial over this question typically involves a parade of witnesses—educators, social scientists, and group representatives—who present testimony, much of it conflicting. Cross examination takes place, legal objections are raised and ruled on, and arguments and counterarguments are made by a retinue of lawyers. The proceedings are of an adversary nature with the court being asked, in effect, to make (1) value choices that are more appropriately the province of representative bodies (whether, for instance, quality education or integration is to be given priority); and (2) technical judgments for which it lacks the necessary expertise (such as the impact of busing on children). Whatever question one may have about the role of the courts with respect to these matters, direct judicial intervention and oversight can be expected to continue in the absence of more affirmative action in social issues by the other two branches of government.

TRADITIONAL INTEREST GROUPS

The democratic dogma assumes an order based on control through the consent of the governed. As long-standing community institutions have been modified or dissolved under the impact of technology and urbanization, the nature of popular control has changed also. The Jacksonian ideology of rule by friends and neighbors has given way to the realities of mass society with its impersonal, large-scale, and bureaucratic institutions. In the process new participation patterns, a new organizational topography, and new citizen attitudes toward the community and its governmental instrumentalities have evolved.

If, as Durkheim and other social theorists have emphasized, the plural organization of society is a precondition for freedom, it follows that people must be joined together in groups that stand between the isolated individual and the state or government. These groups, which Greer and Orleans refer to collectively as the parapolitical structure of the community, serve as mediating agencies between the individual or family and the institutions of mass society.[20] They permit people of like interests to combine and pool

[20]Scott Greer and Peter Orleans, "The Mass Society and the Parapolitical Structure," *American Sociological Review* 27 (October 1962): 634–646.

their resources for a wide variety of purposes. Although relatively few such organizations are specifically oriented to politics or public affairs in their major activities, many of them are "politicized"; that is, they seek occasionally or often to further their aims through the medium of government. As such, they provide a potential mechanism for individuals to make their influence felt in community affairs and to be represented meaningfully in the decision-making process.

The congeries of voluntary associations, from garden clubs to labor unions, which form the organizational structure of the urban community, differ greatly in the number and character of their membership. They also differ markedly in territorial scope, from the strictly neighborhood group to one drawing membership from the entire metropolis and even beyond. Organized around a broad spectrum of interests, their purposes vary from simple social interaction to influencing governmental policy. Because these combinations of individuals form, in reality, subsystems of power that compete and cooperate in the community, they are vital to the maintenance of a pluralistic society.

Business

Economic power in the United States has become increasingly concentrated, with corporate mergers and takeovers a common item of news in the *Wall Street Journal*. The 100 largest firms control 55 percent of the nation's industrial assets and the 50 largest financial institutions control well over two-thirds of its bank assets.[21] Big business, however, is little interested in most community issues. Its main concerns relate to matters over which local areas have little control, such as interest rates, import–export policies, energy, inflation, productivity, environmental regulations, and national fiscal policies. Its participation in community affairs is confined largely to passive membership in local chambers of commerce and good government groups and occasionally in backing civic enterprises of a "brick and mortar" nature, such as the construction of a convention center or war memorial.

The case may be different in a "company-dominated" town or in a small city where the Main Street merchants call the signals; but today it is the exception rather than the rule for business leaders to play the role of civic overlords. To say this is not to imply that they are without influence. As one observer has noted, if we look at the

[21]Thomas R. Dye, *Who's Running America: The Carter Years* (Englewood Cliffs, N.J.: Prentice-Hall, 1979).

outcomes of local government decisions over long periods of time, we find that the interests of businesspeople taken as a group tend to be served more often than, to take the most contrasting case, the interests of blacks and Puerto Ricans.[22] The influence of business in local affairs is not so much directly exercised as it is anticipated. Rather than being based on conspiracies or control of wealth, this influence rests on the usefulness of the economic notables to others, such as political leaders, who seek the prestige and legitimacy which the corporate elite can lend to civic undertakings. It also rests on the fear of economic reprisal, such as an industry relocating its plant elsewhere because of dissatisfaction with local policy.

Until well into the nineteenth century the economic influential and the political leader were identical in most American cities. With the ruling elite sharing the same social and economic perspectives, community controversy was minimized and consensus on overall policy readily reached. By the end of the century, however, the situation had changed. As cities grew in size and heterogeneity, demands on the public sector increased in scope and magnitude. Local governments found it necessary to assume new functions and undertake new services to meet the mounting needs of a rapidly expanding urban society. The demands on them became more burdensome, and at the same time the stakes of local public office grew more attractive. The stage was now set for a new breed of community leader, the professional politician.

Cooperating closely at first with the economic influentials who were gradually withdrawing from active public roles, the new leaders soon established their own independent basis of support. Instead of social position and wealth, their principal resource was the strength of numbers. Appealing to the rising class of workers, the immigrants and low-income groups, they offered them access to opportunities and rewards that had been denied them under the passing system of oligarchical control. "Machine politics," the "boss," and the "ward heeler" became the prevalent symbols of local government as the nineteenth century drew to a close. The response of the economic dominants in the large cities—and ultimately of the middle class in general—to the new "working-class" politics was withdrawal. One finds an analogue to this in the

---

[22]Peter B. Clark, "Civic Leadership: The Symbols of Legitimacy," Paper presented at the 1960 annual conference of the American Political Science Association. The prevalent assumption that corporate interests are confined to the economic sphere is questioned, however, in Lauren Seiler and Gene Summers, "Corporate Involvement in Community Affairs," *Sociological Quarterly* 20 (Summer 1979): 375–386.

present-day flight from the central city to suburbia. The exodus in a sense dramatizes what has long been true in most large urban areas: the noninvolvement of the upper and middle classes in the political and civic affairs of the core city.

After relinquishing the political reins, commercial and industrial leaders became content to influence the conduct of government indirectly through various citizen groups and reform leagues. More important, they began to play predominant roles in the private welfare sector of the community. Service on boards such as the Community Chest, Red Cross, and hospitals became a substitute for political involvement. Activity of this type served several purposes for the economic and social elites. It furnished them with a means of satisfying their traditional sense of civic obligation without becoming immersed in local politics. It provided them with a highly prestigious and noncontroversial role in civic affairs. And finally, it enabled them to retain certain responsibilities within control of the private sector of the community that otherwise would have to be assumed by government.

Changes in business organization and styles also contributed to the separation of economic and political power in local affairs. In place of the local proprietors, the family- and home-owned establishments, came the large and impersonal corporate enterprises, frequently branches of national firms or controlled largely by outside capital. Along with them came the modern business elite, the organization men described so graphically by William Whyte of *Fortune* magazine. The new managers and engineers of economic power were not imbued with the sense of personal commitment to the community that had characterized their predecessors. Mobile, subject to frequent transfer from city to city, engrossed in their careers, they were individuals of limited civic commitment. Their involvement in the affairs of the local community was minimal and generally restricted to the specialized economic interests of their organizations. For the most part, business came to expect public officials to handle community problems and, unless seriously dissatisfied, rarely intervened. Today the larger firms, mainly to enhance their corporate image, often encourage their middle-management executives to play a more active role in community affairs. Much talk is also heard of business assuming greater responsibility for the solution of urban problems, but aside from a few well-publicized instances—a $1 billion pledge by the insurance companies for mortgage and home improvement loans in core areas is an example—relatively little has been done (or can be anticipated) in this regard. The nature of the economic system with its profit-making demands minimizes the extent to which the private sector can voluntarily engage in social amelioration efforts.

Labor

A popular conception of "who gets what" in American society centers around the triad of "Big Business, Big Labor, and Big Government." The contest in the public arena is pictured as a struggle between the first two giants with the third acting as mediator and controller and, in the eyes of some, as dispenser of lavish favors to those on the "in." This view is not limited to the national and state scenes; even at the local or metropolitan level murmurs are heard about business or labor running the community or being the recipients of political largess. The evidence, as noted previously, offers little to substantiate the mythology of business dominance in community affairs, particularly in the large cities. The case with respect to labor is no different.[23]

In discussing labor's role in community affairs, one may make several observations at the outset. First of all, if unions and business are contesting for power over local civic matters, the struggle is taking place behind the scenes. Seldom do clashes over issues of a noneconomic character stir the community waters. In civic causes trade union leaders will often be found in the same camp with the business notables assisting a chest or hospital drive, endorsing a bond issue for public improvements, working to establish a cultural center, or supporting an urban redevelopment project. Second, like business, labor is not a monolithic aggregation of power. Differences among and even within unions militate against any effective system of centralized control. Third, union leadership is likely to be most effective in mobilizing support for those issues that the membership considers legitimate concerns of the organization.

The generalization that American unions do not display great interest in local governmental affairs has empirical support. When labor intervenes and uses its strength in the metropolitan arena it usually does so because matters of direct relevance to the economic interests of its members are involved. The construction trade unions, for example, will resist building code changes that threaten to reduce the job potential of their constituents. Or the joint AFL–CIO council will lend its support to public employee unions in disputes over wages and working conditions. Labor leaders will also speak out at times on various noneconomic matters of local concern, such as educational and recreational needs, but they will try to avoid the more controversial questions such as racial discrim-

---

[23]As in the case of big business, the decisions of most concern to labor are not made at city hall but at the national and state levels (wage and price guidelines, fair labor practice legislation, right to work laws, workmen's compensation, and unemployment insurance are among the issues of particular concern).

ination in housing and job opportunities. Even though the national leadership of organized labor takes strong stands on issues of equality, the local leadership treads cautiously in this realm. The rank and file of union membership is by no means committed to the abolition of discrimination, particularly in its own house or at its own doorstep. For local union officials to act militantly in issues of this kind presents threats to their continuance as leaders.

Labor's principal access to influence in local affairs is through the political officials who are concerned with the mass mobilization of numbers. In the large cities labor is usually found closely allied to the Democratic party; and where partisan elections for local office are held, it normally supports candidates of this political faith. On occasions, the union will line up behind local political leaders to oppose charter reform measures that threaten to diminish the patronage or other perquisites of their allies in government. Their support of "friendly" candidates and their interests gives them access to the governmental structure and entitles them to certain symbolic rewards, such as appointments of labor officials to various local boards and commissions.

Organized labor also attaches considerable importance to participation in activities of the private welfare agencies and other local institutions where its guarantee of financial support provides a means of penetration. Union officials are now found on community welfare councils and similar boards and on various civic commissions. Beyond these trappings of recognition, however, labor still does not occupy a place in the power structure commensurate with its numbers or economic strength.[24] Its influence in community affairs lags well behind the power it exercises in economic matters in the industries with which it is involved. One reason for this lag is the tendency to see itself not as a group that assumes leadership in local policymaking but as one with which business and the political sector must deal if major community proposals are to be implemented.

The White Ethnics

The term "white ethnic" as commonly used refers to first- or second-generation Americans, many of them working class, whose cul-

[24]William H. Form, "Organized Labor's Place in the Community Power Structure," *Industrial and Labor Relations Review* 12 (July 1959): 526–539. Also see Schley R. Lyons, "Labor in City Politics: The Case of the Toledo United Auto Workers," *Social Science Quarterly* 49 (March 1969): 816–828.

tural heritage is neither Anglo-Saxon nor Protestant. Ethnic ties persist even in some suburbs where third-generation families still tend to socialize with people of the same nationality background. The four largest ethnic groups in the United States are the Irish, Polish, Italians, and Jews (Hispanics, although classified as white by the Census Bureau, are not referred to as "white ethnics"). The voluntary associations they have formed are primarily religious and fraternal in nature (several Jewish organizations, such as the Anti-Defamation League, are conventional-type interest groups). Some neighborhood associations are composed largely of white ethnics, but the basis of organization in such cases is usually territory, not ethnicity.

Nationality groups formed the nucleus of the old party machines that provided immigrants with a measure of social mobility and access to government jobs at the local level. Because of this affiliation ethnics became firmly entrenched (and remain so) in many of the large city bureaucracies of the Northeast and Midwest. In New York City, for instance, the police department continues to be heavily Irish, the sanitation department Italian, and the school system Jewish. Politically also, ticket balancing continues in cities with large nationality populations, such as New York, Chicago, and Boston. Studies indicate that ethnic ties have a major influence on voting behavior.[25] Even though white ethnics are not organized as politically active groups, there is an Irish, Italian, Jewish, and Polish vote.

An ethnic name is a prerequisite for victory in some electoral units; in several of Chicago's congressional districts, for instance, voters have consistently selected candidates with Polish surnames. It is even more important in nonpartisan contests where many voters, in the absence of party identification to guide them, tend to look for nationality labels. Ethnic voting in the case of whites is today less a matter of self-interest than of pride in seeing a member of one's ethnocultural background achieve public recognition. In fact, ethnic politics as contrasted to that of interest groups, such as business and labor, is largely the politics of status.[26] Public figures have long been aware of this sensitivity.[27]

---

[25]See Richard F. Hamilton, *Restraining Myths: Critical Study of U.S. Social Structure and Politics* (Beverly Hills, Calif.: Sage, 1975).

[26]This point is made in Robert L. Lineberry and Ira Sharkansky, *Urban Politics and Public Policy*, 3d ed. (New York: Harper & Row, 1978), p. 109.

[27]Gerald Ford, for example, drew quick rebukes from Polish and Slavic leaders in this country when he made the mistake in the 1976 presidential debates with Jimmy Carter of saying that Eastern Europe was not under Soviet domination.

Neighborhood Associations

Neighborhoods have become a focal point of national policies for aiding the large cities.[28] An outgrowth of the social legislation of the 1960s with its stress on community participation, the notion of resurrecting the neighborhood as the key element in urban revitalization has generated considerable interest at all levels of government. The availability of general revenue sharing and community development block grant funds to localities has encouraged many neighborhoods to organize in hopes of influencing the territorial distribution of these monies within the individual municipalities.[29]

Economic factors have also contributed to the neighborhood movement. People who do not like the way things are going in their residential environs have three alternatives: resign themselves to the situation and do nothing; move out; or stay and attempt to remedy conditions.[30] For the upwardly mobile and those with sufficient resources to afford them a choice, the popular response has been to exit for suburbia; for the less advantaged it has usually been resignation. During the last several years the option of fleeing has become less available, with many families being priced out of the new housing market. An increasing number who find themselves in this position now tend to favor the third alternative: remaining and participating in locality-based organizations that articulate the needs of the neighborhood and translate them into demands on the relevant public and private institutions.

Many kinds of neighborhood associations currently operate in American cities. They range from highly structured units with professional staffs to groups loosely organized on an ad hoc basis for the purpose of influencing a single issue such as the closing of a nearby school. They also differ widely in their goals and objectives as well as their tactics and strategies. Some come into being for the implicit, if not explicit, purpose of keeping out racial minorities; others hope to achieve an orderly transition from an all-white to a

---

[28]Evidence of the new interest in neighborhoods at the national level can be seen in the creation of an Office of Neighborhoods, Voluntary Associations, and Consumer Protection in the Department of Housing and Urban Development and in the Neighborhood Statistical Act of 1977, which provides for the aggregation of census data on a neighborhood basis.

[29]Federal legislation and regulations refer to neighborhood associations and other local citizen groups as community based organizations (CBOs).

[30]These alternatives are discussed in John M. Orbell and Toru Ono, "A Theory of Neighborhood Problem Solving: Public Access vs. Residential Mobility," *American Political Science Review* 66 (June 1972): 471–489. They are derived from Albert O. Hirschman, *Exit, Voice, and Loyalty: Responses to Decline in Firms, Organizations, and States* (Cambridge, Mass.: Harvard University Press, 1970).

racially balanced neighborhood; and still others are interested primarily in obtaining funds for revitalization projects. Broad as these differences are, neighborhood associations fall essentially into two categories: conflict oriented and cooperative oriented.

The conflict or social protest model, as it applies to local communities, is the work largely of Saul Alinsky, a onetime union organizer who sparked the neighborhood movement in Chicago in the late 1940s. The model assumes the existence of a wide cleavage between working- and middle-class sections of the city and the controlling agencies of society. It also assumes that the demands of these neighborhoods will not be fulfilled by proceeding through normal political and institutional channels but only through militant confrontation with the power holders.[31] In the words of one Alinsky follower, the establishment does not give rights—"people take rights or they don't get them."

The organizing strategy of the protest model is to involve neighborhood residents in a major campaign built around a single issue, such as redlining (the refusal of financial institutions to make mortgage loans or of insurance companies to write policies on property within certain areas of the city). Its purpose is to give people a sense of power by engaging them in conflict with the established agencies ("neighborhood hell raising" as some angry officials refer to it). Once having seen that public and private institutions are vulnerable to confrontation, neighborhood groups, according to the Alinsky model, are stimulated to extend their newly discovered influence to other issues. This approach was popular with many of the community organizers in the poverty and model cities programs. They contended that the underprivileged have no other course open to them because they lack access to the decision-making centers and are without resources to function as conventional pressure groups.

One of the more viable organizations embodying the conflict model is the Association of Community Organizations for Reformed Neighborhoods (ACORN), a federation of neighborhood groups principally in the South and Midwest. ACORN provides organizers and assists its member units in shaping strategies. Its major concentration has been on utility rates, redlining, and taxes. These issues, following the model, constitute the focal point around which the local groups are organized.

[31]According to Alinsky and his followers, the neighborhood organization must identify the "enemy," engage its membership in action against it, and use every means short of violence to dramatize the issue and elicit a favorable response. See Saul Alinsky, *Rules for Radicals: A Practical Primer for Realistic Radicals* (New York: Random House, 1971).

Another, and probably the largest, neighborhood coalition that employs confrontation tactics is the Chicago-based National Peoples Action. One of its recent efforts is a typical example of protest politics. On a Sunday afternoon it brought 18 busloads of neighborhood leaders from across the country to the posh suburban home of James Schlesinger, then head of the Department of Energy, to demonstrate against utility rate hikes and oil company profits. Armed with placards and bullhorns the group trampled over his lawn and hung him in effigy from a garage basketball hoop. From there it proceeded crosstown to another high-income section of Washington where it accorded the same kind of treatment to Patricia Harris, at that time secretary of the Department of Housing and Urban Development.

The cooperative or consensual model corresponds closely to conventional interest group ideology and strategies. Neighborhood associations that follow it utilize the normal channels of access to decision makers and employ the same types of pressures commonly used by special interest groups. They make their demands known through their political representatives or the bureaucracies themselves, endeavoring to establish mutually rewarding relations with them. They also monitor the provision of public services such as street cleaning and garbage collection and assemble evidence of building code violations or other infractions that detract from the quality of a residential area. The appropriate officials are then contacted for corrective action. Those who fail to cooperate are singled out for electoral reprisal. On matters that transcend their individual neighborhoods they form coalitions with other territorially defined associations to aggregate influence resources.[32]

Neighborhood organizations seldom conform wholly to either the consensual or conflict model, usually embodying elements of both in varying degrees. Associations oriented to the conflict model enjoyed their greatest popularity during the social protest years of the 1960s and early 1970s. Since then their numbers have decreased and their militancy moderated. Alinsky's death was a blow to the movement, but a more important factor in their decline was the loss of interest in confrontation by a people weary of a decade of disruptive domestic conflict. With the change in social climate the

---

[32]The effectiveness of citywide coalitions is hampered by goal conflicts among member organizations, particularly between white and black groups. The Philadelphia Coalition of Neighborhood Organizations, for example, has succeeded in holding together an interracial coalition only by avoiding the most serious issues confronting neighborhoods and the community as a whole, such as school busing and the location of subsidized housing.

conventional forms of neighborhood associations again became prevalent. According to a study of community organizations in ten cities, the successful groups are cooperative rather than conflict oriented, possess some resources, and know how to negotiate for results that are politically realistic.[33]

The number and viability of neighborhood associations vary from one metropolitan area to another. In Chicago, Philadelphia, and Baltimore strong coalitions have emerged to demand locality involvement in housing, crime prevention, and youth employment programs. In Pittsburgh a coalition of 30 groups (Pittsburgh Neighborhood Alliance) has enjoyed a measure of success in influencing city budget decisions and securing a new home rule charter that provides for elected neighborhood advisory boards.[34] In St. Louis neighborhood groups have been able to effect some changes in the distribution of community development block grant funds. And in Washington D.C. and Atlanta, among others, the city government has granted legal recognition to neighborhood councils. Despite their current viability, however, the capacity of these groups to sustain themselves over the long run remains uncertain.

MINORITY GROUP POWER

Until about the mid-1960s, the black movement for greater equality concentrated on the goal of integration. The strategy was to desegregate the schools, disperse black families in white neighborhoods, end discrimination in employment practices, and improve the social conditions of the nonwhites. As expectations rose but progress toward equality in fact proved distressingly slow, black leaders increasingly turned to direct action to speed up the process: sit-ins, demonstrations, rent strikes, economic boycotts, poverty marches, and similar forms of pressure. Integrationists urged the nation to respond to these developments by accelerating the rate of material and social advance. The report of the Commission on Civil Disorders was a brief for this position. It called for both stepping up the pace of social programs and creating strong incentives to facilitate black movement out of central city ghettos.

By 1965 the emphasis had shifted from integration to power mobilization. As described by one writer, "The hopes of the Negroes that racial equality and democracy could be obtained through

[33]Frank X. Steggert, *Community Action Groups and City Government: Perspectives from Ten American Cities* (Cambridge, Mass.: Ballinger, 1978).
[34]See in this connection Edward Schwartz, "Neighborhoodism: A Conflict in Values," *Social Policy* 9 (March/April 1979): 8–14.

legislation, executive action, and negotiation, and through strong alliances with various white liberal groups were supplanted by disillusionment, bitterness and anger which erupted under the cry of 'Black Power' . . . ."[35] Those who advocated black power often had little more in common than the desire to redress the historical pattern of black subordination to white society.[36] The term, in fact, took on many meanings ranging from ideological commitment to violence and the creation of a separate black nation within the United States ("black nationalism") to the development of political and economic strength within the ghetto.

The argument of black power proponents rests on the assumption that the black population must first overcome its feelings of powerlessness and develop pride in its color and ethnicity before it can function effectively in the larger society. For this purpose blacks must have control over decisions that directly affect them. Implicit here is the creation of some form of neighborhood control and the promotion of "black capitalism" within the confines of the ghetto. This concept of black power is based on the proposition that the nonwhite minority must achieve a position of strength through solidarity if it hopes to bargain effectively with the rest of society— the majority is far more likely to make concessions to power than to justice or conscience.[37]

The movement for minority rights entered a new period in the mid-1970s marked by a decline of militancy and an emphasis on conventional politics. The great drive that gave racial equality a top spot on the nation's agenda in the 1960s had lost much of its momentum. A decade of tumult and confrontation had sapped its strength and exhausted its leadership. Also the liberal coalition that had helped to sustain the minority surge had begun to disintegrate from disaffection, despair, and simple combat fatigue. By this time also many of the older black leaders who had played key roles in the events of the preceding decade had passed from the national scene. Concurrently many of the new generation of young blacks who had been active in the civil rights movement—Andrew Young, former United States ambassador to the United Nations, is an outstanding example—either entered the political arena or were recruited into the ranks of the established agencies.

[35]Kenneth Clark, "The Present Dilemma of the Negro," *Journal of Negro History* 53 (January 1968): 35.
[36]Martin Kilson, "Black Power: Anatomy of a Paradox," *Harvard Journal of Negro Affairs* 2 (1968): 30–35.
[37]Martin Duberman, "Black Power in America," *Partisan Review* 35 (Winter 1968): 34–48.

The number of black elected officials has risen steadily during the last decade, although they still constitute less than 1 percent of the total (4,500 out of 522,000 in 1978 according to the *Directory of Black Elected Officials*).[38] Almost one-half of all elected blacks hold municipal offices and another one-fourth serve as school board members. Fewer than 1 percent occupy federal and statewide posts. Eighteen are members of the lower house of Congress but no black is presently in the Senate. State supreme courts remain virtually all white, as well as overwhelmingly male and predominantly of Anglo-Saxon ancestry.[39] As late as the mid-1970s only two blacks were serving on these tribunals across the nation. The record is considerably better on the federal bench, where the members are appointed rather than elected as in most states. At the end of 1980 blacks held almost 60 of the approximately 675 federal judgeships including one on the Supreme Court. (Two-thirds of this number were appointees of President Carter.)

More significant than the numbers, blacks now occupy the office of mayor in two of the country's five largest cities (Los Angeles and Detroit) and in several other major municipalities, among them Atlanta, Birmingham, Gary, New Orleans, and Newark. Although these electoral successes reflect a new political consciousness on the part of blacks, they are coming into political ascendancy in cities that are typically older, poorer, and more nonwhite than most American communities.[40] Black officials must usually function in a setting in which both the municipal bureaucracy (particularly the police and fire departments) and the major social and economic institutions remain in the hands of whites. They face a formidable task under these circumstances in seeking to meet the needs and expectations of their constituents.[41]

Hispanics are also demonstrating greater political awareness although generally they have made less use of the electoral process than blacks. In 1980 individuals with Spanish surnames held only

[38]In 1969 there were only 1185 black elected officials.

[39]Bradley C. Canon, "Characteristics and Career Patterns of State Supreme Court Justices," *State Government* 45 (Winter 1972): 34–41.

[40]Los Angeles is an obvious exception to this statement. So also are a number of smaller communities, such as Boulder, Colorado, College Park, Maryland, and Chapel Hill, North Carolina, which have black mayors and black populations of less than 10 percent (all three incidentally are state university communities where a more liberal electorate can be expected).

[41]On this point see Michael D. Preston, "The Limits of Black Urban Power: The Case of Black Mayors," in Louis Masotti and Robert Lineberry (eds.), *The New Urban Politics* (Cambridge, Mass.: Ballinger, 1976); also Edmond J. Keller, "Electoral Politics in Gary," *Urban Affairs Quarterly* 15 (September 1979): 43–64.

about three-tenths of one percent of the elective public offices in the United States including five congressional seats, eleven less than blacks. They also occupy fifteen federal judgeships. At the local level they are beginning to make their political muscle felt in communities where they are highly concentrated, such as Miami where the mayor and a majority of the city council are Hispanics.

WHO PARTICIPATES?

Pluralist theory, as noted earlier, assumes the existence of a society in which power is widely dispersed. To be assured of sharing in this influence, individuals must participate as political actors and organizational members. It is here that we are confronted with an apparent contradiction between democratic dogma and practice. As numerous studies show, political affairs are not central concerns in the lives of most Americans. Well over one-third of the adult population can be characterized as politically apathetic, with no more than 5 percent actively involved beyond going to the polls.[42]

The problem is not so much the relatively low level of participation, undesirable as this may be from the standpoint of civic vitality and individual development. The important question is whether the system is responsive to the interests of all sectors of the community. If those who take part in public affairs are randomly distributed throughout the population, there is less likelihood that the system will be more responsive to one group than another. If, on the other hand, the nonparticipators are disproportionately concentrated in certain socioeconomic categories, the chances are considerably greater that their needs will receive less attention than those of the politically active groups.

Voting

Political participation has many shades of meaning, from the simple act of voting to direct involvement in the formulation and execution of public policy.[43] Voting is a minimal act of participation, requiring only a small amount of time and energy. Yet less than 60 percent of American adults cast ballots in presidential elections and a far smaller proportion—usually no more than 30 percent—go to the polls in local contests. There are various theories as to why people vote or fail to do so. Generally, the studies on this question point to three sets of factors that are related to electoral participation—per-

[42]Lester Milbrath, *Political Participation: How and Why Do People Get Involved in Politics* (Chicago: Rand McNally, 1965).
[43]See Sidney Verba and Norman Nie, *Participation in America* (New York: Harper & Row, 1972) where 12 separate types of participation are listed.

sonal characteristics of the individual, structural features of the governmental system, and the stakes at issue.

Persons high on the socioeconomic scale, as the findings uniformly show, are more likely to vote than lower status individuals; those between the ages of 25 and 65 more than the young and elderly; homeowners more than renters; and long-term residents more than relative newcomers to the community.[44] Social rank evidences a particularly strong association as demonstrated in a typical municipal election in Toledo, Ohio. Sixty-one percent at the top of the scale went to the polls compared to one-fourth at the bottom. Nonvoters were thus more representative of the city's residents than those who took part in the election.[45] These figures show how low voting levels intensify the impact of socioeconomic differences, giving a disproportionate voice to upper-status voters over the election results.[46]

Structural variables, such as form of government and type of election, also affect the participation rate. A study of voting in municipalities above 25,000 population found that cities with mayor–council governments and partisan ballots have higher turnouts in local elections than those with council–manager and nonpartisan contests.[47] One explanation is that mayoralty contests attract greater

---

[44]The most recent systematic study of elections concludes that education is by far the most important determinant of voting, with age second. Raymond E. Wolfinger and Steven J. Rosenstone, *Who Votes?* (New Haven, Conn.: Yale University Press, 1980). Other studies indicate that psychological factors are also related to participation. Individuals who feel personally or politically inefficacious or who are alienated from their political institutions are less likely to be involved than those with a high sense of efficacy and a feeling of trust in government. See James D. Wright, *Alienation and Democracy in America* (New York: Academy Press, 1976).

[45]Howard D. Hamilton, "The Municipal Voter: Voting and Nonvoting in City Elections," *American Political Science Review* 65 (December 1971): 1135–1140.

[46]The voting rate of blacks is less than that of whites. The difference, however, is not great when controlled for socioeconomic status. Electoral participation for persons of Hispanic heritage, although increasing, remains substantially below that of both whites and blacks. In the 1976 presidential election, for instance, six of every ten whites and one of two blacks of voting age went to the polls compared to about one of three Hispanics. The fact that both blacks and Hispanics are disproportionately represented among the poor lowers the overall participation rate for these minorities.

[47]Robert R. Alford and Eugene C. Lee, "Voter Turnout in American Cities," *American Political Science Review* 62 (September 1968): 796–813. A 1975 survey of municipalities over 25,000 generally supports these findings, although it shows that voter participation in local elections has fallen since the early 1960s, notably in the "unreformed" cities. Albert Karnig and B. Oliver Walter, "Municipal Elections: Registration, Incumbent Success, and Voter Participation," *Municipal Year Book,* 1977, pp. 65–72. A recent study of 16 large cities, however, found that form of ballot made little difference in voter turnout. See Owen E. Newcomer, "Nonpartisan Elections: A Look at Their Effect," *National Civic Review* 66 (October 1977): 453–456.

interest than the election of council members because the office itself is more visible and symbolic and enjoys greater significance in the eyes of the public. Similarly, the influence of partisan elections on voting reflects the fact that parties serve as agents of political mobilization as well as mechanisms for aggregating and articulating interests.

The issue climate of a community is a further factor influencing participation rates. When residents are reasonably well satisfied with the way their local governments are operating and there are no controversial items on the public agenda, the incentive for going to the polls is not impelling. This situation is more likely to exist in socially homogeneous and stable communities of small size than in the large and heterogeneous cities where divisive issues are common and competing groups numerous. For this reason voting turnouts for local elections in central cities usually compare favorably with the extent of participation in suburban contests despite the differences in social rank. However, in national elections where the issues are salient to all classes, the voting rate of the suburbs is normally higher.

Organization Membership

Special interest groups play a major role in determining the allocation of public resources. In a democratic and pluralist society, individuals not represented by such organizations are likely to be without political power. Who belongs is thus as important as who votes. There is, in fact, a high correlation between membership in voluntary associations and electoral participation.[48] Those who belong are more likely to be politically active than the nonjoiners. The percentage of adults who are members of organized groups corresponds closely to the proportion who vote in national elections. But as in political participation, those who are actively involved in organizational affairs constitute a very small minority of the population.

When the demographic features of membership in voluntary associations are examined, a pattern similar to that found in electoral participation emerges. Belonging to formal organizations is closely related to social rank (education, occupation, income) and age. More than one of every two adults with less than a high school education belongs to no formal organization, whereas only about

---

[48]A study of four middle-sized cities found organizational activity, social rank, and home ownership the most important characteristics associated with local political involvement. Robert R. Alford and Harry M. Scoble, "Sources of Local Political Involvement," *American Political Science Review* 62 (December 1968): 1192–1206.

one of five college graduates falls into this category. Similarly, 60 percent or more in the low-income brackets are nonjoiners as against 20 percent in the upper levels, thus indicating the class-linked nature of organizational affiliation. Age is also a determinative factor, with membership highest among individuals between the years of 35 and 65. Associational membership, however, has been increasing slightly but noticeably in recent years, the rise occurring all along the socioeconomic continuum and especially among the poorer segments of the population.[49]

From the standpoint of a democratic polity the most serious problem reflected by the statistics on membership is that the organizations dominating both community and national life simply do not represent all interests or segments of the society. Political scientist E. E. Schattschneider, in his study of pressure groups, found that most of the well-entrenched organizations are composed mainly of businesspeople and upper-class joiners. In his words, "Probably about 90 percent of the people cannot get into the pressure system."[50] This exclusionary bias falls most heavily on the disadvantaged among the population. It is evident even in the case of powerful associations that include lower-class or minority constituencies. The extent, for example, to which the building-trade unions have served the interests of blacks or to which the major farm organizations have represented the rural poor may well be questioned.

The Legacy of the 1960s

Whatever may be said about their successes or failures, the social programs of the 1960s led to the entry of new groups into the political arena and the enlargement of the participatory process for the disadvantaged and later for the middle class as well. The Economic Opportunity Act of 1964 (the war on poverty legislation) provided the impetus for this important development. Its requirement that community action programs financed by federal funds be planned and administered with "maximum feasible participation" on the part of those intended to be served was a bellwether for citizen involvement going beyond conventional political activity. No one was really certain as to what the provision meant or how it was to be carried out, but its intention appeared clear: to afford citizens a

---

[49]See Herbert H. Hyman and Charles R. Wright, "Trends in Voluntary Association Membership of American Adults," *American Sociological Review* 36 (April 1971): 191–206.

[50]E. E. Schattschneider, *The Semi-Sovereign People: A Realist's View of Democracy in America* (New York: Holt, Rinehart and Winston, 1960), p. 35.

more direct voice in the formulation and execution of bureaucratic policy. Although few middle-class groups were sympathetic to community action programs, many came to appreciate their participatory aspect during the 1970s as frustration over governmental decisions at the local level mounted.

Taking part in community action is viewed in two ways. One group of theorists and practitioners regards it as therapeutic; the other as a means of gaining power. According to the first, this type of involvement raises the self-esteem of individuals, aids them in overcoming feelings of hopelessness, gives them a sense of control over matters affecting their lives, and equips them to cope in a competitive society. Participation, in this conception, is desirable for its own sake irrespective of what it accomplishes in material terms. The second school of thought considers involvement basic to the achievement of power. So viewed, its primary purpose is to influence or exercise control over actions of decision makers in the relevant public and private institutions—or, expressed somewhat differently, to make the bureaucratic delivery systems more responsive to the needs and desires of those whom they serve. The therapeutic rationale is closer to the classical conception of political involvement as an essential part of an individual's development. The power view, on the other hand, is more compatible with modern interest group theory and is the motivation for most current organizing efforts.

The war on poverty and model cities at no time involved large numbers of people in the decisional process but they did develop a new cadre of leaders from the ranks of the poor and racial minorities. The community action groups of this period, along with the parallel black power movement, also awakened other types of minorities to the potentialities of direct involvement. The elderly (one group even calling itself the "Gray Panthers"), the physically handicapped, and homosexuals emerged as not-to-be ignored actors on the political scene. The results in many cases have been impressive. The handicapped, to cite one example, have enjoyed considerable success in securing the removal of architectural barriers in public buildings so as to accommodate persons in wheelchairs.

The social action milieu of the 1960s also spawned a host of public interest groups (so called because their expressed goals relate to the concerns of the public at large and not to the personal advantage of the individual members). These range from organizations for the preservation of wildlife to those dedicated to the protection of consumers. Many such groups conduct extensive research, participate actively in public hearings, engage in lobbying, and present alternatives to decision makers. Those concerned with environmentally related issues have been particularly effective, aided by federal legislation requiring an environmental impact statement (EIS) before major projects such as the construction of highways and power plants can be undertaken. As a final weapon, public interest organizations that are dissatisfied with legislative or administrative decisions can turn to the courts where litigation can tie up proposed measures for long periods of time. Some observers worry that the stepped-up involvement of citizen groups is unduly prolonging the policy-formulating process and making it increasingly difficult for government to arrive at decisions in such matters as public works projects. Their concern poses the classical dilemma of efficiency versus broad participation.

POWER IN PERSPECTIVE

Metropolitan residents are caught in the maelstrom of modern society with all its advantages and liabilities. Their reaction to this environment takes many forms: from social conformity to deviance, from aggressive behavior to submissiveness, from community involvement to withdrawal, from commitment to the system to estrangement. Within the borders of the metropolis, amorphous as they may be, individuals vie for the rewards that society has to offer. As businesspeople, professionals, skilled crafts workers, or just common laborers, they daily pursue their social and economic objectives in a milieu too complex to understand and too large to conquer. In their role as community citizens these same individuals participate in a political system whose function is to maintain order, provide services, adjust conflicts among its members, and shape an environment conducive to the achievement of human goals.

Society, it is true, is structured in such a way that many of the crucial decisions relating to the local community are made miles away from it: in the halls of Congress, in the offices of federal agencies, in the state highway commissions, at the headquarters of national associations, or in corporate board rooms in the skyscrapers of New York. Despite this movement of power to higher levels, the residual functions of the urban polity involve stakes of great significance to the local citizenry. Where a park is located, how land is zoned, what portion of community resources is allocated for educational purposes are but a few such activities. Of even more importance, the successful execution of many national policies and programs, whether pertaining to housing, racial discrimination, equality of opportunity, or crime reduction, depends largely on the actions of local and areawide governments.

The numerous clusters of power characteristic of most large

and politically fragmented metropolises in the United States provide the residents with many opportunities to further their personal goals and interests. Unfortunately not all individuals or groups have the means or capabilities to take advantage of these opportunities, so that some profit unduly while others suffer. The critical problem for the metropolitan community (and for society as a whole), in terms of a democratic system, is to find ways of more equitably allocating power resources to assure that all sectors of the populace are fully represented in the public decision-making process.

Chapter 6
The Intergovernmental Web

Urban government cannot be looked at in isolation from other levels of the political system. It is part of a larger structure that includes both the state and national tiers of public authority. Despite the rhetoric of grass-roots autonomy, municipalities and other local units have become increasingly dependent on higher echelons for assistance in carrying out their basic responsibilities. There are, in fact, few urban functions—whether law enforcement, education, public health, transportation, or community revitalization—that do not involve all three levels of government. Although local units continue to deliver the bulk of these services, their role in financing them has decreased dramatically during the last two decades. At the same time also, their administration of activities traditionally considered local in nature has been subjected to a growing number of standards and restrictions imposed by national and state authorities (including the courts). These developments have brought about changes in intergovernmental relations and cast the federal system in new perspective.[1]

FEDERALISM

Federalism in legal terms is a form of political organization in which powers and functions are constitutionally divided between two or more levels of government. In political terms it is a system of interdependent tiers of government sharing activities and relating to each other in an accommodating, although at times contending, fashion. Because of the great volume of interaction that now takes place throughout the political structure—from Washington and the state capitals to city hall and the county court house—the opera-

[1]For recent comprehensive analyses of the federal system in the United States see Parris N. Glendening and Mavis M. Reeves, *Pragmatic Federalism: An Intergovernmental View of American Government* (Pacific Palisades, Calif.: Palisades Publishers, 1977) and Deil S. Wright, *Understanding Intergovernmental Relations* (North Scituate, Mass.: Duxbury, 1979).

tions of urban communities must be viewed within the framework of the federal system as a whole.

Although federalism in theory defines the relationship between levels of government, the concept in the United States has gone through four broad phases, commonly characterized as dual, cooperative, creative, and new. The distinction among these historical phases is not clear-cut—some authors also identify other stages—but each represents a different conception of the relationship between the national government and the states and localities.[2]

The Polar Model

Dual federalism emphasizes a clear demarcation between the powers of the national government and the states. Chief Justice Roger Taney gave legal expression to this doctrine just prior to the Civil War in holding that the two levels are "separate and distinct sovereignties, acting separately and independently of each other, within their respective spheres."[3] As constitutional law, dual federalism prevailed until the 1930s when it was overruled by a series of decisions upholding New Deal legislation. Long before this time, however, the variance between doctrine and practice had become evident. The network of interrelations that developed historically between the national government and the states during the late nineteenth and early twentieth centuries had negated the notion of two parallel strata of public authorities operating in their individual compartments with little or no crossover from one to the other.[4]

The Cooperative Model

Cooperative federalism, the term first used during the New Deal period to describe intergovernmental relations, signifies the common sharing of public functions by two or more levels of government. Originally, it referred only to the relations between Washing-

---

[2]There is no commonly agreed on identification of stages in the development of intergovernmental relations. See, for instance, Deil S. Wright, "Intergovernmental Relations: An Analytical Overview," *Annals of the American Academy of Political and Social Science* 416 (November 1974): 1–16.

[3]*Ableman* v. *Booth,* 21 Howard 506 (1858).

[4]Morton Grodzins, one of the major theoreticians of federalism, characterized the American system of government as analogous to a marble cake even though it is structured formally like a three-layer cake. See his "The Federal System," in American Assembly, *Goals for America* (Englewood Cliffs, N.J.: Prentice-Hall, 1960), p. 265.

ton and the state capitals because direct contacts between national agencies and local units were relatively few. Whatever federal assistance urban communities received—and it was meager—was channeled through the state governments.

Cities are creatures of the state, totally unrecognized by the Constitution. The celebrated Dillon's rule (named after the justice of the Iowa Supreme Court who wrote the opinion) made this clear in metaphorical language: "Municipal corporations owe their rights to, and derive their powers and rights wholly from, the legislature. It breathes into them the breath of life, without which they cannot exist. As it creates, so may it destroy. If it may destroy, it may abridge and control."[5]

Despite their inferior legal status, the position of the cities has seldom been supine. As one observer of intergovernmental relations has noted, something like a federal system developed early within states, the municipalities enjoying a substantial degree of self-rule and the two levels sharing power over many functions.[6] Federal–local relations, on the other hand, remained insignificant until the depression years of the 1930s when funds for public works projects and housing were allocated to the cities as emergency measures.

The issue of whether the national government should deal directly with the cities came to a head after World War II over a proposed program of aid for municipal airport development. State officials argued vigorously that the funds should be administered by them. Representatives of the cities, on the other hand, called for direct grants, maintaining that airports are peculiarly urban facilities. Mayor Fiorello LaGuardia of New York, speaking for the large municipalities, minced no words in telling Congress that there was simply no place in the picture for any intermediate state agency. The big cities, aside from the proposal at hand, were anxious to obtain explicit statutory endorsement of direct federal–local relations in matters of urban concern. The states were equally determined to prevent the formalization of any such precedent. After prolonged controversy the position of the cities prevailed in principle, Congress specifying that any public agency might apply directly for an airport development grant.

---

[5]*City of Clinton* v. *Cedar Rapids and Missouri River Railroad,* 24 Iowa 455 (1868). The decision was subsequently upheld by the U.S. Supreme Court. Some state constitutions now grant home rule status to the larger cities (and counties), thus giving them legal standing independent of the legislature.

[6]Roscoe C. Martin, *The Cities and the Federal System* (New York: Atherton Press, 1965), pp. 28–35.

The airport act of 1946 did not immediately change the prevailing practice. Most grants for urban purposes continued to be routed through the states. As late as 1962 direct payments to local governments were under $700 million annually. The act nonetheless had given recognition to the localities as the third partner in the federal system and it was only a matter of time before national–city relations would be considerably expanded. The "Great Society" programs of the 1960s and the new-type urban grants of the 1970s saw to this by vastly increasing the amount of funds flowing directly into municipal and county coffers. In the process the path from city hall to Washington became well worn.

The Creative Model

Creative federalism goes beyond the cooperative concept in calling for extensive involvement of the national government in urban problem solving and emphasizing the establishment of relations between federal agencies and nonpublic organizations and institutions at the local level. The concept was advanced by President Lyndon Johnson in a commencement address at the University of Michigan in 1964. Referring to the overwhelming problems of the cities, he declared that they "require us to create new concepts of cooperation—a creative federalism—between the National Capital and the leaders of local communities." The poverty program embodied this concept with its provisions for the direct funding of community action agencies.

The creative federalism phase with its clarion call for the expansion and broad use of social programs was of relatively short duration. As public disillusionment with the social engineering efforts of the 1960s set in, the emphasis shifted from federal intervention in the solution of urban problems to state and local control. But even though creative federalism did not survive long in the national vocabulary, the concept itself left a more lasting legacy. Its basic premise that government can make little headway toward solving the problems of the cities without enlisting the active participation of community groups and business interests has become common doctrine. The Carter Administration's urban policy statement released in March 1978, for example, called for a "new partnership" involving all levels of government along with citizen based organizations (CBOs) and the private sector generally. Rational as this approach is, it still remains at the rhetorical level. American political ingenuity has not yet succeeded in finding effective ways of joining together these disparate elements in coordinated efforts to raise the quality of urban life.

New Federalism Model

New federalism, the latest stage in intergovernmental relations, is a product of the Nixon presidency.[7] Early in his first term in office, Nixon described the essence of the new doctrine when he said that his administration would restore "power, funds, and authority to those governments closest to the people . . . to help regain control of our national destiny by returning a greater share of control to state and local authorities." His successor, Gerald Ford, used similar rhetoric in calling for the return of power "from the banks of the Potomac to the people in their own communities." The thrust of new federalism, as these statements indicate, is to deemphasize the national government's role in local and state affairs. This objective is to be pursued by shifting control over the administration of grant programs from Washington to lower levels in the federal system.

To further the decentralization goal, Nixon proposed both general revenue sharing (unrestricted grants to the states and localities) and special revenue sharing (grants for broadly defined areas, such as education and law enforcement, with state and local officials given maximum discretion in their use). As conceived by the president, the national government's role in urban affairs was to be limited to raising the problem-solving capabilities of local and state governments through financial assistance.[8]

Nixon's efforts to decentralize power, to "restore the balance in the federal system," fell far short of accomplishment. Too many influential interests stand to lose by a devolution of authority over the grant programs—the federal bureaucracies administering such aids, the congressional committees overseeing them, the constituent groups benefiting from them. Nixon, however, did achieve some success in increasing state–local discretion over the use of federal funds. He maneuvered general revenue sharing through Congress and was instrumental in furthering enactment of the community development block grant program, a limited version of one of his special revenue-sharing categories.

The Carter Administration's "new partnership" can hardly be called an additional phase in the intergovernmental saga; if anything, it represents a modified version of new federalism. The con-

---

[7]This phase is treated in Michael D. Reagan, and John Sanzone, *The New Federalism.* 2d ed. (New York: Oxford University Press, 1980).

[8]The Nixon Administration's efforts to decentralize the grant programs are described in Douglas Haider, *When Governments Come to Washington: Governors, Mayors, and Intergovernmental Lobbying* (New York: Free Press, 1974), pp. 257–282.

cept of decentralizing responsibility and limiting the urban role of the national bureaucracies was congruent with Carter's populist sympathies. Consistent with the new federalism philosophy, he favored the strategy of avoiding direct federal intervention by giving financial aid to local and state governments to enhance their problem solving capacity. Unlike Nixon, however, he demonstrated a genuine concern for the difficulties of the cities and a willingness to give high priority to their amelioration within economic restraints. In addition, he favored targeting funds to the areas most in need rather than spreading them across the whole spectrum of state and local governments. Under the Reagan Administration the new federalism doctrine is finding wide acceptance because of its basic compatibility with political conservatism.

THE FEDERAL GRANT BAG

Total federal aid to local and state governments almost doubled every five years during the past quarter century, from $3.2 billion in 1955 to approximately $83 billion in 1980 (Table 6.1). Such assistance now provides about one-fourth of the revenue of the state–local sector, whereas federal and state grants combined constitute almost 45 percent of the revenue of local jurisdictions. These funds are provided through several types of grants and hundreds of individual programs for purposes ranging from bikeway construction and urban rat control to general government support and community development. Many of these programs have become institutionalized and well entrenched in the political system.

Table 6.1 FEDERAL AID TO STATE AND LOCAL GOVERNMENTS, 1955 TO 1980

YEAR	AMOUNT FEDERAL AID (IN BILLIONS OF DOLLARS)	PERCENT INCREASE
1955	3.2	—
1960	7.0	119
1965	10.9	58
1970	24.0	120
1975	49.8	108
1980	82.9	66

SOURCE: Advisory Commission on Intergovernmental Relations, *Significant Features of Fiscal Federalism 1978–79* (Washington, D.C.: U.S. Government Printing Office, May 1979), p. 1.

Grant Types

Federal grants are of three major types: categorical, block, and revenue sharing. Categorical or special purpose aids are the oldest and most prevalent form of fiscal assistance. They are directed at specific, narrowly defined activities, such as the furnishing of hot lunches to needy school children or the building of a sewage disposal plant. Nearly 500 such programs are now in existence, representing three-fourths of the total grant money distributed annually by the national government. The principal categorical aids for urban areas are in the fields of public works (sewers, water supply, roads, public buildings), airport development, low-income housing, education, welfare, and mass transit.

One of the latest categorical aids is the urban development action grant (UDAG), referred to by President Carter as the centerpiece of his urban program and by developer James Rouse as "the most remarkable program dealing with the American city I have seen in my lifetime." UDAG provides for grants to distressed cities to stimulate private investment, whether in the renovation of an historic hotel in Louisville, the establishment of an industrial park in a blighted Chicago area, the construction of a galleria linking an office center and hotel in St. Paul, or a neighborhood revitalization project in Baltimore. UDAG functions on a far smaller scale than the former urban renewal program and is designed to trigger off projects that otherwise would not occur. It is highly popular with municipal officials and private developers because, unlike most federal programs, it gives the city wide latitude in the choice of projects, involves a minimum of red tape, and permits undertakings that can show rapid results.

Block grants, in contrast to categorical aids, are awarded for use within a broad functional field, such as law enforcement or community development. They are a relatively recent innovation, the first one being initiated by Congress in 1966. Most such grants have been created by combining several existing categorical aids, as the four major programs of this type show.

1. The Partnership for Health Act of 1966 was the pioneer block grant program in this country. It consolidated 20 categorical aids to combat specific diseases into a new system of broad awards for comprehensive public health services.
2. The Omnibus Crime Control and Safe Streets Act of 1968 provided for block grants to the states for the purpose of upgrading police forces and law enforcement methods. At least 75 percent of the funds must be channeled to local com-

munities. The act also established the Law Enforcement Assistance Administration (LEAA) in the Department of Justice to administer the program.

3. Title 1 of the Comprehensive Employment and Training Act of 1973 (CETA) combined 17 categorical aids in the manpower field into a single block grant. The act authorizes federal aid to "prime sponsors"—cities, counties exceeding 100,000 population, and state governments—to plan and operate training programs for the unemployed and underemployed. Other sections of the act provide categorical assistance for the funding of public service employment (PSE) and summer jobs for youths. Two-thirds of CETA funds go directly to local units and one-third to state governments.

4. Title I of the Housing and Community Development Act of 1974 merged seven existing categorical programs—urban renewal, model cities, water and sewer facilities, open space, neighborhood facilities, rehabilitation loans, and public facility loans—into the community development block grant (CDBG). Unlike the other block grants in which the states participate, all CDBG allocations go to local general purpose governments (municipalities and counties). Over 2500 such units are presently recipients of community development funds.

The third type of grant, revenue sharing, was inaugurated by the State and Local Fiscal Assistance Act of 1972. Referred to as general revenue sharing (GRS), funds totaling more than $7 billion are distributed annually to state governments and some 38,000 municipalities and counties, many of which had never received a federal grant prior to passage of the act.[9] Two-thirds of the money goes directly to the localities and the remainder to the states. Recipients may spend the funds for virtually any service or function they see fit. Surveys show that local governments have used the money primarily for police and fire protection, public works, and welfare programs; and the states have earmarked much of their portion for pub-

---

[9]The participation of nonmetropolitan communities in federal grant programs is, as one observer notes, perhaps the most important development in small-town government and policymaking for many decades. The GRS grant alerted these units to a new revenue source and shortly thereafter many of them began to tap into other federal programs. For a study of the experience in one state see Alvin D. Sokolow, "Small Towns, Big Grants: Federal Aid and Nonmetropolitan Local Governments in Illinois," *Illinois Government Research* (Urbana: Institute of Government and Public Affairs, University of Illinois, November 1979).

lic education, social services, and capital improvements. Renewal of the revenue sharing program came under heavy attack from national lawmakers in 1980. In a compromise measure Congress extended the program for three years but suspended authorization of the states' portion for fiscal 1981. A House amendment to the bill, moreover, requires the states to return federal funds earmarked for special programs, such as education, in an amount equal to the revenue sharing allotment. The strings attached to the state portion reflected in part congressional irritation at the resolutions passed by more than 30 state legislatures calling for a constitutional amendment to mandate balanced federal budgets.

A proposal that the national government share the federal income tax with the states was first offered in 1958 by Melvin Laird of Wisconsin who introduced a bill to this effect in the House of Representatives. A similar plan was put forward in 1964 by Walter Heller, then chairman of the Council of Economic Advisers in the Johnson Administration, but attention was diverted from it by the accelerating American involvement in Vietnam. When Nixon took over the presidency, he saw revenue sharing as an ideal tool of new federalism and set about to secure its passage.

Although the GRS legislation did not incorporate Heller's plan of allocating a specified percentage of the federal income tax to the states and localities, it established the principle of sharing the national tax base as a source of intergovernmental revenue. Many observers are favorably disposed to this development, convinced that the national government should assume greater fiscal responsibility for local needs because of its superior taxing and income redistribution capabilities. They are also sympathetic to the idea of a more decentralized system of administration and more programmatic discretion for lower levels of public authority. What bothers some of them, nevertheless, is that once restrictions on the use of the funds are removed, local and state governments will be inclined to spend the money to satisfy their most influential constituencies rather than to implement national policies in such fields as low-income housing and civil rights.[10] Others, such as Senator Mark Hatfield of Oregon, express the traditional concern that separating tax collecting from spending responsibilities weakens federalism by making state and local authorities more dependent on the central government.

---

[10]All grants, regardless of type, are subject to routinely imposed requirements, such as those pertaining to affirmative action, citizen participation, and accounting practices.

Other Grant Characteristics

Grants-in-aid may be further distinguished by the two principal bases on which they are awarded; formula and project. In the case of formula-determined awards, eligible jurisdictions are automatically allotted financial assistance according to an equation established by Congress or administrative regulation. General revenue sharing and all block grants are distributed in this way.[11] GRS allocations, for example, are computed on the basis of population size, per capita income, and tax effort, and CDBG awards on population, extent of poverty, and age of housing.[12]

Project grants, unlike those of the formula variety, do not involve automatic entitlement but require aspiring recipients to compete for funds by submitting detailed applications. (Here grantsmanship, the ability to package a proposal in such a way as to appeal to the awarding agency, is sometimes a more important factor than the question of need or equity.) Most categorical aids are of the project type, a prominent example being the now-discontinued urban renewal program. Other activities supported in this way cover a broad spectrum of functional areas, including air and water pollution control, community health centers, and mass transit. Many of the grants in this class require recipients to match a portion of the federal funds with state or local contributions.

A portion of federal urban aid, as noted before, is channeled through the state governments. In some instances the states serve merely as conduits; in others they are given various degrees of discretionary authority over the reallocation of the money to their political subdivisions. Since 1960 most of the new urban grant programs, including GRS and CBDG, provide for direct payments to local governments. The aggregate amount distributed in this way is now almost equal to the pass-through funds. In 1977, for instance, locality units received a total of $15.5 billion directly from the national government and another $14.3 billion in aid routed through the states.

---

[11]The CDBG program requires eligible recipients to file applications outlining plans for use of the funds. The process, however, is not a competitive one. Each jurisdiction is assured the amount determined by formula as long as it complies with the general guidelines.

[12]The original CDBG formula worked to the disadvantage of the older cities in the Northeast and Midwest which are losing population. The new formula reflecting the age of housing benefits them substantially. Opposition to the change from southern and western members of Congress was softened by increasing the total funding of the program so that allocations would not be reduced for any city or state.

Local agencies also benefit indirectly from federal grants received by the state governments for their own programs. The availability of these funds tends to reduce the overall budget restraints of the states and enables them to make larger allocations of aid to their school districts and other locality units than would be the case if such resources were not at hand. The amounts made available in this way are referred to as "indirect pass-through" funds. A study of the intergovernmental grant system estimated that in 1977 local governments received $5.6 billion in the form of state aid that can be attributed mainly to federal grants.[13] Taking this amount into account along with direct payments and direct pass-through funds, local units collectively received over $35 billion of the approximately $60 billion in federal assistance awarded the state-local sector in that year.

Current Trends

By the end of the 1970s two new trends in the intergovernmental aid pattern had emerged, one relating to the growth of federal assistance and the other to the degree of control exercised by the national government over the administration of grant programs. Based on the allotments of the last several years, the rapid increase in the magnitude of federal fiscal assistance now appears to have leveled off. From 1970 to 1975 grants to state and local governments rose by 108 percent, and from 1975 to 1980 by only two-thirds. In aggregate figures the amount increased by about $4 billion in 1979 and by less than $1 billion in 1980 (adjusted for inflation, the latter total represents an actual decline). As a proportion of state–local expenditures, federal aid reached a peak of almost 27 percent in 1978 and dropped to below 24 percent in 1980 (Figure 6.1). If this trend continues, as is likely, state and local governments will find it necessary to depend on their own revenue sources for an increasingly larger share of their budgets.

The second development is the reversal, or at least containment, of the movement to decentralize federal aid programs. No new block grant has been established since 1974 and those presently in existence have been subjected to expanding national requirements. Local discretion, in fact, has been circumscribed by legislative directions and administrative guidelines almost to the

[13]G. Ross Stephens and Gerald W. Olson, *Pass Through Federal Aid and Interlevel Finance in the American Federal System 1957 to 1977: A Report to the National Science Foundation* (Kansas City, Mo.: University of Missouri—Kansas City, August 1979).

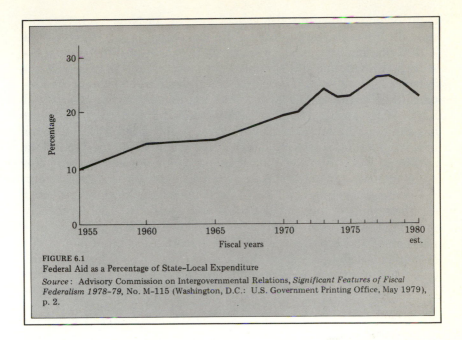

FIGURE 6.1
Federal Aid as a Percentage of State–Local Expenditure

Source: Advisory Commission on Intergovernmental Relations, *Significant Features of Fiscal Federalism 1978–79*, No. M-115 (Washington, D.C.: U.S. Government Printing Office, May 1979), p. 2.

point where some of the block grants are beginning to resemble categorical aids, a process referred to as "recategorization." Some decentralization sentiment, however, reappeared in Congress in late 1980 when the lawmakers directed HUD to study the feasibility of a housing assistance block grant program as an alternative to the existing housing categoricals.[14]

THE STATES AND THEIR LOCALITIES

Wide divergencies exist among the 50 states in the role they play toward their political subdivisions. Some tend to exercise close control over their local units whereas others allow them considerable latitude. Some are generous with fiscal aid, others are penurious. The service delivery pattern, moreover, is so varied among and even within states as to defy generalization. What is locally administered in one jurisdiction may be the responsibility of state government in another. In Hawaii, for example, the state depart-

[14]None of the housing assistance programs was included in the community development block grant legislation. However, some local community development agencies (CDAs) have used CDBG funds for housing purposes as well as other revitalization needs.

ment of education runs the school system; in New York City responsibility is divided between the municipal board of education and 32 community school districts. In Rhode Island the state operates the Providence and Newport bus systems, and in Missouri gubernatorially appointed commissions have charge of the police departments of the state's two largest municipalities, St. Louis and Kansas City. In Rhode Island and Wisconsin the state government has assumed the localities' share of costs associated with the major federal programs related to income maintenance: aid for dependent children, Medicaid, and food stamps. Any comparisons between cities or states must take these wide variances into consideration.

State governments for many years have been sharply criticized for their indifference to urban-related problems. Until recently most legislatures were badly malapportioned in favor of rural constituencies and reflected the anticity bias that has been part of our cultural heritage. As late as 1962, state aids to local governments (exclusive of federal pass-through funds) totaled less than $10 billion. By the end of the decade, however, many states were beginning to demonstrate greater concern on the urban front. This new consciousness is evidenced in several ways—increased fiscal assistance to local governments, assumption of functional responsibilities, and adoption of measures related to urban development.

Fiscal Aid

State financial assistance to local governments takes the form of either grants-in-aid or shared taxes.[15] Most grants-in-aid are of the formula type with allocations earmarked for the support of particular services or facilities and distributed with at least nominal reference to some measure of local need. In the case of shared taxes, the state returns a portion of the yield from various levies to the local units according to a distribution formula or on the basis of origin of collection. In New York, 18 percent of the personal income tax is shared with local governments, half of the amount being earmarked for city usage; and in North Dakota, 5 percent of all revenues from sales and income taxes are channeled to the localities. Florida, Kansas, Michigan, and Wisconsin are among the other states utilizing the shared tax device.

State aid to local units (exclusive of direct federal pass-through funds) totaled $48.1 billion in 1977, an eightfold increase since

[15]For an analysis of state fiscal aid see Advisory Commission on Intergovernmental Relations, *The States and Intergovernmental Aids* (Washington, D.C., February 1977), No. A-59.

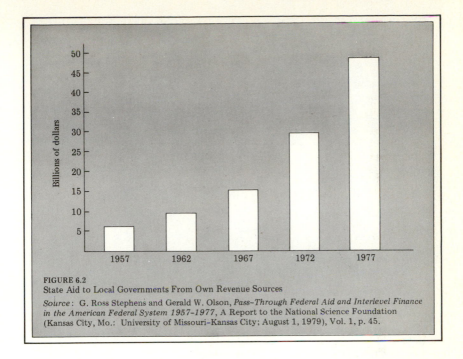

FIGURE 6.2
State Aid to Local Governments From Own Revenue Sources
Source: G. Ross Stephens and Gerald W. Olson, *Pass–Through Federal Aid and Interlevel Finance in the American Federal System 1957–1977*, A Report to the National Science Foundation (Kansas City, Mo.: University of Missouri–Kansas City; August 1, 1979), Vol. 1, p. 45.

1957 (Figure 6.2).[16] The largest portion, almost two-thirds, was allocated to the public schools. About one-eighth of the funds was designated to support the general operational or housekeeping costs of the municipalities and counties, and most of the remainder was earmarked for such traditional local services as welfare, roads, and health (Figure 6.3). During the last several years a small but increasing amount of state aid has been in the form of project grants for functions of a distinctly urban character, such as mass transit, day-care facilities, and land use planning.

Functional Aid

Along with providing fiscal assistance, many states have taken over the administration of various functions formerly performed by the local units. In some instances they have created special authorities to assume responsibility for a service, as in New York State where regional transportation agencies have been set up in a number of

[16]When reports refer to the magnitude of state aid, it is important to determine whether the figures include federal pass-through funds. The Census of Governments, for example, includes such funds in its compilation of state assistance.

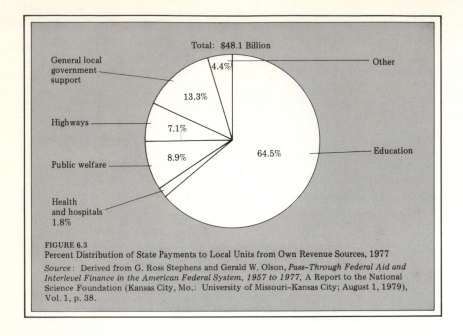

FIGURE 6.3
Percent Distribution of State Payments to Local Units from Own Revenue Sources, 1977
Source: Derived from G. Ross Stephens and Gerald W. Olson, *Pass–Through Federal Aid and Interlevel Finance in the American Federal System, 1957 to 1977*, A Report to the National Science Foundation (Kansas City, Mo.: University of Missouri–Kansas City; August 1, 1979), Vol. 1, p. 38.

metropolitan areas. In other cases the state governments themselves have preempted the activity, as in Rhode Island where the legislature abolished city and town health departments and transferred their duties to the state health department. Other functions that have been assumed by various states include property assessment, welfare, and environmental pollution abatement.

Although local units have willingly acceded to state takeovers in some instances, they generally have shown little disposition to divest themselves of any service, preferring to follow the grant-in-aid path. Studies show that in those states with extensive assistance programs, the bulk of services tend to be provided by local units, whereas in those where such aid is meager, the state government plays a larger direct role in the delivery system. Wisconsin, for example, ranks high in fiscal aids but low in state-delivered services. Hawaii, on the other hand, ranks low in fiscal grants to its local units but high in terms of state-administered functions.

The New Interest

Of more importance in the long run than monetary or functional assistance, state governments are beginning to take an interest in how their communities are growing and the consequences of this growth. The laissez-faire system of local planning and development that has prevailed historically in the United States is coming under increasing attack as environmental and energy considerations become more acute. Florida is one of the first states to require that all its cities and counties prepare and adopt state-approved land use plans. Few others have gone this far because control over the use of land has been a jealously guarded local function. Most have limited their efforts in this field to coastal zoning, floodplain restrictions, and requirements for sewage facilities.

State governments in recent years have evidenced greater concern over the related problems of metropolitan sprawl and inner-city deterioration but few have directly intervened to alter local development patterns. However, many are attempting to encourage growth management planning indirectly through the use of fiscal incentives and capital expenditures. Massachusetts, as an example, has adopted a policy of locating new state office buildings and giving priority status to the construction of transportation and higher educational facilities in urban centers. It has also enacted legislation granting preferential tax treatment for inner-city commercial development and providing fiscal and technical assistance to neighborhood improvement programs.

Michigan and Minnesota are among the states that make funds available to their political subdivisions to upgrade industrial sites and facilities designed to attract additional investment by the private sector, a use of public money known as "leveraging." (Alabama adds a unique feature to industrial development activities by offering customized manpower assistance to incoming businesses through the use of mobile training units.) Indiana, Missouri, and Pennsylvania have community assistance programs that provide tax credits to firms that invest in distressed neighborhoods, and several, including New York, make grants to neighborhood organizations to aid them in carrying out community conservation measures. A majority of states have now created housing finance agencies to promote credit availability for new home construction and rehabilitation programs. Forty-five have established departments or offices of local governmental affairs to address community problems, 30 such agencies enjoying cabinet-level status.[17]

Despite these modest beginnings to aid local units, state governments have yet to demonstrate their willingness and capacity to deal with large-scale urban problems. Few have moved aggressively in this field; most continue to show reluctance to become involved in any major capacity. Moreover, the big urban govern-

[17]A compendium of recent state action to assist local units is contained in Advisory Commission on Intergovernmental Relations, *State Community Assistance Initiatives: Innovations of the Late 70s* (Washington, D.C., May 1979).

ments (despite their often-repeated complaints of federal interference) usually prefer to deal with national rather than state agencies. Not only are they mindful of the poor track record of the states toward the cities but they also tend to be more wary of state control than federal intervention. Relations between the states and their large municipalities continue to be marked more by suspicion and conflict than mutual trust and cooperative action. The past always seems to get in the way of establishing closer ties between these two elements in the federal system.

The last two decades have witnessed considerable improvement in the relative position of the states within the intergovernmental web. Their revenue systems have been made more responsive to economic growth and their tax structures have become less regressive because of the widespread adoption of the personal income tax (presently used by 44 states). Their own source funds have risen at a rate almost double that of federal revenue and 40 percent more than locally derived receipts. As a group they now raise $1.40 for each $1 collected at the local level compared to a one-to-one ratio in 1963. Because of these favorable developments, most states are reasonably well situated from a financial standpoint. None has defaulted on its bonds as several cities, such as New York and Cleveland, have done. Many, in fact, have accumulated substantial surpluses in recent years. Wisconsin in 1979 declared a two-month moratorium on income taxes because of excess funds in its treasury, and California's surplus of over $5 billion was used to bridge most of the revenue gap at the local level initially caused by Proposition 13. Other states have been using a portion of their funds to provide local property tax relief.

The superior fiscal capacity of the state governments compared to their political subdivisions is strong reason for them to assume a larger role in urban problem solving. Two recent developments, however, militate against the likelihood of such action. First, the financial well-being enjoyed by the states during the 1970s is attributable in part to federal funding, with revenue derived from their own sources well below their spending levels. Any significant curtailment of federal aid will cause the surpluses to disappear quickly. Second, the tax revolt symbolized by Proposition 13 is now reaching up to the state governments, further restricting their fiscal freedom.

IMPACT OF FEDERAL INTERVENTION

For most of the nation's history the predominant issue in intergovernmental relations has been the assumption of power by the national government at the expense of the states. In recent decades, however, the most important development relating to the federal system has been the expansion of Washington's involvement in urban problem solving. Critics of this trend charge that direct federal intervention at the local level has weakened the urban role of the states and made local units little more than administrative arms of the national government. Those who take this position equate the growth of federal aid with increased national control over the states and localities.

How Much Control?

Concern about the impact of federal intervention in urban affairs is generally overdrawn. The charge that direct grants to local units have weakened the relationship between the states and their political subdivisions is less ominous than it sounds. State governments historically have played a relatively minor part in helping their large cities cope with the problems of urbanization. Their failure to assume a more supportive role in this respect has been a contributing factor to the expansion of federal involvement at the local level. Finally, it must be remembered that the growing interdependence of the society has exerted strong pressures for the centralization of power at higher levels in both the public and private sectors, and these pressures would exist regardless of federal aid.

The old adage that those who pay the piper call the tune is obviously applicable to the fiscal assistance programs but certainly not to the extent that some critics contend. When the former Department of Health, Education and Welfare (HEW was divided into two departments in 1980, Health and Human Services and Education), to cite one classic example, cut off funds to the city of Chicago for failure to comply with federal guidelines, Mayor Richard Daley wasted no time in getting the money flowing again with a call to President Johnson. As this incident shows, influence in the federal system is not a one-way street. State and local governments are not helpless in the face of the federal bureaucracy. They are able to exert pressure through Congress, other political channels, and their own interest groups.[18]

Both the localities and states have well-staffed organizations

[18]On this point see Suzanne Farkas, *Urban Lobbying: Mayors in the Urban Arena* (New York: New York University Press, 1971). A recent study by Joseph Zimmerman, based on an extensive survey of state and local officials, found no evidence that the expansion of federal powers in urban affairs has resulted in the atrophy of local governments. These units retain considerable discretionary authority, are able to influence congressional and administrative policies, and remain the chief providers of public services. "Federal Preemption and the Erosion of Local Discretionary Authority," Paper presented to Congress of Cities, Atlanta, Georgia, December 1980.

that represent them in the nation's capital. Often referred to as public interest groups (PIGs), these associations monitor legislation, cultivate ties with lawmakers, White House aides, and administrative personnel, engage in lobbying, and keep their members informed of developments on the Washington front. Each category of local units has its own organization. The U.S. Conference of Mayors is the arm mainly of the large cities; the National League of Cities (a broadly based federation of state leagues of municipalities with a combined membership of nearly 15,000) reflects the position of the medium- and small-sized communities; and the National Association of Counties looks out for the interests of the counties.[19]

The major organizations of state officials are the National Governors Conference, the National Conference of State Legislatures, and the Council of State Governments (principally a research and service agency complementing the other two groups). Metropolitan agencies—Councils of Governments (COGs) and regional planning commissions—are represented by the National Association of Regional Councils. Local and state bureaucratic officials are also organized into national groups, including the International City Management Association, Municipal Finance Officers Association, American Public Works Association, and the American Association of State Highway and Transportation Officials.

The government organizations are not always united in their positions because their basic interests do not coincide at times. Differences between the large and small cities, between the municipalities and the counties, and between local governments and the states frequently arise over federal legislation and policies. The original passage of general revenue sharing, to note one instance, was jeopardized for a time by disagreements over the allotment of funds. The major organizations, however, recognize that no single one is self-sufficient in its influence. They consequently engage in extensive negotiations with each other in efforts to resolve differences and present a united front to the federal establishment. Accommodation among the groups on policy stands involving issues of mutual concern is more common than conflict.

Spending Patterns

Federal grants, particularly those with matching requirements, have been criticized for distorting the budgetary policies of state and local governments by inducing expenditures on aided functions to the neglect of others. The question here is whether such

---

[19]The operation of government interest groups is treated in Haider, *When Governments Come to Washington.*

assistance stimulates spending on a service or program above the amount the grantee would otherwise make or whether it simply substitutes for state–local funding, thereby freeing the latter for other needs or reducing taxes. Clearly, a grant would be stimulative (at least to the extent of the matching money) if it caused the recipient to undertake a new program or responsibility. It would also be stimulative if it induced the grantee government to allocate more of its own funds to an established functional area than it would normally do. Stimulation of spending on a particular service, however, does not necessarily mean that other items in the budget will suffer because the recipient may continue to maintain them at the same level by increasing its own-source revenues.

Research findings provide no definitive answer to this issue. A majority of them indicate that federal grants overall have a stimulating effect. According to several, the availability of such assistance leads to increased outlays by local and state governments not only for the function to which it is directed but also for complementary and even unrelated activities.[20] Other research, however, contradicts this finding, holding that federal grants cause a significant reduction of local–state spending on unaided or little-aided items.[21]

Most of the research in this area precedes the adoption of revenue sharing and block grants that presumably have a less distortive effect on local and state budgets because of greater discretion by recipients over their use. One would assume from fragmentary evidence that general revenue sharing is essentially substitutive, especially in the large cities (employed to hold down taxes), whereas CDBG is mildly stimulative in its effects (encourages additional spending by the localities to speed up revitalization efforts).[22] An analysis of the impact of the earlier block grants in ten large urban communities partially supports this assumption. It showed that for

[20]Jack W. Osman, "The Dual Impact of Federal Aid on State and Local Government Expenditures," *National Tax Journal* 19 (December 1966): 362–372; David L. Smith, "The Response of State and Local Governments to Federal Grants," *National Tax Journal* (September 1968): 349–357; and John C. Weicher, "Aid Expenditures and Local Government Structure," *National Tax Journal* 25 (December 1972): 573–583.

[21]T. Pogue and L. G. Sgontz, "The Effects of Grants-in-Aid on State-Local Spending," *National Tax Journal* 21 (June 1968): 190–199; Thomas O'Brien, "Grants-in-Aid: Some Further Answers," *National Tax Journal* 24 (March 1971): 65–77; and J. C. Olds and T. J. Wales, "Supply and Demand for State and Local Services," *Review of Economics and Statistics* 54 (November 1972): 424–430.

[22]The assumption that most revenue sharing funds are used to maintain or expand regular operating programs is supported in F. Thomas Justes (ed.), *The Economic and Political Impact of General Revenue Sharing* (Ann Arbor: Survey Research Institute, University of Michigan, 1977). See also Patrick Larkey, *Evaluating Public Programs: The Impact of General Revenue Sharing* (Princeton, N.J.: Princeton University Press, 1979).

every dollar in federal aid, local expenditures were raised by 25 cents and taxes reduced by 75 cents, indicating that on the whole the grants were more substitutive than stimulative.[23]

The importance of the form of aid from a public policy standpoint was emphasized in a recent ACIR study.[24] The commission's findings indicate that important impact variances are associated with grants of different characteristics. Project awards, for instance, are more inducive of state–local spending than formula-type aids and those with high-matching requirements more than low. This relationship suggests that the formal features of grants should be tailored to serve the objectives intended by policymakers. A program such as revenue sharing, in other words, may be appropriate if the purpose is to help local governments in carrying out their normal functions and inappropriate if the objective is to further a particular national goal.

The debates over federal assistance programs generally fail to recognize this relationship between the type of grant and the end to be served. A well-designed aid system, as two ACIR analysts have noted, must contain three distinct elements: (1) categorical grants to stimulate and support programs in specific areas of national interest, such as the provision of low-income housing; (2) block grants to give the recipient governments greater flexibility in meeting needs in broad functional areas, such as law enforcement; and (3) general revenue sharing to lessen fiscal disparities among local (and state) governments and allow them to fashion their own programs to meet their unique needs.[25]

The Coordination Problem

The problem in the intergovernmental aid system is less one of federal control over the states and localities than of program proliferation and lack of coordination. In 1976, as an illustration, 18 dif-

[23]E. M. Gramlich and H. Galper, "State and Local Fiscal Behavior and Federal Grant Policy," *Brookings Papers on Economic Activities* (Washington, D.C.: The Brookings Institution, 1973), pp. 15–58.

[24]Advisory Commission on Intergovernmental Relations, *Federal Grants: Their Effects on State-Local Expenditures, Employment Levels, Wage Rates* (Washington, D.C., February 1977). Supporting this conclusion is a recent study showing that grants with strong statutory directives for assisting minorities result in more local targeting of benefits to this group than do programs involving less federal control. Rufus Browning, Dale Rogers Marshall, and David Tabb, "Implementation and Political Change: Sources of Local Variations in Federal Social Programs," *Policy Studies Journal* 8 (1980): 616–632.

[25]Will Myers and John Shannon, "Revenue Sharing for States: An Endangered Species," *Intergovernmental Perspective* 5 (Summer 1979): 10–18.

ferent categorical aids dealt with urban transportation, 23 with pollution control, and 36 with social services. Frequently a local project will involve grants administered by four or five federal agencies, each guarding its own turf.

The coordination of federal grant programs in urban areas has long been a matter of serious concern. The problem exists at both the national level where policy is made and at the local level where it is executed. Various steps have been taken over time to develop closer linkages among the urban-related activities of federal agencies. The creation of the Department of Housing and Urban Development (HUD) in 1965 and the Department of Transportation (DOT) in the following year was prompted largely by the need for more unified direction over urban programs. In 1978 President Carter formed the Interagency Coordinating Council (composed of 16 department and agency representatives and chaired by the Assistant to the President for Intergovernmental Affairs) to eliminate conflicts between federal agencies in the operation of such programs. His action was typical of efforts made by previous administrations to promote greater order in the intergovernmental system.

Various steps have also been taken to foster cooperative action at the local and metropolitan levels. The Johnson Administration designed the model cities program as an instrumentality for coordinating the Great Society's attack on urban slums, but the strategy met with little success. It also established through legislative channels the A-85 and A-95 review processes (so called after the numbers of the circulars issued by the Office of Management and Budget spelling out the procedures to be followed). The first is designed to give state and local officials opportunity to react to proposed grant regulations before final decisions are made. The second requires that applications for a wide range of urban grants be submitted to an areawide clearinghouse for review and recommendation before being forwarded to Washington. None of these steps has proved very effective in coordinating program activities at either the national or local levels.

As part of its new federalism thrust to decentralize the national bureaucracy, the Nixon Administration established 10 Federal Regional Councils comprised of the regional directors of 11 major agencies. These bodies were directed to coordinate federal programs at the field level and to eliminate friction and duplication in their administration. Although the councils continue to exist, they play a relatively minor role in the intergovernmental system. One drawback is that the Washington bureaucracy has never fully committed itself to their use. Another is that all departments do not delegate the same degree of administrative and programmatic discretion to their regional offices. Some observers, however, see the councils as potential instrumentalities for conducting what they refer to as "negotiated federalism." This is a process in which the federal agencies and the localities (and states) negotiate a package of aid programs tailored to the needs, problems, and priorities of the individual areas. The Chicago council is experimenting on a small scale with this approach but there is little likelihood of its extensive use in the near future.[26]

General Policy Impacts

Although there is no adequate way of measuring the overall impact of federal grant programs on the social and physical conditions of metropolitan areas, the assistance they provide has enabled fiscally distressed cities to avoid bankruptcy, prevented the collapse of mass transit systems, upgraded housing for a large number of low- and moderate-income families, and stimulated the renovation of many central business districts. Yet important as the aid programs usually thought of as "urban" (those administered by HUD, for example) are to the nation's cities, their impact has been insignificant compared to various national policies unrelated to local fiscal assistance (such as those pertaining to home mortgage guarantees and tax incentives).[27]

A number of national programs have, in fact, worked to the serious disadvantage of the large central cities. The metropolitan portion of the interstate highway system has provided easy access for both businesses and families to the formerly agricultural land on the periphery. FHA and VA mortgage guarantees, by favoring new residential construction over rehabilitation, influenced the outward push to the suburbs and encouraged urban sprawl. Favorable tax treatment of home ownership (mortgage interest payments and local property levies are allowable deductions on federal income tax returns) gave additional impetus to the suburban boom of the post-World War II period.

Federal policies, although not the major force, have also contributed to the deconcentration of industry. Until 1976 tax laws gave firms more generous deductions for investing in new construction than in rehabilitation. Freight regulations have favored

[26]Rochelle L. Stanfield, "Federal Regional Councils—Can Carter Make Them Work?," *National Journal* (June 18, 1977): 949–953.

[27]Peter Morrison, Robert Vaughan, Georges Vernez, and Barbara Williams, *Recent Contributions to the Urban Policy Debate* (Santa Monica, Calif.: Rand Corporation, March 1979).

trucking over railroads, thereby depriving many cities of one of their major advantages. New environmental and safety regulations have made compliance more costly in the older central municipalities than in the newer and less densely settled areas. Highway construction has not only opened up suburban sites to commercial and manufacturing use but has also made many sections of the South accessible to industry for the first time. These developments in their totality have dealt a serious blow to many of America's core cities.[28]

FEDERALISM IN REVIEW

The federal system in the United States is characterized by resiliency and accommodation, by shifting emphasis on the centralization and decentralization of power, by the ebb and flow of national involvement in local affairs, and by increasing complexity. Intergovernmental relations in this system reflect socioeconomic and political realities. Just as these realities are constantly changing, so also are the relations among (and within) the three levels of public authority.[29] At any given time the pattern of governmental interaction will be influenced by the state of the economy, social conditions, citizen attitudes, and political alignments.

The current intergovernmental scene, as indicated in this chapter, is marked by three major trends—the peaking of federal aid; increased activity by the states toward their urban areas; and the reimposition of national controls over the grant programs. Federal assistance to local and state governments, at least during the Reagan Administration, is unlikely to increase above present levels and may even decline. This curtailment in the expansion of grant monies will fall heaviest on the larger and older metropolitan communities where social and physical problems are most severe. Targeting aid to these areas, as originally proposed by the Carter Administration, would necessitate a reduction in the allocations now received by the less disadvantaged units, a solution not likely to find political acceptance.

State governments, concerned over increasing federal–local ties, are in the process of discarding their long-standing policy of

---

[28]OMB Circular A-16 issued in August 1978 as part of the Carter Administration's urban program requires federal agencies to prepare an urban and community impact analysis (UCIA) for any proposed new program, outlining its potential effects on cities, suburbs, and nonmetropolitan areas.

[29]Intergovernmental relations among local units are treated extensively in Chapters 11 and 12.

"benign neglect" toward the large urban areas. This recognition of urban responsibility comes at an opportune time because the leveling out of federal aid funds will make increased state assistance more imperative. Despite the resurgence of state government as a more viable partner in the federal system, however, the prospects of large-scale local involvement on their part is considerably diminished by the antitax mood that is currently prevalent. The willingness or ability of the states to step up fiscal aid significantly to their large urban communities in the face of this resistance is questionable.[30]

The federal system in the United States permits wide diversity among its parts. At the same time it creates an intricate web of intergovernmental relationships that seeks to maintain a reasonable balance among its tiers of political authority in the pursuit of national, state, and local goals. This pattern of relations has undergone substantial change in recent years, caused principally by the unprecedented growth of grants-in-aid and by federal judicial intervention. The future will see many more such changes as adjustments are made to keep the system operative in the face of new developments and challenges.

---

[30]A long-standing complaint of local units is that the states mandate them to take on new responsibilities or incur new costs (such as delivering special services to the handicapped or giving police and firefighters more generous benefits) without providing funds to carry them out. This practice, however, is becoming less prevalent because of the increased sensitivity of state government to locality needs. California and Rhode Island, for example, now reimburse local units for costs incurred in providing certain state-mandated services. On the general impact of state and federal mandates see the symposium edited by Max Neiman and Catherine Lovell in *The Urban Interest* 2 (Spring 1980); also Catherine Lovell and Charles Tobin, "Mandating—A Key Issue for Cities," *Municipal Year Book, 1980*, pp. 73–79.

Chapter 7
Urban Planning

Urban planning is as old as civilization itself. Community building based on clearly determined plans can be found in the cities of ancient Greece and Rome, the trade centers of medieval Europe, and the elaborately designed settlements of the Incas and Mayas. The Spanish code of the Indies of 1573 contained specific directions as to how towns were to be laid out in the Americas; and the early New England colonists planned their localities to cope with the harsh realities of a hostile environment.

City planning during the nation's early existence was confined mainly to the mapping of streets and the siting of public buildings. Until well into the nineteenth century many of the new cities and towns that sprang up were laid out by surveyors hired by developers and land speculators. The gridiron street pattern still common to many communities is a heritage of the surveyor's level. Pierre L'Enfant's design for the physical layout of the national capital is one of the more outstanding instances of early American planning, but other examples can also be found in places such as Savannah, Georgia; Williamsburg, Virginia; and Philadelphia. It was not until the late 1800s, however, that the movement for planning and controlling the overall physical development of urban settlements began to emerge, triggered chiefly by the growing congestion and blight in the industrial cities.[1]

Despite the rapid urban expansion in the period following the Civil War, planning and land use regulation did not become established as legitimate functions of local government until after World War I. The first municipal planning commission in this country was created in Hartford, Connecticut, in 1907; the first urban planning course was offered by Harvard in 1909 (the same year that the world's first school of city planning was founded in Liverpool, En-

---

[1]The historical development of land use planning and control in the United States is treated in Irving Schiffman, "The Politics of Land Use Planning: A Review Essay and Annotated Bibliography," (Davis, Calif.: Institute of Governmental Affairs and Institute of Ecology, University of California, Davis, 1979).

gland); and the first comprehensive zoning ordinance was adopted in New York City in 1916. Thus for most of the nation's history decisions about the use of land have been made by business interests, realtors, private developers, financial institutions, and householders, subject to little or no formal public control.

The legal and social recognition of land development regulation as a proper governmental activity did not come easily. In a culture marked by individualism and the sanctity of private property, the notion that owners cannot use their land as they see fit was (and still is) difficult for many Americans to accept. Zoning, in fact, had its origins in the law of nuisances and was rationalized by the courts as a means of protecting property values rather than of controlling development in the public interest.

Today the need for planning and regulating urban change is no longer seriously questioned. The debate has now shifted to more complex issues. How can growth be managed within the limitations of the physical resource base and environmental considerations? Because planning has long been focused on growth, how can it be reoriented to serve areas with stable or declining populations? What is the proper scope of urban planning and the role of the professional planner? To what extent should citizens be involved in the planning process? How can effective metropolitan planning be achieved without depriving locality residents of a meaningful measure of control over the immediate area in which they live? What role should the state and national governments play in urban planning? Before turning to these questions the present chapter first examines planning as it has been traditionally defined and practiced and the principal implementing tools associated with it.

THE CONVENTIONAL APPROACH

Planning in the broadest sense is simply the process of deciding in advance what to do in order to achieve desired goals. It is a means of reaching decisions about what specific objectives are to be pursued and what action taken to attain them. As such it provides inputs for individual and group choices that involve consideration of the future. Urban or city planning as conventionally understood relates primarily to land use: the shaping of the community's physical environment and the spatial distribution of activities—residential, commercial, industrial, cultural and recreational, governmental—within its confines.

The planning process involves four basic sets of functions: research (Where is the community now?); goal formulation (Where does it want to go?); plan making (How does it get there?); and implementation (What means can it employ to achieve its goals?). The first three categories relate to the preparation of a general plan (also referred to as a comprehensive or master plan) for guiding development; the fourth refers to the strategies and instrumentalities for carrying it out. The means of execution include both regulatory devices (principally zoning, subdivision controls, and building and housing codes) and the more affirmative measures available to local governments (construction of public facilities and the use of federal and state grants for community development purposes).

The General Plan

The general plan theoretically serves as the basis for both short- and long-range decisions that pertain to the physical development of the city and the quality of its environment. As traditionally defined, it consists of three major elements: land use, community facilities, and circulatory network (in recent years additional components such as housing and conservation have been mandated by state and federal regulations). The first refers to the location and extent of the residential, commercial, and industrial areas; the second to the variety of public activities that involve neighborhood and citywide needs, such as schools, parks, utilities, and government buildings; and the third to the street system and mass transit.[2]

Not all municipalities have formulated general plans. Most smaller units have only a broad conception of their desired future state and on this basis determine their zoning and other land use regulations (nationally about two-thirds of all zoning activities are taken without benefit of any land use plan). Most large cities, however, have adopted such a development guide. In some cases the plan consists of an explicit set of objectives documented by a map and proposed timetable. In others, it comprises a more general statement of policy objectives pertaining to different sections of the city, with the accompanying map serving only to illustrate the type of alternative arrangements available for achieving the stated goals. Whatever its form, the plan seeks to project a physical development pattern to which the municipality is to aspire over a given period of time, usually 10 to 20 years. Its overall thrust will vary according to the type of community it serves. In the older cities the principal development problem is conservation and revitalization; in the ma-

[2]The classic treatise on the conventional land use plan is T. J. Kent, Jr., *The Urban General Plan* (San Francisco, Calif.: Chandler, 1964). A more recent treatment is Daniel Mandelker, "The Role of the Local Comprehensive Plan in Land Use Regulation," *Michigan Law Review* 74 (1976): 889–973.

ture and affluent suburbs it is protection; and in the urban fringe areas and newer sunbelt municipalities it is the control of growth and expansion.

The general plan, even though it may be formally adopted by the legislative body of a municipality, is not legally binding on anyone. Only those elements of it that governmental policymakers see fit to incorporate into law through zoning and other implementary means have this effect.[3] The execution and enforcement of the plan, in other words, are strictly political acts. Unless the chief executive and council are willing to employ it as the basis for decisions on land use, space allocations, circulation patterns, and public improvement projects, it will stand merely as a collection of noble statements and attractive maps.

Zoning

Zoning, the principal means of regulating urban development in the United States, is an exercise of the police power. It originated in efforts to segregate noxious activities from residential areas and to prevent land use incompatibilities at the neighborhood level. Comprehensive or communitywide zoning is accomplished by means of an ordinance which sets up the type of districts into which the city or town is to be divided and specifies the permissible uses in each. The districts are then allocated throughout the municipality by means of an official zoning map that is adopted as part of the ordinance. Three broad categories of zones are customarily established—residential, commercial, and industrial—with a number of subclassifications in each. In addition to governing the kind of development permitted in each type of district, the zoning ordinance also contains regulations pertaining to such features as building height, minimum lot and house size, and the proportion of the lot the structure may cover. Once adopted, the ordinance is enforced by the building commissioner, who has authority to deny building and occupancy permits for structures or uses not complying with its provisions.[4]

Zoning has come under growing criticism in recent years. One of the major complaints relates to its use as an instrument for reinforcing racial and class segregation. It is common knowledge that

[3]There are indications in pending litigation that the general plan may, like zoning, assume the force of law in some jurisdictions where such plans are mandated by state law.
[4]Zoning and other land use regulatory devices are reviewed in the report of the National Commission on Urban Problems, *Building the American City* (Washington, D.C., 1968).

many suburban municipalities employ large lot size and minimum floor space standards (and some also ban apartment construction) to increase housing costs within their communities and thereby keep out low- and moderate-income families. In some cases the motivation for such standards may be less racial or class than fiscal (the desire to attract land uses that pay more in taxes than they entail in municipal services), but the exclusionary effect on the less affluent sectors of the metropolitan population is the same.[5] The only remedy against practices of this nature is judicial intervention because there is no administrative check on local planning and zoning by any higher level of government. Legal action is a costly and time-consuming procedure in which few developers are willing to engage; and civil rights and housing advocacy groups have only limited resources for challenging the constitutional validity of land use regulations. Legislative remedies have been sought in the form of state zoning review boards and in laws to require metropolitan area communities to accept a "fair share" of low-income housing, but efforts in this direction have proved mostly futile.

Other Regulatory Instruments

Subdivision regulations, building codes, and housing codes, the three other major control devices, also involve the exercise of the police power. Like zoning, subdivision regulations are of relatively recent vintage. They came into widespread use after World War II in response to the housing boom. Administered usually by the planning agency of the municipality, their primary objective is to govern the process by which lots are created out of larger tracts and made ready for improvements. They specify the standards to be followed by developers in designing and constructing streets, providing utilities and open space, and preparing building sites in general. To some extent they overlap zoning, particularly in cases where large-scale development is undertaken.

Building codes in one form or another date back to the earliest days of urban society. They consist of a series of standards and specifications designed to establish minimum safeguards in the construction of buildings. Although the necessity for such control is universally acknowledged, building codes have come under heavy

[5]Many middle- and upper-class families are not content to rely on economic factors to separate them residentially from low-income groups but tend to use the local political system to keep out those whose presence they consider a threat to their personal security and property values. See Michael N. Danielson, *The Politics of Exclusion* (New York: Columbia University Press, 1976).

fire for unduly adding to the cost of housing. Critics point to the difficulty of getting them amended (often in the face of opposition from the construction trades unions) to permit the use of new materials and new methods, such as prefabrication. They also call attention to the lack of uniformity in code provisions commonly found among municipalities in metropolitan areas and across the country generally. It is estimated that if building regulations were standardized nationwide, the use of industrialized processes and interchangeable parts could decrease construction costs by as much as 20 percent.[6]

Housing codes are the newest regulatory device for implementing urban planning. As late as 1956 fewer than 100 cities had adopted such controls; now the number exceeds 5000. The original stimulus for this increase came from the 1954 Housing Act which required communities, as a condition of eligibility for urban renewal funds, to have a "workable program" with a housing code element. Unlike the other control instruments, which are designed primarily to guide new development and new construction, housing codes attempt to bring existing dwelling units up to minimum standards of health and safety. Although intended to apply citywide, code enforcement tends to be carried out only in limited areas, mainly where it is believed that blight can be arrested and dwellings upgraded. This practice, encouraged initially by federal policies on the availability of funding, often leads to the neglect of enforcement in those sections of the community where the housing is worst. Local officials, moreover, are often hesitant to enforce strict compliance in such areas for fear of driving needed low-cost housing out of the market.

Capital Improvement Program

Zoning and other types of regulations are primarily protective devices and, as such, are restrictive and permissive rather than creative and promotive. They serve to prevent land use development that communities deem undesirable, but of themselves they have no power to create the kind of physical environment envisioned in general plans. Zoning an area for expensive homes is no assurance that such units will be built; or redesigning the central business district is no guarantee that the merchants and property owners will make the necessary investments to effectuate the plan. Implemen-

---

[6]Joseph F. Coates, "The Physical Nature of the American City in the Year 2000," *Municipal Year Book, 1979,* p. 19.

tation, in other words, is dependent more on the response of the private market than on any public regulatory action.

One implementary device of an affirmative character that contributes both directly and indirectly to plan execution is the capital improvement program. This program is simply a schedule of public projects designed to meet present and future community needs. Its importance to overall planning is at least twofold. First, it provides for carrying out that portion of the general plan calling for government investments, such as the acquisition of open space, the development of recreational facilities, or the construction of a civic center. Second, it influences private investment decisions by the allocation and timing of public expenditures for various programs. Thus a governmental decision to give priority to upgrading an older section of the city over a program to extend streets and sewer and water mains into a new area would have a decisive impact on private developmental decisions.

In addition to the conventional public works–type items, capital improvement programs in the larger cities now normally include provisions for neighborhood rehabilitation and subsidized housing. Funded predominantly by federal grants, these projects provide local governments with added tools of an affirmative nature for furthering their developmental goals. But even in respect to these aspects, successful execution of community plans remains heavily dependent on the response of the private market. The most that governmental programs at all levels can hope to do is to make the local situation attractive to developers and investors by seeing that suitable locations are available, providing site improvements, and offering tax incentives.

PLANNING TRENDS

The traditional concerns of city planning practices have been severely challenged in the contemporary setting. The intense pressures of rapid social change as reflected in the urban turbulence of the 1960s shattered the "rational world" of the planners and hastened the reassessment of planning theory and practice. The debate has revolved principally around four issues: the scope of planning; the utility of the general plan; the political nature of planning; and citizen involvement.

Scope of Planning

The constitution of the American Institute of Planners (AIP), the national society of urban and regional planners in the United

States, long reflected the group's emphasis on land use.[7] As the document stated until recently, the profession's particular sphere of activity is the planning of urban communities and their environs "through determination of the comprehensive arrangement of land uses and land occupancy and the regulation thereof." This qualifying clause was finally deleted in 1967 in response to charges of social insensitivity and to pressures within the organization itself for extending the scope of community planning beyond the physical environment.[8]

It was not that planners were unaware of the social realm; the profession had its roots in the reform tradition that saw planning as a means of ameliorating social problems and improving society. It was rather their espousal of a theory of environmental determinism—the influence of physical factors over social behavior—that shaped their approach. Many of the earlier planners believed that upgrading the physical environment with well-designed homes, schools, playgrounds, and public facilities would significantly reduce social disorganization and pathology. This notion still persists in some quarters, as evidenced in a recent remark by one of the developers of Irvine, California, a mammoth new community south of Los Angeles. "The basic concept in our new town," he said, "is that we are not interested in sociological things. . . . Our concept is that if we could build a better community physically, the social things would take care of themselves."[9]

It may seem strange that planners relied so heavily on manipulating the physical environment to affect human behavior rather than on seeking to deal with the social factors more directly. Yet in a profession dominated for many years by architects, engineers, and landscape designers, such an approach was probably inevitable. Only in recent years has the clarity of the planner's perspective been shaken by contemporary events and empirical research that have punctured the myth of environmental determinism. As Melvin Webber points out, "The simple one-to-one cause-and-effect links that once tied houses and neighborhoods to behavior and welfare are coming to be seen as but strands in highly complex

---

[7]In 1978 AIP merged with the American Society of Planning Officials (ASPO) to form the American Planning Association. AIP had been the professional association and ASPO a broad-based organization of planning commission members, other public officials, and interested citizens as well as professional planners and academicians.

[8]The change was also prompted by federal aid programs such as model cities that called for a mixture of physical components and social services.

[9]Quoted in *Fort Myers (Florida) News Press*, April 2, 1978.

webs that, in turn, are woven by the intricate and subtle relations which mark social, psychic, economic, and political systems."[10]

AIP in 1977 adopted a new policy statement for the profession that broadens the concept of urban planning well beyond its former land use orientation. As defined in the new document, planning is "a comprehensive, coordinated, and continuing process, the purpose of which is to help public and private decision makers arrive at decisions which promote the common good of society." So delineated, it encompasses functional or policy areas relating to growth management, housing, economic development, environmental quality, historic preservation, transportation, health, education, public safety, recreation, and cultural opportunities. According to the statement, local government is to play a leading role in "land use and facility planning and in operational and implementation planning (including planning for social and economic goals as well as physical and environmental goals)."[11]

Despite this policy declaration, the scope of urban planning remains an unsettled issue among members of the profession. Many provisions of the statement are couched in terms so general that they can be interpreted to suit the preferences of those with divergent views. Its definition of planning, for example, is compatible with the generic concept (planning as an all-inclusive process embracing all aspects of the city) espoused by the modernists. At the same time the sections relating to local government responsibilities support the position of the traditionalists who regard city planning as limited essentially to the physical dimensions of the community.[12]

Planning for functional and social service activities, such as health (how many hospital beds will be required), education (what school facilities will be needed and where), job training (what will be the demands of the employment market), and welfare (how can the needs of the poor be met), have historically been performed by

[10]"Comprehensive Planning and Social Responsibility," in Bernard J. Frieden and Robert Morris (eds.), *Urban Planning and Social Policy* (New York: Basic Books, 1968), p. 10.
[11]*AIP Planning Policies* (Washington, D.C.: American Institute of Planners, October 1977).
[12]The broadened definition of planning in the AIP statement has not met with universal acceptance among the planning profession. The chairman of the Department of City and Regional Planning at the University of California, Berkeley, for example, maintains that urban planning for the physical environment can be responsive to social issues without taking formal responsibility for social planning. Allan B. Jacobs, *Making City Planning Work* (Chicago: American Society of Planning Officials, 1978).

the individual departments or agencies charged with administering the programs. The AIP policy statement would enlarge the role of the city planning department to include the coordination if not actual formulation of these plans.[13] This inclusion continues to be regarded with disfavor by many local officials and planners.

Utility of General Plan

Aside from the dispute over the scope of the planning agency's responsibilities, the notion of a general plan has been under attack since the early 1960s by critics within and outside the profession.[14] Pointing to evidence that the purpose of formulating such a plan— to shape the development of a city (or metropolitan area) in accordance with a preconceived design—is not being accomplished, they list a formidable array of objections. These include the inability to predict the future much beyond a few years; the dependence of local action on external forces that cannot be controlled or accurately foreseen; the impossibility of accommodating the varied and conflicting interests of a pluralistic society in a plan that expresses a single hierarchy of values; the "pie-in-the-sky" goals that are unrelated to the real issues of urban communities; and the absence of a capacity in metropolitan areas for central direction and coordination. As one veteran observer expressed it, little of what is called comprehensive city planning is effective. "In older cities it ratifies what the market did before planning and land use controls were established. In suburban and newly developing areas it sanctions what the market will do anyway."[15]

The new approach shifts the perspective from the product-oriented activity of the classical model (formulation of a general plan) to planning as a process within a decision-making environment. Instead of detailed and long-range blueprints, it emphasizes a framework of policy guidelines and projects—a bundle of policy plans— aimed at specific and intermediate levels of achievement. This conception is more in line with the views of those who argue that

[13]Several planning schools inaugurated programs in the 1960s to train social policy planners. However, social policy planning still remains an enigma in definition and identity.

[14]See, for example, Alan A. Altshuler, *The City Planning Process* (Ithaca: Cornell University Press, 1965).

[15]William Wheaton, "Metropolitan Allocational Planning," *Journal of the American Institute of Planners* 33 (March 1967): 103. Those who support this position point to the experiences of Houston, the only large city in the United States that has no zoning. See Bernard Siegan, "Non-Zoning in Houston," *Journal of Law and Economics* 13 (April 1970): 71–147.

the logic of comprehensive planning is inconsistent with the need for action.[16]

The *Cleveland Policy Planning Report* issued in 1975 by the Cleveland planning commission is the most extreme example of the policy approach. Rather than mapping out a desired future in terms of land uses, facility locations, and transportation routes, it sets forth objectives and courses of action in a limited number of functional problem areas including housing and mass transit. Acknowledging that land use planning may be appropriate in developing communities, the report notes that Cleveland has stopped growing and is even declining. As such its problems have "less to do with land uses, zoning, or issues of urban design—the traditional domain of city planners—and more to do with personal and municipal poverty, unemployment, neighborhood deterioration and abandonment, crime, and inadequate mobility."[17]

Many members of the planning profession, however, are not prepared to reject the basic importance of the general plan as conventionally conceived. A 1976 report by the Southeastern Wisconsin Regional Planning Commission epitomizes this view. Noting that the validity of comprehensive land use planning has been called into question, the commission affirmed its belief in such an approach as a viable means of coping with development and environmental problems generated by urbanization. "The comprehensive plan not only provides the necessary framework for coordinating and guiding growth . . . but provides the best conceptual basis available for the application of systems engineering skills to the growing problems. . . ."[18]

Those who support the notion of a general plan commonly acknowledge the importance of social and economic concerns in physical development planning and the need for constant updating. At the same time they point out that public investments in facilities such as expressway systems, mass transit, sewers, and utilities inevitably fix the shape of a community for an indefinite future. To make heavy commitments to such projects without the guidance of an overall plan is, in their opinion, unwise and irresponsible. Debate over the merits of the general plan is far from over and its

[16]John Friedmann, "The Future of Comprehensive Urban Planning: A Critique," *Public Administration Review* 31 (May/June 1971): 318.
[17]The approach is described in Norman Krumholz, Janice Cogger, and John Linner, "The Cleveland Policy Planning Report," *Journal of the American Institute of Planners* 41 (September 1975): 298–304.
[18]Southeastern Wisconsin Regional Planning Commission, *1976 Annual Report* (Waukesha, Wis., October 1977), p. 7.

employment is not likely to be terminated in the near future. Even the AIP policy statement calls for the enactment of "statutory requirements for adoption of a comprehensive plan by the local legislative body as a prerequisite for the exercise of land development controls and eligibility for federal or state capital project grants." Several states have already taken this step, mandating their municipalities and counties to prepare comprehensive land use plans.[19]

Planning and the Political Process

The role of the planner in the political process is also a matter of debate. Some members of the profession hold that planners should be in a position to exercise their expertise in the public interest free from political pressures. Others maintain that planning is an integral part of the political process and therefore must be closely related organizationally to those responsible for the making and execution of policy. Some argue that planners should be value free or neutral technicians advising decision makers on how to achieve given objectives. Others insist that they must also be advocates of policies and actions that they perceive—based on their professional judgment—to be in the best interest of the community.[20]

The planning function historically has been assigned to a commission appointed by the mayor or council. This body, as most often constituted, is vested with authority to hire its own professional staff, prepare and adopt a master plan, and submit recommendations on zoning to the lawmakers. The location of these duties in an agency outside the regular governmental channels was largely the result of reformist zeal. Pressure for planning (or more accurately zoning) originated with civic improvement groups during the municipal reform era early in the present century. By assigning these responsibilities to an independent commission, the reformers hoped to insulate the planning and zoning functions from politics and politicians.

[19]The efforts of Florida to control growth are described in John M. DeGrove, "Regionalism and Growth Management: A Lost Opportunity?" in Charlie B. Tyer (ed.), *Substate Regionalism in the United States: Perspectives and Issues* (Columbia, S.C.: Bureau of Governmental Research and Service, University of South Carolina, 1978), pp. 47–59.

[20]See in this connection Richard E. Klosterman, "Foundations for Normative Planning," *Journal of the American Institute of Planners* 44 (January 1978): 37–45. J. Vincent Buck notes that urban planners are being pulled toward both professional and political involvement, with the scale tipped slightly toward the political. "Politics and Professionalism in Municipal Planning," Sage Professional Papers in Administration and Policy Studies (Beverly Hills, Calif.: Sage, 1976).

Since the 1940s autonomous planning agencies, although continuing to predominate in numbers, have lost favor as support has increased for integrating the planning function into the regular administrative structure of government.[21] Chicago was one of the first cities to make the change when it reconstituted its planning agency as a full-fledged executive department in 1957 and retained the commission only as an advisory board.[22] A survey by the International City Management Association of changes in organizational form from 1960 to 1970 showed that the number of independent agencies declined by 12 percent during the period, whereas planning departments responsible to municipal chief executives increased by 38 percent.

Contrary to the view of some professionals, the planning function is not a neutral activity or art. Every plan that is proposed or adopted is a political instrument. It promotes the interests of some individuals or groups, often at the expense of others. It represents trade-offs and accommodations among values and objectives as well as among special interests. Planners who are close to the centers of political power are in strategic positions to introduce into the decisional process a broad perspective of the community interest to temper the often narrower concerns of the political officials.

The "new federalism" programs of the 1970s, such as CDBG and local public works, have given added impetus to placing the planning function under more direct political control. Because most projects under these grants are relatively small in scope and call for quick action—in contrast to the large-scale and long-range urban renewal efforts of past decades—they require close cooperation between the planning staff and the policymakers in their design and implementation. Cities such as Milwaukee and St. Louis have given recognition to this fact by placing planning and the administration of urban revitalization programs in the same unit, commonly named the city or community development agency (CDA). This type of restructuring makes planning an instrumentality of an operational agency directly responsible to the chief executive. The new programs have also caused many planners to accept the fact

[21]Although the planning profession has taken no official stand on the question of structure, the chairman of one of its committees told a congressional subcommittee that "the proper position of the planner and the planning office is directly under the chief executive and through him to the legislative body." Hearings before the Subcommittee on Urban Affairs of the Joint Economic Committee, Congress of the United States, *Regional Planning Issues,* part 3 (Washington, D.C., 1971), p. 398.
[22]For a discussion of the arguments relating to the various types of organizational arrangements see David C. Ranney, *Planning and Politics in the Metropolis* (Columbus, Ohio: Merrill, 1969), pp. 45–60.

that they must think in shorter-range and less ambitious terms if they are to be effective in the current milieu of fewer resources and lowered expectations.

Despite the structural and normative handicaps that planning faces, it can no longer be content with fashioning the "city beautiful" or remain preoccupied with land use compatibilities, population densities, open space ratios, and traffic movement. As Victor Gruen once remarked, the planners who have taken refuge in an allegedly value-free application of techniques to achieve goals set by others have now been shoved willy-nilly into the ideological arena. They are being asked whom they are planning for, whose values they are advocating, whose interests they are serving, and what they are doing about the critical social issues of the day. Urban planners have not as yet resolved these questions to their own satisfaction. Neither have the policymakers nor the public in general decided on the role they are willing to have planners play or on the organizational structure appropriate to the planning function.

Citizen Involvement in Planning

Until recently citizen participation in the planning process was little more than nominal. It was the common practice of planning agencies to formulate plans and then present them at a public hearing for purposes of fulfilling legal requirements and providing information. This procedure affords opportunity to the public only to react, under very inappropriate circumstances, to proposals about which they have little knowledge and no input. The situation showed signs of changing during the 1960s due mainly to the mobilization of the disadvantaged by community action programs, the rising opposition of residents to expressway and urban renewal projects that threatened their neighborhoods, and federal mandating of citizen involvement in aided programs.[23]

Urban planners today accept the need for citizen involvement; that battle is over. What remains is to find ways of making the concept a reality because participation, despite the rhetoric of "planning with people," remains a weak component of the planning process. Views differ as to the meaning of participation and neither

[23]Arguments in support of citizen participation are found in Louise G. White, "Rational Theories of Participation: An Exercise in Definition," *Journal of Conflict Resolution* 20 (June 1976): 255–278; F. Stevens Redburn, "On Human Service Integration," *Public Administration Review* 37 (May/June 1977): 264–269; and Louise G. White, "Approaches to Land Use Policy," *Journal of the American Planning Association* 45 (January 1979): 62–71.

public officials nor members of the planning profession have any clear idea as to how to make it work. There is broad agreement that the views of all concerned parties should be solicited and given serious consideration in formulating plans. Beyond this there is little consensus.

Many professionals look upon lay participation as a means of learning about public preferences, informing people, and generating support for implementation. Many, however, are skeptical of the contributions that citizens can make to the actual shaping of the plan itself, feeling that most groups display little social consciousness. They are concerned about the numerous instances where neighborhood residents disrupt efforts to design a coordinated plan for the overall development of a community or push for upgraded zoning to keep out racial minorities or low-income families. They are also concerned that enlarged public involvement unduly prolongs debate and action, raises questions as to representativeness (for whom do the participants speak), and often results in deadlock.[24]

The question whether citizens are sufficiently knowledgeable to participate meaningfully in the planning process is a common one. A number of planners during the 1960s attempted to respond to it by advancing the concept of advocacy planning—the use of experts by organized groups to analyze the actions of governmental agencies, evaluate officially proposed plans, and offer alternative approaches. As a leader in the movement reasoned, if citizens are to be included in the process, they must not only have the opportunity to be heard but must also be able to respond to proposals in the technical language of planners.[25] Although the concept encompasses representation in the public arena of all special interests through planners who express their clients' point of view, the emphasis has been placed on its application to low- and moderate-income groups.

As the designation implies, the concept of *advocacy planning* is derived from the legal model or analogy. Individual organizations retain planners to represent them before planning commissions or local legislative bodies and plead for their position much as

---

[24]For a discussion of the advantages and disadvantages of citizen participation see W. R. Derrick Sewell and J. T. Coppock, *Public Participation in Planning* (New York: Wiley, 1977) and Roger Kasperson and Myrna Breitbart, *Participation, Decentralization and Advocacy Planning* (Washington, D.C.: Association of American Geographers, 1978). See also a review essay by Albert K. Karnig, "Planning and the Search for Answers," *Urban Affairs Quarterly* 15 (September 1979): 101–110.

[25]Paul Davidoff, "Advocacy and Pluralism in Planning," *Journal of the American Institute of Planning* 31 (November 1965): 332.

lawyers do for clients in legal proceedings. Although unknown by the term prior to the 1960s, advocacy planning is by no means new. Business establishments have long retained consultants to review and challenge public proposals or provide expert support for sought-after land use changes. Groups of homeowners have similarly employed professional planning firms to assist them in opposing highway alignments, zoning modifications, or various physical facility developments. The novelty of the situation in the 1960s was the nature of the clientele: people with few resources and little access to the established centers of power. Not unexpectedly, local officials showed little enthusiasm for the move to provide community groups with their own expertise independent of municipal and county agencies. Many professional planners also regarded it with skepticism and even some hostility. Trained in the ethic that stresses the public interest rather than fidelity to an individual client, they questioned the appropriateness of transferring the advocacy principle from the legal system to the governmental planning process.[26]

Advocacy planning found its most highly publicized expression in organizations such as Architects Renewal Committee of Harlem (ARCH), Urban Planning Aids of Boston (UPA), and Community Design Center of San Francisco (CDC), which provided assistance to low-income neighborhoods and communities in urban renewal and expressway construction disputes.[27] The advocacy approach achieved a small measure of success in blocking the implementation of plans but proved unproductive in winning acceptance for alternative proposals put forward by citizen groups. The initial enthusiasm that it engendered faded as basic conflicts between the professionalism of the planner and the dynamics of protest politics surfaced (advocacy planning continues to exist but on a greatly reduced scale). Other factors also contributed to its decline: lack of funding (it is almost wholly dependent on government and foundation grants); the relative absence of stable organizations in low-income neighborhoods; and the difficulty of drawing the disadvantaged into a planning process. Many locality groups, also, prompted by the opportunities available in the CDBG program with its neigh-

[26]Advocacy planning has also taken on two other forms. One is that of the "clientless" professional who feels that important community issues are not being properly raised or dealt with and who, in Ralph Nader fashion, activates a supporting constituency. The other is that of the "inside" advocate, the planner who works for a public agency but endeavors to articulate the interests of the disadvantaged or unrepresented groups in the formulating of plans.

[27]See Allan Heskin, "Crisis and Response: A Historical View on Advocacy Planning" *Journal of the American Planning Association* 46 (January 1980): 50–63.

borhood emphasis, have turned from adversaries to collaborators with city development agencies. Some observers, however, fear that citizen organizations are being co-opted by local administrators in the process.

DEVELOPMENT STRATEGIES

Various strategies or development philosophies are discernible among local governments in the United States. In some instances they are expressly stated; in others they are implicit. Two overall approaches that have attracted considerable attention and aroused much controversy are triage and nongrowth: the first applicable to the older and declining central cities; the second to the newer and expanding suburban communities.

Triage

Triage is a battlefield term that refers to the assignment of priorities for treatment among casualties so as to make the best use of available surgical aid. Victims are divided into three categories: those who will live whether given immediate attention or not; those who will survive only if operated on at once; and those who are so seriously wounded that they will likely die whether or not operated on. Under triage the second group of casualities receives the bulk of the aid and the other two are given pain-killing medicine to ease their suffering.

The relevance of the triage concept to city redevelopment was first suggested by Anthony Downs, an economist and planning consultant. Downs proposed that neighborhoods be classified into three categories: healthy; in need of assistance (beginning to evidence signs of blight and decline); and very deteriorated. Resources available for community redevelopment, such as CDBG funds, would be allocated to each type on a basis similar to triage. The healthy neighborhoods would receive only token assistance to produce high visibility effects such as the installation of water fountains or the planting of trees. The marginally declining areas would be given the preponderance of aid to restore them to a healthy state. The badly deteriorated sections would be allotted funds primarily for health and safety purposes, such as demolishing abandoned or dangerous structures. No major investments, however, would be made to upgrade these areas because they would absorb all the resources at hand without producing any significant physical improvement.[28]

The strategy, as described by Downs, is to empty out the unsalvageable neighborhoods by encouraging residents to move to less deteriorated sections, those in the second category, where public funds would be spent in large amounts to stop or reverse decline. In this way scarce resources, at least in theory, would be used most effectively, neither wasted on neighborhoods too far gone to be saved or given to the more affluent areas that have the capacity for self-help.[29]

Few if any governmental bodies openly espouse a triage strategy—such a course would be morally and politically condemned as heartless. Yet officials in many of the older and declining cities are sympathetic to the approach and in some cases are implicitly following its general tenor in their allocational decisions. Triage, even if lacking in compassion, may appear to be the logical course for such communities to pursue, yet it suffers from the same basic weakness inherent in other redevelopment strategies. As the poorest of the poor are pushed out of the badly blighted sections into the areas of the city being shored up with public funds, they bring with them all the social and economic problems that contributed to the deterioration of the neighborhoods they are leaving. The likelihood of this process repeating itself in the new setting is great.

The Nongrowth Movement

The nongrowth movement first emerged in the early 1970s as a number of relatively affluent suburban communities began to place restrictions on the rate and extent of their population expansion. Petaluma, California, for example, limited new housing to 500 dwelling units yearly (for projects of five or more units) based on a rating system related to factors such as design and availability of facilities. Boca Raton, Florida, set a population limit of 100,000 for the city, the ordinance specifying that no residential development would be permitted beyond this ceiling. Eastlake, Ohio, a Cleveland suburb, enacted an ordinance that subjects all proposed zoning changes to popular vote, a requirement equivalent to barring

[28]Anthony Downs, "Using the Lessons of Experience to Allocate Resources in the Community Development Program," *Recommendations for Community Development Planning* (Chicago: Real Estate Research Corporation, undated), pp. 1–28.
[29]For a discussion of triage see William C. Baer, "On the Death of Cities," *The Public Interest*, No. 45 (Fall 1976): 3–9.

the rezoning of any land for apartment complexes in that community.

Nongrowth policies do not always stem from the same motivations. For some communities they are simply a means of keeping out lower-class families and racial minorities. By wrapping their exclusionary measures in an environmental protection cloak, these localities hope to avoid constitutional pitfalls as well as social criticism. Other municipalities act out of genuine concern for the quality of life and the potential impact of unlimited expansion on a fragile resource base. In still others the motivations for restrictive growth policies are mixed: opposition to the entry of certain kinds of people and the desire to preserve environmental amenities.[30]

Antigrowth measures have received a generally favorable reception from the Supreme Court. Those that provide for limited expansion under carefully defined criteria, such as the Petaluma ordinance, appear judicially acceptable as a valid exercise of the police power. On the other hand, those that attempt to bar all growth or set absolute ceilings on population size (as in the case of Boca Raton) are regarded as infringements on the constitutional right of freedom of movement. Zoning by referendum (as in Eastlake) has received judicial acceptance. By a five to three vote in 1976 the Supreme Court upheld the Eastlake ordinance, rejecting the contention that it deprived property owners of due process of law by subjecting the permitted use of their land to the whims of an uninformed public.[31]

The management of growth has become a more critical issue as the problems of energy, resource shortages, and threats to the environment have mounted. Controlling the rate and direction of population expansion in urban areas is a legitimate, but sensitive, public responsibility. In exercising it, government must balance the power to restrict development with considerations of social equity that arise when some citizens are deprived of the opportunity to obtain the same residential benefits enjoyed by others. The existing system of land use control in which each community individually determines its own posture toward expansion is conducive to unfair treatment. Growth policies within urban areas, in the opinion of many experts, should be set at the metropolitan or state level

[30]On the subject of nongrowth generally see Edgar Rust, *No Growth: Impacts on Metropolitan Areas* (Lexington, Mass.: Heath, 1975). A defense of the nongrowth movement is Earl Finkler, William Toner, and Frank Popper, *Urban Nongrowth: City Planning for People* (New York: Praeger, 1976).
[31]*City of Eastlake* v. *Forest City Enterprises*, 426 U.S. 668 (1976).

and be binding on the local units. Only in this way are the ends of social equity likely to be promoted.

METROPOLITAN PLANNING

The United States evolved from a rural society into a predominantly metropolitan nation without any sort of centralized guidance or direction. No explicit national policy relating to the size and location of population settlements was ever promulgated, nor were any controls (other than those adopted by local governments) exercised over the urban development that took place. The situation is not materially different today. Despite talk of a national urban policy and the assumption of a more active role by the states in protecting the environment, the metropolis continues to be a product of decentralized decision making mediated by only a modest degree of coordinated planning.

Federal Initiatives

Metropolitan or substate regional planning was little more than a subject of discussion in this country until after World War II. A few isolated efforts had been made earlier, such as the formulation of the "Regional Plan for New York and Its Environs" sponsored by a private foundation in the late 1920s, but for the most part the shaping of urban areas was left to the random collection of local plans and policies. Whatever areawide planning occurred was performed by special districts and highway commissions for purposes of carrying out their functional responsibilities.

The last two decades have witnessed greater interest in metropolitan or regional approaches. Much of the initiative in this respect has come from the national government. With the proliferation of urban aid programs in the 1960s the need for coordinated planning on an areawide basis became increasingly evident to federal authorities. Impetus for such planning came from two sources: (1) Section 701 of the Housing Act of 1959 (as amended) that authorized funds for regional planning purposes (originally 701 funds were limited to municipal planning agencies) and (2) the provision of the 1962 Highway Aid Act that no road projects would be approved in the future unless they were part of a comprehensive regional transportation plan.

The most important stimulus to metropolitan planning came in 1966 with the passage of the Demonstration Cities and Metropolitan Development Act (Model Cities). Section 204 of the legislation (as supplemented by the Intergovernmental Cooperation Act of

1968) stipulates that all applications by local units for federal grants and loans covering a wide range of programs must be submitted for review to an areawide "clearinghouse" designated by the Office of Management and Budget. In spelling out this requirement, OMB Circular A-95 specifies that the comments and recommendations of the clearinghouse shall include information concerning "the extent to which the project is consistent with or contributes to the fulfillment of comprehensive planning." There are now more than 500 such reviewing bodies and the number of grant programs covered by the process exceeds 200.

Part 4 of the OMB circular also requires that national and state agencies make maximum use of common geographic boundaries for the planning and coordination of federal aid programs. In response to this provision 45 states have set up substate districts, most of them headed by regional planning commissions or councils of governments (COGs) with A-95 review authority.[32] Some federal departments work closely with these districts in carrying out their functional responsibilities. The Environmental Protection Agency, for example, relies on them to prepare regional plans for water quality and waste treatment. Not all federal programs, however, move in this direction; a number of them require the establishment of single-purpose planning districts as in the case of the new health systems agencies (HSAs).

This lack of consistency in federal regional policy has led to a proliferation of multicounty planning units limited to a single functional area.[33] A bill to remedy this situation—the proposed Intergovernmental Coordination Act—was introduced in the ninety-sixth Congress (1978–1980). It provided for: (1) use of substate districts for administration and coordination of all federally aided areawide planning programs; (2) designation of a single planning agency in each district for all such programs; and (3) melding of all federally assisted areawide planning programs in each region into a single coordinated work program.[34] No action was taken on the bill,

---

[32]James Glass and Keith Ward, "The Origins and Development of Substate Districts," in Charlie B. Tyer (ed.), *Substate Regionalism in the United States*, pp. 10–20.

[33]According to the ACIR there are 30 federal programs that require or encourage the creation of single-purpose regional agencies for their administration. See Advisory Commission on Intergovernmental Relations, *Regionalism Revisited: Recent Areawide and Local Responses* (Washington, D.C., 1977), pp. 11–19.

[34]For an evaluation of substate regionalism by an assistant director of ACIR see David B. Walker, "Substate Regionalism: The Situation in 1977," in Charlie B. Tyer (ed.), *Substate Regionalism in the United States*, pp. 21–31.

and prospects for the passage of such a measure in the near future are not promising because the requirements would tread on too many bureaucratic toes.

Metropolitan Planning Agencies

Metropolitan planning (or regional planning as it is commonly referred to) originated with organizations that were established and financed by private groups. Only a few such agencies, the New York Regional Plan Association is the most prominent, remain in existence, the remainder having given way to public bodies. Metropolitan planning agencies are set up on a multijurisdictional basis. They include units that serve two or more counties, a combination of counties and municipalities, and a city and county jointly. A 1962 survey by the National Municipal League showed 63 such bodies operating in SMSAs.[35] A similar survey conducted six years later by the Graduate School of Public Affairs at the State University of New York-Albany listed 351 metropolitan planning commissions, including countywide agencies both within and outside SMSAs.[36] Since that time the number of multijurisdictional units with planning powers (including COGS and economic development districts) has increased to almost 700.[37] Not all of these can be described as planning bodies in any true sense of the term; yet their very existence reflects the emphasis that the national government (and to a much lesser extent the states) has placed on areawide planning and coordination in recent years.

The organizational structure for metropolitan planning takes several forms. The most desirable arrangement, from the standpoint of potential effectiveness, exists when responsibility for the function rests in an areawide general government. Such a situation is found in Toronto (Canada) where the metropolitan planning board is a component unit of a government possessing jurisdiction over an impressive array of activities. It is likewise the case in consolidated city–county governments, such as Nashville–Davidson County (Tennessee) and Jacksonville–Duval County (Florida). Similar centralization of the planning role also occurs in the rela-

[35]An annotated list of these agencies is found in *National Civic Review* 51 (July 1962): 384–390. A companion list is found in Housing and Home Finance Agency, *National Survey of Metropolitan Planning* (Washington, D.C., 1963).

[36]*1968 Survey of Metropolitan Planning*, Local Government Studies Center, Graduate School of Public Affairs, State University of New York, Albany, pp. 15–26.

[37]A few multijurisdictional planning bodies cross state lines, such as the Tri-State Regional Planning Commission established by interstate compact among Connecticut, New Jersey, and New York.

tively few instances where a county agency is vested with areawide planning authority. The Broward County Planning Council (Fort Lauderdale) is one such example; it has power to prepare a land use plan for the entire county and to require that the plans of the individual municipalities comply with it.

The areawide planning function in virtually all cases is performed by either a regional planning commission or a council of governments. The first, created by state legislation or agreement among local units and endowed with only advisory powers, is not an integral part of any political entity with corresponding territorial jurisdiction. This detachment divorces planning from the programmatic and policy making processes of an ongoing public unit with implementing authority. The second type, a voluntary association of local governments, also leaves the areawide planning function detached but provides an indirect means of integrating it more closely with the operating agencies. Most COGs were created in SMSAs where no multijurisdictional planning body existed previously. Some, however, such as the Metropolitan Washington Council of Governments (District of Columbia) and the Southeast Michigan Council of Governments (Detroit) replaced already functioning metropolitan planning commissions.[38]

The method of selecting those who serve on regional planning agencies varies greatly. In many instances the membership consists solely of local government officials from the area. In other cases the governor is the appointing authority; and in still others different combinations of selection methods are employed. The Broward Planning Council, for example, is composed of 15 members, including municipal officials and lay citizens, appointed by the county board; the Metropolitan Area Planning Council in the Boston SMSA consists of 127 members: one representative from each of the 96 municipalities in the area, 21 gubernatorial appointees, and 10 ex-officio members from important state and city agencies; and the Southeastern Wisconsin Regional Planning Commission has a membership of 21, including 7 appointed by the county boards and 14 by the governor. No empirical studies have been done to show whether there is any relationship between the method of selection and the effectiveness of such bodies.

Nature of Metropolitan Planning

Like its counterpart at the local level, metropolitan planning has until very recently concerned itself almost exclusively with the physical components of the region. As late as 1968 land use and

[38]Councils of governments are treated more fully in Chapter 12.

transportation studies predominated, with social issues almost totally ignored (see Table 7.1). This orientation was generally stipulated by state enabling laws under which most regional commissions were established and by the legislative and administrative guidelines of the 701 program that originally restricted the use of federal funds for planning to the physical aspects of metropolitan areas.

Paralleling developments in the municipal field, efforts have been made to expand the scope of regional planning beyond the physical realm. The push in this direction has come largely from the national government. In 1967 the Office of Management and Budget (then the Bureau of the Budget) formulated a "physical-economic-human resources" definition of comprehensive planning as part of its official guidelines for federal financial support of multijurisdictional planning activities. Shortly thereafter the 701 assistance program was enlarged to include human resource development and governmental services as eligible fields for planning funds. And in 1968 Congress specified that comprehensive planning by local and metropolitan agencies must contain a housing component as a precondition of continued 701 aid.

These initiatives have resulted in a significant broadening of the planning activities of regional commissions. Although no late national survey is available, a study of state-mandated subdistricts in Tennessee provides a fairly representative picture of developing trends. These agencies, which function primarily as regional planning and A-95 review authorities, are engaged in formulating plans for a variety of functional areas. Their concerns include manpower, law enforcement, housing, programs for youth and the elderly, drug abuse, and economic development, as well as the traditional objects of attention such as land use, transportation, solid waste disposal, and sewer and water facilities.[39]

Metropolitan planning, as viewed by most practitioners and theorists—and certainly by most public officials—is supplementary to city planning and not a substitute for it. Its purpose is to provide a broad framework within which local units can plan for their own growth and development. According to a policy statement by the American Institute of Planners in 1962, still relevant except for its emphasis on the physical environment, a metropolitan planning agency should seek establishment and acceptance of goals, both long-range and immediate, for the metropolitan area's physical development (with due regard to economic and social factors). These

[39]Charlie B. Tyer, "State Mandated Substate Districts: Mission, Programs, and Priorities," in Charlie B. Tyer (ed.), *Substate Regionalism in the United States*, pp. 103–131.

Table 7.1 TYPES OF STUDIES CONDUCTED, METROPOLITAN
PLANNING COMMISSIONS, BY REGION, 1968

TYPE	TOTAL	NORTHEAST	SOUTH	MIDWEST	WEST
Land use	123	37	37	34	15
Transportation	114	33	36	31	14
Water resources	63	27	16	14	6
Air pollution	31	9	12	6	4
Community facilities	83	24	27	24	8
Recreation	11	2	3	5	1
Open space	19	8	4	4	3

SOURCE: *1968 Survey of Metropolitan Planning,* Local Government Studies Center,
Graduate School of Public Affairs, State University of New York, Albany, p.8.

goals should be the basis for the formulation of the comprehensive
metropolitan area plan—and that plan, in turn, should serve as a
framework within which may be coordinated the comprehensive
plans of municipalities, counties, and other units of government in
the metropolitan area.[40]

As the AIP statement indicates, the function of metropolitan
planning bodies is to work cooperatively with local units and the
relevant departments and agencies of the national and state governments in establishing goals and formulating overall plans for the
development of the area. Ideally they are to serve as a strong coordinating influence, a catalyst or broker as it were, in integrating the
efforts of all affected public and private interests in the shaping of
the metropolis. Practically, they must be content with a far less ambitious role given the limited powers they now possess.[41]

THE PLANNING OUTLOOK

The president's *Report on National Growth 1972,* the first such
document to be issued, turned away from proposing an overall development policy for the nation as a whole. In doing so it pointed to
the difficulty of achieving consensus on the specific goals and pri-

[40]American Institute of Planners, "The Role of Metropolitan Planning," (Washington, D.C., 1962), pp. 4–5.
[41]Dennis Rondinelli, pointing out that regional planning operates in a policy-making system that is inevitably multinuclear, sees areawide planning agencies playing
an "adjunctive" role in which they serve as brokers among interdependent decision-
making organizations, act as a regional lobby and a catalyst for action, and mobilize
resources to achieve marginal change. "Adjunctive Planning and Urban Development Policy," *Urban Affairs Quarterly* 6 (September 1971); 13–39. Along similar
lines see Donald N. Rothblatt, "Multiple Advocacy: An Approach to Metropolitan
Planning," *Journal of the American Institute of Planners* 44 (April 1978): 193–199.

orities to be served by such a policy.[42] The report, however, did indicate approval of the practice of low density development, noting that it reflects the preferred life-style of a majority in the society. The Carter Administration, at least in theory, rejected this endorsement of urban expansionist trends in favor of "community conservation guidelines" that are aimed at slowing sprawl and utilizing existing facilities. A HUD official in 1978 stressed that the department's strategy was designed to encourage state and regional planning agencies "to adopt plans that try to control growth, try to direct it back toward the urban core, and try to stop the wasting and overconsumption of energy and agricultural lands."[43] Such a strategy, however, runs up against the political strength of suburban America and is not likely to be pursued by the Reagan Administration.

The prevalent attitude among public decision makers and professionals is that planning can serve as the basis for action only if it remains within the limits imposed by the value system of the majoritarian society and the realities of the power distribution pattern. For this reason many planners accept the prevailing trends in growth and population settlement as givens and seek not to resist but to bend these forces in the interest of a more livable environment. Even this approach encounters difficulty because planning, whether at the local or regional level, involves proposals and commitments that pertain to an uncertain future. People find it much easier to act when they are confronted with an immediate problem or when a decision is forced on them by the pressure of circumstances. They are less ready to support public planning that involves present sacrifices on their part in return for some projected future benefit.

Current trends point toward stronger roles for both the national and state governments in the control of urban growth. Because of entrenched local interests their intervention is crucial in strengthening planning and program coordination at the metropolitan level. HUD in the late 1970s announced its intention to reorient the 701 program to give more emphasis to state and regional planning, and proposals have been made by federal officials to channel additional aid to those metropolitan areas that formulate plans supportive of national objectives. An increasing number of states, including Cali-

---

[42]The 1970 Housing Act directs the president to report biennially on a national growth policy. This provision has been met in name only. For all intents and purposes the nation remains without such a policy.
[43]Quoted in Rochelle Stanfield, "HUD's Robert Embry Talks About the New Urban Policy," *Planning* 44 (June 1978): 21.

fornia, Massachusetts, and North Carolina, are developing urban growth policies. Hawaii has become the first state to adopt a comprehensive statewide plan and Florida is in the process of doing so.[44] These efforts are likely to be stepped up as fiscal resources decline and environmental and energy problems intensify.

In the present context of national and local trends, the role of metropolitan or areawide planning assumes ever greater significance. Whether its detachment from the political arms of government and its almost servile dependence on other public agencies for its funding and the implementation of its plans can enable it to serve contemporary urban needs is questionable. The encouragement of regional planning activities by the national and state governments offers assurance that at the least incremental adjustments in development patterns will continue to be made. This typical American approach, however, is no longer sufficient. The future with its need for strong conservation policies will require large, not small, changes in our life-styles and the way in which we manage growth. Unfortunately, the nation is not yet ready to face up to this reality.

[44]See Richard A. Mann and Mike Miles, "State Land Use Planning: The Current Status and Demographic Rationale," *Journal of the American Planning Association* 45 (January 1979): 48–61.

Chapter 8
Financing Urban
Government

The end of the 1970s found many local governments in financial straits. The city of Cleveland was on the verge of bankruptcy, the Chicago school system was unable to meet its payroll, and Wayne County (Detroit) was planning drastic layoffs of its personnel because of huge operating deficits. Several years earlier, in the most dramatic case of all, Congress and the New York state government had to rescue the city of New York from fiscal chaos. Other large municipalities—Detroit, Newark, Philadelphia, and St. Louis among them—were also struggling with severe budgetary problems. Local authorities, moreover, could draw little consolation from public attitudes, the polls showing that most Americans believe governmental spending has "gotten out of hand." A committee of the International City Management Association put the situation in perspective when it stated that the nation's cities face a decade of fiscal scarcity, political skepticism, and reduced services.[1]

Urbanization has brought great benefits to society but it has also placed a mammoth burden on the public sector to cope with the needs and problems it has generated. The weight has fallen heavily on the local level of government where the municipalities and other units are most directly involved in keeping the urban system operative. Because of the magnitude of this task, huge amounts of economic resources in the form of goods and services are allocated through the local public economy as distinguished from the private sector. The events of the past decade have not lessened the need for such action but they have imparted a sense of urgency to questions relating to the fiscal structure of the existing system.

Economists commonly conceive of governments as having three broad objectives in the use of taxes and expenditures: stabili-

[1]The long-run outlook is one of continued fiscal strain for small communities as well as for large. See Herrington J. Bryce (ed.), *Small Cities in Transition: Dynamics of Growth and Decline* (Cambridge, Mass.: Ballinger, 1977).

zation of the economy, allocation of resources, and redistribution of income.[2] The first rests almost exclusively with the national government and is pursued through policies that seek to maintain a high level of resource utilization and a stable monetary system. The second is mainly the function of local units. It involves the assembling and use of resources in the production of more of certain types of goods and services, such as libraries and health protection, than could or would be supplied on a wholly private basis. The third, which aims at changing the distribution of income in the society from that brought about by the workings of the private market, is principally the responsibility of the national government and, to a lesser extent, that of the states and localities. This redistribution process takes place in two ways: direct money payments to the less affluent in the form of welfare benefits, rent supplements, food stamps, and similar subsidies; and the provision of public services, such as education and police protection, available equally to all citizens, regardless of how much or how little their tax contributions. The present chapter relates mainly to the second of these objectives—the financing of urban public services—but it is also concerned with the redistributional or equalizing impact of the various forms of local taxes and charges.[3]

THE EXPANDING PUBLIC SECTOR

The fiscal woes of metropolitan areas arise from many causes—inflation, expanded service requirements, inefficient management, demands of public employee unions, and state-mandated programs with no provision for funding.[4] For the older central cities (and some of the mature suburbs as well) the problem is aggravated by a shrinking tax base and an increasing proportion of low-income residents. For the newer communities in the urban ring, the spiraling costs of capital facilities needed to accommodate growth—roads, sewers, parks, jails, firehouses—create financial headaches. Balancing the urban budget has become more difficult in recent years

[2]Richard A. Musgrave, *The Theory of Public Finance* (New York: McGraw-Hill, 1959), chap. 1.
[3]An inventory of current research in the field of state and local government finance is John E. Petersen, Catherine L. Spain, and Martharose F. Laffey, *State and Local Government Finance and Financial Management* (Washington, D.C.: Government Finance Research Center, August 1978).
[4]See John Shannon and L. Richard Gabler, "Tax Lids and Expenditure Mandates: The Case for Fiscal Fair Play," *Intergovernmental Perspective* 3 (Summer 1977): 7–12.

as needs have intensified and the costs of goods and services have risen sharply.[5]

The expenditures of national, state, and local governments (exclusive of social security and similar trust fund payments) aggregated $63 billion in 1950. A quarter of a century later the amount had jumped to over $500 billion. By the end of the 1970s local units alone were spending in excess of $175 billion annually (including federal and state aid monies). In 1940 the combined outlays of all local governments in the nation were less than New York City's current budget, a telling commentary on the changes that have taken place in urban areas since then. Excluding the allocations for foreign aid, defense, and social security, the expenditure of public funds for domestic programs and services is about equally divided between the national and state–local levels. Municipalities, counties, school districts, and special districts account collectively for about one-third of the total, and the states, the remaining one-sixth (computing grants-in-aid as part of the recipients' budget).

The upward spiral of governmental costs, startling as it may seem, must be viewed in the light of complementary developments. The increase has been accompanied by an expanding economy, a growing urban population, rising standards of living, higher personal incomes, demands for more and better services, and mounting national defense requirements. Functions such as welfare and mass transit have been transferred from the private to the public sector. New regulatory activities in the fields of conservation, consumer protection, and occupational safety have been assumed by government in response to social needs. Much of the rise in recent years, moreover, is due to the strong inflationary pressures that have pushed up the costs of all goods and services, both public and private. This factor alone is responsible for more than 50 percent of the dollar increase in governmental spending over the last decade.[6]

When viewed in relation to economic growth, the statistics on local government finance point to no massive diversion of income or capital to public purposes. They do show that the expenditures

[5]It is worth noting that most services provided by local government do not readily lend themselves to increases in productivity or cost-saving innovations, as is the case with many privately supplied goods. Teachers, for instance, are not easily replaced by machines. See in this connection D. F. Bradford, R. A. Malt, and W. E. Oates, "The Rising Cost of Local Public Services: Some Evidence and Reflections," *National Tax Journal* 22 (June 1968): 185–202.

[6]Public sector growth is not unique to the United States. Measured by total taxes as a percent of gross national product, the United States ranks fifteenth out of the twenty most industrialized nations.

of local units in the aggregate have increased at a faster rate than the natural rise in the yield of currently used sources of revenue, such as the property tax and municipal sales tax. They also reveal that local government spending has gone up more rapidly than the GNP (gross national product or total output of goods and services valued at market price). Local and state outlays increased from 8.2 percent of GNP in 1959 to 11 percent in 1979; and those of the national government from 18.7 percent to 21.6 percent.

REVENUE SOURCES

Local taxes fall into two broad categories: property and nonproperty. The first is an assessment on the value of real estate and personal goods. The second includes a broad array of levies, with income and sales being the major revenue producers. Under the fiscal system as it has evolved in the United States, a rough division of funding sources exists among the three levels of government. The national tier derives the bulk of its revenue from income taxes on individuals and corporations; states rely heavily on sales taxes (by 1980 all but six of them had also turned to the income tax levy); and local government, since the turn of the century, has had almost exclusive title to the general property tax. Municipalities, counties, school districts, organized townships, and many special districts all share this levy, relying on it in varying degrees for a portion of their revenue (Figure 8.1).

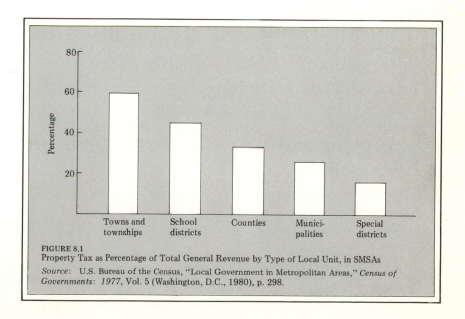

FIGURE 8.1
Property Tax as Percentage of Total General Revenue by Type of Local Unit, in SMSAs

Source: U.S. Bureau of the Census, "Local Government in Metropolitan Areas," *Census of Governments: 1977*, Vol. 5 (Washington, D.C., 1980), p. 298.

General Property Tax

The property tax (principally a levy on land and buildings and on tangible personal property such as household goods and motor vehicles) has provided the historical base of support for local government since colonial times. Next to federal income and excise taxes it has been the most lucrative source of public revenue in the American political system. As late as 1932 the property tax produced more funds than all other federal, state, and local taxes combined, providing almost three-fourths of local government receipts. Although its yield has continued to rise—from $18 billion in 1962 to $60 billion in 1977—its relative importance has declined due to the utilization of other forms of taxes and the substantial increase in federal and state aid. Today the property levy finances slightly more than one-third of the aggregate operating budgets of local units in SMSAs (Figure 8.2).

The extent of dependence on property taxes varies considerably among urban areas. In New England, where the use of other types of local levies is virtually unknown, SMSAs rely on this source for 80 to 90 percent of their locally raised revenues. By contrast, in metropolitan communities where local sales taxes are employed, the proportion is from 65 to 70 percent; and where municipal income taxes are in effect, the ratio is only about 60 percent. Property taxes generally finance a greater portion of public services

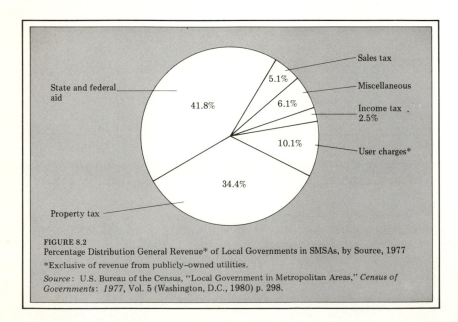

FIGURE 8.2
Percentage Distribution General Revenue* of Local Governments in SMSAs, by Source, 1977

*Exclusive of revenue from publicly-owned utilities.

Source: U.S. Bureau of the Census, "Local Government in Metropolitan Areas," Census of Governments: 1977, Vol. 5 (Washington, D.C., 1980) p. 298.

in the suburbs than in the large cities where additional types of taxes are more common.

Because of the heavy reliance on the property levy, a community's tax base (assessed value of the property) is an important measure of its financial ability to support services. Property subject to the tax in the United States was officially assessed at $695 billion in 1971 and $1230 billion in 1976, a substantial portion of the increase attributable to rising real estate values and inflation rather than to new construction.[7] (The relationship between assessed value and market or sales price varies considerably from jurisdiction to jurisdiction, with the national average about one-third of market value.) Nonfarm residential units account for 60 percent of the real estate assessment, and industrial and commercial establishments, 25 percent.

The balance or mix between the various land uses within individual communities is critical because the ratio between service demands and tax receipts for each type of property differs substantially. Residential units, except those of more than average value, normally pay only a portion of the costs of the public services they receive, whereas commercial and industrial uses contribute as much as two to three times the local outlays generated by them. This variance underlies the competition for industry frequently observed among SMSA municipalities.

From the standpoint of tax base, the well-balanced municipality is one that has a mix of residential and nonresidential properties. So also the well-balanced metropolis is one that contains a similar blend of land uses. In the latter case, however, it would be no more possible or even desirable for each autonomous unit in the area to embody this mix than it would be for each neighborhood of the central city to do so. Yet an effort to achieve this very end takes place within SMSAs as each local government seeks to attract the kind of development that will produce more in tax revenues than it costs in public services. What generally happens is that communities with the wealthier taxable capacity spend more on public services than their less affluent neighbors, but not so much as their superior tax base would permit. Consequently, the rich localities often have lower rates than the poorer units. This inversion has two deleterious effects. It encourages economic activity to locate in low-tax jurisdictions (at times distorting overall metropolitan devel-

---

[7]Real property accounts for more than four-fifths of the assessed total and personal, the remainder. Approximately one-third of all real estate in the United States is exempt from the property tax. Government-owned property constitutes 70 percent of this amount and religious and charitable organizations the other 30 percent.

opment patterns) and encourages communities to plan their land use for fiscal advantages rather than on the basis of broader considerations.[8]

The general property tax has been the target of severe criticism for many years. It has been condemned as regressive (not based on ability to pay), difficult to administer fairly, disproportionately burdensome on homeowners, and a serious impediment to the revitalization of central city housing stock. Some fiscal experts argue that logically it should pay only for property-related services, such as police and fire protection, whereas person-related functions such as education and welfare should be financed by income and other types of taxes. Many observers say that the heavy reliance on the levy is more the result of history and necessity than rational choice.

However valid the arguments against the property tax, the fact remains that it has long existed, produces large revenues, and shows surprising elasticity (the responsiveness of its base to changes in GNP). Recent research also indicates that the levy is far less regressive than critics contend and possesses the greatest potential of any local tax source for revenue growth during periods of inflation.[9] Supporters acknowledge that the tax falls most heavily on elderly and low-income houseowners but maintain that this situation can be corrected through homestead exemptions (a portion of the assessed value of the property is not subject to the tax). The debate over the property levy will continue but the lack of any satisfactory and politically realistic alternatives assures its employment as a major source of local government revenue for some time to come.

Nonproperty Taxes

Rising costs and mounting public needs in the nation's urban areas following World War II outran the ability of the property tax to provide sufficient revenue without large rate hikes. Confronted with the necessity of finding additional funds to supplement returns from the property levy, local officials pursued two courses of action: They sought increased federal and state aid and tapped new sources of income. The results of their efforts are evident today. Financial assistance from higher levels of government supports a significant portion of local public budgets (intergovernmental aid is

[8]These points are elaborated on in Dick Netzer, *Economics of the Property Tax* (Washington, D.C.: The Brookings Institution, 1966), pp. 125–130.
[9]See Henry J. Aaron, *Who Pays the Property Tax: A New View* (Washington, D.C.: The Brookings Institution, 1975).

discussed in Chapter 6), and a broad array of nonproperty taxes is now utilized in many jurisdictions. These include levies on gasoline, motor vehicles, cigarettes, alcoholic beverages, retail sales, income, and gross receipts of utilities and business establishments. (The relative reliance of city governments on the major revenue categories is illustrated in Figure 8.3.)

The municipal income tax, sometimes referred to as an earn-

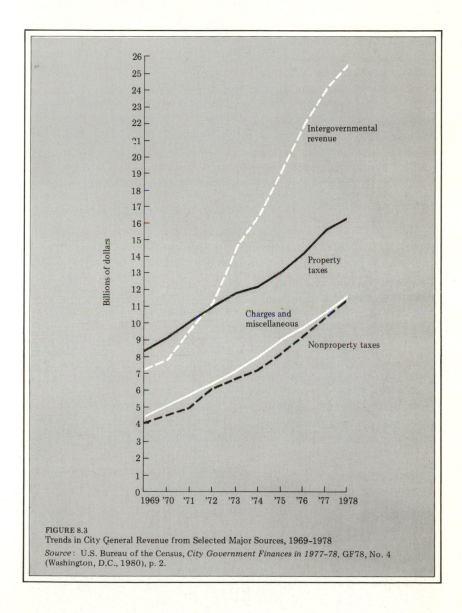

FIGURE 8.3
Trends in City General Revenue from Selected Major Sources, 1969–1978
Source: U.S. Bureau of the Census, *City Government Finances in 1977–78,* GF78, No. 4 (Washington, D.C., 1980), p. 2.

ings or commuter tax, originated in Philadelphia in 1939.[10] Now authorized in ten states, it is utilized by more than 3500 jurisdictions, including a number of school districts. The overwhelming majority of these units, however, are located in three states—Ohio, Pennsylvania, and Maryland. With the exception of Bernalillo County (Albuquerque, New Mexico), the tax is confined to the eastern half of the United States. Most of the user jurisdictions are relatively small in size; only about 25 municipalities of 100,000 or more population have adopted such a levy, but this number includes some of the nation's largest cities such as New York, Detroit, Baltimore, St. Louis, Cleveland, Pittsburgh, and Cincinnati. The tax has usually been introduced under conditions of severe financial distress with the primary objective of obtaining additional revenue.[11] Although it does not account for a large share of municipal tax collections in the country as a whole, it does provide significant amounts of revenue for those cities in which it is employed. Philadelphia, for example, derives over half its municipal tax revenue and St. Louis well over one-third from this source. The proportion runs as high as 60 percent in some of the medium-size cities such as Toledo and Dayton.

The local income tax rate ranges from one-half of 1 percent in Kansas City, Missouri, to 3 percent in Philadelphia. The most common levy is a flat 1 percent of the gross earnings of persons living or working in the municipality and of net profits of businesses from locally conducted activities. Only a few cities allow exemptions or provide for a graduated rate. The feature of the tax that is most attractive to the larger central cities is its application to commuters who work within the core boundaries. This aspect is defended on the grounds of equity in that it enables the host municipality to recoup some of the added costs of the services and other public facilities it must furnish the nonresident working population.[12]

Central cities have long complained of being exploited by their suburban ring in the sense that they are not adequately compensated for services undertaken in the latter's behalf. This "exploita-

---

[10]Background material and an extensive bibliography on local income taxes are contained in Advisory Commission on Intergovernmental Relations, *The Commuter and the Municipal Income Tax* (Washington, D.C., April 1970).

[11]In practice the tax has been used largely to relieve pressure on the property levy. See Elizabeth Deran, "Tax Structure in Cities Using the Income Tax," *National Tax Journal* 21 (June 1968): 147–152.

[12]See in this connection G. Ross Stephens, "The Suburban Impact of Earnings Tax Policies," *National Tax Journal* 22 (September 1969): 313–333.

tion" thesis has been the subject of considerable debate. No one questions the fact that suburban commuters clearly add to the operational and capital costs of the core municipality. Their presence during the workday requires the city to provide road and parking space, public utilities, police protection, and similar services beyond the level that would be necessary to accommodate its resident population. But the costs and benefits are not one-way streets. Commuter-workers spend money in the shops, restaurants, and entertainment spots of the central city, and these expenditures are reflected in increased tax returns for the municipality. They also help operate the business and industrial enterprises that enrich the tax base of the host municipality while relieving it of the burden of educating their children.

The extent to which these costs and benefits balance out has not been conclusively demonstrated.[13] Much depends on the factors that are taken into consideration in making the determination. If only the expenses directly related to servicing the working commuter are put into the equation, subsidization is more difficult to show. If, however, the poverty-related costs of the central city (which houses a disproportionate share of the area's poor, elderly, and unskilled) are regarded as a metropolitan responsibility—as they should properly be—a significant degree of exploitation does take place. To recoup this portion of costs through a commuter tax might be questioned, because suburbanites who do not work in the core municipality escape its imposition.

The second major revenue innovation, the local sales tax, is currently utilized by over 4000 municipalities and counties in 27 states. More than one-half of the cities with populations in excess of 100,000 draw on this source of funding. The heaviest use occurs in California and Illinois where the tax has been almost universally adopted by municipalities and counties. It is also employed widely in Alabama, Oklahoma, Texas, Louisiana, Utah, Virginia, and

[13]Support for the subsidy thesis is found in William B. Neenan, *Political Economy of Urban Areas* (Chicago: Markham, 1972), pp. 45–139. The nonexploitation argument is supported in Phillip E. Vincent, "The Fiscal Impact of Commuters," in Werner Z. Hirsch (ed.), *The Fiscal Pressures on the Central City* (New York: Praeger, 1971), pp. 41–143. Most studies ignore the fact that city residents with above average income in effect pay a "poor" tax to subsidize the services provided to low-income families, a situation that does not exist in most suburban communities. For a discussion of this issue see David Bradford and William Oates, "Suburban Exploitation of Central Cities and Government Structure," in Harold Hochman and George Peterson (eds.), *Redistribution Through Public Choice* (New York: Columbia University Press, 1974), pp. 43–90.

Washington.[14] Although receipts nationwide from the levy do not constitute a large proportion of local government revenue, reliance on the tax is pronounced in jurisdictions where it is in effect. New York City and Chicago, for example, derive approximately 15 percent of their locally raised tax money from this source and Los Angeles and St. Louis, nearly 20 percent. In a number of large municipalities—including Birmingham, Denver, New Orleans, Oklahoma City, and Phoenix—the ratio is over 30 percent. The rate varies among the user units, ranging from one-half of one to 3 percent, with 1 percent the most common figure. The local levy is usually "piggybacked" on to that of the state sales tax, thus providing a convenient and economical method of collection.

Local sales taxes have the advantage of revenue productivity, low cost of administration, and a means of tapping nonresidents who otherwise would not contribute to the municipality's coffers. Like most nonproperty levies, however, such a tax is not without its drawbacks when employed in metropolitan areas. The most obvious is that merchants in a sales tax municipality may be penalized if residents can avoid the levy by shopping in an adjacent city or town. Some of the deficiencies of this and other nonproperty taxes can be eliminated by imposing them on a countywide or metropolitan basis, because in this way all individuals and businesses in the area are uniformly reached. Other defects, however, would remain, such as the regressiveness of most of these taxes and their general nuisance to the citizen. The "hand-to-mouth" operations that have characterized metropolitan area financing in recent decades have given little consideration to long-range effects and objectives, or even to the relations among the various types of levies and their impact on different segments of the population. The search for new revenue sources has been more in the nature of frantic improvisation than a constructive approach to a sound fiscal system.

User Charges

In addition to taxes and grants-in-aid, local governments derive a portion of their income from fees of various kinds. The most important of these nontax revenues in terms of total dollars are user charges that are collected in return for measurable benefits provided. Consumers who are furnished with a specific service by their local units pay for it in the same way they would if the sup-

[14]A survey of its use is contained in John L. Mikesell, "Local Government Sales Tax," in John F. Due (ed.), *State and Local Sales Taxation: Structure and Administration* (Chicago: Public Administration Service, 1971), pp. 266–305.

plier was a private firm. The provision of water by a municipality or special district is a case in point. Consumers are billed for the amount of water they use, that is, for the benefits they receive. Under this method of financing a householder will pay less than the florist or factory owner whose water needs are greater. The same principle has been applied in many jurisdictions to such services as sewage disposal and garbage collection. These utility-type operations by local public agencies are essentially indistinguishable from similar activities carried on under private auspices.[15]

User charges amount to almost one-third of municipally generated revenue, a proportion that has remained relatively stable in recent years.[16] They enjoy several advantages in addition to generating income for the local units and removing important costs from the general tax levy. First of all, they constitute a rationing device for those products or services that would be significantly wasted if they had a zero price, such as unmetered water. Second, they help solve the problem of geographic spillovers of benefits from one jurisdiction to another by enabling the supplying government to recoup its costs from the benefiting users wherever they reside. Third, by providing consumer signals as in the private marketplace, they enable public agencies to adjust the quantity of a service to bring it more closely in line with demand. Finally, the prices charged for various items or activities can be used as a means of control to further community objectives.[17] Wilbur Thompson, for instance, has suggested that a sophisticated manipulation of tolls, parking fees, and motor vehicle licenses could be resorted to by a local unit to promote certain forms of urban transportation and to discourage others.[18]

If viewed as taxes, user charges could be classified as regressive because they are not based on the ability to pay. The same observation, however, can be made about similar-type goods or services—electricity, gas, telephone—provided by nongovernment utilities. When consumers buy in the private market they individu-

---

[15]Selma J. Mushkin, "Public Prices for Public Products," *Municipal Year Book, 1971*, pp. 245–253.

[16]Calvin A. Kent, "Users' Fees for Municipalities," *Governmental Finance* 1 (February 1972): 2–7.

[17]The advantages of user charges are discussed in Dick Netzer, *Economics and Urban Problems* (New York: Basic Books, 1970), pp. 185–191.

[18]*A Preface to Urban Economics* (Baltimore: Johns Hopkins Press, 1965), pp. 280–286. The wide range of possible applications of user fee financing is treated in Jerome W. Milliman, "Beneficiary Charges and Efficient Public Expenditure Decisions," in U.S. Congress, Joint Economic Committee, *Analysis and Evaluation of Public Expenditures*, vol. 1 (Washington, D.C., 1969), pp. 318 ff.

ally make their own allocational decisions as to what to purchase and how much. User charges for specific services extend this principle of individual choice to the public sector, where normally such decisions are collective or political judgments that find reflection in governmental budget allotments.

Although user fees might be more extensively exploited by local governments, they also have their limitations. They are inappropriate for services such as education that have substantial income redistributive effects and for financing what economists refer to as a "pure public good," or one of such nature that no person can be denied its benefits, regardless of whether he or she pays for it. Pollution control, street lighting, and the maintenance of public safety are examples of such a good. Services of this kind do not lend themselves to the pricing mechanism characteristic of the private market. Another limitation of the user charge relates to those functions that could be financed on a fee basis but seldom are because they produce community benefits aside from those enjoyed by the individual consumer. Public policy dictates that the use of goods or services in this category (libraries and education are examples) should not be discouraged by the imposition of a fee.[19] The subsidizing of public transit systems from tax revenue is similarly justified because of the benefits they generate external to the user.

RESOURCE DISPARITIES

Because neither needs nor resources are evenly distributed among the governmental jurisdictions within SMSAs, those sections with the most serious public wants frequently have the least means to meet them. This lack of congruence between needs and fiscal capacity is particularly evident in the case of public education. Due to the almost complete reliance of school districts on the general property tax levy for their locally derived revenue, those with low assessed valuations per capita are at a serious financial disadvantage. A jurisdiction with little industrial and commercial development and mostly low-cost residential units will be hard pressed to meet its minimum educational requirements while a neighboring district with a strong property tax base is able to enjoy the benefit of well-financed schools at less tax effort.

Fiscal inequities in the provision of public education came under judicial attack in the early 1970s when the California supreme

---

[19]Economists refer to goods and services of this nature as "merit goods," those that society decides are so important that some minimum quantity is regarded as a fundamental right.

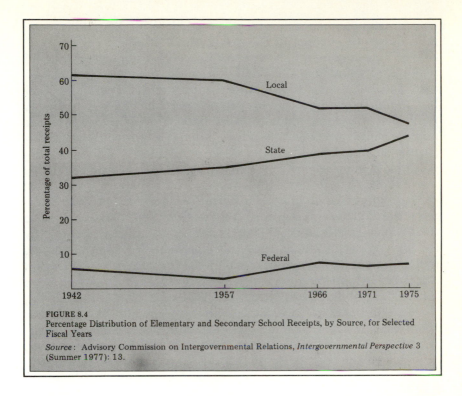

FIGURE 8.4
Percentage Distribution of Elementary and Secondary School Receipts, by Source, for Selected Fiscal Years

Source: Advisory Commission on Intergovernmental Relations, *Intergovernmental Perspective* 3 (Summer 1977): 13.

court (in the widely cited *Serrano* v. *Priest* case) struck down the state's system of school financing as in violation of the California constitution.[20] The court held that the heavy reliance on local property taxes denied the equal protection of the law to children in the poorer districts. As an example of the disparity, it noted that Beverly Hills was producing $1500 for the education of each pupil on a tax rate of $2.60 per $100 assessed valuation while West Covina, a less affluent community, was deriving only $700 for each student on a tax rate 65 percent higher. Judicial intervention in California and elsewhere was prompted principally by the reluctance of state governments to assume greater financial responsibility for their school systems. As late as 1975 state aid provided on the average less than 45 percent of elementary and secondary school revenues (see Figure 8.4).

The California decision was followed by similar holdings in other jurisdictions, including Connecticut, Kansas, Michigan, Minnesota, New Jersey, and Texas. The rulings caused considerable

[20]*Serrano* v. *Priest*, 96 California Reporter 601 (1971).

consternation among state officials, leading to modifications in aid formulas and increases in the states' share of educational costs.[21] School financing reform, however, received a major setback in 1973 when the United States Supreme Court (in *San Antonio Independent School District* v. *Rodriguez*) reversed the Texas case by a five-to-four vote. Speaking for the majority, Justice Lewis Powell ruled that education is not a fundamental right guaranteed by the national constitution and therefore judicial relief for financial disparities among school districts is not available.[22] Although disappointing to advocates of fiscal equalization, the decision does not prevent state courts from invalidating existing arrangements that are found in violation of state constitutional provisions (unlike *Serrano,* the *Rodriguez* case involved the Fourteenth Amendment to the national constitution).[23] This power was in effect sanctioned by the high tribunal's refusal to review *Clowes* v. *Serrano* (a followup of the original *Serrano* case) in which the California supreme court mandated a 1980 deadline for the state legislature to equalize the funding of public education.[24]

In the matter of fiscal equalization generally, Minnesota has taken a novel step toward metropolitan tax sharing (an example not yet followed by any other state). The Fiscal Disparities Act passed by the legislature in 1971 established a tax-base sharing program for the Minneapolis-St. Paul metropolis. Under the law 40 percent of the assessed value of all new industrial and commercial growth, wherever it occurs in the area, becomes part of a pooled tax base for the SMSA. A separate metropolitanwide tax levy is then applied to this base and the proceeds shared by all local units in accordance with an equalization formula that takes into account population and fiscal capacity. The Minnesota plan enjoys the advantage of requiring no new taxing authority or new administrative layer of govern-

[21]Some economists argue that the principal beneficiaries of state assumption of educational costs would be the relatively well-to-do homeowners in suburbia, who are already taxing themselves substantially for this function. Their solution for correcting interjurisdictional inequities is a shift to statewide property taxes that would finance in some measure not education alone but all basic local services. See George E. Peterson and Arthur P. Solomon, "Property Taxes and Populist Reform," No. 30, *The Public Interest* (Winter 1973): 60–75.

[22]*San Antonio Independent School District* v. *Rodriguez*, U.S. Supreme Court Reports, 36 Lawyers Edition 2d, 16 (1973).

[23]Ferdinand P. Shoettle, "Judicial Requirements for School Finance and Property Tax Redesign: The Rapidly Evolving Case Law," *National Tax Journal* 25 (September 1972): 455–472.

[24]*Clowes* v. *Serrano*, 432 U.S. 907 (1977). Largely because of the concern caused among state officials by the *Serrano* decision, the states' share of public school costs nationally had increased to almost 50 percent by the end of 1980.

ment. However, it can contribute meaningfully to the reduction of disparities only in those SMSAs that are undergoing substantial growth, because none of the tax base existing prior to the law is shared.[25]

EXPENDITURE PATTERNS

Local units within a metropolis serve up different packages of public programs. At one extreme is the government of the small dormitory suburb that operates with part-time personnel, relies on volunteers instead of professional fire fighters, avoids installing curbs and sidewalks, and provides no parks or recreation facilities. At the other end of the spectrum is the large central-city government with its broad range of services encompassing everything from tiny-tot play areas to hospitals and museums. The same differences, although not so extreme, prevail among school districts. Beyond meeting the minimum requirements of the state department of education, local districts vary widely in their educational offerings and facilities. One may provide courses in music, art, and specialized types of vocational training, employ school psychologists and nurses, and conduct extensive recreational programs. Another may offer few of these activities, limiting itself to a "skin and bones" educational program. In some instances the differences may be due to the voluntary choice of the residents; in others, to the lack of ability to pay for a higher level of services.

The total revenues, expenditures, and outstanding debts of all governments in the United States—national, state, and local—increased during the 1970s at an average annual rate of about 11 percent. At the local level municipalities are the largest spenders followed closely by school districts, the two types accounting for 70 percent of the aggregate expenditures by substate units in metropolitan areas. Functionally, public education consumes the largest share (over two-fifths) of the collective operating budgets of local governments. No other service including public safety, health and welfare, and sewage and refuse disposal exceeds 15 percent of the total outlay (Figure 8.5). Defense constitutes the largest expenditure item for the national government and education (including grants-in-aid to local school districts) for the states.

Within the large SMSAs per capita expenditures by central city governments for municipal purposes exceed those of the suburban

[25]Walter H. Plosila, "Metropolitan Tax-Base-Sharing: Its Potential and Limitations," *Public Finance Quarterly* 4 (April 1976): 205–224. The law was tied up in litigation for almost five years before it went into effect.

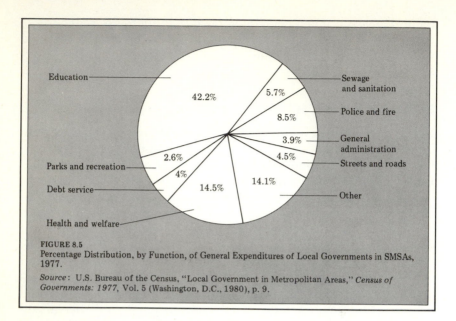

FIGURE 8.5
Percentage Distribution, by Function, of General Expenditures of Local Governments in SMSAs, 1977.

Source: U.S. Bureau of the Census, "Local Government in Metropolitan Areas," *Census of Governments: 1977*, Vol. 5 (Washington, D.C., 1980), p. 9.

units, often by a substantial margin. The variance, however, is much less in the case of public education, with outlying school districts frequently spending more per pupil than the core city system. Overall, households in the central municipalities usually pay a greater proportion of their personal income in local taxes than do suburban dwellers, averaging almost one-third higher in the most populous SMSAs. This difference is offset only partially by the wider range of services they normally receive.

Table 8.1 PER CAPITA OPERATING EXPENDITURES OF MUNICIPALITIES BY SELECTED FUNCTIONS AND POPULATION SIZE, 1978 (in dollars)

POPULATION SIZE	POLICE	FIRE	ROADS	HEALTH AND HOSPITALS	HOUSING AND REDE- VELOPMENT	SEWERAGE
1 million or more	98	40	17	78	35	10
500,000 to 999,999	73	38	20	53	20	16
300,000 to 499,999	60	41	20	30	15	17
200,000 to 299,999	51	36	22	28	18	14
100,000 to 199,999	48	35	22	17	18	13
50,000 to 99,999	45	33	21	15	16	13
Less than 50,000	34	18	23	11	8	13
All municipalities	50	28	21	26	15	13

SOURCE: U.S. Bureau of the Census, *City Government Finance in 1977–78*, GF, No. 4, (Washington, D.C., 1980), p. 11.

Table 8.2 CAPITAL EXPENDITURES BY LOCAL GOVERNMENTS IN SMSAs 1972 AND 1977 (in billions of dollars)

	1972		1977	
FUNCTION	AMOUNT	PERCENTAGE OF TOTAL	AMOUNT	PERCENTAGE OF TOTAL
Education	3.9	25.1	4.1	18.6
Streets and roads	1.7	10.9	2.2	10.0
Local utilities	2.6	16.6	5.3	24.0
Hospitals	0.4	2.6	0.7	3.1
Sewerage	1.9	12.1	3.7	16.7
Housing and redevelopment	1.4	9.0	1.1	5.0
Parks and recreation	0.9	5.8	1.0	4.5
Other	2.8	17.9	4.0	18.1
Total	15.6	100.0	22.1	100.0

SOURCE: U.S. Bureau of the Census, "Local Government in Metropolitan Areas," *Census of Governments, 1972*, Vol. 5, (Washington, D.C., 1975), pp. 241–242; and "Local Governments in Metropolitan Areas," *Census of Governments, 1977*, Vol. 5, (Washington, D.C., 1980), pp. 298–299.

The amounts spent by cities on certain type services tend to vary with population size. In the large municipalities per capita expenditures for law enforcement, health and hospitals, and housing and urban redevelopment are generally higher than in the smaller communities. Per capita outlays for police protection in 1978 were $98 in cities of one million or more; in those under 100,000 they were less than one-half this amount. Spending for some functions such as street maintenance and sewage disposal are more comparable among all size categories (Table 8.1). Expenditures in the smaller cities and towns are usually spread out over a more limited range of activities than in the populous communities, with educational allotments in some instances running as high as 65 percent of the total outlay of local government.

Capital Expenditures

Along with meeting operational needs, governmental bodies make substantial investments in public improvements. In 1977 expenditures by local units in SMSAs for capital purposes aggregated $22.1 billion (compared to $15.6 billion in 1972). The largest proportion of this amount (one-fourth) was for local utilities, including water supply, mass transit, and electric power (Table 8.2). The percentage spent on educational facilities—slightly under one-fifth of the total—declined significantly from the 1972 ratio, a reflection of the drop in school enrollment and the lessened need for new classrooms. (Other statistics indicate that the percentage of personal income preempted by school taxes is also decreasing in most areas of the country.)

Local governments in the urbanized sections of SMSAs continue to have large-scale capital requirements. In the central cities and older suburbs the emphasis is primarily on the renewal of social capital (schools, libraries, recreational facilities, sewers, streets), and in the newer fringe area communities (and sunbelt cities) on its creation. Public investments in suburbia have generally exceeded those in the core municipalities since World War II. In the St. Louis SMSA almost two-thirds of the area's total capital outlay during the early 1970s was made by suburban units and in the Washington, D.C. metropolis the proportion was 60 percent. This pattern has been common to virtually all of the well-populated SMSAs, the major exceptions occurring in cases where the central municipality boundaries have been expanded through either large annexations (as Oklahoma City) or city–county consolidation (as Jacksonville, Florida).

The accumulated public debt of the nation in 1977 was $969 billion, or approximately $4500 for every man, woman, and child. Federal indebtedness represents the largest portion (73 percent) of the total, local units 17 percent, and the states 10 percent. The principal debt generators at the local tier are the governments situated within SMSAs. These jurisdictions collectively account for over 80 percent of the outstanding obligations of public agencies below the state level. The municipalities are the largest debtors by a wide margin (45 percent of the total) followed in order by special districts (25 percent), school districts (15 percent), county governments (13 percent), and townships (2 percent). The total debt of local units in metropolitan areas was $139 billion in 1977, or about $875 per capita.[26]

EXPENDITURE DETERMINANTS

The expenditure patterns of American local governments are characterized by variances of wide range both among and within SMSAs. These differences are not confined to central city–suburban comparisons; they also exist among core municipalities and

---

[26]Approximately two-thirds of the long-term indebtedness of local governments is represented by general obligation bonds and the remainder by revenue or nonguaranteed obligations. The first are backed by the full credit and taxing powers of the issuing unit; the latter are paid out of the proceeds of revenue-generating operations, such as water supply systems and parking garages, and have no claim on the general taxing powers of the debtor government.

among the fringe area communities themselves. Part of this diversity is due to interstate (and even intrastate) variations in the assignment of functional responsibilities between the state and local governments and in arrangements for the financing of locally performed services. Differences of this nature exist particularly in the case of public welfare, hospitals, and education. In New York City, for example, both welfare and education are financed out of the municipal budget; in Boston education but not welfare is funded by the municipality; in Chicago welfare is primarily a state function and education the responsibility of a school district; and in Honolulu both services are financed and administered by the state. Even when assignability is taken into account, however, substantial differences in aggregate expenditures per capita among SMSA governments still remain.

During the last two decades numerous efforts have been made to explain the reasons for these variances through statistical analyses.[27] The research has concentrated on a limited number of variables as possible determinants of spending patterns. These include median family income, population size, density, degree of urbanization, rate of growth, and grants-in-aid.[28] Although the findings are mixed, four factors are cited most frequently as influencing expenditure levels: per capita income of households; federal and state aid; proportion of SMSA residents living outside the central city; and size of population.

The studies indicate, not surprisingly, that the availability of resources is the most important single determinant of local public expenditure levels. The greater the per capita income differential among localities, the larger the variance is likely to be in their service outlays. Wealthy communities, in other words, tend to allocate more for their public needs in the same way that affluent individuals spend more than the poor on their private wants.[29]

The second variable, grants-in-aid, also pertains to resources. Like income, it bears a positive relationship to spending because it

[27]For a list of such studies see John C. Fredlund, *Determinants of State and Local Expenditures: An Annotated Bibliography* (Washington, D.C.: Urban Institute, 1974).

[28]Emil M. Sunley, Jr., "Some Determinants of Government Expenditures Within Metropolitan Areas," *American Journal of Economics and Sociology* 30 (October 1971): 345–364.

[29]Seymour Sacks and Robert Harris, "The Determinants of State and Local Government Expenditures and Intergovernmental Flow of Funds," *National Tax Journal* 17 (March 1964): 75–85; and Woo Sik Kee, "City-Suburban Differentials in Local Government Fiscal Effort," *National Tax Journal* 21 (June 1968): 183–189.

increases the funds available for community purposes.[30] The third factor, central city–suburban population ratio, is associated with different per capita expenditures between the two sections. The higher the proportion of fringe area dwellers in an SMSA, the greater the variance in spending (with the major city showing the larger amount). This relationship is usually regarded as a reflection of suburban exploitation of the core municipality. The assumption is that disproportionate increases in the outlying population impose additional and uncompensated burdens on the central community.[31]

The importance of the fourth factor, population size, on expenditures has been the subject of considerable debate. The question of such a relation early became a political issue, with central city partisans contending that the outlying units are uneconomical and inefficient because of their small size and suburban defenders arguing that there are diseconomies of scale in the larger governments.[32] Initial studies gave support to the assumption that the populous cities spend more per person for similar operations than the smaller. Later research—by taking other factors such as availability of resources and service levels into account—casts doubt on the existence of such an association.

Some analysts feel that a better picture of the impact of size can be obtained by examining functions individually because the optimum scale for each is likely to be different. Economist Werner Hirsch found that one group of activities (including air pollution control and sewage disposal) benefited from economies of scale as population exceeded the 100,000 mark, whereas another set (including education, law enforcement, fire protection, and libraries) resulted in no such savings when provided by units above this figure.[33] An ACIR study in three states also found that size generally had no effect on per capita outlays and number of public employees

---

[30]Roy W. Bahl, Jr. and Robert J. Saunders, "Determinants of Change in State and Local Government Expenditures," *National Tax Journal* 18 (March 1965): 50–57.

[31]A study by Alan K. Campbell and Seymour Sacks found that the three variables—income, state aid, and central city–suburban population ratio—accounted for two-thirds of the variance in per capita expenditures by urban communities. *Metropolitan America: Fiscal Patterns and Governmental Systems* (New York: Free Press, 1967).

[32]Some studies indicate that cities up to 250,000 population do not demonstrate any major economies or diseconomies of scale. Others conclude that units from 100,000 to 150,000 have the advantage in terms of efficiency. See in this connection William L. Henderson and Larry C. Ledebur, *Urban Economics: Processes and Problems* (New York: Wiley, 1972), pp. 94–98.

[33]"Local Versus Areawide Government Services," *National Tax Journal* 17 (December 1964): 331–339.

in cities of 25,000 to 250,000 for most functions of a typically local nature (such as those in Hirsch's second set). However in the case of the larger municipalities, the effects of population size showed up clearly in higher spending and employment for these items.[34] The impact of size has not been settled by these various studies but two observations may be drawn from them. One, there is general consensus that higher per capita expenditures for most urban functions are associated with large population size (the numerical definition of "large" elicits less concurrence); and two, wide disagreement continues over the economies of scale issue (do higher per capita outlays in the big municipalities reflect diseconomies or simply better services?).

THE PROPOSITION 13 SYNDROME

The Jarvis–Gann amendment to the California constitution, popularly known as "Proposition 13" (its designation on the ballot), was approved by a two-to-one majority of the state's voters in June 1978. Placed before the electorate by initiative petition, the amendment gave dramatic impetus to the developing nationwide trend to impose legal limitations on tax increases and public spending. Under its provisions the real property levy is limited to 1 percent of market value, with upward adjustments in assessments not to exceed 2 percent per year. The situation in California was somewhat unique in that property taxes were 40 percent above the national average and the state had a surplus of over $5 billion in its treasury. The overwhelming endorsement of the measure, however, reflected a growing national sentiment that the tax burden had become too heavy and public spending excessive. It also reflected the cynicism toward government generally and the distrust of public officials now felt by a large number of the electorate.

Although Proposition 13 is the symbol of the tax revolt, it was not the first measure adopted in the 1970s to control the costs of government. In 1976 New Jersey placed caps (ceilings) on the budgets of all local governments in the state, limiting increases to no more than 5 percent a year; and in March 1978 Tennessee voters by a wide margin passed a constitutional amendment tying the rate of increase in state spending to the rate of growth of the state's economy. During the latter half of the 1970s efforts were also initi-

[34]Advisory Commission on Intergovernmental Relations, *Urban and Rural America: Policies for Future Growth* (Washington, D.C., 1968), p. 62. Also see the ACIR publication "Size Can Make a Difference: A Closer Look," *Information Bulletin*, No. 70-8 (September 1970).

ated to put legislative and constitutional curbs on congressional spending. The well-publicized Kemp-Roth bill provides for the reduction of federal income taxes on individuals by 10 percent annually for three consecutive years; and economist Milton Friedman's proposal (sponsored by the National Tax Limitation Committee) calls for a constitutional amendment to prohibit federal spending from rising faster than the GNP.[35]

By the end of the 1970s 15 states and the District of Columbia had enacted some form of new restraints on local and state taxing and spending powers. In some instances, as in the case of Proposition 13, limits were placed on specific taxes, and in others on the overall taxing or expenditure level. The current trend is to relate increases to economic factors such as growth in personal income and rate of inflation.[36] Some states have adopted so-called "circuit breaker" laws to provide relief to those most adversely affected by tax hikes, such as low-income households and the elderly. Relating principally to the general property levy, these enactments specify that no further increase may occur once a family's tax bill reaches a certain proportion of its income. Restrictive measures of these various types are too recently adopted to assess their impact on the operation and services of local governments. If nothing else, they foretell an era of fiscal austerity in the public sector.[37]

[35]The Friedman proposal also calls for "indexing" the federal income tax. Under an indexation measure, fixed dollar provisions of the tax law, such as income brackets, personal exemptions, and the standard deduction, are adjusted to compensate for increases in the general price level, thus eliminating the tax rise that would otherwise occur because of the effect of inflation on a progressive tax. See Advisory Commission on Intergovernmental Relations, "The Balanced Budget Movement," *Intergovernmental Perspective* 5 (Spring 1979): 6–7. A number of states, including Arizona, California, Colorado, Minnesota, and Wisconsin, already apply indexing to their state income taxes.

[36]Paul Gann, cosponsor of Proposition 13, proposed in 1979 an additional amendment—Proposition 4—to the California constitution that limits the growth of state and local government budgets to a level determined by the rate of inflation and population increase. The voters approved the proposal by a three-to-one margin in November of that year. A second Jarvis-sponsored amendment (Proposition 9) that would have cut state income taxes on individuals by one-half was defeated in June 1980.

[37]See Astrid E. Merget, "The Era of Fiscal Restraint," *Municipal Year Book, 1980,* pp. 179–191. A Rand Corporation report for the California Department of Justice on the preliminary results of Proposition 13 found that cities and counties tended to cut their budgets first on services not affected by state or federal mandates, such as police, fire, and parks, while fully funding certain social services required by state law or for which federal matching funds were available. This result is contrary to what most observers had anticipated.

FISCAL INEQUITY REMEDIES

If the socioeconomic community and the political city were coter-minous in urban areas, as was essentially the case until the early years of this century, the spatial distribution of wealth and eco-nomic activities within their boundaries would not give rise to in-equities in the provision of services.[38] Both the low-income or "def-icit" sections and the more affluent neighborhoods would share the same tax base. Because this situation has not existed in most large SMSAs for more than 50 years, other means short of political con-solidation have been used to alleviate the disparity problem. These include (1) superimposing new agencies on the existing govern-mental structure, (2) shifting responsibilities or functions to units of broader territorial scope, (3) financing services on a metropoli-tanwide basis, and (4) redistributing income through federal and state action.

The first approach is represented by the familiar device of the special district. By permitting the pooling of area resources for car-rying out certain functions, these units help reduce the effects of territorial differentiation in taxable capacity. The special school district for handicapped children in St. Louis County, Missouri, illustrates this point. Invested with power to levy a countywide property tax to support its activities, the district is able to draw on the wealth of the area to serve handicapped children regardless of their place of residence in the county. In this way those who live in the poorer districts where lack of funds would prevent such serv-ices are able to benefit from the tax resources of the larger commu-nity. This approach is not without its disadvantages, because it adds to the political fragmentation of metropolitan areas.

The second method, transfer of functions to governmental units of larger territorial scope, has the same effect as the use of special districts. If responsibility for such items as public health and hospitals is assumed by the county, or if welfare programs are administered directly by the state, the problem of logistics—getting the service distributed where it is most needed—is solved. There is, in short, a close positive association between the equitable ful-fillment of needs and the proportion of the local service package

---

[38]Service inequities can, of course, exist within the same governmental jurisdiction. Many instances can be cited where the level of activities (such as street maintenance and sanitation) is lower in poor or minority neighborhoods than in the wealthier sections of the community. Court decisions have held this inequity to be in violation of the Fourteenth Amendment. See *Hawkins* v. *Town of Shaw*, 437 Federal 2d, 1286 (1971).

that is handled by spatially inclusive units. The greater the number of activities of a local nature administered by the county, areawide special districts, or the state government, the less territorial variance will exist in the system between need and fiscal capacity. Although desirable for reasons of equity, the upward transfer of responsibility also has its disabilities because it takes control of a function out of local hands and places it in a larger bureaucracy.

The third device, areawide financing, offers another means of overcoming the uneven spatial distribution of resources. One form this technique assumes is for the county or a metropolitan taxing agency to collect and distribute funds to the local units according to some equalization formula (the Minnesota Fiscal Disparities Act moves in this direction). The practice is followed in the Toronto metropolis in the case of education. A metropolitan school board finances the local school districts through an areawide levy. The arrangement permits the retention of local districts but—by tapping the resources of the total metropolitan community—assures sufficient funds to each unit to maintain comparable levels of education. Critics of this type of solution maintain that the redistribution of tax funds encourages the continued existence of inefficient and poorly operated systems. Advocates counterargue that by separating the responsibility for financing a function from responsibility for its administration equity can be promoted, further bureaucratization prevented, and local control retained.

Income redistribution, the fourth equalizing device, depends largely on the willingness of higher levels of government to take on fiscal responsibility for certain costly functions of a person-related nature, particularly public welfare and education. The action most commonly proposed is that the states (with some federal aid) provide total funding for their school districts and the national government assume the full costs of public welfare. These steps would eliminate the gross disparities now existing in educational expenditures within states and in welfare benefits among states. They would also ease the financial pressures on local units of government and enable them to maintain other services at an adequate level. Progress was made on both these fronts during the last decade, but the current tax mood of the country gives little encouragement to the assumption of new fiscal obligations by either the national or state governments.

Given the politically divided nature of most large urban areas, attempts to resolve the disparity dilemma at the metropolitan level merely add to its ramifications because local units invariably resort to devices that tend to generate more, rather than less, inequity. This level, moreover, does not provide a promising arena for effecting any significant measure of income redistribution either through the service delivery system or direct subsidies to the less advantaged. Political pressures are too close and too intense for local policymakers to embark on any such course even if they were so inclined. There is little likelihood, for example, that the wealthy school district will voluntarily share its affluence with its poor neighbor or that the suburban community will voluntarily impose additional taxes on itself to aid the central city poor. It is only at more remote levels of government that political settlements involving the removal or diminution of inequities in the provision of services to metropolitan residents can be negotiated.

Chapter 9
Housing, Desegregation, and Crime

For several decades the "urban crisis" has been a common theme in much of the writing on American cities. There has been little consistency, however, in defining the nature of this crisis or identifying its major features. Some observers see it primarily in terms of physical problems, such as sprawl, blight, and environmental abuse; others view it essentially as a failure of governmental and social institutions to function in the public interest; and still others regard it as a matter of social disorganization resulting mostly from poverty and racial discrimination. From an individual perspective the crisis is likely to be defined on the basis of personal experiences and values. To the elderly householder residing in a high crime area, the dominant urban problem may be one of insecurity; to the low-income family, inadequate housing; to the young black, unemployment; to the rush hour commuter, traffic congestion; to the public official, lack of fiscal resources.

Views of what is wrong with urban society vary widely among analysts. Conservative writers, such as Edward Banfield, argue that the problems of the cities are greatly exaggerated. Pointing out that most urban dwellers live more comfortably and conveniently than ever before, they maintain that it is rising expectations, not actual conditions, that are the source of current dissatisfaction. For Banfield, the one troublesome issue is the existence of an "irresponsible" lower class that can only be contained and kept in check rather than reformed.[1] *Time* magazine in a 1977 cover story echoed this theme.

> Behind its [the ghetto's] crumbling walls lives a large group of people who are more intractable, more socially alien, and more hostile than almost anyone had imagined. These are the unreachables: the American underclass. . . . Its members are victims and victimizers in the cul-

[1]Edward C. Banfield, *The Unheavenly City Revisited*, rev. ed., (Boston: Little Brown, 1974).

ture of the street hustle, the quick fix, the ripoff and, not least, violent crime.[2]

As described by *Time*, this underclass produces a highly disproportionate number of the nation's juvenile delinquents, school dropouts, drug addicts, and welfare recipients, as well as much of the adult crime, family disruption, and urban decay. If Banfield is correct, government can do little to remedy this situation and social programs such as the war on poverty and model cities are exercises in futility. The best that can be done, so the argument goes, is to let nature take its evolutionary course. Eventually poverty will diminish (and with it much social disorganization) as the rate of production increases and population growth stabilizes. The answer, in short, lies in economics, not governmental intervention.

Considerable pessimism also exists among liberal writers. Many of them, disillusioned by the seeming failure of the social legislation of the 1960s, are resigned to lesser remedies and more reliance on action by the private sector. Those at the extreme end of the liberal spectrum maintain that the structure of our institutions must be radically changed before we can cope effectively with the critical problems of society. Economists of this persuasion hold that the difficulties confronting us are the inevitable consequences of a capitalistic system which generates income inequalities among the people, severely damages the environment in the scramble for profits, and creates social classes with contradictory interests.[3] Complementing this view is the "conspiracy" theory that an undefined group, commonly referred to as "The Establishment," controls the basic institutions of American society and deliberately refrains from promoting significant social change because its members profit from existing arrangements.

Such veteran analysts of the urban scene as political scientist Norton Long and planner George Sternlieb also tend to take a dim view of the prospects of the older central cities. Long refers to them as "Indian reservations" for the poor, the deviant, and the federally subsized bureaucracy that manages them.[4] Sternlieb in a similar vein conceptualizes them as "sandboxes," places where the alien-

[2]*Time* (August 29, 1977): 13. Reprinted by permission from *Time*, The Weekly Newsmagazine; Copyright Time Inc., 1977.

[3]A series of essays reflecting this view is contained in David M. Gordon (ed.), *Problems in Political Economy: An Urban Perspective*, 2d ed., (Lexington, Mass.: Heath, 1977).

[4]Norton Long, "The City as Reservation," *The Public Interest*, No. 25 (Fall 1971): 21–38.

ated and those left behind with limited skills can be kept occupied (with the aid of government programs), while the rest of society gets on with its main task—business.[5] Not all observers, however, are as pessimistic. Economists Alexander Ganz and Thomas O'Brien, for example, call the older cities "dynamos," the chief beneficiaries of the transformation from a manufacturing to a service-dominated economy.[6] They see this change leading to the revitalization of core areas to accommodate the new and expanding service industries.

Public officials engaged in the daily task of coping with urban "crises," whatever their nature and magnitude, become impatient with academic critics who question the usefulness of governmental intervention or call for major restructuring of societal institutions. They point to gains as well as to failures and see more cause for hope than for despair. Contrary to the dogma fashionable among critics that all social programs are little more than placebos, they maintain that many partial but genuine successes in ameliorating urban problems have been achieved.[7]

Underlying these views of the urban scene is the question of whether we possess the knowledge to solve the difficulties of our cities. Insofar as most physical problems are concerned, such as pollution and transportation, the technology exists or can be developed given sufficient resources, but economic considerations deter its full application. Similarly, in the case of some social issues— health care would be one—political and economic realities rather than lack of know-how are the principal impediments. On the other hand, in the matter of complex social problems such as crime and racism the causes are not entirely understood and no firm body of knowledge exists to guide policymakers in dealing with them. The conflicting testimony often given by social scientists to congressional committees and other governmental bodies (and to the courts as in school desegregation cases) points up this deficiency.

Other chapters in this book deal with various service and organizational difficulties confronting metropolitan areas. Here we focus on three social issues that are of great concern to many communities and to the nation as a whole—housing for the poor, school

[5]George Sternlieb, "The City as Sandbox," *The Public Interest*, No. 25 (Fall 1971): 14–20.
[6]Alexander Ganz and Thomas O'Brien, "The City: Sandbox, Reservation, or Dynamo?" *Public Policy* 21 (1973): 120–126. This more optimistic view is questioned in Franklin J. James, Jr., "The City: Sandbox, Reservation, or Dynamo? A Reply," *Public Policy* 22 (1974): 39–51.
[7]See in this connection Eli Ginzberg and Robert Solow, "Some Lessons of the 1960s," *The Public Interest*, No. 34 (Winter 1974): 211–220.

desegregation, and crime. Other social and economic problems exist—every person has a favored list—but none is currently more divisive or disruptive in its impact on the populous SMSAs than these. Like most urban difficulties, all levels of public authority are involved in their solution but, like the others also, the immediate burden and the consequences of the actions taken fall directly on the local community.

HOUSING THE URBAN POOR

Until the last half-century the task of providing housing for the nation's diverse population, both rich and poor, was left to the private market. Government's role in this field was limited to the enactment and enforcement of such regulatory measures as local building codes and zoning ordinances. Today all aspects of the housing market are affected directly or indirectly by public action. The national government, now the key policymaker in this sector of the economy, first became involved during the depression years of the 1930s. Its intervention took two forms: restructuring the home financing system through creation of the Federal Housing Administration (FHA) to insure mortgages and subsidizing the construction of low-cost shelter for the poor. The adoption of these measures brought to an abrupt end the long tradition of exclusive private responsibility for the provision of housing.[8]

The Wagner–Steagall Act of 1937, hailed by President Franklin D. Roosevelt as inaugurating "a new era in the economic and social life of America," authorized loans and subsidies to local housing authorities (LHAs) for construction of low-cost dwelling units.[9] In 1949 Congress passed a more comprehensive bill (that included urban renewal as well as public housing) with the expressed goal of assuring "a decent home and a suitable living environment for every American family." Since then a broad range of measures has been enacted. These include various programs subsidizing below-market interest rates for the poor, direct loans at low interest rates to nonprofit sponsors of rental housing for the elderly, incentives to builders to encourage the streamlining of production

---

[8]For a critical evaluation of federal housing policy see Arthur P. Solomon, *Housing the Urban Poor* (Cambridge, Mass.: MIT Press, 1974). A more journalistic critique of the housing industry is Martin Mayer, *The Builders* (New York: Norton, 1978).
[9]LHAs are created by municipal and county governments under state enabling legislation to develop and operate low-rent public housing projects. They usually finance the construction of such housing through the sale of long-term bonds. HUD makes annual contributions to the LHAs to pay off this indebtedness.

methods (known as "Operation Breakthrough"), grants to home-owners for rehabilitation, and rent supplements.

Historically, the housing stock in the United States has under-gone successive reuse by occupants of ever lower income levels. The construction of new homes for the more affluent released dwelling units for those less well off. Thus as middle- and upper-class households moved outward from the centers of the larger cities during the early years of the century, they left behind homes that were taken over by working-class families, many of them European immigrants. By the late 1940s the process of succession was once more in full swing as white families (including many blue collar) left the inner-city neighborhoods for suburbia. With their departure large numbers of older dwelling units again filtered down to accommodate the new wave of urban migrants (this time southern blacks and to a lesser extent rural whites and Hispanics).[10]

As indicated by the population decline in the large core cities during the last several decades, the inflow of newcomers—even though large in number—has not been sufficient to offset fully the white outmigration. Normally under such circumstances the sur-plus supply of older homes on the market would lead to a drop in price (rent), thereby making more units available to the poorer fam-ilies. This process, however, has not occurred. Because of the low income of many inner-city households, old but habitable properties have not been able to command rents high enough to maintain them at an adequate level of repair. As a consequence, large quanti-ties of housing have filtered out of the market through landowner abandonment instead of trickling down to low-income urbanites.[11]

Government programs to provide shelter for the poor have par-alleled the operations of the private market since the 1930s. How successful these efforts have been is a matter of dispute. Observers generally agree that the nation's housing stock has improved over the last two decades but they differ as to the extent. Critics charge that as many as 6 to 9 million families remain poorly sheltered.[12]

[10]The drawbacks to this process are analyzed in Frank S. Kristof, "Federal Housing Policies: Subsidized Production, Filtrations, and Objectives," *Land Economics* 48 (November 1972): 309–320 and 49 (May 1973): 163–174. Studies also indicate that filtering down cannot be relied on exclusively to meet the housing needs of disad-vantaged families. See Gary Sands, "Housing Turnover: Assessing Its Relevance to Public Policy," *Journal of the American Institute of Planners* 42 (October 1976): 419–426.

[11]Glenn A. Clayton, "Abandoned," *Journal of Housing* 28 (June 1971): 271–276 and Report of the Comptroller General of the U.S., *Housing Abandonment* (Washington, D.C., August 10, 1978).

[12]See David Birch, *America's Housing Needs: 1970 to 1980* (Cambridge, Mass.: Joint Center for Urban Studies, MIT and Harvard, December 1973).

Government officials, on the other hand, point to the progress that has been made in enlarging the supply of housing and upgrading its quality. They cite census figures showing that the number of occupied dwelling units within SMSAs increased from 38 million in 1960 to 54 million in 1976, whereas the proportion lacking plumbing facilities declined from 13 percent to less than 2 percent.[13] What statistics of this nature fail to show, however, is the condition of the neighborhoods in which the housing is situated. Structures may meet physical standards but the families living in them are not properly sheltered if the dwellings are located in unsafe and deteriorating neighborhoods—as in the case, for instance, with most public housing.

Public Housing

The housing efforts of the national government in behalf of economically disadvantaged families and the elderly poor fall into two major categories: public housing (owned and operated by local government agencies) and housing assistance (programs to aid low-income families in the private market).[14] From the passage of the first housing bill in 1937 to the early 1950s, shelter accommodations for the poor were provided exclusively through public housing. Since that time federal policy has deemphasized the government's role as a supplier and landlord and has increasingly relied on various assistance programs.

Public housing, plagued by problems and massive failures, fell into disfavor during the 1960s. The program was suspended by the Nixon administration in 1973 and only recently revived on a small scale. At the time of its suspension there were 1.1 million units under management or available for occupancy, a total that has increased only slightly since then (Table 9.1). At least one project is located in every city (except San Diego) with a population of more than 250,000. A few, such as the ill-fated Pruitt-Igoe complex in St. Louis, have been demolished or stand unoccupied because of their state of disrepair. Most, however, continue to function, providing

---

[13]Most of the gain (70 percent) in the number of dwelling units occurred outside the central municipalities. Many of the larger and older cities experienced substantial losses.

[14]Projects that are developed, owned, and operated by LHAs are commonly referred to as "conventional public housing." Those constructed by private developers under a contract in which LHAs agree to purchase the units on completion are known as "turnkey projects." Also, LHAs in a limited number of instances lease property from private owners and make the units available to poor families.

Table 9.1 NUMBER OF PUBLIC HOUSING UNITS,* 1960–1978 (in thousands)

YEAR	NUMBER OF FAMILY UNITS	NUMBER OF UNITS FOR ELDERLY	TOTAL
1960	477.1	1.1	478.2
1965	568.7	36.2	604.9
1970	750.1	143.4	893.5
1975	892.1	288.3	1,180.4
1977	892.7	295.0	1,187.7
1978	898.3	299.7	1,198.0

*Under management or available for occupancy.
SOURCE: U.S. Bureau of the Census, *Statistical Abstract of the United States, 1979,* (Washington, D.C., 1979), p. 790.

shelter for slightly over 1 percent of the nation's households.

Public housing has been the subject of controversy from its inception. Real estate and home building interests have assailed it as socialistic; liberals have faulted it as insensitive to human values; and the General Accounting Office has charged it with gross mismanagement. Housing for the poor in federal programs has always been subordinate to other goals, and this fact has contributed greatly to the difficulties it has experienced. The purpose of the 1937 legislation, for example, was to stimulate the depressed economy and to clean up slums as well as provide accommodations for those unable to afford private housing. The 1949 act also combined the goals of supplying low-income housing with renovating blighted urban areas. The problem also rests in part on the federal requirement (in effect until 1969) that the operating and maintenance expenses of the projects be financed through rents. For such a policy to be viable, the tenants must be able to pay a level of rent sufficiently high to cover these costs, a situation that prevailed only during the first two decades of the program.

Public housing fared well during its early years. Its tenants were mostly working-class poor who could not find reasonably priced accommodations in the tight private market. These were the people that many members of Congress had in mind when they passed the first housing act in 1937: the temporary but upwardly mobile poor (referred to by some cynics as the "deserving poor") who had at least some income and could afford to pay a modest rent. Government-provided housing, in brief, was intended as temporary shelter for those who, once their economic status improved, would move on to the private market. Consistent with this philosophy, the projects were managed as business enterprises, with realistic rent levels, careful screening of prospective tenants, and adequate maintenance.

By the mid-1950s the character of public housing had begun to change. The migration of rural blacks and whites into the cities, coupled with the demolition of thousands of slum area homes by urban renewal and expressway projects, intensified the problem of providing shelter for the very poor. The 1949 act, in anticipation of this situation, had lowered the income eligibility requirements and specified that displaced families were to be given priority in obtaining public housing accommodations.[15] Within slightly more than a decade occupancy of family units changed from the poor who held jobs most of the time to the chronically unemployed, from stable families to problem households, and from racially mixed to almost totally black. The systematic removal of occupants who reached the income ceiling and the exodus of others who became alarmed at the changes drained the projects of the most successful tenants and their stabilizing influence. And because the newcomers were unable to pay sufficient rent to cover operating and maintenance costs—many of them, in fact, had no income other than what they received from welfare programs or social security—physical deterioration was extensive, to the point where many units and even entire projects became uninhabitable.

Both the national government and local housing authorities have made various efforts over the last decade to improve public housing conditions. Congress in 1969 belatedly authorized subsidies for operating expenditures (under provisions of the law the Department of Housing and Urban Development pays all costs exceeding 25 percent of the tenants' income), and in more recent years it has appropriated funds for major physical improvements. It has also placed a ban on the further construction of high rise buildings for families with children.[16] Local housing authorities, urged by HUD, have sought to secure a better economic mix of tenants (with little success) and have experimented with various devices, such as tenant management, to encourage occupants to become involved in making the projects more habitable. Despite these efforts, public housing remains a serious problem. Many buildings continue to be poorly maintained; more than 400 projects are in financial trouble; and crime, vandalism, and drugs plague the large complexes.

---

[15]The redirection was prompted also by complaints from building and real estate interests that public housing was interfering with private enterprise.
[16]High rise construction was dictated by costs, with little consideration given to its impact on tenant families. The low rise projects with fewer units have generally proved more successful.

Housing Assistance

The urban violence of the mid-1960s sparked the enactment of new programs to better the condition of the poor. One such measure was the Housing and Redevelopment Act of 1968 which President Lyndon Johnson exuberantly called "the most farsighted, the most comprehensive, the most massive housing program in all American history." The act set a ten-year goal of 6 million new and rehabilitated dwelling units for low- and moderate-income families. This goal was to be met primarily through the private market by means of interest subsidies to developers and home purchasers. (As Table 9.2 shows, achievement fell far short of this goal.) Section 235 of the legislation authorized mortgage interest subsidies for low- and moderate-income families to enable them to buy dwelling units.[17] The notion of enabling the poor to become homeowners was advanced by Senator Charles Percy of Illinois and others who argued that such ownership would motivate disadvantaged families by giving them a stake in the community. The companion program, Section 236, provided similar interest subsidies to organizations and private developers to encourage the building of rental apartments for low-income families.

Both the 235 and 236 programs were successful in producing housing although not to the extent anticipated in the 1968 law.[18] They were not successful, however, in reaching the families most in need because the income eligibility requirements all but ruled out the very poor. By 1972 both programs were in deep trouble due largely to mismanagement and fraud as well as to economic conditions. Families that purchased rehabilitated homes, presumably approved by HUD inspectors, were often faced with major repairs within a short time after occupancy. Already operating with marginal resources, such households seldom had the means to replace a worn out heating system or leaky roof, not to mention defective plumbing and wiring. Many of the homes also were located in older and less stable neighborhoods already in various stages of deterioration, thus making it virtually impossible to obtain improvement loans. The common reaction of the new owners who found themselves in this situation was simply to abandon the property, leaving HUD to take over as guarantor of the mortgage loan.

The 236 program also failed to function as intended. High maintenance costs, inflation, and economic recession caused many

---

[17]In the 235 program, as originally adopted, HUD insured the mortgages and made payments to the lenders to reduce the interest to 1 percent.
[18]Approximately 260,000 units were built or rehabilitated under Section 235 and 545,000 under Section 236.

Table 9.2 SUBSIDIZED HOUSING TARGETS AND ACHIEVEMENTS
UNDER 1968 ACT,* JULY 1, 1969 TO JUNE 30, 1978 (units in thousands)

TWELVE MONTHS ENDING JUNE 30	NEW CONSTRUCTION	REHABILITATION	TOTAL NEW AND REHABILITATION
Total ten years			
Target	5000	1000	6000
Actual	2370	325	2695
1978—Target	585	137	722
Actual (Estimated)	226	34	260
1977—Target	595	135	730
Actual	195	27	222
1976—Target	595	135	730
Actual	118	19	137
1975—Target	595	135	730
Actual	111	17	128
1974—Target	600	130	730
Actual	141	30	171
1973—Target	595	100	695
Actual	289	42	331
1972—Target	575	75	650
Actual	388	41	429
1971—Target	445	60	505
Actual	440	42	483
1970—Target	260	50	310
Actual	293	34	328
1969—Target	155	43	198
Actual	165	37	202

*Achievements do not include use of the existing housing inventory without reha-
bilitation to meet the housing needs of low- and moderate-income families, an option not considered in the 1968 target. Over 570,000 such units were added to the
subsidized inventory from 1969 to 1977.
SOURCE: Department of Housing and Urban Development, *1977 Statistical Year
Book* (Washington, D.C., 1979), p. 341.

of the sponsoring organizations and developers to default on their
mortgage payments. As a result of foreclosures in the two programs,
HUD became the nation's largest "slum landlord," holding over
200,000 units at one time. The failures brought an end to 236 rental
housing, but the 235 ownership program has managed to survive
although in a modified and sharply reduced form.

The Housing and Community Development Act of 1974 marks
the latest major change in federal housing policy, shifting the emphasis from the supply to the demand side of the equation (earlier
efforts had concentrated primarily on making units available to low-

income families either through public housing or subsidies to the private market).[19] Section 8 of the legislation authorizes rent subsidies for low- and moderate-income families in privately owned units. Under the law, LHAs certify eligible parties and contract directly with owners to pay the difference between fair market rental and 25 percent of the tenant's income. The tenants in turn execute separate leases with the landlords to pay their share of the rent. At the end of 1978, more than 700,000 households were being accommodated under this program, over 85 percent of them living in preexisting dwelling units (Table 9.3).

The Section 8 program, although socially and theoretically more desirable than public housing, has several drawbacks. First, because of opposition to government-subsidized housing in the more affluent neighborhoods and suburbs, many of the units made available for occupancy are located in the less desirable, and often deteriorating, areas of the inner city. Second, the program generally does not reach the very poor or those with large families because landlords are reluctant to accept them as tenants. Third, there is a question of equity for only a small percentage of the potentially eligible households can be accommodated.[20] Finally, no subsidized rent program such as Section 8 can alone meet the shelter needs of the disadvantaged. Under most market conditions it is necessary to provide complementary assistance on the supply side to

Table 9.3 HOUSING AVAILABLE UNDER SECTION 8 (as of December 31, 1978)

SOURCE OF HOUSING	NUMBER OF FAMILY UNITS	NUMBER OF ELDERLY UNITS	TOTAL UNITS
New construction	22,429	64,830	87,259
Rehabilitation	6,259	7,994	14,253
Existing housing (without rehab.)	441,461	173,747	615,208
Total	470,149	246,571	716,720

SOURCE: Department of Housing and Urban Development, *1978 Statistical Year Book* (Washington, D.C., 1980), p. 227.

[19]Several of the earlier programs, particularly rent supplements, were designed to stimulate the private market by increasing the demand ability of low-income families but the major subsidies went to the developers.

[20]Generally, a household may qualify for Section 8 assistance if its income does not exceed 80 percent of the median family income in the metropolitan area. It is estimated that under this formula 40 percent of the nation's 76 million households are eligible for Section 8 aid. By the early 1980s the federal government had already obligated itself to pay more than $200 billion in rent subsidies to landlords and developers over the next 40 years.

encourage the construction of new housing or the rehabilitation of marginal units.[21]

Displacement

During the urban renewal period of the 1950s and 1960s many thousands of families were uprooted from their homes by slum clearance projects and expressway construction. The days of massive clearance and extensive highway building in urban areas have ended but the problem of displacement—although of less magnitude—remains. It impacts most heavily on the poor, racial minorities, and the elderly, but middle-class urbanites are now also being affected. Displacement is precipitated in several ways: by housing rehabilitation and neighborhood upgrading; by the conversion of rental apartments to condominiums and co-ops; and by disinvestment.

Improvement of the dwelling units and physical amenities of a neighborhood normally increases the value of its housing and results in higher rents. Thus when gentrification occurs, when public funds are invested in locality improvements, when private developers and landlords engage in extensive rehabilitation efforts aided by federal subsidies, the rental (or sales) prices of dwelling units in the area rise beyond the means of many of the original residents. Householders in this situation have little alternative but to move elsewhere. Revitalization activities under urban development action grants (UDAG) also cause some displacement but mostly of small, low-profit businesses that are unable to remain in the project area because of higher rents.

National legislation and administrative mandates require local authorities to provide relocation assistance, including financial aid, to families and businesses displaced under federal programs. The evidence is mixed as to the success of such efforts. Some community development agencies have established reasonably effective procedures for this purpose, but many—reminiscent of the poor relocation record under urban renewal—tend to give low priority to the problem. The Section 8 rental subsidy (by increasing the ability of lower income residents to pay rent) provides a tool for preventing displacement of the less affluent or facilitating their relocation in adequate housing. However, because of the limited funds available for this program, only a small minority of potentially eligible families can be accommodated.

[21]See Jill Khadduri, Katharine Lyall, and Raymond Struyk, "Welfare Reform and Housing Assistance: A National Policy Debate," *Journal of the American Institute of Planners* 44 (January 1978): 2–12.

Unlike gentrification and neighborhood rehabilitation which involve the displacement largely of low-income families, condominium (and co-op) conversion affects mainly middle-class households. A recent phenomenon, the practice has been prompted by the relatively low rate of return on rental property, tax advantages, and the opportunity to make a quick profit. When conversion takes place the tenants are given the option of purchasing their unit or getting out. Many households, even if they have sufficient money to meet the required down payment, are compelled to move because the monthly costs of a condominium (including mortgage payments, taxes, and maintenance fees) are usually much higher than the previous rent. Due to widespread conversions—an estimated 100,000 to 200,000 annually since 1977—moderate rental apartments are now in extremely short supply in many SMSAs. Alarmed at the trend and pressed by tenant groups, local authorities have sought to slow down the conversion rush by means of moratoriums and other measures (bills for this purpose have also been introduced in state legislatures and Congress), but it is questionable how far government can intervene without violating the constitutional rights of property owners.

In contrast to urban revitalization, disinvestment in a declining neighborhood or section of the city takes the form of landlord abandonment, demolition without replacement of housing stock, business withdrawal, and the withholding of public funds for physical and service improvements. Disinvestment of this type inevitably leads to displacement because deteriorating conditions and the loss of dwelling units through nonmaintenance compel residents to seek shelter accommodations elsewhere. Families are displaced, in other words, not by newcomers of higher economic status but by abandonment and blight. This form of displacement is far more widespread in many of the older central cities—witness the large tracts of vacant land and boarded-up buildings—than that caused by gentrification and neighborhood upgrading.

Housing Discrimination

Racial discrimination in the provision of housing for urban dwellers is a long-standing practice in the United States, condoned until recent decades by both the courts and the political arms of government. The favorite device employed for many years was the restrictive covenant by which homeowners (and subdividers) bound themselves and their successors from selling or renting the property to blacks, Jews, or other minorities. It is estimated that at one time 80 percent of the land in Chicago was proscribed against black occupancy. As late as 1947 the FHA Underwriting Manual recommended the use of restrictive covenants, warning that "the presence of incompatible groups in a neighborhood tends to lessen or destroy owner-occupancy appeal." And up to 1950 the official code of the National Association of Real Estate Boards prohibited its affiliates from introducing into a neighborhood "members of any race or nationality" whose presence would be detrimental to property values. Suits to overthrow restrictive covenants were unsuccessful until 1948 when the Supreme Court (in *Shelley* v. *Kraemer*) ruled that they were unenforceable through governmental processes.[22]

Since 1960 both the legislative and judicial branches of the national government have taken steps against housing discrimination. In 1968 Congress passed the Fair Housing Act prohibiting landlords from discriminating against prospective tenants on the basis of race. (A large number of municipalities also adopted "open housing" ordinances, the equivalent of the national legislation.) Federal courts have invalidated suburban zoning and other subterfuges designed to keep out low-income families. Some state tribunals have also intervened, the New Jersey Supreme Court, for example, holding that localities must assume their fair share of housing for the region's poor.[23]

Under the community development block grant program inaugurated in 1974, local governments are required to formulate a housing assistance plan as a prerequisite to receiving funds. HUD in recent years began to employ this provision to pressure suburban governments, insisting that they not only develop such plans but also move ahead with their implementation through use of the Section 8 program. Its efforts in this regard have met with vigorous protests from local units. Although most of them have proceeded at least formally, if grudgingly, to comply with the demand, a few have simply forfeited the money; others have sought to meet the requirement by providing the less controversial housing for the elderly poor; and some have brought legal action to compel HUD to release the funds.

The problem of providing low-income shelter is further compounded by the racial issue. Public housing projects in the 1930s and 1940s were predominantly white (up to 1950 about two-thirds

---

[22]334 U.S. 1 (1948).
[23]*Southern Burlington County NAACP* v. *Township of Mount Laurel,* 67 New Jersey 151; certiorari to the U.S. Supreme Court denied, 423 U.S. 808 (1975). In this case the court struck down a zoning ordinance permitting only single-family detached dwellings in the township.

of the units were occupied by white families). By the 1960s, however, most of the complexes, except those for the elderly, were virtually all black and geographically segregated in the inner city. The Chicago situation is typical. In 1966 a number of black tenants sued the Chicago Housing Authority for excluding public housing from white neighborhoods. Before the case ended ten years later, HUD and the suburban municipalities had been brought into the litigation. The evidence showed that (1) all new units built after 1950 were located in black neighborhoods of the city and (2) the Housing Authority was operating 60 projects containing 29,000 units with 99.5 percent black occupancy and 4 projects (constructed prior to 1950) with a tenancy 95 percent white. After a long series of legal maneuverings, the case was finally concluded in 1976 when the Supreme Court in *Hills* v. *Gautreaux* sustained a lower court order directing an areawide solution.[24]

Hailed as a landmark decision by some housing advocates and as a meaningless gesture by others, *Hills* v. *Gautreaux* actually took away as much as it gave. On the one hand, it held that district courts could order HUD to provide low-income dwelling units in outlying areas; but on the other, it emphasized that the decision "would neither force suburbs to submit public housing projects to HUD nor displace the rights and powers accorded local governments under federal or state housing statutes or existing land use laws [zoning]."[25] HUD's ability to open up suburban areas to low-rent accommodations is, in short, severely limited. It cannot provide public housing because the initiative for such projects must come from local authorities. It can contract directly with private developers and organizations to supply Section 8 units, but these parties are experiencing considerable difficulty in obtaining suitable sites because of local opposition and zoning regulations.[26] And although HUD can withhold community development block grant (CDBG)

[24]425 U.S. 284 (1976).

[25]For a critique of the decision see Irving Welfeld, "The Courts and Desegregated Housing: The Meaning (if any) of the Gautreaux Case," *The Public Interest*, No. 45 (Fall 1976): 123–135.

[26]Through a series of zoning decisions, the Supreme Court has restricted the ability of housing advocates to use the judiciary as a means of remedying residential segregation. See, for instance, *Village of Arlington Heights* v. *Metro Housing Development Corporation*, 429 U.S. 252 (1977), in which the Court upheld zoning that had the effect of keeping out a subsidized housing development. Also, in this connection see Kenneth Pearlman, "The Closing Door: The Supreme Court and Residential Segregation," *Journal of the American Institute of Planners* 40 (April 1978): 160–169.

funds to noncooperative communities, political realities circumscribe the extent to which this strategy may be employed.

The location of significant amounts of subsidized dwelling units (except for the elderly) outside the ghetto areas of the inner city or the deteriorating sections of the older suburbs is unlikely in the foreseeable future. The stigma that became attached to the large public housing projects during the last two decades has seriously prejudiced the move to provide shelter for poor families in better neighborhoods. Many whites associate all housing assistance programs, including Section 8, with lower class blacks and welfare recipients, "the undeserving poor," who are perceived as carriers of social disorganization, crime, and blight. Efforts to provide low-income units in more desirable locations have also been hindered by the white backlash against further changes in race relations.

National housing policy has theoretically been committed to two goals—providing adequate shelter for the poor and desegregating residential dwelling patterns. Action to implement these objectives has been ambivalent. Originally, the emphasis was solely on supplying housing with no attention given to desegregation. Later HUD began to prod central city LHAs to furnish low-income accommodations outside the ghettos on "scattered sites." Attempts to implement this approach have drawn strong public reaction and intensified the resistance of middle-class neighborhoods to government-assisted housing. Bowing to this fact, HUD announced in late 1980 that it would permit large cities to build subsidized housing in predominantly black neighborhoods. As if to illustrate the goal dilemma, however, a federal district court in St. Louis—almost simultaneously with the announcement—ordered HUD and the city to submit plans to ensure that Section 8 and other housing assistance programs in the St. Louis area support efforts to desegregate the central city schools.

SCHOOL DESEGREGATION

Desegregating the public schools—which today means busing to most people—continues to dominate educational issues. Even in communities where large-scale transportation of students to achieve racial balance has been in operation for several years, many residents remain unreconciled although resigned to it. Nationally, as revealed in a 1978 Harris poll, 85 percent of white and 43 percent of black Americans oppose busing. Violence over the issue has subsided although sporadic outbreaks still occur (as in Boston in late 1979). Congress and the states periodically pass antibusing legislation, and many white parents continue to turn to suburban systems or private schools for educating their children. Litigation over desegregation plans has been long and costly and shows few signs of abating (about 20 cases reach the Supreme Court each year, with at least several of them being accepted for review).

Despite the intensive efforts of the last quarter century, four of every ten black children still attend schools in which they constitute 90 percent or more of the student body.[27] The South, long the target of criticism over its racial policies, is the most integrated, with less than one of each four black children in predominantly black schools. This situation contrasts with that of the Midwest where the proportion is well above one-half. In 1974, a year for which statistics are available, 45 percent of black students in 11 southern states attended schools where white pupils constituted a majority. This proportion was twice as high as that in 32 northern and western states (Table 9.4). Placing students of different races in the same school, however, is not always the end of educational discrimination. Data assembled by researchers indicate that in many southern districts (and the same is true in some school systems outside the South) disproportionate numbers of black students are expelled, suspended, placed in classes for the retarded, or retained in grade. They also show that blacks are frequently underrepresented on the faculties of the integrated schools.[28]

Busing, the common remedy in desegregation efforts, is not an end in itself; it is only a means to secure the constitutional rights of

Table 9.4 BLACKS AS PERCENT OF TOTAL ENROLLMENT IN PUBLIC SCHOOLS BY SPECIFIED AREAS, 1970 TO 1974

RACIAL COMPOSITION OF SCHOOLS	1970 (%)	1974	
		32 NORTHERN AND WESTERN STATES (%)	11 SOUTHERN STATES (%)
Under 50% black	33	23	45
50 to 100% black	67	77	55
95 to 100% black	38	50	20
100% black	14	14	8

SOURCE: U.S. Bureau of the Census, *Statistical Abstract of the United States, 1978* (Washington, D.C., 1978), p. 151.

[27]Nationally, black children comprise 15 percent of the total public school enrollment.

[28]This problem is discussed in Charles S. Bullock, "Defiance of the Law: School Discrimination Before and After Desegregation," *Urban Education* 11 (October 1976): 239–262.

those in the society who are suffering racial discrimination in the nation's public schools. As the Supreme Court made clear in the 1954 landmark case of *Brown* v. *Board of Education of Topeka,* educational equality under the law means desegregated education.[29] This right is no longer questioned; only the means of achieving it are in dispute. Beyond the constitutional issue, however, is the unanswered question whether interracial mixture in urban school systems leads to improvement in the scholastic achievement of children from minority and disadvantaged families. Another uncertainty is the extent to which desegregation efforts precipitate the "flight" of white families out of the central city, thereby lessening the opportunities for attaining racial balance in the public schools.

The Legal Battle

From the time of the *Brown* decision (which overturned the "separate but equal" doctrine first enunciated in 1896 in *Plessy* v. *Ferguson*)[30] to the present, the courts have been the most active public instrumentalities in the desegregation of public schools. Holding *de jure* segregation (that caused by state law or official action) unconstitutional, the Supreme Court in the *Brown* case ordered desegregation to proceed "with all deliberate speed." In doing so it gave federal district courts broad and flexible discretion in devising remedies. The ruling struck a decisive legal blow at the dual school systems of the South but its impact was minimal for some time. More than ten years after it was rendered, the overwhelming majority of black children in the South were still attending all-black schools.

While southern officials were using all sorts of legal ploys to prevent or delay integration, *de facto* segregation (that which results primarily from residential housing patterns or other factors outside government control) was increasing rapidly in the rest of the country. By the mid-1960s three of every four black children in 75 of the nation's most populous cities were attending schools with enrollments of 90 percent or more black. Not until 1973 did a case involving a nonsouthern school district reach the Supreme Court. It had been generally assumed that whatever racial imbalance existed in the schools outside the South was *de facto* and not the result of deliberate action by state governments or local boards of education.

The violence surrounding the civil rights militancy of the 1960s underscored the slowness with which legal gains were being

[29]347 U.S. 438 (1954).
[30]163 U.S. 537 (1896).

translated into political realities and set off a flurry of legislative and judicial action. Television and press coverage exposing the violent measures adopted by some southern officials in reaction to the demonstrations and sit-ins shocked many Americans and paved the way for passage of the Civil Rights Act of 1964. That portion of the law relating to education authorized the Justice Department to bring suit against any school district that maintained a segregated system and barred federal grants to such a unit under any aid program. The Supreme Court also responded by ordering a speedup in the desegregation process. In a 1968 case it ruled that school officials must act "aggressively, affirmatively, and immediately" to eliminate all vestiges of the dual system;[31] and in 1971 it explicitly approved busing as an accepted means of desegregation, rejecting arguments that such a remedy would destroy the traditional neighborhood school. Chief Justice Warren Burger, speaking for a unanimous court, stated, "All things being equal, with no history of discrimination, it might be desirable to assign pupils to schools nearest their home. But all things are not equal in a system that has been deliberately constructed and maintained to enforce racial segregation."[32]

The Supreme Court in 1973 directed its attention for the first time to the question of segregation in schools outside the South. Upholding the plan ordered for the Denver system, the Court ruled that school districts can be required to desegregate if they have engaged in intentional acts of segregation, such as might be involved in demarcating attendance boundaries, locating school sites, and assigning teachers.[33] *De jure* segregation, in other words, must be found before judicial intervention is warranted. Justice William Douglas, although concurring in the result, argued that no constitutional difference exists between *de jure* and *de facto* segregation, a position the Court continues to reject.

Subsequent to the Denver case, the question of proving intent to discriminate on the part of school officials became a critical issue. Civil rights lawyers maintained that intention can be demonstrated by the impact or effect of a policy. If, for example, the redrawing of attendance boundaries by a school board is followed by increased racial imbalance in the system, the result constitutes proof of intent. The Supreme Court refused to accept this argument, holding that effect is not sufficient grounds to show discrimi-

[31]*Green* v. *County Board of New Kent County*, 391 U.S. 430 (1968).
[32]*Swann* v. *Charlotte-Mecklenberg Board of Education*, 402 U.S. 554 (1971).
[33]*Keyes* v. *School District No. 1, Denver*, 413 U.S. 189 (1973).

natory purpose.[34] However, in two recent decisions involving sweeping desegregation plans for the cities of Columbus and Dayton, Ohio, the Court appears to have softened its position on this point. In upholding the busing remedies imposed by lower federal tribunals, it ruled that policies adopted by school boards that have the "foreseeable consequences" of affecting minorities differently from whites are "relevant evidence to prove the ultimate fact, forbidden purpose."[35] Although the opinions stated that the district courts had remained within the requirements of the earlier decision as to intent (more than consequences were shown), the weight they gave to impact was a welcome indication to desegregation proponents.

The important question now remaining is whether the Supreme Court is moving toward the acceptance of interdistrict or areawide remedies. The justices rejected such an approach in 1974 by a five-to-four vote when they overruled a district court order to bus children between the Detroit city school system and 53 suburban districts. The right to integrated education gave way in that case to the right of local communities to manage their own school affairs. "No single tradition in public education," the majority said, "is more deeply rooted than local autonomy."[36]

The Detroit decision, however, did not completely close the door to a metropolitan solution. The opinion, written by Chief Justice Burger, stated that

> an interdistrict remedy might be in order where the racially discriminatory acts of one or more school districts caused racial segregation in an adjacent district, or where district lines have been deliberately drawn on the basis of race . . . [but] without an interdistrict violation and interdistrict effect, there is no constitutional wrong calling for an interdistrict remedy.

Subsequent to the Detroit ruling the Court left standing a lower court order to consolidate the heavily black school system of Wilmington, Delaware, with 11 suburban districts. In this instance clear evidence existed to show that state and local officials had acted deliberately to keep the city schools black and those in the outlying areas white. (The Delaware legislature in 1968 had mandated the state board of education to proceed with school district

---

[34]The ruling as to intent was made in an employment discrimination suit. See *Washington* v. *Davis*, 426 U.S. 229 (1976).
[35]*Columbus Board of Education* v. *Penick*, 61 Lawyers Ed. (2d) 666 (1979). *Dayton Board of Education* v. *Brinkman*, 61 Lawyers Ed. (2d) 720 (1979).
[36]*Milliken* v. *Bradley*, 418 U.S. 717 (1974).

consolidation throughout the state but had specifically excluded the Wilmington system from such action.)[37]

Intradistrict remedies were possible in both the Dayton and Columbus cases because black students constituted a minority of the enrollment. The situation is different in most of the large cities of the Northeast and Midwest (and a growing number in the South and West) where the student bodies are overwhelmingly black or Hispanic. (Minority pupils outnumber whites in all but 8 of the nation's 29 most populous municipalities.) In these instances the fate of desegregation efforts hinges on the Court's future posture toward metropolitan solutions. It is difficult to conceive of any way of designing meaningful intradistrict plans for school systems such as Washington, D.C. where 95 percent of the enrollment is black, or Detroit where the proportion is 80 percent. As one educator has said, "There simply are not enough white children in the central city to go around." (This reality was underscored when classes began in St. Louis City in September 1980 under a court-ordered desegregation plan. With enrollment in the system over three-fourths black, less than one-third of the students were assigned to integrated schools.) Although recent rulings indicate some receptivity on the part of the high tribunal to consider evidence of suburban discrimination in fashioning desegregation remedies, it is doubtful that the court will commit itself to an areawide approach in the foreseeable future. This unlikelihood is reinforced by the current social and political climate, the advent of an administration strongly opposed to forced busing, and the probability that one or two of the more liberal justices on the Court may soon retire.

Educational Consequences

Integrated education is advanced not only as a constitutional right but also as a means of raising the scholastic achievement of minority group children and promoting racial harmony. What can be said about the fulfillment of these expectations after more than a decade of large-scale efforts to desegregate the public schools? The answer is "very little," given the mixed and even contradictory findings and the bitter disputes among researchers.[38]

---

[37]*Evans v. Buchanan*, 423 U.S. 963 (1975). The Supreme Court continues to be unreceptive to cross-district remedies as evidenced in its recent (May 1980) decision affirming (without a written opinion) a lower court's rejection of a plan to bus children between Atlanta's predominantly black school system and nine surrounding suburban districts. *Armour v. Nix*, 40 CCH Supreme Court Bulletin, B2121.

[38]A recent Rand Corporation paper also reached this conclusion. See Anthony Pascal, "What Do We Know About School Desegregation?" (Santa Monica, Calif.: Rand Corporation, January 1977).

The first extensive study of the effects of various programs and remedies, including integration, on educational achievement was conducted in the late 1960s by sociologist James S. Coleman for the United States Civil Rights Commission. Based on a nationwide survey of public schools, Coleman concluded that organizational efforts at educational improvement, such as reduced class size and special or compensatory programs, exercise little independent effect on pupil progress when family background factors are statistically controlled. According to his findings, the major favorable influence on the academic accomplishment of minority group students is the presence in the classroom of higher achieving children from more advantaged backgrounds. Although the gain is incremental and not nearly sufficient to overcome the disabilities of poor environment, the effects are greater than those resulting from compensatory programs.[39] Whether the improvement is due to class or racial mixture, these findings would argue for school desegregation as the only means of bringing minority children into contact with significant numbers of advantaged students.

Coleman has since backed away from his original findings, saying that it is now clear that desegregation does not, by itself, produce important educational benefits. His views in this respect, as well as his negative attitude on busing, have been challenged vigorously by some social scientists and supported just as stoutly by others.[40] Sharp as the differences are among researchers on these questions, some broad areas of congruence are indicated in their findings.

1. Modest gains in educational achievements, whatever their cause, are made by minority students in integrated schools.
2. Black children progress more in schools that are predominantly but not overwhelmingly white.
3. The academic progress of white pupils does not suffer as a result of desegregation.
4. Greater interracial contact has little effect on the self-esteem or self-confidence of minority students.[41]

[39]James S. Coleman et al., *Equality of Educational Opportunity* (Washington, D.C., 1968). The Coleman study, as virtually all research in this field, measures academic progress by standardized achievement tests administered on a national basis. Many objections have been raised as to the validity of these tests, particularly as they apply to children from minority and disadvantaged families.

[40]See James S. Coleman, Sara Kelly, and John Moore, "Trends in School Desegregation, 1968–73" (Washington, D.C.: The Urban Institute, 1975). This paper and Coleman's public statements touched off the debate.

[41]For a collection of studies on the accomplishments of school desegregation see Ray C. Rist (ed.), *Desegregated Schools: Appraisals of an American Experiment* (New York: Academic Press, 1979).

One of the major arguments for desegregated schools is that they promote social harmony by providing opportunity for extended contact between children of different races. Here again the evidence is unclear. Available research suggests that little change of a positive nature takes place in the attitudes of either black or white youngsters toward each other or in their friendship patterns. Some studies indicate that schools with nearly equal percentages of minority and white students have the highest levels of tension. Others purport to show that desegregation, particularly when accomplished by mandatory busing, heightens racial solidarity rather than promotes interracial harmony. These findings, however, are highly tentative and tell us little about the long-range effects of exposure to those of a different race during a child's school years.[42]

"White Flight"

One of the major objections raised by critics of court-ordered busing as a means of desegregation is that it precipitates a decline of white enrollment in the central city public schools. (This is now the position of Coleman who originally appeared to support busing.) Many white families, it is maintained, either exit to suburban districts or send their children to private schools. White students who remain in the system are predominantly from lower income families that do not have the resources to flee or afford private institutions. As a consequence, one of the major purposes of integration— to mix not only the races but also social classes—is defeated.[43]

Integration proponents deny that white flight of any significant degree is caused by desegregation. Pointing to the fact that the white exodus from the central cities began long before school busing was an issue, they cite other factors—particularly the drop in the birthrate—as the major contributors to the decline in the number of white students.[44] The key question is what the enrollment

[42]A discussion of how desegregation efforts have affected blacks is contained in Robert L. Gill, "The Impact of United States Supreme Court Decisions on the Lives of Black People, 1950–1974," *Negro Educational Review* 27 (April 1976): 92–115.

[43]Coleman's position is supported, among others, by Diane Ravitch, "The 'White Flight' Controversy," *The Public Interest*, No. 51 (September 1978): 135–149; and David W. Armor, *White Flight, Demographic Transition, and the Future of School Desegregation* (Santa Monica, Calif.: Rand Corporation, 1978). The Armor study indicates that white flight is strongest in districts that have more than 20 percent minority students and available white suburban systems.

[44]Those who maintain this position include Christine Rossell, "School Desegregation and White Flight," *Political Science Quarterly* 90 (Winter 1975): 675–695 and Thomas F. Pettigrew and Robert L. Green, "School Desegregation in Large Cities: A Critique of the Coleman 'White Flight' Thesis," *Harvard Educational Review* 46 (February 1976): 1–53.

situation would be in the absence of court-mandated busing. Research findings give no definitive answer. No one disputes the fact that white enrollment has been declining in virtually all school systems, not only in the central cities but in the white suburban districts as well. The problem is to separate out the losses attributable to busing from those due to fewer births and the outmigration of white families for reasons unrelated to forced desegregation.[45]

Although the debate among social scientists over the busing issue has been heated and acrimonious, certain tentative conclusions can be drawn from the research.

1. Some white flight does occur as a result of busing but its magnitude remains a matter of dispute.
2. The greatest incidence of flight is during the initial year of implementing the court order.
3. The decline in white enrollment is materially increased if the desegregation plan involves the busing of white children to black schools.
4. The white flight is greatest in areas where suburban school systems are readily available; it is the least in consolidated city–county districts, such as Louisville and Nashville, where families would have to move long distances to avoid integrated education.[46]
5. The white flight is likely to be more extensive, the higher the percentage of black children in the central city system.

The decline of white enrollment in the central city schools, no matter what its cause, is a development of grave concern. It would be tragic to return to a dual system—one for whites and the other for blacks (and Hispanics)—as a number of the large metropolitan areas are coming dangerously close to doing. Obviously, the goal of integrated education cannot be achieved in a system that is predominantly black or Hispanic. Nor can the mixture of social classes in school settings be attained if only the children from disadvantaged families, regardless of race, are left in the central city district.

---

[45]For a general overview and analysis of the busing problem see Gary Orfield, *Must We Bus? Segregated Schools and the National Policy* (Washington, D.C.: The Brookings Institution, 1978).

[46]For a study showing that busing did not trigger white flight from a consolidated city–county district see J. Dennis Lord and John C. Catau, "School Desegregation, Busing, and Suburban Migration," *Urban Education* 11 (October 1976): 275–294. To the same effect is Michael Giles, Everett Cataldo, and Douglas Gatlin, "White Flight and Percent Black: The Tipping Point Reexamined," *Social Science Quarterly* 56 (June 1975): 85–92.

URBAN CRIME

One of the nation's most acute social problems is the rising crime rate. Survey after survey shows that lawlessness and the fear of crime rank high on the list of urban issues for most Americans. Public concern is reflected in the large quantities of protective devices bought for home and personal safety (guns, watchdogs, burglar alarms, mace); in the neighborhood "crime watches" and citizen patrols that have been organized in every region of the country; and in the intensification of demands for harsher treatment of lawbreakers. It is also evident in the rapid growth of private security forces, the refusal of taxicab drivers to enter certain neighborhoods, the buses that carry no change, the bumper stickers that read "Support Your Local Police," and the huge sums spent by law enforcement agencies on new anticrime weapons and techniques.

The total cost of crime is immense, although its precise magnitude is unknown.[47] It is estimated, for example, that well over $1 billion annually is lost in automobile thefts, $150 million in robberies, and more than $500 million in residential burglaries. Dollar figures cannot measure the trauma and personal suffering associated with criminal activity, particularly the 20,000 murders, 75,000 rapes, and 850,000 cases of aggravated assault that occur each year. Nor can they reveal the deterring effects that urban crime has on the revitalization of inner-city neighborhoods. Areas within a community that suffer from high crime rates are not likely to attract investments by households or business enterprises no matter what governmental incentives are offered.

The Johnson Administration, prompted by growing national concern, launched a "war on crime" at almost the same time that it inaugurated the "war on poverty." In the conceptual framework of the "Great Society," the problem of lawlessness was not separable from that of poverty. The major thrust of the Johnson programs was aimed at what many experts consider the root causes of crime: poverty, unemployment, and racial discrimination. The Nixon Administration also placed a high priority on fighting lawlessness, but it conceived the problem as primarily one of law enforcement rather than social pathology. Nixon's views had been made known during the 1968 presidential campaign when he took a "get tough" law-and-order stance, pledging to reduce crime by strengthening the nation's police forces and stopping the coddling of criminals. Both

---

[47]The Joint Economic Committee of Congress estimated that the total cost of crime in 1977, including outlays for maintaining the criminal justice system, was $125 billion.

the Johnson and the Nixon wars failed. Today, chastened by the lack of success, many criminologists and law enforcement officials have lowered their expectations in searching for new ways to reduce the incidence of criminal activity.

The Extent of Crime

According to the *Uniform Crime Reports* compiled by the Federal Bureau of Investigation, the rate of serious crime rose from 3680 violations per 100,000 inhabitants in 1969 to 5522 in 1979, an increase of 50 percent. Violent crimes (murder, rape, robbery, and aggravated assault) went up 63 percent during this period and property crimes (burglary, larceny, and automobile theft), nearly 50 percent (Table 9.5). These figures indicate that crime has increased at a substantially faster rate than the growth in population.

The highest degree of lawlessness is found in the large urban centers where the opportunities are greatest and the chances of apprehension least. As Table 9.6 shows, the crime index (which is based on the serious offenses previously listed) is approximately twice as high in cities above 250,000 as in those below 10,000. The higher incidence of crime in the larger urban areas, moreover, occurs in all seven classes of serious offenses listed by the FBI. The difference is particularly great in the case of robbery, where the rate in SMSAs as a whole is almost 5 times that of the smaller nonmetropolitan cities and towns and over 12 times the rural average (Table 9.7). However, the incidence of crime in these less populous areas has also taken a sharp turn upward as people and industry have moved into places outside SMSAs.

Table 9.5   CRIME INDEX, 1969 TO 1979 (rate per 100,000 inhabitants)

YEAR	CRIME INDEX TOTAL	VIOLENT CRIMES	PROPERTY CRIMES
1969	3680.0	328.7	3351.3
1970	3984.5	363.5	3621.0
1971	4164.7	396.0	3768.8
1972	3961.4	401.0	3560.4
1973	4154.4	417.4	3737.0
1974	4850.4	461.1	4389.3
1975	5281.7	481.5	4800.2
1976	5266.4	459.6	4806.8
1977	5055.1	466.6	4588.4
1978	5109.3	486.9	4622.4
1979	5521.5	535.5	4986.0

SOURCE: Federal Bureau of Investigation, *FBI Uniform Crime Reports, 1979* (Washington, D.C., 1980), p. 41.

Table 9.6 CRIME RATE BY CITY SIZE GROUP, 1979

POPULATION SIZE	TOTAL NUMBER OF SERIOUS CRIMES (IN THOUSANDS)	CRIME INDEX (NUMBER PER 100,000 INHABITANTS)
Under 10,000	951	4323
10,000 to 25,000	1192	4954
25,000 to 50,000	1254	5860
50,000 to 100,000	1292	6629
100,000 to 250,000	1225	7742
250,000 to 500,000	1043	9007
500,000 to 1 million	1079	8688
Over 1 million	1402	7929

SOURCE: Federal Bureau of Investigation, *FBI Uniform Crime Reports, 1979* (Washington, D.C., 1980), pp. 163–164.

The suburbs, long considered bastions of safety, have likewise been plagued by an increasing amount of burglaries, drug abuse, vandalism, and even robberies and rapes. The incidence of criminal activity is higher in the older communities situated within the inner ring but is beginning to rise in the outlying areas as well. Regionally, the greatest increases are taking place in the rapidly growing metropolises of the sunbelt states where industrialization is imposing its social costs along with its economic benefits. The central cities of the Northeast and Midwest, on the other hand, have been experiencing smaller rises, reflecting in part declining densities and population losses.

National crime statistics contained in the *FBI Uniform Crime Reports* must be viewed with two cautions in mind. First, the compilations are based on the counts of "actual offenses known" sent to the Bureau by some 11,000 law enforcement agencies. The reliability of the data therefore depends on the accuracy with which these

Table 9.7 CRIME RATE BY AREA, 1979 (rate per 100,000 inhabitants)

CRIME INDEX OFFENSES	TOTAL U.S.	SMSAs	CITIES OUTSIDE SMSAs	RURAL
Murder	9.7	10.9	5.7	7.4
Rape	34.5	41.1	18.3	15.1
Robbery	212.1	276.2	57.9	22.1
Aggravated assault	279.1	312.5	248.0	142.8
Burglary	1499.1	1708.8	1134.4	770.8
Larceny-theft	2988.4	3353.1	3218.0	1072.2
Motor vehicle theft	498.5	610.6	266.3	137.1

SOURCE: Federal Bureau of Investigation, *FBI Uniform Crime Reports, 1979* (Washington, D.C., 1980), p. 40.

many units record and report crimes (the FBI has made a concerted effort in recent years to upgrade reporting procedures). Second, the statistics greatly underrepresent the amount of criminal activity because they reflect only offenses reported to the police by victims; and as surveys show, more than two-thirds of all unlawful acts go unreported. Persons who fail to report a crime give as their principal reason that they feel nothing can or will be done about it.[48]

As is apparent, the way local police agencies count offenses or the extent to which the public reports crime can significantly affect the FBI tabulations. It is possible (as some criminologists contend) that the *actual* rate of crime nationally has remained relatively stable during the last decade, whereas the *recorded* rate has soared because of more complete reporting.[49] The reality probably lies somewhere between these extremes. But whether or not the incidence of crime has risen, citizen fear of it—as polls show—has grown considerably.[50] In the perception of most urbanites, lawlessness has greatly increased, posing a serious threat to the security of their person and property.

Organized Crime

Organized crime has long flourished in the United States. This type of activity involves the operation of illegal enterprises by a hierarchically structured group. Labeled variously by such terms as the Mafia, the mob, or the syndicate, the organization (or group of organizations) controls a large part of illegal gambling, commercialized prostitution, narcotics distribution, and the numbers game in urban areas. It has infiltrated certain labor unions and is now heavily involved in legitimate businesses (including restaurants, hotels, vending machine operations, and even banks), using the huge profits reaped from its illicit activities to move into these fields.

Although organized crime reaches up to the state and national echelons of the political sphere, its widest penetration has been at the local level. Evidence as to the extent to which public officials are involved is fragmentary and sketchy, but the instances that periodically come to light indicate the gravity of the problem. The

[48]Since 1973 victimization surveys based on representative samplings have been carried out for the Law Enforcement Assistance Administration (LEAA) by the Bureau of the Census. The surveys are designed to measure the extent to which city residents and commercial establishments are the objects of serious crime.

[49]On crime statistics generally see Suzanne de Lesseps, "Crime Reduction: Reality or Illusion," *Editorial Research Reports* 11 (July 15, 1977): 539–556.

[50]See, for example, U.S. Department of Justice, LEAA, *Boston: Public Attitudes About Crime* (Washington, D.C., June 1979).

American Bar Association has stated that the largest single factor in the breakdown of law enforcement dealing with organized crime "is the corruption and connivance of public officials;" and a presidential commission has observed that the mob flourishes only where it has corrupted government personnel.

Examples of the influence of the underworld in local affairs are numerous. Hugh Addonizio, elected mayor of Newark in 1962 with the support of known mobsters, was later convicted of 66 counts of extortion and acceptance of kickbacks while in office. In 1972 Mitchell Schweitzer, a New York City judge, retired in the face of allegations that he had accepted a bribe to impose a light sentence on a defendant with syndicate ties. A legislative committee found at the time that defendants in the New York City courts who were known to be associated with organized crime had their cases dismissed or won acquittal five times as often as other accused individuals. Only recently two top aides of the Chicago mayor resigned under charges that they had caused the demotion of several police officers who were enforcing the antigambling laws too vigorously.

Currently there is evidence of the existence of organized crime in 25 metropolitan areas, including Buffalo, Chicago, Detroit, Denver, Kansas City, Los Angeles, and San Francisco. This activity, moreover, is not confined to the large cities. It touches such communities as Madison, Wisconsin, Rockford, Illinois, and Pueblo, Colorado. John Gardiner's study of political corruption in Wincanton (a pseudonym given to a city of 75,000 population) shows how the syndicate, in more extreme cases, becomes closely intertwined with the political system. The payoff by mob leaders to control law enforcement action against commercialized gambling and prostitution ranged from turkeys and bottles of liquor for the beat officers to several thousand dollars a month for key public officials, including the mayor and police chief. Campaign contributions and other forms of favors were also commonplace means of gaining influence over the local government.[51]

The costs to the public resulting from organized crime are enormous. An investigating committee estimated that in California alone such operations are costing the state's citizens over $6 billion annually. Films such as *The Godfather* have glamorized the underworld crime empire but have failed to convey a sense of how dam-

---

[51]"Wincanton: The Politics of Corruption," in William Chambliss (ed.), *Crime and the Legal Process* (New York: McGraw-Hill, 1969), pp. 103–135. Also see Donald R. Cressey, *Theft of the Nation: The Structure and Operations of Organized Crime in America* (New York: Harper & Row, 1969).

aging and dangerous this type of activity is to the well-being of American communities. Like the shortage of oil, many people continue to doubt the seriousness of the problem.

Causes of Crime

Many theories have been advanced to explain the causes of crime and its apparent increase. Some commentators on social mores attribute lawlessness to a breakdown in family life; others, to the emphasis that Americans place on material goods; and still others, to permissiveness and a general weakening of the moral and religious fiber of the nation. Criminologists and policymakers are similarly split among several competing theories about the nature of crime; and empirical findings as to its causes are indeterminate. As one criminal justice planner has observed, the most important conclusion to be drawn from the numerous theories and studies is that we know little about crime and less about how to reduce it.[52]

Theories about the causes of crime and the remedies for it fall basically into three categories. One (blame the individual) views lawlessness as a failure of character and stresses punitive action against offenders as the most effective deterrent. A second (blame society) sees crime as essentially a product of social factors such as poverty, unemployment, racial discrimination, and deprived childhood. The cure, in this conception, is to restructure society so as to eliminate conditions that breed wrongdoing. A third (blame both the individual and society) regards crime as the product of many human and environmental factors that defy precise analysis. To those who subscribe to multicausal theories, the remedy is by no means certain but embodies elements of both reform and punishment.

Empirical studies suggest that at the individual level criminality is associated with factors such as poverty, a repressive environment, and the disruption of family life and at the community level with demographic variables such as density and age.[53] Some research indicates that population density and residential overcrowding are the strongest predictors of crime rates. According to these findings, the greater the density (people per square mile) and the

[52]William Drake, "The Local Official and Criminal Justice Policy," *Nation's Cities* 13 (December 1975): 27.
[53]Wesley G. Skogan, "The Changing Distribution of Big-City Crime," *Urban Affairs Quarterly* 13 (September 1977): 33–49.

Table 9.8 CITY ARRESTS FOR SERIOUS CRIMES, BY AGE, 1979

TYPE OF CRIME	PERCENTAGE UNDER 18	PERCENTAGE UNDER 21	PERCENTAGE UNDER 25
Murder & manslaughter	10.1	25.5	45.9
Rape	17.2	35.1	57.0
Robbery	33.0	55.6	74.9
Aggravated assault	16.8	32.5	51.4
Burglary	50.0	69.8	83.0
Larceny–theft	41.5	58.3	71.2
Motor vehicle theft	50.6	70.1	83.1
Recap: Violent crimes	21.9	40.0	59.3
Property crimes	44.5	62.2	75.2
Total all serious crimes	40.4	57.9	72.1

SOURCE: Federal Bureau of Investigation, *FBI Uniform Crime Reports, 1979* (Washington, D.C., 1980), p. 206.

more overcrowding in households (persons per room), the higher a community's crime rate is likely to be.[54] Other research concludes that sociocultural factors, such as sex and race, are the more important indicators. Males, to mention one obvious relationship, are the predominant offenders, accounting for approximately 85 percent of all individuals arrested for serious crimes in urban areas (lawlessness, however, has risen among women in recent years). Racially, the crime rate is higher among blacks and Hispanics than among whites but so also is the incidence of poverty, unemployment, and other social factors commonly associated with unlawful behavior.

Many authorities point out that the crime rate is a reflection of the age structure of a community.[55] Young people, as arrest records show, are responsible for a disproportionate share of the nation's crime. Those between the ages of 14 and 21, although they constituted only about one-seventh of the nation's urban population, accounted for nearly three-fifths of all city arrests for serious offenses in 1979 (Table 9.8). The rate started to show appreciable gains in the 1960s as the baby boom that followed World War II began to swell the ranks of the teenagers. Criminologists now predict that

[54]John McCarthy, Omer Galle, and William Zimmern, "Population Density, Social Structure, and Interpersonal Violence," *American Behavioral Scientist* 18 (July/August 1975): 771–791.

[55]Kyriacos Markides and G. S. Tracy, "The Effect of the Age Structure of a Stationary Population on Crime Rates," *Journal of Criminal Law and Criminology* 67 (September 1976): 351–355. A study finding no significant relation between age composition and crime rates in suburban communities is John Stahura, C. Ronald Huff, and Brent Smith, "Crime in the Suburbs?" *Urban Affairs Quarterly* 15 (March 1980): 291–316.

the rate will decrease in the 1980s on the basis of change in age composition alone. They anticipate such a decline as the proportion of young people in the population falls because of the lower birthrate of the last two decades. According to some experts, however, the high level of lawlessness in American society is so pervasive that it has become a permanent feature of the national scene.

Obviously, no local government or combination of local units can hope to eradicate crime or cope with all forms of social disorganization. No public agency can eliminate prejudice or the cultural factors that build up resentment and frustration by depriving certain groups of the opportunity to participate fully in the society. Nor can government assume the role of the family, church, and other private institutions that inculcate and reinforce socially conforming behavior. Inadequate and inefficient law enforcement by municipal and county authorities may contribute to increased crime rates, but in the final analysis the problem transcends the metropolitan community and its governmental system.

THE PROBLEM MAZE

Urban and metropolitan communities differ widely in the severity of their social and economic problems. Not all of them are confronted with crises; many, in fact, are relatively free of serious difficulties. Some, such as Houston and Fort Worth, enjoy budget surpluses, whereas others, such as New York and Cleveland, struggle to avert bankruptcy. Some problems are more pervasive than others; drug use, for instance, is common to central cities and suburbs alike, no matter what their size or social composition. Others, such as traffic congestion and pollution, differ in their intensity from area to area. Generally, the larger municipalities are plagued with the more critical problems, but many nonmetropolitan cities and towns have suffered severe declines with the thinning out of the rural population. Only in the last decade or so have the fortunes of some of these improved.

Two of the problems considered in this chapter—inadequate housing for low-income families and crime—are found in varying degrees in most urban areas. The third—school desegregation—is less universal and confined to those communities with significant racial minorities. Certain broad observations, however, can be made from an examination of the three:

1. Strong ideological differences exist as to how to deal with the problems, and the experts themselves are in disagreement as to both causes and remedies.

2. National programs are almost impossible to tailor to fit the divergent needs of individual localities because of the wide variances among metropolitan areas and the conditions within them.
3. Race relations is an enduring dilemma that underlies and hinders efforts at urban problem solving.
4. Local governments (including school districts) generally lack the organizational and technical capabilities to deal effectively with major social issues, a deficiency not remedied by federal fiscal assistance.
5. No adequate mechanism exists to coordinate the policy and programmatic endeavors of federal, state, and local public agencies in coping with urban-based difficulties.
6. The courts are the key policymakers in school desegregation, and their decisions also impact on matters pertaining to low-income housing and crime control.
7. The approach to the problems of the cities has shifted from grandiose plans and large-scale projects—the war on poverty and model cities are examples—to less ambitious programs of an incremental nature. The changed attitude was well expressed by the commissioner of Baltimore's Department of Housing and Community Development when he said that Americans must learn "how to think small again."

The intense activism of the 1960s and early 1970s has given way to pessimism on the part of some social reformers and to a lowering of sights on the part of others. The movement to secure better housing for the poor and disadvantaged has looked to both the legislative chambers and the judiciary whereas attempts to desegregate the schools have relied almost wholly on the courts. In both issues the basic support has come from the federal bureaucracy (HUD, Department of Justice, Department of Education) and from civil rights and public advocacy groups. The championing of these objectives by a broader segment of the populace waned in recent years as disillusionment with reform efforts set in among many liberals. The critical question is whether the conservative trend now dominant in American politics and society in general can prevail without precipitating renewed social disruption.

Chapter 10
The Delivery of Services

The local governments of SMSAs perform a myriad of functions. They protect life and property, maintain order, move traffic, supply water, dispose of waste, educate children, enforce building and housing codes, guard public health, operate recreational and cultural facilities, and regulate a broad spectrum of activities. The magnitude of these tasks is graphically portrayed by Wallace Sayre and Herbert Kaufman in their study of New York City.

> It takes two billion gallons of pure water a day, removal of four million tons of refuse, thousands of miles of sewers and huge sewage disposal plants, regulation and inspection of food and food handlers and processes, disease control to prevent epidemics, air pollution control to prevent the poisoning of the atmosphere, and a fire-fighting organization capable of handling every kind of blaze from small house fires to immense conflagrations in tenements, skyscrapers, industrial structures, and the waterfront. The basic physical and biological requirements of urban life are either provided or guaranteed by government.[1]

New York, of course, is exceptional. No other American metropolis approaches it in population size or density. Yet the local units in each of the nation's SMSAs have similar responsibilities for providing essential services to their residents; only the scale of the task is smaller and the problems less overwhelming. Urbanites everywhere look to their grass-roots governments to maintain an environment in which they can pursue their daily activities with safety and convenience. No matter what the size of a metropolitan area, the attractiveness of this environment is dependent in part on the quality of public services and the organizational structure for delivering them.

The governmental pattern of SMSAs, as described in Chapter 4, is largely a patchwork product that has evolved over time in response to the needs of an expanding population. In the process all

[1]Wallace Sayre and Herbert Kaufman, *Governing New York City* (New York: Russell Sage Foundation, 1960), p. 34.

levels and types of government have become involved in the service delivery system, often in seemingly irrational fashion. The present chapter sorts out some of these developments, first reviewing several attempts to formulate a conceptual basis or set of criteria for determining the assignment of public functions within urban areas. It then examines six major services: transportation, environmental protection and its related aspects, law enforcement, fire protection, parks and recreation, and health.

FUNCTIONAL ASSIGNMENTS

No widely accepted theory exists to direct the placement of functional responsibilities among governmental units in SMSAs. Whether particular urban services should be administered by municipalities, counties, regional authorities, or states has been determined in piecemeal fashion more by political and historical factors than by any carefully thought out policy of allocation. Attempts to formulate a rational basis for assigning functions have produced various sets of standards and objectives, but each such formulation gives rise to difficulties in its application.

The test most commonly proposed for the placement of service tasks in SMSAs rests on the distinction between local and areawide activities. The first are those that can be adequately provided by municipalities or other units having jurisdiction over only a portion of an urban area; the second are those that require execution of a wider territorial scope. The area approach is said to be necessary when the function is of such nature that it transcends municipal, and in some cases, county boundaries (such as the control of air and water pollution), or is economically unfeasible when performed individually by local units (such as the operation of a sewage disposal plant). Reformers seeking to reorganize the governmental structure of metropolitan areas in the 1950s and 1960s relied on this distinction in formulating their proposals.

The Advisory Commission on Intergovernmental Relations (ACIR) developed a broader set of assignment standards in 1963, pointing out that efficiency and economy are not the only goals to be sought in the distribution of service responsibilities. Along with economies of scale, it listed the minimization of spillover costs or benefits, public accountability, opportunity for citizen participation, and a balancing of needs and resources. Recognizing that governmental activities do not fit neatly into the two categories of local and areawide, the commission ranked 15 urban functions on a scale from most local to least local, based on the criteria it had formulated (Table 10.1).

Table 10.1 RANK ORDER OF URBAN FUNCTIONS FROM MOST
LOCAL TO LEAST LOCAL

	RANK	FUNCTIONS
	1	Fire protection
	2	Public education
Most local	3	Refuse collection and disposal
	4	Libraries
	5	Police
	6	Health
	7	Urban renewal
	8	Housing
	9	Parks and recreation
	10	Public welfare
	11	Hospitals and medical care facilities
	12	Transportation
Least local	13	Planning
	14	Water supply and sewage disposal
	15	Air pollution control

SOURCE: Advisory Commission on Intergovernmental Relations, *Performance of Urban Functions: Local and Areawide* (Washington D.C., 1963), pp. 9–23.

The ranking is largely subjective and, like any such listing,
elicits disagreement. Some observers view public education less
local than police and health more areawide than parks and recreation, to mention two differences. The ranking also fails to take account of the fact that many of the individual functions have both
local and areawide aspects. Police protection, for instance, can normally be handled by municipalities (assuming they are large
enough to support a professional department). Yet certain components of this service, such as communications, training, central records, and laboratory facilities, can often be furnished more efficiently and economically on a county or metropolitan basis.[2]

The ACIR in 1974 recast and amplified its original guidelines.
In their new form they call for the placement of functions in jurisdictions that can provide the particular service:

1. Most economically (at the lowest possible cost).
2. Most equitably (have adequate fiscal capacity and are large
   enough to encompass costs and benefits or spillovers).
3. With adequate political accountability (are accessible to and
   controllable by those served and offer maximum opportunity for active citizen participation).

[2]The administration of a function can also be separated from its financing. The federal or state government, for instance, may assume fiscal responsibility for a particular service, such as education or public welfare, but leave its administration in the
hands of local units.

4. Most effectively (have necessary legal and jurisdictional authority and administrative capability).[3]

Some of these criteria argue for local units to perform a given function; others point to metropolitan or state assumption of responsibility. Those that depend on continuous citizen control or popular participation for satisfactory performance—such as elementary and secondary education and social services—fall into the first category. Those that involve economies of scale, significant externalities or spillovers, fiscal equalization, and geographical adequacy—such as mass transit, community colleges and vocational schools, and waste disposal—are more appropriate to the second group.

Guidelines such as those proposed by ACIR and others are generally a mixture of economic, administrative, and political tests that often point in different directions. To achieve economies of scale may call for a governmental unit of such large size that citizen accessibility and control are limited. Conversely, the maximization of public or client participation in the performance of a service may lessen efficiency and lower administrative effectiveness. The criteria, in short, are not value neutral standards that can be objectively applied. They involve normative choices—whether, for instance, higher priority is to be placed on efficiency than public accessibility or on citizen involvement than the equalization of services. It is only through trade-offs that these various guidelines can be balanced or combined to provide direction for the placement of functions.

Some planners and social scientists, taking account of the value dimensions involved in the assignment of services, suggest a division based on the distinction between place-related and nonplace-related functions.[4] The first are those activities that directly impinge on the life-styles and amenities of individuals within a given urban space. They involve the quality of the residential environs and the security of one's person and home. Functions in this category include public education, zoning, housing code enforcement, refuse collection, neighborhood recreational facilities, and police

[3]Advisory Commission on Intergovernmental Relations, *Governmental Functions and Processes* (Washington, D.C.: February 1974). The Tri-County Local Government Commission in Portland, Oregon, formulated a set of similar criteria for its guidance in making reorganization proposals. These are summarized in *National Civic Review* 65 (July 1976): 349–350. Another list is provided in Melvin Mogulof, *Governing Metropolitan Areas* (Washington, D.C.: Urban Institute, 1971), p. 10.
[4]See Melvin M. Webber, *Explorations in Urban Structures* (Philadelphia: University of Pennsylvania Press, 1964) and Oliver Williams, *Metropolitan Political Analysis* (Philadelphia: University of Pennsylvania Press, 1971).

and fire protection. The second group relates to those services that are essential to the operation of the overall urban system but only incidentally associated with space and life-styles. Among these are transportation, pollution control, water supply, sewage disposal, and central facilities such as airports and zoos.

According to this distinction, functions that affect life-styles should be kept at a scale where meaningful resident involvement and control are possible. By so doing, it is felt that the debilitating effects of large public bureaucracies on citizen attitudes and behavior can be countered. The nonplace-related or systems functions, on the other hand, are said to warrant centralization because they help bind together the specialized but interdependent parts of the metropolis into an effective operating unit. Like the other tests, this approach to the assignment of responsibilities presents difficulties. Many services have both place and nonplace characteristics. Planning and zoning are examples. They can be used as tools for shaping the kind of locality that residents want, but they can also be employed to thwart the interests of the larger metropolitan community through exclusionary practices directed against the poor and racial minorities. A possible solution to this dilemma rests in viewing both types of functions as divisible rather than as integrated wholes. In this way assignment criteria can more appropriately be drawn on to determine which aspects of an activity should be centralized and which decentralized.

TRANSPORTATION

The transportation system of a metropolitan area involves more than the moving of people and goods. It affects virtually all aspects of community life, including the quality of the environment, the spatial location of residential and business activities, and even the degree of social interaction among various segments of the population. For more than a half-century the automobile has dominated urban transportation in the United States. Mass transit, once the principal means of conveyance in the large cities, peaked around 1920 and then began a long and sharp decline. Only recently, with the emergence of energy and environmental considerations, has the drop in ridership halted.

Some critics blame the automobile for many of the nation's urban problems. They charge it with precipitating sprawl, polluting the air, undermining the economic viability of the central city, causing congestion, and destroying the beauty and social cohesion of neighborhoods by generating unsightly expressways. Defenders of this mode of transportation are hard put to deny these charges,

Table 10.2 MOTOR VEHICLE REGISTRATION AND MILES TRAVELED,
1950–1978

YEAR	NUMBER OF PASSENGER CARS (IN MILLIONS)	NUMBER OF TRUCKS & BUSES (IN MILLIONS)	MILES TRAVELED WITHIN URBAN AREAS (IN BILLIONS)
1950	40.3	8.8	218
1960	61.7	12.2	330
1970	89.2	19.2	576
1975	106.7	26.2	728
1976	110.4	28.2	776
1978	117.1	31.9	NA

SOURCE: U.S. Bureau of the Census, *Statistical Abstract of the United States 1979*, (Washington, D.C., 1979), p. 645.

but they note that the motor vehicle has met the needs of rapid population and industrial growth and given individuals greater freedom of residential choice and considerably more mobility to pursue their cultural and recreational goals. They also point to its role in the American economy. Automotive retail sales—passenger cars, trucks, accessories, parts, repairs, and fuel—total more than $250 billion each year; and about one of every seven wage earners is employed in jobs related to motor vehicles and highway transportation.[5]

The statistics on automobile growth are staggering. In 1920, 9 million passenger cars, trucks and buses were registered in the United States; now the total exceeds 150 million. Seven of ten metropolitan households owned cars in 1960, 14 percent of them having two or more; today the overall proportion is close to 80 percent, with almost one of every three families possessing more than one vehicle. Within urban areas the street and road mileage doubled between 1950 and 1976, and motor vehicle travel jumped from 218 to 776 billion miles annually (Table 10.2).

As the number of automobiles grew, mass transit patronage steadily decreased. In 1940 public transportation carried 13 billion passengers; in 1977 the total was 7.6 billion.[6] The low point was reached in 1972 when 6.6 billion riders were recorded (Table 10.3). Since that time ridership has increased due principally to gasoline shortages and prices. During the long decline in transit usage most

[5]The enemy is not the automobile, as one writer puts it, but the long prevalent policy of putting all our transportation eggs in the motor car basket. John Jerome, *The Death of the Automobile* (New York: Norton, 1972).

[6]For a general treatment of mass transit see Martin Farris and Forrest Harding, *Passenger Transportation* (Englewood Cliffs, N.J.: Prentice-Hall, 1976).

Table 10.3 TRANSIT PASSENGER TRIPS,* 1940–1977 (in millions)

YEAR	RAIL	TROLLEY COACH	MOTOR BUS	TOTAL
1940	8,325	534	4,239	13,098
1945	12,124	1,244	9,886	23,254
1950	6,168	1,658	9,420	17,246
1960	2,313	657	6,425	9,395
1970	2,116	182	5,034	7,332
1972	1,942	130	4,495	6,567
1975	1,810	78	5,084	6,972
1977	2,251	70	5,295	7,616

*Passengers are counted each time they board a transit vehicle.
SOURCE: American Public Transit Association, *Transit Fact Book,* 1977–1978 ed. (Washington, D.C., 1979), p. 26.

private lines either went out of business or were taken over by governmental agencies. As late as 1960 there were only 54 publicly owned transportation systems; now the number is more than 450. About one-third of these account for four-fifths of all revenue, passengers, and employees in transit operations.[7]

Nationally, only about 8 percent of the workers in SMSAs ride transit facilities to get to and from their places of employment. The heaviest use occurs in the larger and more densely populated cities of the Northeast and Midwest. New York City heads the list with more than three-fifths of its resident workers traveling to their jobs on public transportation. At the other extreme are the newer sunbelt municipalities, largely a product of the automobile age. In Los Angeles less than 10 percent of its labor force uses public transit; in Houston the proportion is under 8 percent and in San Diego, below 6 percent (Table 10.4).[8]

The Federal Role

The national government has played an important role in the development of urban transportation systems. Its support of highway construction to the almost total neglect of mass transit has been a contributing factor to the spatial decentralization of metropolitan

[7]George A. Avery, "Breaking the Cycle: Regulation and Transportation Policy," *Urban Affairs Quarterly* 8 (June 1973): 424.
[8]San Francisco is the only large western city where a significant portion (about one-third) of its resident labor force uses public transportation facilities. It is also the most densely populated city in the West and the only one with a rapid rail system. The percentages in Table 10.4, it should be noted, apply only to workers living in the central city. The proportion of suburbanites who commute to work by mass transit is substantially less in most of the areas listed.

Table 10.4 PUBLIC TRANSIT USE BY WORKERS LIVING IN SELECTED CITIES, 1970

CITY	TOTAL NUMBER OF WORKERS (IN THOUSANDS)	PERCENTAGE USING PUBLIC TRANSIT	DENSITY (POPULATION PER SQUARE MILE)
New York	3,094	61.8	26,343
Boston	258	39.3	13,936
Washington, D.C.	334	37.8	12,321
Philadelphia	737	37.1	15,164
Chicago	1,336	36.2	15,126
San Francisco	317	35.7	15,764
Baltimore	343	27.0	11,568
Cleveland	277	22.1	9,893
St. Louis	223	21.3	10,167
Atlanta	204	21.3	3,779
Detroit	533	18.4	10,953
Dallas	362	10.6	3,179
Los Angeles	1,113	9.3	6,073
Houston	504	7.8	2,841
San Diego	283	5.5	2,199

SOURCE: U. S. Bureau of the Census, *Statistical Abstract of the United States, 1978* (Washington, D.C., 1978), pp. 24–25, 657.

areas. Expressway building, funded largely by federal matching grants, became the popular response to street congestion in the period following World War II. The big boost for this solution came in 1956 with the passage of the Highway Revenue Act reorienting national highway policy from an emphasis on a rural pattern of roads to a dominantly interurban system. The act provided for the construction of an interstate network of 42,500 miles, including 5,500 miles of urban freeways that skirt or penetrate virtually all cities over 50,000 population. Because the law authorized subsidies to the states and localities covering 90 percent of the costs of such roads, urban governments made little effort to find alternative solutions to their transportation problems. Over 85 percent of the interstate system is now complete and the remainder (except for segments that have been dropped because of local opposition) is expected to be finished soon.[9]

[9]The 1956 act also established the highway trust fund to be used exclusively for road building purposes. All receipts from federal taxes on gasoline, tires, and automotive parts go into this fund. During the last two decades these sources produced as much as $5 billion annually. Proponents of public transportation have waged a long battle to open up the fund to transit use. Their efforts, strongly resisted by highway interests, have met with only limited success.

The first attention given to public transportation at the national level occurred during the 1960s when Congress authorized relatively small sums of money for planning purposes and demonstration projects and created the Urban Mass Transit Administration (UMTA) within the Department of Housing and Urban Development. (UMTA has since been moved into the Department of Transportation.) The first significant aid bill for public transit was passed in 1970; it provided $10 billion over a 12-year period for capital improvements, such as the purchase of buses. The landmark legislation in this field was enacted in 1974 when Congress for the first time authorized the use of federal funds to subsidize the operating costs of mass transit systems.[10]

The states have been even more neglectful of mass transit than the national government. As late as 1971 they spent over 98 percent of their total transportation budget on highways and roads. More recently many of them have created departments of transportation with a public transit component, but most such agencies continue to be dominated by the highway bureaucracy and its allied interests. The states have had little to do with the new federal aid programs for transit purposes because these generally provide for direct grants to the agencies serving the larger urban areas. This procedure is in sharp contrast to the handling of highway funds, all of which are allocated through the states.

Policy Trends

Emphasis on the highway program has now shifted from building new roads to upgrading and maintaining existing ones. Political consensus supporting highway construction began to break down in the late 1960s as costs escalated and public opposition to the disruption of urban neighborhoods by freeways mounted.[11] In addition, increasing demands began to be made on transportation funds for major maintenance purposes. Both the interstate system and the nation's other highways are experiencing rapid deteriora-

---

[10]The last transportation bill enacted during the 1970s was the Surface Transportation Assistance Act of 1978. It authorized an expenditure of $54 billion in federal aid over a four-year period, with approximately one-fourth allocated to public transit.
[11]See in this connection David W. Jones, *Transportation in the Bay Area: A Challenge to Institutional Reform* (Berkeley: Institute of Governmental Studies, University of California, 1978).

tion (particularly around the large metropolitan areas) due to weather and heavy truck usage; and huge sums of money will be required to bring them up to standard. According to estimates of the Federal Highway Administration, 900,000 miles of road urgently need repairing or upgrading.

Federal interest in mass transit has also shifted from elaborate new subway or rapid rail projects to improving and expanding existing surface systems. During the late 1960s the need to ease traffic congestion in the large urban areas with the least environmental damage had sparked a consideration of rapid transit as a solution. The first completely new undertaking of this nature since completion of the Philadelphia subway in 1907 was the San Francisco Bay Area Rapid Transit project (BART) which went into operation in 1972.[12] That same year Washington, D.C. broke ground for its new multibillion dollar system and Atlanta and Miami followed several years later. A similar undertaking was also approved for Detroit contingent on the commitment of large business investments in the transit corridors.[13] The Department of Transportation, however, gave notice in the late 1970s that further projects of this magnitude would receive little consideration for federal funding, a position reaffirmed by the Reagan Administration.

The dwindling federal interest in conventional rail or subway transit is caused by spiraling costs and disappointment in the results of the BART experience. The tremendous outlays involved in such projects have virtually priced them out of the market. The Washington system, when completed, will exceed $5 billion and Atlanta's, well over $2 billion. (Harvard economist John Kain has calculated that the interest alone to finance Atlanta's project would cover the cost of increasing the area's bus service by 50 percent and providing it free to riders.) Equally important, BART has demonstrated the limitations of rapid transit as a solution to the transportation problem. Aside from the technical difficulties that have plagued the system from its beginning (five years after it opened BART provided its passengers with a day of free rides as a gesture of apology), its impact on traffic congestion and environmental pollution has been minimal. Ridership has been well below original projections—it handles less than 150,000 passengers on week-

---

[12]The only other American cities with rapid transit rail systems are Boston, Chicago, Cleveland, and New York.
[13]A "people mover," a scaled-down version of a rapid transit system that operates primarily in the congested central area, was also approved for several cities but its fate is now in doubt.

days—and it has drawn over half of its users from buses. Even when it is operating at full capacity, the system will reduce the vehicle miles of travel in its service area by only an estimated 3 percent.[14]

Various alternatives of a less ambitious nature than rapid transit are now receiving renewed attention and use. These include giving buses priority over other vehicular traffic through exclusive bus lanes, providing incentives for the organization of car pools, eliminating fares, upgrading services, and controlling the flow of traffic by electronic sensory devices.[15] Of these alternatives, the use of exclusive bus lanes on expressways has proved the most successful in diverting individuals from their cars. Some transportation experts argue that placing restraints on the use of automobiles is the only effective solution, but there are formidable political obstacles to this approach.[16]

No matter what alternatives are employed, the development of a more balanced transportation system in urban areas must face two often overlooked facts. First of all, even if the number of transit riders in the large cities doubled, the impact on congestion would be slight. More than 90 percent of SMSA travel would continue to be accounted for by automobiles. Second, existing mass transit facilities, including those under construction, could accommodate no more than a small fraction of urban residents now using private cars. As Brock Adams, while serving as secretary of the Department of Transportation, told an audience, "If you were to reduce the automobile traffic in United States cities by 5 percent to 10 percent, you would overwhelm any public transportation you have. You couldn't get on the bus. There aren't enough subways."[17]

[14]For evaluations of BART see Henry Bain, "Origins and Impacts of BART, the San Franciso Bay Area's Newest Travel Mode," in Joel A. Tarr (ed.), *Retrospective Technology Assessment—1976* (San Francisco: San Francisco Press, 1977) and Melvin M. Webber, "The BART Experience: What Have We Learned?" *The Public Interest,* No. 45 (Fall 1976): 79–108.

[15]Denver recently conducted (with federal funding) a one-year experiment with systemwide free fare that boosted daily ridership by almost 45 percent. See Thomas Crosby, "Free Fares: Will It Work?" *Mass Transit* 6 (May 1979): 16–17.

[16]A recent study by the New York Regional Plan Association maintains that the ultimate solution to the urban transportation problem does not lie in devising new forms of public transit but in bringing about radical changes in land use policy to minimize intrametropolitan travel. Boris S. Pushkarev and Jeffrey M. Zupan, *Public Transportation and Land Use Policy* (Bloomington: University of Indiana Press, 1977).

[17]Quoted in *Mass Transit* 6 (August 1978): 8.

Administrative Pattern

Urban transportation by any logical criteria is basically an areawide function. The network of major roads, arteries, and mass transit facilities in an SMSA must be treated as a system rather than a set of unrelated segments divided up by local governmental jurisdictions. As origin and destination surveys show, a large portion of the trips that begin in one section of a metropolitan area terminate in another, passing through the boundaries of two or more localities in the process. To facilitate this movement for efficiency and environmental reasons, one must consider the entire urbanized area as the geographic base for planning and coordinating the operation of the system.

The organizational arrangements for the operation of mass transit systems in the United States vary widely among urban areas. The predominant form of administration is by public authorities and special districts. In the Atlanta area the Metropolitan Atlanta Rapid Transit Authority was created in 1965 to design and operate a regional transit system; and in the Minneapolis–St. Paul SMSA a Metropolitan Transit Commission appointed by the Twin Cities Metropolitan Council has similar responsibilities. The Chicago metropolis has the nation's most comprehensive transit management agency, the Northeastern Illinois Regional Transportation Authority. The eight-member board, consisting of representatives from the six-county area, is charged with the planning and funding of all public transit facilities within its territorial boundaries. It contracts for services with rail and bus lines and has jurisdiction over the Chicago Transit Authority (CTA) which operates the rail transit system and most of the city's bus services. In virtually all instances the authority or special district responsible for transit is a single-purpose agency. The Seattle arrangement, however, is an exception; there the metropolitan district that operates the mass transportation system also handles sewage disposal.[18]

Municipal departments in a relatively small number of cities (including Dallas, Houston, and San Diego) operate the transit facilities; and in a few urban areas (Milwaukee is an example) the county government has taken over the function. Several states—Connecticut, Maryland, and Rhode Island—have also entered the

[18]A summary of the organizational aspects of mass transit is Institute of Public Administration, *Financing Transit: Alternatives for Local Government* (Washington, D.C.: U.S. Department of Transportation, July 1979), pp. 277–304. For arguments in support of powerful regional authorities see Tabor R. Stone, *Beyond the Automobile* (Englewood Cliffs, N.J.: Prentice-Hall, 1971), particularly pp. 130–140.

field, assuming responsibility for this service in their large population centers. Some areas with public transportation agencies, such as Chicago, also depend partly on private firms (subsidized by public funds). For the most part the long prevalent practice of carving up jurisdiction over mass transit among the individual communities in SMSAs has disappeared in the face of economic realities. Consolidation of public transportation facilities has also been stimulated by federal requirements such as the provision that the states designate a single planning body (preferably the A-95 review agency) in each of their SMSAs to coordinate requests for highway and transit assistance grants.

Although the urban transit function is now centralized in most areas, the problem of developing an integrated system is far from solved. One difficulty is that transportation planning typically remains separated from general planning. In the case of Chicago, for example, the Chicago Area Transit Study (CATS) is the designated agency for transportation planning, whereas the Northeastern Illinois Planning Commission is the official regional planning body. (Atlanta has improved on this situation by merging its transportation planning agency with the metropolitan planning commission.) Another difficulty is that transportation planning in many instances continues to be dominated by a highway bureaucracy mentality little disposed to mass transit.

Problems persist also on the operational side. Most public transit agencies are dependent on financial assistance not only from federal grants but from state and local governments as well. Fares pay on the average less than 50 percent of the operating costs (not to mention capital needs), and few transportation authorities have independent taxing powers. They must rely, moreover, on the cooperation of local and state governments in transit-related matters that lie outside their control. Streets and roads must be designed to feed the rapid transit lines, parking restrictions and lane reservations for express buses must be imposed by municipalities and counties, and area governments must take into account the impact of their land use policies on the circulatory network. To the extent that any of these elements of cooperation are lacking, the efficiency of the transportation system is impaired.

ENVIRONMENTAL PROTECTION

Once the concern mainly of conservationists such as the Sierra Club and the National Wildlife Federation, the environment became the rallying point at the end of the 1960s for a broad spectrum of groups that cut across age and ideological lines. The celebration

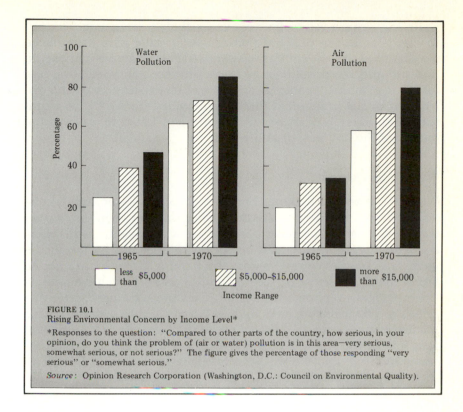

FIGURE 10.1
Rising Environmental Concern by Income Level*

*Responses to the question: "Compared to other parts of the country, how serious, in your opinion, do you think the problem of (air or water) pollution is in this area—very serious, somewhat serious, or not serious?" The figure gives the percentage of those responding "very serious" or "somewhat serious."

Source: Opinion Research Corporation (Washington, D.C.: Council on Environmental Quality).

of Earth Day in April 1970 by millions of Americans dramatically reflected the increased popular interest in environmental matters. As Figure 10.1 shows, public concern over water and air pollution rose sharply among all income groups during the latter half of the 1960s (interest was greatest among the more affluent). The drive to stop pollution and clean up the atmosphere demonstrated strong sustaining power over the last decade even though its thrust was slowed by economic considerations and oil shortages (the latter generating pressure to ease air quality standards so lower grade coal can be burned).

Various federal laws dealing with water and air pollution had been enacted as early as 1948, but by the late 1960s the inadequacy of these measures was generally conceded. (State governments had shown little activity in this field and efforts at the local level were limited chiefly to smoke abatement programs in some of the large cities.) The Environmental Policy Act of 1969 was one in a series of bills passed by Congress in response to the environmental movement. It reiterated national policy that all levels of government share the responsibility for protecting the environment. The following year, as the political parties vied to take advantage of the popular issue, President Nixon exercised his executive reorganization authority to consolidate all major programs for combating pollution in a single agency independent of existing departments. Named the Environmental Protection Agency (EPA), the new unit was given broad powers by subsequent legislation to promote the quality of the nation's air and water.

Water Management

Water management includes both the supply of water and the disposal of sewage. There is a close relationship between the two activities. No matter how large a quantity of water may be available to a community, its quality can be seriously impaired by the inadequate treatment of sewage before discharging the effluent into the area's rivers and streams. Until recent decades, local governments (the principal suppliers of water in urban areas) directed extensive efforts at providing water to their residents and industry but gave scant attention to the problem of waste discharge. In fact, until well into this century it was common practice for cities to dump untreated sewage into the watercourses that conveniently flowed by their doorsteps and from which they drew their water.

Urban areas require water for a variety of purposes including human consumption, waste disposal, manufacturing, and recreation. As in the case of other natural resources, the amount of water consumed has risen steadily. Part of the increase is due to population growth, but a substantial portion is attributable to the rise in per capita use, the result of improved living standards that have made such appliances as automatic dishwashers, washing machines, and air conditioners common household items. The concentration of industry in metropolitan areas has also caused urban water needs to soar. Industrial requirements are enormous; the manufacture of a ton of paper, for example, takes 25,000 gallons of water, and that of a ton of rayon fiber 200,000 gallons. In all, the nation's average daily consumption exceeds 300 billion gallons.

Water has been fairly abundant in most sections of the country—the West being a notable exception—but fears are now being expressed that the quantity may not be adequate to meet future needs. In the eastern cities, where intense urban and industrial concentration has caused severe pollution problems, the quality of water has until recent years been the major concern; now shortages caused by droughts and increased usage are plaguing the area. In the western states quantity remains the crucial factor. There many communities must rely on distant sources for their needed supply. San Francisco's reservoirs are located as far as 150 miles from the city, and Los Angeles and San Diego draw some of their water from as far away as 550 miles.

The problem of water purity received national attention during the 1970s when studies showed that the supply in New Orleans and a number of other large cities was unsafe for drinking. The General Accounting Office also found that only 60 of 446 water systems examined in six states met acceptable standards governing bacterial content and testing frequencies; and the EPA estimated on the basis of various findings that 8 million Americans were drinking below standard water. Responding to these studies, Congress passed the Safe Drinking Water Act of 1974 which authorizes EPA to set national standards in this field. The law gives primary authority for enforcement to the states that adopt criteria at least as strict as those established by EPA and set up adequate surveillance procedures. If a state fails to act, the EPA can bring civil suits against water suppliers to compel correction of violations.

The first intervention by the national government in the control of urban water pollution came shortly after World War II, with the passage of legislation designed to stimulate state action in this field of growing concern. When the state follow-up proved disappointing, Congress enacted the Water Pollution Control Act of 1956, authorizing the Secretary of the Interior to call conferences of public officials and industry representatives in areas where serious pollution problems existed and to institute court action when satisfactory solutions could not be worked out by voluntary means. Slightly less than a decade later Congress took further steps, with adoption of the Water Quality Act of 1965, the first law to establish national standards for water quality.

By 1970 it was evident that the existing federal–state program was totally inadequate. At best, it was only holding the line on common organic pollution of water resources, not improving conditions. Prompted by the upsurge of public interest in environmental matters, Congress in 1972 revised the earlier act and set the goal of eliminating all pollution in the United States waters by 1985. The new legislation provided that (1) states maintain interstate streams and their intrastate tributaries up to federal standards; (2) publicly owned sewage treatment plants furnish a minimum of secondary treatment by 1977 and the best waste treatment technology by 1983; (3) industrial establishments pretreat effluents before discharging them into municipal sewers; and (4) state governors designate water quality areas in their jurisdictions and certify regional agencies to do the necessary planning for meeting the pollution guidelines. Local units are to be denied federal funding for facilities not in conformity with such plans. The legislation also authorized significant fiscal aid to the states and localities: $18 billion in construction grants and $7 billion for general cleanup purposes.

Historically, the approach to water management in metropolitan areas has been fragmented and piecemeal.[19] The New York region, for example, has more than 600 independent water systems and the Chicago SMSA almost 350 separate water suppliers and well over 125 waste disposal systems. Nationwide, along with numerous municipal, county, and private providers, about 3600 special districts are concerned with supplying water to urban communities and 1600 with sewage disposal. Seldom does the multiplicity of local jurisdictions involved in these functions have any relationship to the watershed that collects the water or the drainage area that receives the sewage. This diffusion of responsibility impedes both the efficient delivery of these services and the overall attack on pollution.[20]

The arrangements for supplying water vary from area to area. In the Sacramento SMSA a large number of both public and private agencies are engaged in the task; in the Minneapolis–St. Paul metropolis, municipal ownership is dominant; in Detroit, Cleveland, and Chicago, the central city provides water on contract to some suburban communities (the common practice in such cases is for the core municipality to sell water wholesale to the neighboring jurisdictions and they in turn handle the distribution to consumers); in southern California, a metropolitan water district serves five SMSAs, including Los Angeles and San Diego.

The administrative pattern for waste disposal also varies widely. At least five different types of arrangements are in effect in metropolitan areas: (1) municipal operation of both collection and treatment facilities; (2) administration of the total sewerage system in an urban area by a special district government; (3) operation by a series of special districts; (4) various contractual combinations; and (5) municipal operation of the local collection systems and special district management of the disposal facilities.

A majority of central cities fall into the first category, operating

---

[19]See Advisory Commission on Intergovernmental Relations, *Improving Urban America: A Challenge to Federalism* (Washington, D.C., September 1976), pp. 129–138.

[20]The problem of water supply often extends beyond the boundaries of individual SMSAs. Southern California's struggle with Arizona interests over the use of Colorado River water is one example. Chicago's attempt to utilize additional water from Lake Michigan for sewage disposal purposes, an action opposed by five Great Lake states and Canada, is another.

all aspects of the sewerage function. Some older and larger suburbs likewise maintain their own systems, but most of the smaller communities do not possess adequate resources to warrant construction of treatment plants. The second method, integrated administration on an areawide basis, has not been fully achieved in any major SMSA. In St. Louis, for example, a metropolitan sewer district operates all sewerage facilities in the central city and in most of the urbanized portion of St. Louis County, but the remainder of the area is served by a variety of systems. The third approach, a profusion of special sanitary districts, is becoming less popular as costs mount and the disadvantages of maintaining many separate systems become more apparent. The fourth type, contractual arrangements, is employed with reasonable success in some metropolitan areas such as Detroit where the central city handles sewage from approximately 40 suburban communities. The fifth means, splitting responsibility between local units and a regional agency, has received increasing attention in recent years. Some areas, such as Milwaukee with its Metropolitan Sewerage Commission and Chicago with its Metropolitan Sanitary District, have long employed this device. Others, such as Seattle, are relative newcomers to the practice.

Air Quality

The purity of air as well as that of water has become a matter of growing national concern. Many millions of people reside in communities troubled by polluted air. The plight of metropolitan Los Angeles, penned between the mountains and the ocean, is a well-publicized fact, but many other large population centers such as New York, Chicago, and Philadelphia are also severely affected. The physical damages from air contamination—to horticulture, paint on homes, fabrics, and other commodities—exceed $2 billion annually, according to some sources. More important is the deleterious effects on public health. A National Academy of Science study estimates that air pollution causes 15,000 deaths and 7 million sick days each year. No less than a quarter century ago, the problem of atmospheric contamination was regarded as a soiling nuisance composed mostly of smoke. Today it represents a serious threat to human health, involving as it does a host of gaseous (and carcinogenic) particle pollutants that are difficult to disperse.

Until recent years the regulation of air contamination was left largely to the municipalities and counties. During the 1960s a majority of states adopted programs to curb pollution but few of them provided for the exercise of regulatory powers. The first national legislation in this field was passed in 1955 when Congress directed the Public Health Service to conduct research and to provide technical aid to state and local units. Although other legislation enacted during the 1960s enlarged the national role, it was the Air Quality Act of 1967 and the Clean Air Act of 1970 that marked the beginning of a broad federal attack on atmospheric contamination. These laws were the first to single out officially the automobile as the worst culprit (it accounts for well over one-half of the pollutants).

The 1970 act set May 1975 as the deadline for the states to meet automobile emission standards and mid-1977 for the overall cleanup of air contamination. It also mandated emission standards that motor vehicle manufacturers must build into their cars; consolidated control over air pollution programs in the Environmental Protection Agency; and required the states to submit air pollution control plans to EPA for approval.

By 1975 it was apparent that the dates set for compliance were unrealistic. No state had EPA-approved plans for controlling pollution in operation and automobile manufacturers and other affected parties were calling for extension of the deadlines and modification of the standards. Surveys showed that in at least 30 large cities drastic action (such as limiting traffic or shortening the work week) would be required to bring pollution levels into compliance. Reacting to this situation Congress passed the Clean Air Act Amendments of 1977 giving states until 1982 to meet the standards, with another five-year extension to 1987 for cities with severe automobile exhaust problems. The changes also authorized EPA to cut off federal funds for highway and sewerage facility construction to those states that fail to submit adequate plans for achieving air standards. (The agency took such action against California and Kentucky in 1980.) The Reagan Administration has indicated that it favors a further extension of the Clean Air Act deadlines and a review of existing regulations and standards (as well as of EPA's role and status.)

More so than in the case of most other functions, local units are helpless to protect themselves against the failure of their neighbors to control air pollution. Despite this fact, few abatement programs until recently were administered on an areawide basis. It was not until the 1960s that an appreciable number of urban areas instituted steps to remedy this situation. The measures adopted take several forms. One is to transfer the function to the county government, as in Milwaukee. A second is to create a metropolitan special district, such as operates in the San Francisco-Oakland and Boston areas. A third is to establish an interstate commission, a mechanism first employed collaboratively by New York, New Jersey, and Connecticut.

Areawide approaches, however, are still not in universal use, with many city governments continuing to administer their own abatement programs.

Solid Waste Disposal

More than 150 million tons of solid waste (garbage and trash) are generated by American households and commercial establishments annually. (If industrial matter and sewage are included, the total exceeds 4.5 billion tons a year.) Sanitary landfills where the refuse is compacted and covered with layers of earth remain the common means of disposal, but many urban areas are running out of available sites for this purpose. Of growing concern also is the disposition of hazardous residues, including various kinds of industrial materials, pesticides, and radioactive substances. A congressional subcommittee called attention to this situation in late 1979 when it reported that millions of tons of dangerous chemicals pose an imminent danger to human beings and the environment near hundreds of disposal sites around the country. Calling federal and state efforts in this field totally inadequate, the subcommittee said that the management of these wastes is the most serious environmental problem facing the nation.

There is general consensus that the solution to solid waste disposal (aside from hazardous materials) lies in large-scale recycling or resource recovery. Experiments are being conducted by some cities to run shredded garbage through separators to remove metals, glass, and papers and then burn the residue to produce steam. Few such systems, however, are in operation and as yet no environmentally and economically sound technology has been developed. The problem of disposing of the sludge from the treatment of sewage is also growing. The common means of handling this waste is to dump it into the ocean or lakes or to bury it (in a few instances it has been used to fertilize farmland). Now, however, environmental considerations rule out these methods. The solution, according to most technicians, is to convert the sludge to methane gas, but efforts in this direction are only in the experimental stage. Ironically, the cleaner the waterways are made through the treatment of effluent discharge, the more "undisposable" residue is created.

Dividing the responsibility for solid waste disposal among a host of municipalities in an SMSA, which is now the prevalent practice, is inefficient and costly. With landfill sites becoming scarcer and the need for large investments in resource recovery facilities more acute, disposal must inevitably be relegated to an areawide agency. Hazardous waste is another matter. For technical reasons, this responsibility can only rest with the state and national governments. But even these levels will encounter serious political obstacles in executing it. Colorado state officials, for example, have been unable to find a publicly acceptable site for the disposal of 70,000 cubic feet of soil contaminated with radioactive waste; and New Jersey has been stymied in its efforts to dispose of 40,000 barrels of dangerous chemicals presently stored in a warehouse located in the city of Elizabeth. It was not until late 1980, moreover, that Congress enacted legislation creating a special fund (financed mainly through taxes on chemicals) to clean up existing accumulations of toxic waste.

Noise Pollution

The latest addition to the environmental vocabulary is noise pollution, now recognized as a serious health hazard. Studies show that excessive noise can jeopardize worker safety, impair hearing ability, and cause mental stress. Chicago was the first American city to adopt an ordinance (in 1955) restricting noise emissions in relation to industrial and commercial activities. Other municipalities have followed with similar laws, but enforcement has been lax or nonexistent. At the state level little attention has been given to the problem. California passed a vehicle noise control law in 1967 but no state has enacted comprehensive legislation dealing with this hazard.

Federal involvement in noise regulation first began in 1972 with the passage of the Noise Control Act. Under the provisions of the law the Environmental Protection Agency is directed to set maximum noise levels for commercial products such as motors and air conditioners and for railroads and motor carriers. Because the Federal Aviation Administration is responsible for the regulation of aircraft noise, EPA was authorized merely to advise the agency on how to carry out this function. The 1972 act also specified that the environmental impact statement (EIS) required for all federally funded projects must consider noise and its potential effect on the environment.

Considerable dissatisfaction with the law and the manner in which it is administered has arisen since its enactment. Critics charge that EPA's noise control program enjoys little of the agency's attention or resources. They complain particularly of the lack of improvement in noise levels around airports. EPA officials deny that they are slighting the program, contending that their advice to the Federal Aviation Administration on curbing aircraft noise has gone unheeded. To remedy this latter situation, a bill was introduced in Congress in 1978 to transfer the development and policing of aircraft noise standards to EPA. The measure, however, met defeat over a provision pushed by the airlines that would have authorized federal subsidies to help defray the costs of quieter engines.

The need for regulating this environmental hazard will intensify because the noise level in urban areas continues to increase by an average of one decibel each year. Primary responsibility for controlling emissions (other than aircrafts) will likely remain with local governments even though most of them are ill equipped to handle this function (as they are in the case of most other aspects of environmental pollution).

LAW ENFORCEMENT

Law enforcement (the prevention of crime and the apprehension of violators) has been primarily a local function since the nation's founding. State patrols are a product of the present century and the Federal Bureau of Investigation was not established until 1924. Today a total of approximately 500,000 police officers are employed by municipal and county departments. Next to teachers, they constitute the largest group of public personnel at the local level. Nationwide, outlays for law enforcement now aggregate over $12 billion annually, with more than two-thirds of this amount expended by local governments. If all criminal justice activities, such as prosecution, courts, and corrections, are included, the national total exceeds $21 billion (see Figure 10.2).

Police comprise that branch of the criminal justice system that is responsible for the maintenance of social order.[21] In executing this difficult and complex function, they have considerable power and discretion—from issuing a traffic ticket or giving a warning to shooting under threatening circumstances or withholding fire. Less than one-quarter of their activities is directly concerned with crime prevention; the bulk of their time is spent in providing various services to the public, such as controlling traffic, assisting at accidents and fires, settling family disputes, furnishing information, patrolling, and acting as social counselors.[22] Because of the roles they

[21]The criminal justice system consists of a series of steps from arrest to incarceration or release through which a suspected offender passes. See John R. Snortum and Ilana Hadar (eds.), *Criminal Justice: Allies and Adversaries* (Pacific Palisades, Calif.: Palisades Publishers, 1978).

[22]See James Q. Wilson, *Varieties of Police Behavior* (Cambridge, Mass.: Harvard University Press, 1968) for an analysis of police roles.

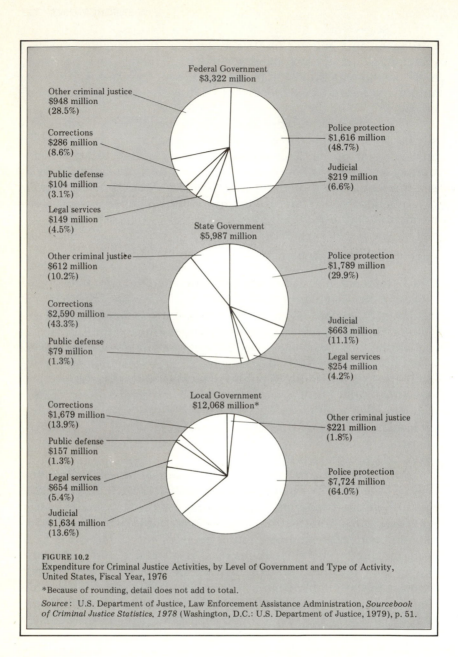

FIGURE 10.2
Expenditure for Criminal Justice Activities, by Level of Government and Type of Activity, United States, Fiscal Year, 1976

*Because of rounding, detail does not add to total.

Source: U.S. Department of Justice, Law Enforcement Assistance Administration, *Sourcebook of Criminal Justice Statistics, 1978* (Washington, D.C.: U.S. Department of Justice, 1979), p. 51.

play and their continuous around-the-clock presence, the police are the most visible public personnel in the community, having more frequent contact with citizens than any other governmental employees.

Although historically the subject of intermittent controversy, the police came under unusually strong attack during the 1960s when overt hostility was manifested toward them by minority groups, college students, and many liberals. Most departments were unprepared psychologically to deal with the civil disorders and community conflicts that marked this period. In their efforts to cope with hundreds of riots, near riots, and other major disturbances, they drew criticism from some groups for alleged brutality, harassment, and insensitivity to human rights and from others for their inability to contain and bring mass violence and disruptions quickly under control.

The incidence of violent demonstrations has subsided but the underlying factors that precipitated them—unemployment, racism, poverty—remain basically unchanged. Allegations of police brutality continue to be common; in Philadelphia, for instance, the Justice Department in 1979 brought a civil rights suit against the mayor and other top city officials, charging them with condoning systematic and criminal violence by the police department (the suit was later dismissed by the court on jurisdictional grounds). A number of cities, including Chattanooga, Miami, Tampa, and Philadelphia experienced riots in their black neighborhoods during the 1980 summer related to police action. Some experts believe that the problem of police behavior is related to the kind of personnel recruited into the system. According to this theory, law enforcement work attracts ideologically conservative and authoritarian-oriented individuals, traits that are assumed to lead to abusive conduct. Other research, however, indicates that improper behavior by police comes more from the pressures of the work than from personality traits or biases.[23]

Effective law enforcement, as most authorities agree, depends heavily on public confidence and support. In efforts to establish greater rapport with the citizens they serve, many departments have expanded their community relations programs beyond mere public relations gimmicks. They have sought to develop ties with neighborhood groups by listening to their grievances and providing them with stepped-up services outside the criminal process. Such

[23]For a concise treatment of police behavior see Clarence Stone, Robert Whelan, and William Murin, *Urban Policy and Politics* (Englewood Cliffs, N.J.: Prentice-Hall, 1979), pp. 286–308.

ancillary activities differ from city to city but in general they include counseling on crime prevention strategies, assigning officers to neighborhood centers to aid residents with their problems and to refer them to the appropriate agencies, assisting young people with police records to find jobs, and developing various youth programs. These efforts have met with mixed success. Where they have been accompanied by more substantive actions, such as the recruitment of blacks and other minorities into the force, attitudes toward the police have shown improvement. For the most part, however, no significant progress has been made in bettering relationships between the law enforcers and residents in the minority and poor neighborhoods of the city.

The police have also moved toward greater professionalization by recruiting more individuals with college degrees, encouraging their personnel to pursue educational programs, providing expanded in-service training, and establishing tighter standards of conduct. (More than 700 colleges and universities in the United States now offer undergraduate and graduate degrees in police science and criminal justice.) The professional thrust has not been enthusiastically welcomed by all of the rank and file. To some, it is another way of saying that they are not performing adequately. Many police deeply resent the charges that have been made against them in recent years. They feel that the public does not understand the nature of their work and is unappreciative of the vital services they provide. The complaint of one officer expresses a prevalent sentiment: "You cry police brutality without knowing what is happening. You talk about crime in the streets but you tolerate courts giving criminals a slap on the wrist. You don't know what a cop is or what he should do."[24] The solidarity fostered by this attitude makes the large police departments almost invulnerable to external control and militates against any basic changes in their philosophy or manner of operation.[25]

Organizational Pattern

The police function has a long tradition of local autonomy in the United States. Regardless of size or financial resources, virtually every city, town, or village regards itself as capable of providing

[24]Quoted in Nicholas Alex, *Black in Blue* (New York: Appleton, 1969), p. 11.
[25]A survey of New York police found that two-thirds agreed with the statement, "The police department is really a big brotherhood in which each patrolman does his best to help all other patrolmen." Thomas E. Bercel, "Calls for Police Assistance," in Harlan Hahn (ed.), *Police in Urban Society* (Beverly Hills, Calif.: Sage, 1970), p. 268.

Table 10.5 AVERAGE POLICE & FIRE EMPLOYMENT PER 1,000 POPULATION, 1978

	POLICE		FIRE	
	NUMBER OF CITIES		NUMBER OF CITIES	
POPULATION GROUP	REPORTING	MEAN	REPORTING	MEAN
500,000 and over	16	2.94	17	1.50
250,000–499,999	26	2.05	26	1.74
100,000–249,999	69	1.81	69	1.69
50,000–99,999	150	1.67	141	1.63
25,000–49,999	267	1.65	241	1.65

SOURCE: Heywood T. Sanders, "Governmental Structure in American Cities," in *Municipal Yearbook 1979* (Washington, D.C.: International City Management Association, 1979), p. 109.

adequate law enforcement within its boundaries. Some 40,000 separate police agencies exist throughout the country, ranging in size from those with no full-time personnel to the New York City force of approximately 30,000. In the larger SMSAs the number of individual departments often exceeds 100. Within a 50-mile radius of Chicago there are nearly 350 locally maintained police forces, and in the five counties surrounding Philadelphia, more than 160.

Wide differences other than size exist among departments. A recent survey of costs and administrative practices among 50 of the large cities found that per capita expenditures ranged from $43 to $83; percentage of personnel assigned to patrol duties from 41 to 86 percent; the proportion of the force at the rank of sergeant or above from 4 to 27 percent; and the number of officers per 1,000 population from 1.4 to 5.7.[26] As Table 10.5 shows, police employment varies directly with population size, the largest cities having on the average almost twice as many officers for each 1,000 people as those between 25,000 to 50,000. Washington, D.C. heads the list with 5.7, followed by Philadelphia with 4.6 and Chicago with 4.3. The average in central cities as a whole exceeds that in the suburbs, but the margin is not great (1.9 to 1.6).

County governments, through the sheriff's office, are usually responsible for law enforcement in rural sections and the urbanized unincorporated areas of SMSAs. A limited number of counties such as Los Angeles and St. Louis offer police services to their municipalities on a contractual basis. Similar arrangements also exist among cities but the practice is not widespread. Special districts, commonly used for other services, are seldom employed for law

[26]John F. Heaphy, "Recent Developments in Policing," *Municipal Year Book, 1979*, pp. 256–258.

enforcement purposes. Various national and local study commissions have recommended the creation of a single police agency for metropolitan areas or at least the consolidation of the smaller forces.[27] Not all observers agree with such proposals. They have been challenged, for example, by political scientist Elinor Ostrom and her colleagues who maintain that no empirical basis exists for assuming that consolidation will result in higher service levels and greater efficiency.[28]

Proposals of a less extreme nature have also been made. One of the more common is that the states establish minimum standards relating to such matters as training and personnel. Another calls for the centralization of certain police functions, such as communications, record keeping, laboratory operations, and training. Recommendations in this latter vein provide for the consolidation of these activities in the county government or other areawide agency (special district or authority), with the local departments responsible for patrolling and the other crime prevention functions. Most researchers, including Ostrom, acknowledge that a metropolitan area might be better served if a larger-scale police agency were created to carry out the more technical functions requiring specialization of personnel and equipment. This division of responsibility offers a means of striking a balance between the criteria of efficiency and citizen control. Few SMSAs, however, have moved toward the adoption of such an arrangement.[29]

Federal authorities, as in other functional areas, have exhibited increasing concern for the improvement of local law enforcement. Three national commissions relating to this field have issued comprehensive reports in recent years. The first centered on the causes

[27]For recommendations supporting the consolidation of small police departments, particularly those with fewer than ten officers, see National Advisory Commission on Criminal Justice Standards and Goals, *Police* (Washington, D.C., 1973).

[28]Elinor Ostrom and Roger Parks, "Suburban Police Departments: Too Many and Too Small?" in Louis H. Masotti and Jeffrey K. Hadden (eds.), *The Urbanization of the Suburbs* (Beverly Hills, Calif.: Sage, 1973), pp. 369–398 and Elinor Ostrom and Dennis Smith, "On the Fate of Lilliputs in Metropolitan Policing," *Public Administration Review* 36 (March/April 1976): 192–200. Ostrom and her colleagues contend that small departments enjoy closer communication and rapport with the residents, are more accessible, and more readily held accountable. For a contrary view questioning the viability of small departments see William Browne, "Resource Needs and Attitudes Toward Finance Allocations: A Study of Suburban Police Chiefs," *Public Administration Review* 34 (July/August 1974): 397–399.

[29]Progress along these lines has been hindered by the strong preference among local police chiefs for autonomy. See, for example, Jon A. Baer, "Cooperation and Conflict: Overlapping Police Jurisdictions," *National Civic Review* 68 (September 1979): 417–422.

of the violent outbursts in the cities during the 1960s; the second dealt with impediments to the effective operation of the criminal justice system; and the third devoted particular attention to the fear accompanying crime and the deleterious effects that lawbreaking has on the quality of urban life. The national government interjected itself more directly into the local law enforcement field when it passed the Omnibus Crime Control and Safe Streets Act of 1968. Although the program has come under heavy criticism as wasting money on Dick Tracy-type police gadgets and failing to alleviate the crime problem, it has persisted thanks largely to the strong constituency it has developed among state and local law enforcement officials.[30] However, Congress in 1979 enacted legislation restructuring the Law Enforcement Assistance Administration (LEAA) and more recently it sharply cut the agency's budget, leaving the future of the program in doubt.

FIRE PROTECTION

Fire protection is another basic function of urban government. An adequately staffed and equipped department not only minimizes the loss of life and property from fire hazards but also substantially reduces insurance costs to the owners of homes, commercial establishments, and factories. The task of protecting a large city against fire is both quantitatively and qualitatively different from that in a predominantly residential suburb. Fighting conflagration in a densely settled community of tall office buildings, apartments, industrial plants, and department stores is a highly complex responsibility. Specialized equipment and expertly trained personnel are indispensable requirements. These needs are far less extensive in the small suburban village where the houses are farther apart and tall buildings few or nonexistent. Here, only a pumper or two and less skilled personnel, even volunteers, are frequently all that is needed to provide an acceptable level of protection.

The fire function has two aspects: protection (detection and extinguishment) and prevention (measures directed toward avoiding the inception of fire). Each year fires cause more than 6000 deaths and several billion dollars in property damage (Table 10.6). Any substantial reduction in these human and material losses depends less on increasing the efficiency of firefighting agencies than on instituting more effective prevention programs. It is in this latter respect that many communities are deficient. Smaller departments,

---

[30]During the first 12 years of the agency's existence (1968–1980) it distributed more than $7 billion to state and local law enforcement agencies.

Table 10.6   FIRE LOSSES, 1950 TO 1978

YEAR	PROPERTY LOSS (IN MILLIONS OF DOLLARS)	LOSS OF LIVES
1950	649	6405
1955	885	6352
1960	1108	7645
1965	1456	7347
1970	2328	6718
1978	4008	6357

SOURCE: U.S. Bureau of the Census, *Statistical Abstract of the United States, 1979* (Washington, D.C., 1979), pp. 80, 550.

staffed wholly or in part by volunteers, seldom have the qualified personnel to carry out the necessary inspections and see that the fire codes are properly enforced. Larger agencies also are often precluded by budgetary limitations from carrying on the full range of prevention activities.

Firefighting is a hazardous activity ranking among the most dangerous occupations, including mining and law enforcement, in terms of casualties and injuries. Even the best training does not eliminate the risks that firefighters must take in the line of duty. Despite this fact, remarkably little research and development have taken place in fire protection and prevention. As a national commission pointed out in 1973, growth in knowledge of how to cope with fire has not kept pace with the expansion of the fire problem.[31]

Departments, particularly in the larger cities, must deal not only with accidental fires but also with those attributable to arson. Insurance companies estimate that 40 percent to 50 percent (these proportions are probably exaggerated) of the money they pay out in claims is for losses resulting from deliberately precipitated fires. In Philadelphia convictions were recently obtained against a landlord who set fire to his unprofitable tenement buildings and a restaurant owner who had his business burned to collect $270,000 in insurance. In Boston and Tampa large arson-for-profit rings involving business people, public officials, and insurance agents were exposed. The problem is most severe in the large inner-city slums,

---

[31]National Commission on Fire Prevention and Control, *America Burning* (Washington, D.C.: 1973), p. 2. The United States experiences higher per capita fire losses than other developed nations where greater emphasis is placed on prevention than on suppression technology. See Maurie W. Ayton, "Advances in Fire Safety," in *Selected Profiles of Future Technology in Urban Settings,* vol. 1 (Washington, D.C.: Congressional Research Service, Library of Congress, 1978), p. 29.

where thousands of buildings are burned down each year, some by vandals and thieves and others by landlords. (In New York City's South Bronx 30,000 dwelling units were destroyed by fire during the last decade, and the problem has greatly increased in Brooklyn as well.)[32]

Organizational Structure

Of the major functions administered by local governments, fire protection is one of the "most local." Spillover effects from the performance of this service are not geographically extensive. Residents in one community receive no direct benefits from the fire protection activities of neighboring municipalities other than those derived from mutual aid pacts or informal understandings of assistance in emergencies. Nor do they suffer any serious disabilities from the failure of adjacent jurisdictions to maintain an adequate level of protection as they do, for instance, in the case of water and air pollution. Although it is true that a fire in one city or village could spread into the surrounding area, the likelihood of this occurring is seldom strong enough to cause any significant expenditures for additional fire-fighting equipment or personnel on the part of other communities.

Nationally, fire protection is provided by 225,000 full-time personnel and many thousands of volunteers. Most cities above 10,000 population have wholly professional departments, those between 2,500 and 10,000 generally utilize a combination of professionals and volunteers; and those below 2,500 rely entirely on volunteers. As in the case of police, wide variations exist among communities in the number of fire fighters employed per 1,000 population. The average for municipalities above 25,000 (1.65) is only slightly less than that for police (1.73). However, in contrast to the police distribution pattern, the largest cities show lower fire employment levels than all other size categories (see Table 10.5). Geography is also a distinguishing factor. Municipalities in the eastern region of the country where density is high and the housing stock old employ two to three times the number of fire personnel per 1,000 population than do the newer cities in the West.

The pattern for administering fire protection in SMSAs is relatively simple. Service in the incorporated areas is usually provided by the municipalities and in some instances by special districts. In the unincorporated sections it is furnished by volunteer depart-

---

[32]For a discussion of this problem in one large central city see Steve Slade, "Arson: Business by Other Means," *Nation* 226 (March 18, 1978): 307–309.

ments, special districts (over 1700 fire districts exist within SMSAs), and county governments and by private companies on a subscription basis. A number of smaller municipalities, and even some of medium size, purchase their protection from other cities or the county government. Numerous mutual aid pacts exist among communities of all sizes providing for each party to render assistance to the others on call.[33]

The states have played only a minimal role in the field of fire protection. Most have established an office of fire marshal to enforce state laws or codes pertaining to prevention and to investigate cases of suspected arson, but in many instances these duties have been delegated to the local departments. The national government, other than setting product safety standards and collecting fire-related data, did not actively enter the field until 1974 when Congress enacted the Fire Prevention and Control Act. The legislation created the U.S. Fire Administration with responsibility to sponsor research, conduct programs of public education, and assist state and local fire service training efforts. Until passage of the law, fire protection was one of the few local services without a federal support program. However, unlike LEAA, its counterpart in the law enforcement field, the U.S. Fire Administration has operated on a meager budget, its grant awards totaling less than $3 million annually.

PARKS AND RECREATION

The rise of recreation as a public responsibility in the United States is largely a product of the present century. The opening of the nation's first playground, a large sandpile in front of a children's home in Boston, did not occur until 1885. Some of the larger cities began to develop park systems earlier, more for their aesthetic qualities than for their recreational potentialities. New York City acquired Central Park in 1853, but the purchase was condemned by many as an extravagant waste of public funds. Most of the smaller municipalities did not begin to acquire park acreage until after 1900, and a majority of the suburban communities created since World War II have ignored this responsibility altogether.

The need for parks and outdoor recreational areas has become more imperative as urban populations have multiplied and as lei-

---

[33]A small number of municipalities, such as Scottsdale, Arizona, contract with a private company to furnish fire services. The experience with this method is discussed in Roger S. Ahlbrandt, "Implications of Contracting for a Public Service," *Urban Affairs Quarterly* 9 (March 1974): 337–358.

sure time has increased because of the shorter workweek, longer vacations, and earlier retirement. Attendance at state parks exceeds 550 million and at national parks and recreational facilities, 250 million annually. Many millions also utilize the 30,000 parks and the more than 150,000 playgrounds under the jurisdiction of local governments. Local public expenditures for this function are now well over $1 billion a year, but the gap between need and availability of facilities continues to be wide.

A number of states, including New York, New Jersey, Massachusetts, and Wisconsin, are providing financial assistance to their local units to acquire parkland in urban areas while the opportunity still exists. The national government's concern in this field has been expressed in various ways. In 1961 Congress authorized federal grants to state and local governments for acquisition of open space sites around urban centers (Housing Act of 1961). In 1962 it created the Bureau of Outdoor Recreation in the Department of the Interior with a mandate to formulate a comprehensive nationwide outdoor recreation plan. And in the following year it passed the Land and Water Conservation Fund Act which earmarks money from various user fees, such as admissions to national parks, for acquiring and developing new park and recreational areas. Also, since the 1960s federal policy has placed increasing emphasis on the expansion of the national park system in the major urbanized regions of the country.

Park Administration

All levels of government are engaged in providing public recreational facilities. The greatest burden falls on municipalities where the day-to-day needs of population concentrations must be met. County participation in this function has increased in recent years but is still relatively minor in comparison to that of the incorporated communities. The special district device is also employed to a limited extent for park and recreational purposes. The 1977 *Census of Governments* reports 427 such agencies in SMSAs, over one-half of them in the state of Illinois and 81 in California. State agencies maintain and operate approximately 3800 parks and the national government almost 300 (exclusive of national forests).

The spillover benefits from parks and recreational facilities rank relatively high among urban functions. A large park, zoo, or public beach invariably attracts many users from outside the immediate governmental jurisdiction in which it is located. Furthermore, open space areas, wherever they are located, enhance the attractiveness of the entire metropolitan complex, give psychic benefits to the residents, and serve an important conservation function by helping to maintain the ecological balance of nature.

The administration of the park and recreation function lends itself to a division of responsibilities largely on the basis of the benefits it confers. Three levels can be identified in this respect. Facilities and services used primarily by local residents (playgrounds, neighborhood parks, supervised recreational programs) are appropriately handled by the municipalities. Facilities serving the entire urbanized area (larger parks, golf courses, zoos, beaches) logically fall under the jurisdiction of counties or special districts. Regional parks or forest preserves (large tracts of land kept in their natural condition for hiking, camping, boating, and fishing) call for state or national administration because they normally serve more extensive areas than individual SMSAs.[34]

Little agreement has yet evolved among the various governments as to their proper roles in the park and recreation field. Each local unit usually has its own ideas as to what it should or should not do, and each proceeds on its own way without reference to any overall plan for the area. With open space in the nation's SMSAs becoming increasingly scarce, this fragmented and uncoordinated approach makes little sense. A growing number of councils of governments and regional planning commissions are trying to remedy this situation by formulating areawide park and open space plans for the guidance of local units and state agencies.

HEALTH

Local governments have traditionally been responsible for public health functions such as communicable disease control, restaurant inspection, and school health services. Many of the larger cities and counties also operate general hospitals, primarily for the indigent, but the number of these facilities has been declining since the advent of Medicare and Medicaid (which enable recipients to utilize private hospitals).[35] Aside from their public health functions, local governments have had little relation to the health delivery system. Passage of the National Health Planning and Resources Development Act of 1974, however, has opened the door for their greater involvement in this field. The system of health planning estab-

---

[34]George D. Butler, "Recreation Administration in Metropolitan Areas," *Recreation* 55 (September 1962): 349–351.

[35]Philadelphia, for example, has closed its public general hospital, St. Louis has done similarly in the case of one of its two publicly operated hospitals, and New York is preparing to shut down four of its municipal hospitals.

lished under the law brings state and local governments into the process of determining overall health needs and priorities and the allocation of federal health funds in their respective areas.[36]

The 1974 act (as amended in 1979) provides for the creation of a network of health systems agencies (HSAs) throughout the country. The governor of each state demarcates the territorial boundaries of such agencies (an HSA must include a minimum population of 500,000 and must not divide an SMSA). The secretary of the Department of Health and Human Services (HHS) then designates the agency to serve as the HSA for each district. A not-for-profit corporation, regional planning body, or unit of local government may be named for this purpose. Whatever type is chosen, a majority of its governing board must be health care consumers who are broadly representative of the socioeconomic and racial characteristics of the population in the area served. The balance of the membership must include health care providers (at least one-third) and local government officials.

HSAs are authorized to develop comprehensive plans establishing priorities for health services and facilities and to review all proposed uses of federal health funds in their areas (the HHS secretary may overrule the agency's disapproval of a grant but must state the reasons for so doing). The act also specifies that each governor shall appoint a state planning agency to prepare a statewide health plan (based on those formulated by the individual HSAs) and establish a mandatory certificate of need program. Such a program, which lies at the heart of efforts to develop an effective health planning process, requires hospitals and other medical providers to obtain a certificate of need from the state planning agency for new facility construction and the purchase of major equipment. Failure to obtain such certification disqualifies the project for federal or state aid.[37]

The legislation places HSAs and state health planning agencies in a position where they can exercise considerable influence over the development of the health delivery system. More than 200 HSAs have been designated and are presently in operation. Most of

---

[36]Congress in 1966 had authorized federal support for the creation of areawide health planning agencies but had left them without authority to enforce their decisions.

[37]The law directs states to relax certification requirements for prepaid group health providers such as health maintenance organizations (HMOs). These groups have been favored by Congress and recent administrations because of their internal economies (they have strong incentives to prevent costly illnesses because they are supported by fixed fees) and their potential to force competing providers to lower prices.

them are not-for-profit corporations. Few regional planning agencies and councils of governments (COGs) made efforts to bring the HSA function under their jurisdiction. Their reluctance to enter this field is in part a reflection of the physical planning orientation that is still dominant among them.

Progress in developing a health planning capability at the state level has been slow. Many states have not as yet set up certification programs (Congress in 1979 postponed a pending cutoff of funds to those that had failed to do so) and few have completed their comprehensive plans. Despite these delays, areawide health planning had seemingly become an integral part of national policy, as evidenced by the 1979 extension of the health care act. The Reagan Administration, however, has indicated its opposition to federal intervention in the health delivery field and its intention to abolish the HSA program.[38]

THE DEPENDENT DELIVERY SYSTEM

The growth of metropolitan areas has brought expanded opportunities for millions of Americans in the form of better jobs, greater social mobility, and improved educational and cultural facilities. At the same time it has also brought problems of far larger magnitude than those experienced by less complex societies. We have discussed some of these difficulties in this chapter and others. We have also observed that urbanization and its accompanying features have diminished the self-sufficiency of individual SMSAs and made them increasingly dependent on national and even international trends and developments. Problems that were once local are now national. Services that at one time were exclusively a local function are now the responsibility of several levels of government.

The governmental units of metropolitan areas are the basic and direct providers of most urban public services. Although they depend heavily on higher levels of public authority—particularly for fiscal assistance and policy initiative in major problem fields—the manner in which they execute their service delivery responsibility is a contributing factor to the quality of life in their communities. To understand the role they play, one should view them within the context of the larger system and not solely from a local perspective. Virtually every problem or function as we have seen—from waste

---

[38]On the role and potential impact of HSAs see William Shonick and Walter Price, "Reorganization of Health Agencies by Local Government in American Urban Centers: What Do They Portend for 'Public Health'?" *Milbank Memorial Fund Quarterly* (now *Health and Society*) 55 (Spring 1977): 233–271.

disposal and noise control to crime and school desegregation—involves federal and state agencies as well as local governments. The effective and efficient operation of this complex and interdependent system requires strong coordinating mechanisms, well-defined divisions of responsibility, clear lines of accountability, and readily available means for citizen participation and input. No metropolitan area today meets these criteria, but the objectives they embody are winning greater recognition.

Chapter 11
Governmental Reorganization:
Comprehensive Approaches

Reorganization of the governmental structure of metropolitan areas has been on the civic agenda for more than a half century. Unlike the earlier municipal reform movement that reflected public reaction to the rampant corruption among local officials, the impetus for metropolitan change grew out of concern over the rapid proliferation of government units in urban areas and the inefficiencies associated with the resulting fragmented system. Attempts to restructure the decentralized pattern now typical of SMSAs have met with a long series of rebuffs, interrupted by only an infrequent success. These efforts document the various approaches to the problem of metropolitan governance and the philosophies and objectives underlying them.

Strongly divergent views are held as to the way in which the political system of urban areas should be organized. The Advisory Commission on Intergovernmental Relations has identified five schools of thought in this connection.[1] At one end of the spectrum are the centrists who favor political consolidation as the most effective means of achieving efficiency, eliminating service inequalities, and managing growth and development. At the opposite pole are the polycentrists who look upon the multiplicity of local units as the most desirable way of promoting the interests of a pluralistic society by maximizing grassroots control and assuring bureaucratic responsiveness.[2]

Between these two extremes are the federationists, local optionists, and pragmatists. The federationists support a two-tier system in which urban-related powers are divided between local units and an areawide body (county or multifunctional metropolitan district). The optionists maintain that no single approach can be pre-

---

[1]Advisory Commission on Intergovernmental Relations, *Regionalism Revisited: Recent Areawide and Local Responses* (Washington, D.C., June 1977), pp. 31–32.
[2]For a theoretical analysis of metropolitan reform approaches see Elinor Ostrom, "Metropolitan Reform: Propositions Derived from Two Traditions," *Social Science Quarterly* 53 (December 1972): 474–493.

scribed because of the great differences among urban areas in their structural characteristics and problems. According to them the states should authorize a broad range of reorganization forms and let the local units in each SMSA adopt the solution they deem most appropriate to their needs. (Some optionists would require the local governments to consider formally the available alternatives whereas others would put this action on a purely voluntary basis.) The pragmatists are willing to accept any reorganization plan— whether consolidation, federation, or strengthened metropolitan councils—that provides a policymaking mechanism for areawide concerns. This is essentially the position taken by ACIR.

The present chapter concentrates on those forms of structural change that are of major scope and involve a large degree of centralization. They include annexation, city-county consolidation, comprehensive urban county plan, and federation, all approaches that fall within either the centrist or federationist category. The following chapter (12) deals with the incremental remedies to metropolitan fragmentation that are of modest dimensions and call for relatively little centralization. They are the type—special districts, cooperative agreements, functional transfers, and councils of governments—that in general find support among the polycentrists, optionists, and pragmatists.

ANNEXATION

Prior to this century, urban expansion in the United States was accommodated governmentally by creating new municipalities and enlarging the boundaries of those already established. As areas became urbanized they were incorporated as cities or towns; and as growth spread beyond their original boundaries, the newly settled fringe areas were annexed to the existing governments. Such extensions were the principal means of keeping pace with population increases in the era prior to 1900; today many of the municipalities that grew by annexation comprise the central cities of modern metropolises.[3]

The early annexation movement involved many municipalities and a considerable amount of territory, much of which was not ex-

---

[3]Richard Bigger and James D. Kitchen, *How the Cities Grew* (Los Angeles: University of California Bureau of Governmental Research, 1952), pp. 143–151, and Kenneth T. Jackson, "Metropolitan Government Versus Suburban Autonomy: Politics on the Crabgrass Frontier," in Kenneth T. Jackson and Stanley K. Schultz (eds.), *Cities in American History* (New York: Knopf, 1972), pp. 442–462, describe the early annexation activities of a number of large cities.

tensively urban at the time of absorption. However, from 1900 until the end of World War II, the process was used infrequently and on a small scale. Only a few cities—Los Angeles is a notable example—accomplished sizable boundary extensions between 1900 and 1945 (Figure 11.1). As noted earlier (Chapter 4), state laws enacted in the late nineteenth century made annexation procedures extremely difficult, either by giving residents in the unincorporated areas the exclusive right to initiate such action or requiring their consent to the absorption by majority vote. At the same time the provisions for incorporating new municipalities—and thereby preventing annexation altogether—remained extremely lax and permissive.

Post-1945 Era

The long period of annexation dormancy ended in 1945 when 152 cities with 5000 or more population extended their boundaries. This trend has continued to the present.[4] From 1970 through 1975, according to the Bureau of the Census, almost 60 percent of the nation's municipalities had at least one boundary alteration due to annexation and several had over 200.[5] The vast majority of these acquisitions were small in size, the average involving less than two-tenths of a square mile and fewer than 100 people. Cumulatively, the impact of the boundary alterations was substantial. They added nearly 5500 square miles and almost 2 million residents to the corporate areas of municipalities over 2500 population. Much of the activity took place in the smaller communities, with cities under 50,000 accounting for more than 70 percent of the total territory annexed during the six-year period (Figure 11.2).

Since the early decades of the twentieth century annexation has had only limited utility for most of the older central cities. Many have become hemmed in totally or partially by other municipalities—Milwaukee and Minneapolis are examples of complete encirclement—thus legally preventing or restricting their expansion. In many cases also, residents of adjacent unincorporated areas have strongly resisted efforts to bring them under the jurisdiction of

---

[4]For annexation data from 1950 to 1967 see John C. Bollens, "Metropolitan and Fringe Area Developments in 1967," *Municipal Year Book, 1968* (Washington, D.C.: International City Management Association), p. 31. For more recent data see the various articles authored or coauthored by Richard L. Forstall in the *Municipal Year Book*.

[5]In a small minority of instances boundary changes occur by the detachment of territory from municipalities.

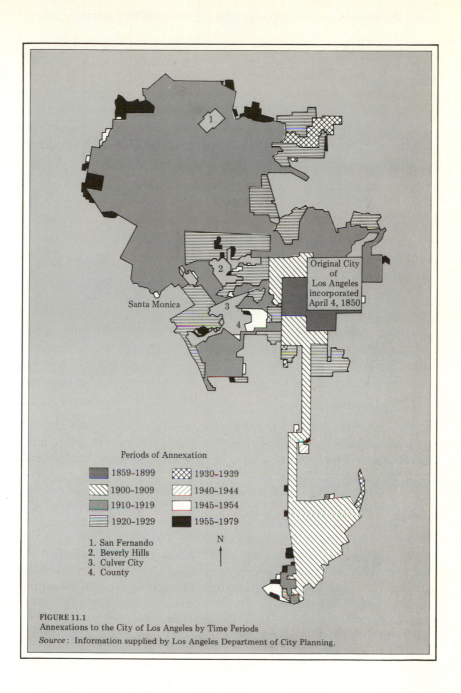

Original City
of
Los Angeles
incorporated
April 4, 1850

Santa Monica

Periods of Annexation

1859–1899		1930–1939	
1900–1909		1940–1944	
1910–1919		1945–1954	
1920–1929		1955–1979	

1. San Fernando
2. Beverly Hills
3. Culver City
4. County

N

FIGURE 11.1
Annexations to the City of Los Angeles by Time Periods

Source: Information supplied by Los Angeles Department of City Planning.

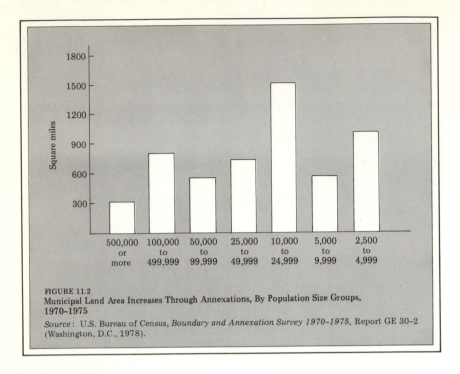

FIGURE 11.2
Municipal Land Area Increases Through Annexations, By Population Size Groups,
1970–1975
Source: U.S. Bureau of Census, *Boundary and Annexation Survey 1970–1975*, Report GE 30-2
(Washington, D.C., 1978).

a city, particularly one that is heavily populated.[6] The record, however, is not totally devoid of successes. As Table 11.1 shows, a number of major municipalities have achieved large-scale land absorptions since World War II.

Oklahoma City has made the most spectacular use of annexation, one of almost incredible scope. At the beginning of the 1950s
it encompassed about 50 square miles; by 1970 it had expanded
more than twelvefold to approximately 630 square miles. It was
easily the largest municipality in territorial size in the continental
United States until Jacksonville and Duval County, Florida, consolidated in 1967 as the city of Jacksonville with an area of 766 square
miles. Large annexations elsewhere have enabled Houston to surpass and Dallas, Kansas City (Missouri), and San Diego to approxi-
mate the geographic size of New York City, by far the nation's big-

---

[6]According to one study, opposition to annexation is likely to be strongest when the
urbanized area is an old settlement, wide socioeconomic differences exist between
the two sections, and the form of government in the municipality is other than council–manager. Thomas R. Dye, "Urban Political Integration: Conditions Associated
with Annexation in American Cities," *Midwest Journal of Political Science* 8 (November 1964): 446.

Table 11.1 CHANGES IN LAND AREA RESULTING FROM
ANNEXATIONS IN SELECTED CITIES, 1950, 1970, AND 1978

CITY	TOTAL LAND AREA (IN SQUARE MILES)		
	1950	1970	1978
Atlanta, Ga	36.9	131.5	131.5
Dallas, Tex.	112.0	265.6	336.3
El Paso, Tex.	25.6	118.3	176.4
Fort Worth, Tex.	93.7	205.0	233.9
Houston, Tex.	160.0	433.9	521.1
Kansas City, Mo.	80.6	316.3	316.3
Memphis, Tenn.	104.2	217.4	280.8
Mobile, Ala.	25.4	116.6	116.6
Oklahoma City, Okla.	50.8	635.7	629.6*
Phoenix, Ariz.	17.1	247.9	277.2
San Antonio, Tex.	69.5	184.0	263.6
San Diego, Calif.	99.4	316.9	323.2
San Jose, Calif.	17.0	136.2	152.4
Tulsa, Okla.	26.7	171.9	177.4

*1978 figure is less than that of 1970 because of different reporting sources.
SOURCE: Published and unpublished Bureau of the Census data and Joel C. Miller, Frances Barnett, and Richard L. Forstall, "Annexations and Corporate Changes, 1970–1977," *Municipal Year Book, 1979* (Washington, D.C.: International City Management Association, 1979), p. 48.

gest population center. In similar fashion, Fort Worth, Memphis, Phoenix, and San Antonio have moved on to encompass more land than Chicago.[7]

Annexation Setting

The large territorial acquisitions have taken place under conditions not present in most SMSAs: favorable annexation laws and the existence of considerable unincorporated areas adjacent to the central city. Both factors are characteristic of sections of the South and West but not of most parts of the Northeast and North Central regions. As a result, virtually all the large land absorptions of recent decades have taken place in southern and western states, the Kansas City, Missouri, case being the only major exception.[8]

[7]For a fascinating case study see John D. Wenum, *Annexation as a Technique for Metropolitan Growth: The Case of Phoenix, Arizona* (Tempe, Ariz.: Arizona State University, Institute of Public Administration, 1970).
[8]The Kansas City annexations are unique in the Midwest including other parts of Missouri. The state supreme court has held that the municipality's constitutional home rule charter gives it power to extend its boundaries by unilateral action.

The procedures most conducive to boundary expansions are those that do not afford the target area opportunity to veto the action.[9] They include annexation by (1) ordinance; (2) popular referendum in the initiating city; (3) special act of the state legislature; and (4) court order. Passage of annexation ordinances made possible the large land absorptions by Oklahoma City, Tulsa, and the Texas municipalities. Kansas City expanded through the affirmative response of its voters on proposals presented as charter amendments. Atlanta's enlargement was accomplished by a single act of the state lawmakers, and boundary extensions in a number of Virginia cities were authorized by special annexation tribunals.

Liberal annexation policies, of course, have little meaning for cities that are surrounded by other incorporated places. When this is the case, expansion can take place only through consolidation, a process that almost universally requires the consent of each municipality. The newer cities of the South and West, such as Dallas, Houston, and Phoenix, were located next to large tracts of unincorporated land when they launched their annexation drive. This situation had vanished long before the middle of the twentieth century in most of the large SMSAs in other parts of the country. Their central cities could profit only by a liberalization of the consolidation laws, but few states have been willing to move in this direction. The local autonomy ideology tends to throw a protective cloak around municipalities once they are established.

The large annexations since 1950 have done more than increase the territorial size of the central city; they have prevented extensive political fragmentation in the affected SMSAs and assured them of a unified governmental structure. Because of sizable land acquisitions by the core municipality some of the newer metropolises of the South and West remain relatively uncluttered in terms of incorporated units despite large population increases. As late as 1977 Metropolitan El Paso had 3 municipalities, San Diego 13, and Phoenix 19. These numbers contrast with the typical pattern found in many of the older SMSAs such as Cleveland with 89 incorporated entities, St. Louis with 194, and Chicago with 261.

For most major urban settlements the annexation route does not represent an adequate solution to the problem of metropolitan governance. First of all, such areas are already characterized by considerable governmental complexity, with many municipalities

[9]An analysis of central city annexation activity in urbanized areas between 1950 and 1960 that finds a clear relationship between liberal laws and substantial land absorptions is presented in Raymond H. Wheeler, "Annexation Law and Annexation Success," *Land Economics* 41 (November 1965): 354–360.

and other units that are not subject to absorption. Second, regardless of the total amount of land acquired through this device in recent years, the boundaries of most big cities still fall short of being coterminous with the territorial limits of the total metropolitan complex. Before 1900 annexation was repeatedly used to keep all the urbanized area within a single municipality; since then it has seldom produced a similar result. Third, in the absence of strong state requirements for incorporating, annexation tends to generate the defensive formation of new municipalities, thereby contributing to further governmental proliferation. Almost one-third of all new incorporations during a recent five-year period occurred in Texas and Oklahoma at a time when extensive annexation efforts were under way in those states.

Supervised Municipal Expansion

During most of this century, the problem of urban fringe growth has been approached more often on the basis of counteracting maneuvers by cities and adjacent unincorporated areas than on rational considerations. Prior to the late 1950s Virginia was the lone state to adopt an orderly process for adjusting municipal boundaries. As far back as 1904 its legislature provided for judicial determination of annexation and consolidation proposals by a special tribunal composed of three circuit court judges. It also prescribed standards (although in the very general terms of "the necessity for and the expediency of" the change) to be followed by the court in ruling on the proposals.

The Virginia procedure has received wide acclaim, both inside and outside the state. Some criticism has been expressed over two of its features: the use of circuit court judges instead of persons possessing special technical competence and the review body's lack of jurisdiction over proposed incorporations. However, the basic idea of the process—vesting power to decide boundary changes in an impartial body with authority to approve, modify, or deny proposals on the basis of prescribed standards—is supported by most observers.[10] Despite the longtime acknowledgment of the merits of the Virginia plan, no other state adopted a similar approach until recent years.

Breakthroughs in methods of dealing with urban fringe areas

---

[10]A detailed analysis of the judicial determination process in Virginia is given in Chester W. Bain, *Annexation in Virginia: The Use of the Judicial Process for Readjusting City-County Boundaries* (Charlottesville: University Press of Virginia, 1966).

(and to a lesser extent with various small municipalities that are uneconomic and functionally inept) came on two fronts around 1960, one involving restrictions on incorporation, the other review of incorporation and annexation proposals and the establishment of standards for evaluating them. These procedures constitute encouraging departures from the prevalent haphazard practices. Yet, in many states that have adopted them, the measures are relatively weak and enforcement is often lax.

The first approach, embodied in "anti-incorporation" laws, prohibits or imposes severe restrictions on the creation of additional incorporated places in the vicinity of existing municipal entities. The purpose is to create a buffer zone not subject to incorporation unless the existing city consents to such action or refuses to annex territory within the area when requested by residents. The approach has proved less effective than anticipated because of several factors. First, the laws embodying it are preventive rather than remedial; none has a retroactive effect. Second, only a few of the states utilizing the procedure require municipalities to absorb part or all of the "frozen" territory when conditions dictate such action; those that have this requirement mandate annexation only when the fringe area is the initiator. Third, the technique has not generally taken hold in states having the heaviest concentrations of metropolitan population. Fourth, the process tends to favor the existing municipalities and therefore does not always work in an equitable fashion.[11]

The second approach represents a more thorough and impartial process than the anti-incorporation mechanism. It calls for the establishment of a permanent administrative body (usually a commission) with quasi-judicial powers to review proposed incorporations and annexations. It also provides standards or guidelines to be used by the reviewing authority in evaluating and making determinations about the sought after action.[12] Disapproval of a proposal terminates its progress (in some instances it may be reactivated after a specified period of time), whereas approval is generally a screening action allowing the matter to proceed to a popular vote. In some states the reviewing body may modify or attach conditions to a proposal before endorsing it.

[11]The Texas law recognizes that fringes tend to reemerge beyond municipal boundaries despite the extension of the city limits through municipal annexation. The legislation specifies that the no-incorporation zone expands outward as the city increases territorially.

[12]Approximately 40 states now have standards for municipal incorporation. Most confine the criteria to factors such as population, size of area, and assessed valuation of property. Only a few require the ability to supply specific urban-type services.

The concept of review by a disinterested agency has slowly gained acceptance, with about ten states now utilizing the device. None adopting the procedure has abandoned it and the overall appraisal is favorable, although in some jurisdictions the authority has not been vigorously employed.[13] Evaluations indicate that the impact of such commissions may extend far beyond the determination of individual boundary adjustments. In California, for example, the actions of these bodies have prompted the designation of city expansion zones, some simplification of the governmental pattern in several metropolitan areas, a reduction in scattered development for speculative purposes, and studies of long-term governmental needs.[14] The reluctant acceptance of the review concept and the limitations usually placed on the agency responsible for implementing it—inability to initiate proposals and exclusion of municipal consolidations from its jurisdiction—are unfortunate. For if properly implemented, the device even at this late date can contribute to the more rational fashioning of the governmental pattern in expanding SMSAs.

CITY–COUNTY CONSOLIDATION

City–county consolidation, a broader centrist approach than either municipal annexation or consolidation, has a long history. The process usually consists of the merger of a county government with the principal city or all the municipalities within its borders.[15] Despite the extensive consideration it has received, this type of governmental restructuring is operative in only 12 SMSAs. Four of

---

[13]Ronald C. Cease, *A Report on State and Provincial Boundary Review Boards* (Portland, Ore.: Portland Metropolitan Study Commission, 1968), pp. 32–39; Kenneth Tollenaar et al., *Local Government Boundary Commissions: The Oregon Experience* (University of Oregon, Bureau of Governmental Research and Service, April 1978). A critical appraisal of the Oregon commissions is contained in Marvin J. Price, "Local Boundary Commissions: The Oregon Experience," *National Civic Review* 68 (November 1979): 542–548.

[14]California Intergovernmental Council on Urban Growth, *Report on a State-wide Survey of Local Agency Formation Commissions* (Sacramento, 1966), p. 7. For more comprehensive analyses see John Goldbach, *Boundary Change in California: The Local Agency Formation Commissions* (Davis: University of California, Institute of Governmental Affairs, 1970), and Richard T. LeGates, *California Local Agency Formation Commissions* (Berkeley: University of California, Institute of Governmental Studies, 1970).

[15]City–county separation, often confused with city–county consolidation, involves the detachment of a municipality from a county. The four principal separated cities, often erroneously identified as city-counties, all achieved this status many years ago: Baltimore (1851), San Francisco (1856), St. Louis (1876), and Denver (1902).

these cases, moreover, antedate the twentieth century: New Orleans (1813), Boston (1821), Philadelphia (1854), and New York (1898).[16]

All of the pre-1900 consolidations were accomplished by state legislative acts and did not require local voter approval; in each case a remnant county government continued to operate apart from the consolidated unit. The New Orleans and Boston reorganizations involved only one county (called parish in Louisiana) and one city; the Philadelphia and New York actions merged many local governments and also brought public education into the new system. The New York plan was unique in that the city's boundaries were extended to embrace four counties (later one of them was divided into two), and these areas, designated as boroughs, were retained with jurisdiction over several administrative functions such as minor public works.[17] These early mergers stand as notable governmental changes, particularly because each of the cities is the hub of a highly important metropolis. The New York reorganization is especially impressive because even in 1898 the city was preeminent among American urban centers in population (about two million people then) and financial importance.

The period from 1900 to the end of World War II was characterized by considerable interest in city–county consolidation and by the failure of efforts to secure its adoption in any metropolis. During these years suburbanites developed strong resistance to the absorption of their communities into a unified government. The usual arguments that consolidation would result in greater efficiency, economy, and equity and establish a government capable of dealing with areawide problems left them unpersuaded. Instead, they continued to insist on local autonomy, unwilling to place control over their zoning and financial resources in the hands of a larger and possibly less responsive government.

Besides local resistance, the efforts to achieve city–county

---

[16]One of the 12 metropolitan areas is Honolulu which acquired its consolidated city–county status by act of the territorial legislature in 1907 (and retained it after statehood in 1959). City–county consolidations in Virginia are excluded from the list of 12 because of that state's unique practice of removing land annexed by a city from county jurisdiction. (Cities there can conceivably annex all of an adjacent county.) Also excluded are consolidations not in metropolitan areas, such as Juneau and Greater Juneau Borough, Alaska, and Carson City and Ormsby County, Nevada. For a general perspective on city-county consolidations, see Parris N. Glendening, and Patricia S. Atkins, "City-County Consolidations: New Views for the Eighties," *Municipal Year Book, 1980* (Washington, D.C., 1980), pp. 68–72.

[17]New York, however, is not an example of a two-level or federal governmental system because the boroughs have no legislative powers.

merger were also impeded by formidable legal barriers. Many states added municipal home rule provisions to their constitutions, thus prohibiting their legislative bodies from passing laws that would mandate or facilitate consolidation. Even in states where the legislatures still possessed this authority, they were disinclined to use it because of opposition by rural and suburban forces. In the face of these impediments the avenue used in the consolidations of the nineteenth century—state legislative action—was generally sealed off.

To achieve consolidation, reformers had to overcome two legal hurdles: passage of a state constitutional amendment or legislative enabling act authorizing metropolitan areas to take such action and approval of the proposal by the local voters—usually by separate majorities in the central city and the rest of the county. Most consolidation efforts in the 1900–1945 period fell before the first obstacle. Only three city–county proposals reached the stage of local voter scrutiny and all were defeated: St. Louis–St. Louis County; Macon–Bibb County, Georgia; and Jacksonville–Duval County.

The Baton Rouge Precedent

Against the background of unproductive efforts nationally, the consolidation of Baton Rouge and East Baton Rouge Parish (County) in 1947 came as a surprise. Aided by a combination of highly favorable factors,[18] the plan went into effect in January 1949. It involved only partial merger, providing for retention of both the city and parish governments. It also continued the existence of two small municipalities but prohibited them from further territorial expansion. A prominent innovation of the plan was the interlocking of the city and parish governments. The seven members of the city council and two other persons elected from the rural area constitute the parish council. The mayor-president, elected on a parishwide basis, serves as the chief administrator of both governments and presides over the two councils, but has no vote. He prepares the executive budgets of each and appoints the finance director, personnel administrator, public works director, and purchasing agent, all of whom serve both the city and the parish. He also selects the police and fire chiefs, who function only in the city. The parish council appoints the attorney, clerk, and treasurer, who are both city and parish officials. Thus the two governments are integrated at many

[18]Thomas H. Reed, "Progress in Metropolitan Integration," *Public Administration Review* 9 (Winter 1949): 1–10.

key points, although there are separate governing bodies and separate budgets.

A second innovation of the Baton Rouge plan was the establishment of taxing and service zones throughout the consolidated area. The parish was divided into three types of districts: urban, industrial, and rural. The boundaries of the city and the urban district were made coterminous, with the city government responsible for providing police and fire protection, waste collection and disposal, street lighting, traffic regulation, sewerage facilities, and inspectional services within this area. Residents of the urban zone are subject to both city and parish taxes. Municipal-type services needed in the industrial sections are provided by the business firms at their own expense. Bridges, highways, streets, and airports are furnished on a parishwide basis and financed by parish taxes. Portions of the rural zone adjacent to the urban district can be annexed to the latter as they become developed, such action requiring the consent of a majority of the property owners in the area and approval of the city council. The employment of tax and service differentials based on need in the various sections of the parish gave the city–county approach an important degree of flexibility that had previously been lacking. This feature has been emulated in later reorganization plans.

Shortly after the Baton Rouge merger went into effect in 1949, opposition groups unsuccessfully sought major changes in the reorganization. During the next four years more litigation developed over local governmental operations than had occurred previously in the entire history of the parish. The plan seemed at the point of disaster in 1950 when a bond issue for public improvements was thoroughly defeated and opponents called the system hopeless. Spurred into action the city council levied a 1 percent sales tax and within two years extended services to the whole urban area. These measures restored confidence in the new governmental arrangement and assured its continued existence.

Two of the most important attainments since the Baton Rouge plan became operational have been the adoption of a comprehensive zoning ordinance and the enactment of subdivision regulations applicable throughout the parish. These controls have been accompanied by building codes, a minimum housing standards ordinance, and major street, drainage, and sewerage programs. Some shortcomings nevertheless persist under the partial consolidation achieved by the plan, such as the overlapping jurisdictions of the two law enforcement agencies (city and parish) and the separate civil service systems for the police and fire departments. In addition, certain offices that remain independent under the state constitution cannot be effectively controlled by the merged government.[19]

The Nashville Breakthrough

Interest in city–county consolidation accelerated in the 1950s with merger proposals being submitted (all unsuccessfully) to local vote in various SMSAs (Table 11.2). Other than the St. Louis case, all such attempts through the early 1960s were concerned with medium- and small-sized metropolitan areas, predominantly in the South.[20] Virtually all of them required dual majorities of the popular vote—one in the major city, the other in the rest of the county. The propositions usually obtained voter approval within the central municipality but failed to do so in the outlying territory. This drought of success, however, came to an end in 1962 in Nashville–Davidson County, the country music capital of the world. A merger proposal for the area, requiring dual majorities, obtained almost as large a proportion of affirmative votes in the fringe sections as in the city of Nashville itself. At the time of the consolidation the county contained 533 square miles and approximately 415,000 inhabitants.

The merger established a single government (referred to as Metro) for the Davidson County area, replacing the old central city and county units. Six suburban municipalities (which collectively contained only about 16,000 residents) were permitted to retain their incorporated status but were barred from expanding their boundaries. Because of the different service requirements of the rural and urban portions of the county, the reorganization plan provided for the establishment of two districts: the General Services District (GSD), covering the entire area, and the Urban Services District (USD), encompassing the former city of Nashville. The USD may be expanded by annexation as the need for urban-type functions arises in the outlying area, but such services must be provided within one year after USD taxes go into effect.

The metropolitan government performs a wide range of functions in the countywide district, including law enforcement, hospitals, streets and roads, planning and zoning, refuse disposal, and

[19]William C. Havard, Jr., and Floyd L. Corty, *Rural-Urban Consolidation: The Merger of Governments in the Baton Rouge Area* (Baton Rouge: Louisiana State University Press, 1964).
[20]Unlike a similar reorganization proposal of 1926 that required dual local approval, the St. Louis area consolidation effort of 1962 was attempted by means of a state constitutional amendment. The proposal lost by 3 to 1 in the state, by 6 to 5 in St. Louis, and by almost 4 to 1 in St. Louis County.

Table 11.2 VOTER DEFEATS OF CITY–COUNTY CONSOLIDATION IN CURRENT SMSAs SINCE 1950

YEAR	AREA
1950	Newport News–Warwick County–Elizabeth City County, Virginia
1953	Miami–Dade County, Florida
1954	Albany–Dougherty County, Georgia
1958	Nashville–Davidson County, Tennessee
1959	Albuquerque–Bernalillo County, New Mexico (also 1973)
	Knoxville–Knox County, Tennessee (also 1978)
1960	Macon–Bibb County, Georgia (also 1972 and 1976)
1961	Durham–Durham County, North Carolina (also 1971 and 1974)
	Richmond–Henrico County, Virginia
1962	Columbus–Muscogee County, Georgia
	Memphis–Shelby County, Tennessee (also 1971)
	St. Louis–St. Louis County, Missouri
1964	Chattanooga–Hamilton County, Tennessee (also 1970)
1967	Tampa–Hillsborough County, Florida (also 1970)
1969	Roanoke–Roanoke County, Virginia
1970	Pensacola–Escambia County, Florida
1971	Augusta–Richmond County, Georgia (also 1974 and 1976)
	Charlotte–Mecklenberg County, North Carolina
	Tallahassee–Leon County, Florida (also 1973 and 1976)
1972	Macon–Bibb County, Georgia (also 1976)
1973	Columbia–Richland County, South Carolina
	Savannah–Chatham County, Georgia
	Wilmington–New Hanover County, North Carolina
1974	Charleston–Charleston County, South Carolina
	Evansville–Vanderburgh County, Indiana
	Portland–Multnomah County, Oregon
	Sacramento–Sacramento County, California
1975	Salt Lake City–Salt Lake County, Utah (also 1978)

SOURCE: Prepared by authors from various sources.

public education. All residents pay the GSD property tax levy to help finance these activities. Householders in the USD receive additional services from Metro, such as more intensive police protection, fire protection, water, sanitary and storm sewers, street lighting, and refuse collection (and pay an additional tax). There are no special districts or independent authorities in Davidson County. Residents outside the USD must rely on private haulers for garbage and refuse collection and on private departments for fire protection.

Metro is presided over by a popularly elected mayor and a council of 41 members, 35 of whom are chosen by district and the remainder at large. All elections are nonpartisan and all terms are for four years. The mayor appoints the heads of the ten executive departments and, with council confirmation, all members of the 34 boards and commissions that are responsible for various functions, including parks and recreation, libraries, public housing, and the public schools.

Some political observers have called the Nashville reorganization the most successful example of city–county consolidation in the current century. This enthusiasm is tempered by the fact that only a small number of mergers have taken place since 1900. There is little doubt, however, that the unified government has become an established part of the Nashville scene. Few local leaders, civic or political, would seriously think of questioning its existence or returning to the old system. Attitude surveys among both whites and blacks indicate general acceptance of it. Most analysts agree that the restructuring has improved the efficiency of the area's government, upgraded public services, provided an institutional framework for more comprehensive problem solving, and brought about a more coordinated approach to the development of the metropolis. Some, however, are critical of the government for what they regard as its lack of initiative in promoting the interests of racial minorities and the poor.[21]

On balance, the reorganization has resulted in some noteworthy accomplishments. Open space for recreational needs has been acquired in the county's outer portions, thereby stopping the loss of suitable sites to residential development. A massive sewer construction program has been undertaken, and areas outside the old city of Nashville are receiving library service for the first time. Service inequities have been reduced by shifting a number of functions to a countywide tax base. From the standpoint of administration, accountability is now clearly defined, some duplication of activities has been eliminated, and some economies of scale realized. The merger has also created an effective mechanism for securing and allocating federal and state aid, many officials attributing the selection of Nashville for a model cities program to the community's unique governmental system and the national prominence of its first mayor.

---

[21]Daniel R. Grant, "A Comparison of Predictions and Experience with Nashville 'Metro'," *Urban Affairs Quarterly* 1 (September 1965): 38–42, 47–48; Robert E. McArthur, "The Metropolitan Government of Nashville and Davidson County," in *Regional Governance: Promise and Performance* (Washington, D.C.: Advisory Commission on Intergovernmental Relations, 1973), pp. 29–32; James C. Coomer and Charlie B. Tyer, *Nashville Metropolitan Government: The First Decade* (Knoxville: University of Tennessee, Bureau of Public Administration, 1974); and James F. Blumstein and Benjamin Walter (eds.), *Growing Metropolis: Aspects of Development in Nashville* (Nashville: Vanderbilt University Press, 1975), particularly chap. 9.

City–county merger has obviously worked no miracles in Nashville–Davidson County. It has not succeeded in wiping out an extensive, longtime backlog of unsatisfactorily met public needs, although it has made general progress in this direction. Not surprisingly, taxes have gone up and user charges have been adopted in the wake of service expansions. In the social field the metropolitan police department has been accused of insensitivity in race relations and the government's first chief executive was criticized for moving too slowly in developing social programs and exercising leadership in the desegregation of the schools. Bitter controversies have also arisen over an urban renewal project and the construction of an interstate highway through a black section of the community.

How well blacks (who constitute one-fifth of the area's population as compared to 38 percent in the former city) fare under the new structure is difficult to assess. They presently hold 6 of the 41 council posts and 2 of the 9 school board seats. They have made gains in obtaining higher level positions in the governmental and school bureaucracies, advances that may have occurred under the old structure as well, given the current emphasis on affirmative action programs in employment. The merger of the city and county school districts, a major feature of the reorganization plan, eliminated inequities that existed between the old systems and (although not foreseen at the time of adoption) enabled the courts to mandate an areawide solution to the school integration problem. Despite considerable vocal opposition, desegregation through large-scale busing was put into effect without violence. The more important school issue now is the quality of education, which many residents view as unsatisfactory.[22]

The Jacksonville Merger

Another city–county consolidation, that of Jacksonville and Duval County, materialized in 1967, when voters throughout the county voiced their approval by a margin of almost 2 to 1. Four small municipalities totaling about 20,000 inhabitants were given the right of separate vote on the proposition by the state legislature, and all decided against inclusion. They now receive from the consolidated government the services formerly provided to them by the county. At its inception the new government, officially named the City of

[22]Henry J. Schmandt, George D. Wendel, and John T. Manns, *Government, Politics, and the Public Schools: A Preliminary Study of Three Cities* (St. Louis: St. Louis University, Center for Urban Programs, September 1977), pp. 45–68.

Jacksonville, had more than a half million people and a land area of 766 square miles.

Similar to the Nashville plan, the merged area is divided into two service districts: general and urban. In the former, which contains the total territory, the new government supplies services such as fire and police protection, health, recreation and parks, schools, streets and highways, and welfare—all financed by areawide funds. In the latter, which encompasses the former city of Jacksonville, the new unit furnishes water, sewerage, street lighting and cleaning, and garbage and refuse collection, for which an additional charge is made. This district may be enlarged by the council as the need for these urban-type services spreads.[23]

Metro operates under a mayor–council system characterized by a fair degree of administrative integration. The independently elected mayor appoints most of the department heads, subject to council confirmation, and selects a chief administrative officer. The council is composed of five members elected at large and fourteen chosen from single-member districts. The sheriff, tax assessor, tax collector, supervisor of elections, civil service commission, and school board are also popularly elected but are now under the mayor's budgetary control. Independent agencies such as the electric power, port, and hospital authorities are subject to a lesser degree of control by the consolidated government.

The Jacksonville reorganization, as that in Baton Rouge, experienced difficulties in its initial stages, even though the charter provided for a seven-month period of orderly transition from the old system to the new. Some outgoing officials placed various obstacles in the path of the incoming government. The old city council, for example, voted sizable salary increases to the fire fighters to take effect immediately before the consolidated unit went into operation, an action financially embarrassing to the new government. Opponents also filed a lawsuit challenging the constitutionality of the merger in an effort to nullify the entire reorganization. The state supreme court, however, unanimously upheld the legality of the consolidation.

The first mayor of the merged city–county, initially unopposed

---

[23]Differential property taxation is now common in consolidated city-counties. Andrew G. White, "Different Property Taxation in Consolidated City-Counties," *National Civic Review* 63 (June 1974): 301–305, 331. For an analysis of the Jacksonville merger see John M. DeGrove, "Southern Regionalism" in Kent Mathewson (ed.), *The Regionalist Papers,* 2d ed. (Southfield, Mich.: Metropolitan Fund, 1978), pp. 98–108.

for the post and later reelected by defeating a former governor who symbolized the old-style preconsolidation politics, had an impeccable record as a judge and was widely respected. He appointed qualified administrators and worked closely with the budget director on developing a rational financing plan. Since the reorganization, a recreational program has been advanced, a minimum housing code adopted and rigorously enforced, an aggressive program of attracting federal funds initiated, and industrial development vigorously promoted. Community leaders, irrespective of race, judge the place of blacks in the new political structure as a marked improvement over the preconsolidation period. There has been a sharp rise in public jobs for blacks; they now hold 4 of the 19 council seats, and they have received at least one appointment to each board or commission of the consolidated government. Costs did increase after the merger but the property tax has decreased and the quality and range of services have substantially improved.

The Indianapolis Unigov

The fourth major city–county consolidation since World War II took place in 1969 with the merger of Indianapolis and Marion County, an area of nearly 400 square miles and 800,000 inhabitants. Unlike the previous adoptions, this consolidation was effected by act of the Indiana legislature, a procedure unprecedented in any state in this century. No local popular vote was involved, and the reorganization went into full effect the following year. Known as "Unigov," the Indianapolis plan resembles in some respects the Nashville and Jacksonville models. Certain urban-type functions, principally health and hospitals, planning and zoning, roads and streets, parks, and urban redevelopment, are provided on a countywide basis. Others, including police, fire, sanitation, libraries, and public housing, are furnished through fringe area municipalities and special service and taxing districts of varying territorial size smaller than the county. The reorganization left virtually untouched the previously existing 17 suburban municipalities, 11 school districts, and 9 townships.[24]

The principal officers of Unigov, chosen at partisan elections, are the mayor and a council of 29 members, all but 4 of whom are selected from single-member districts. More than 50 previously

---

[24]For a consideration of the Indianapolis consolidation, see York Willbern, "Unigov: Local Reorganization in Indianapolis," in *Regional Governance: Promise and Performance*, pp. 59–64.

separate and autonomous agencies were grouped into 6 strong administrative departments under the chief executive. A new transportation department took over the functions formerly exercised by the county highway department, city street department, park board, and mass transportation agency. All council members participate and vote in decisions relating to the county as a whole; but in matters affecting one of the individual service districts, only those representing that area take part. All the old county-elected offices, with one minor exception, remain independent, including the sheriff (who serves the area outside the former city of Indianapolis), auditor, treasurer, and assessor.

It is apparent from this description that the term *Unigov* is a misnomer, even though substantial policymaking and administrative integration has taken place. Basically, the reorganization brought about a merger of the two major local governments in Marion County but made no significant change in the service delivery system or its supporting tax structure. In fact, it created two new service districts—police and fire—within the boundaries of the old central city to keep these functions from being financed from countywide revenues.

The initial phases of the Indianapolis consolidation were plagued with fewer difficulties than the Baton Rouge and Jacksonville cases. Reorganization proceeded vigorously, with special emphasis on management improvement and the installation of streamlined and professional procedures. Some economies of scale were achieved by centralizing certain functions such as purchasing and financial administration. Unigov agencies actually employ fewer personnel than their predecessors, although the salary scale has been significantly increased particularly at the higher levels. Politically, the merger has enhanced the potential for areawide leadership by establishing the elective office of mayor of the consolidated city and county.

Black political strength has undoubtedly been weakened under the reorganization. Although blacks constituted only 27 percent of the population of the old city, they were rapidly becoming a numerical majority in the Democratic party (which usually won municipal elections). Some black leaders had argued that true consolidation, involving a sharing of the resource base of the county, would be beneficial to the black community even though its voting strength would be diluted in the process. The merger bill, however, made little change in the resource base situation. In fact, the basic element of the plan is that the costs of services are to be allocated as closely as possible to the areas where they are provided.

This objective is achieved through the use of multiple service districts, a practice that effectively hinders any general sharing of the county's public resources on the basis of need.

Unigov is now well established. Business leaders and civic groups are generally content with the administrative reforms that have been accomplished. Democrats, although outnumbered on the full council, have managed to exert substantial influence over the operation of the inner city through control of the budgets of the police and fire districts. Blacks, although not happy with the new system because of its avoidance of the resource redistribution issue, have fared better than previously in government appointments and public service positions. Today it is highly improbable that any of the major groups in Indianapolis would mount a frontal attack on Unigov's existence. Nor, on the other hand, would they be likely to make a serious effort to move the system from partial to complete consolidation.[25]

SCHOOL DISTRICT CONSOLIDATION

The vast amount of school district consolidation (many professional educators prefer to call it reorganization or redistricting) in the past several decades contrasts markedly with the small number of city–county and municipal mergers realized during the same period. School districts continued their long-established trend of rapid proliferation until the early 1930s when they reached the huge total of approximately 127,000, constituting almost three-fourths of all governmental units. Since then a steady and at times spectacular decrease has taken place, with the rate of consolidation accelerating considerably since the end of World War II. By 1977 the number had dropped to 15,174, about one-ninth the total of 45 years before. This development represents the first large-scale use of governmental consolidation in the nation's history and the first substantial decrease in number in any category of local units. The movement has been common to many SMSAs as well as nonmetropolitan areas but it has rarely involved the central city system.[26] Now the possi-

[25]Tom Gorton, "Unigov: Can a Partial Merger Be a Total Success?" *Planning* 44 (April/May 1978): 16–21.
[26]For differing attitudes of central city and suburban residents and officials toward a single metropolitan school district see Basil G. Zimmer and Amos H. Hawley, *Resistance to Reorganization of School Districts and Government in Metropolitan Areas* (Providence: Brown University, 1966), pp. 293–316. Factors influencing attitudes toward consolidation are discussed in David W. Scott, "School District Integration in a Metropolitan Area," *Education and Urban Society* 4 (February 1972): 135–154.

bility of merging core area schools with outlying districts has become even more remote in the light of extensive court-ordered desegregation within many central municipalities. This unlikelihood is evident from the strong public opposition to proposals designed to bring about racial and ethnic integration through the establishment of metropolitanwide school districts.

Although the era of large-scale school consolidation has now passed, the reasons for the success of the merger drive remain of interest. Two factors stand out prominently in this connection. One is the willingness shown by state legislatures to foster such action, a readiness prompted by rising educational costs and increasing pressure on the states to assume a greater share of school financing. The other is the strong advocacy of consolidation demonstrated by professional educators and civic leaders who see merger of the smaller districts as imperative to quality education.

State legislatures used two means to promote school consolidation. They amended reorganization laws to eliminate the requirement calling for local initiative of school merger proposals and for majority consent of the voters in each involved district. They also made supplementary financial grants available to consolidated systems, thus offering an enticing incentive. The new legislation took several forms. In some instances county boards of education or specially constituted school reorganization committees were empowered to order merger without local referenda. In others the law specified that as of a certain date all school districts within a given area would be combined. In still others the legislation provided for the formulation of merger plans by special committees, approval by the state superintendent of schools, and submission of the proposals to the voters in the affected districts. Many laws of this last type do not require the consent of voters in each involved district but simply an overall majority in the area of the proposed consolidation.[27]

Professional and lay leadership, the second contributing factor to successful reorganization, was demonstrated in the strong support given to the passage and implementation of school consolidation laws. These efforts were aided by the conviction on the part of many state legislators, educational officials, and private citizens that the merger of school districts would result in higher quality education and more efficient use of public funds. The lack of a comparable conviction by similar elements in respect to municipal and

---

[27]A more detailed analysis of the techniques of school district consolidation is found in John C. Bollens, *Special District Governments in the United States* (Berkeley and Los Angeles: University of California Press, 1957), pp. 192–227.

city-county consolidations helps to explain the low rate of acceptance in that field.

COMPREHENSIVE URBAN COUNTY PLAN: MIAMI

Major structural reorganization of the metropolitan political system has not been confined to the single-government approaches of annexation and consolidation. Starting in the 1950s many reform advocates developed plans based on the principle of federalism, a division of powers and functions between two levels of local government (supporters of submunicipal decentralization or neighborhood control would add a third tier). The new focus was prompted in part by the repeated failures of one-government proposals and in part by the conviction that a federal-type solution would avoid the undesirable features associated with large-scale bureaucracies.

Reorganization based on the bi-level arrangement takes two major forms. One is the comprehensive urban county plan, the other is federation. The first calls for the simultaneous transfer of selected functions from municipalities (and at times from other local units) to the county government.[28] The second features the establishment of a new areawide government (usually in multicounty metropolises) that is assigned a broad range of responsibilities. Both these arrangements represent a halfway house between the extremes of drastic and minor solutions to the governmental problems of metropolitan areas. They seek to preserve much of the existing structure while making only those modifications deemed necessary to combat serious areawide difficulties.

Under the comprehensive urban county plan, the county government, through reassignment of powers and possibly new grants of authority, assumes functions deemed to be of an areawide nature, whereas municipalities and other local units continue to perform local-type services. The geographical fact that many SMSAs (approximately 100) lie within the boundaries of a single county enhances the appeal of this approach. The concept is also relevant for metropolises of more than one county where most of the urbanized area is within the central county. In either case the plan has the advantage of utilizing an existing unit of government rather than adding another public agency to an already fragmented system. Despite its attractive features and the many attempts to secure

---

[28]The combination of two characteristics of this plan—comprehensiveness and simultaneity—differentiates this method of reorganization from other forms of the urban county development that are discussed in Chapter 12.

its adoption, the comprehensive urban county approach has become a reality in only one locality: Metropolitan Miami.

When its charter went into effect in July 1957, Dade County (Miami) became the first metropolis in the United States to put the comprehensive urban county plan into operation. Two barriers to this type of dual-level approach had to be overcome: lack of state constitutional authorization to draft a county charter featuring such a plan and local voter approval of the document. These impediments have proved insurmountable elsewhere.

The state legislative delegation from Dade County played a prominent part in surmounting the first by successfully guiding a proposed constitutional home rule amendment through the Florida legislature in 1955.[29] The proposal, which authorized the preparation of a plan of governmental reorganization for the Miami area, was decisively approved by the statewide electorate in the following year. In 1957 the charter, which had been prepared by a gubernatorial-appointed board, barely gained the required single county-wide majority (44,404 to 42,620). With only about one-fourth of the county's registered voters participating in the special election, heavy support in the city of Miami brought victory for the proposition.

Functions and Organization

The charter provides for a powerful and structurally integrated county government, officially designated as Metropolitan Dade County, and for the continuance of the existing 27 municipalities (Figure 11.3). The county government, encompassing 2054 square miles, is authorized to construct expressways, regulate traffic, and own and operate mass transit systems; maintain central records, training, and communication for fire and police protection; provide hospitals and public health services; furnish parks and recreational areas; and administer housing, urban redevelopment, and air pollution control programs. It is also authorized to prepare and enforce comprehensive plans for the development of the county, thus gaining a grant of power of great significance that is seldom even proposed for a metropolitan government. On related fronts it is permitted to adopt and enforce zoning and business regulations and

---

[29]Following voter defeat of city–county consolidation in 1953, the Metropolitan Miami Municipal Board, a study group appointed by the city of Miami, recommended abolishment of the county government and creation of a federated system. The county's legislative delegation, however, objected to this approach, stipulating that any reorganization plan must be based on retention of the county government.

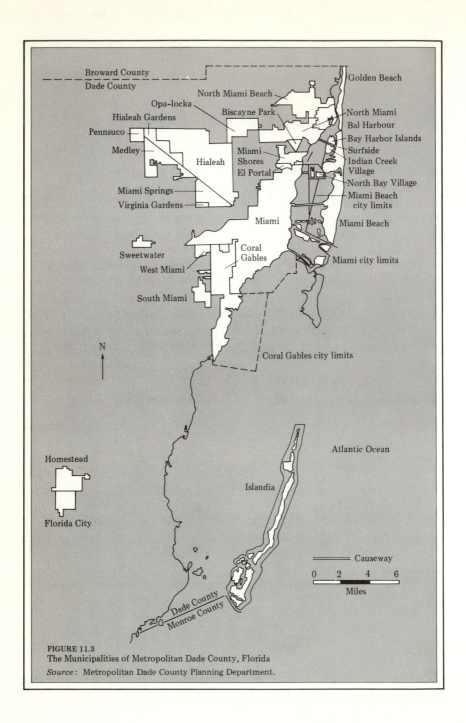

Broward County
Dade County

Golden Beach

North Miami Beach

Opa-locka

Biscayne Park

North Miami

Hialeah Gardens

Bal Harbour

Pennsuco

Bay Harbor Islands

Medley

Miami
Shores

Surfside

Hialeah

Indian Creek
Village

El Portal

Miami Springs

North Bay Village

Virginia Gardens

Miami Beach
city limits

Miami

Miami Beach

Sweetwater

Coral
Gables

West Miami

Miami city limits

South Miami

N

Coral Gables city limits

Atlantic Ocean

Homestead

Islandia

Florida City

Causeway

0   2   4   6
Miles

Dade County
Monroe County

FIGURE 11.3
The Municipalities of Metropolitan Dade County, Florida
Source: Metropolitan Dade County Planning Department.

uniform building and related technical codes throughout its territory.

The county government is also empowered to set reasonable minimum service standards for all local units within its territorial bounds and to take over an activity if there is failure to comply with these criteria (to date, no such assumption of a service has occurred). Additional municipalities can be created and annexations completed only on the authorization of the county governing body and after affirmative majority approval by the voters in the proposed incorporation. However, no municipality existing at the time of the charter's adoption can be abolished except by majority consent of its electors. Finally, the county board may establish and administer special districts and finance their services and facilities by charges made within such areas.

The charter also brought on a thorough revamping of county governmental organization and processes. It specified that the county commissioners, elected on a nonpartisan ballot, are to constitute the legislative and governing body with power to appoint and remove a county manager. Administrative operations were brought under the manager's jurisdiction, a far cry from the supplanted rambling structure. The charter abolished the elective status of the assessor, tax collector, surveyor, purchasing agent, and supervisor of voter registration, and made the holders of these offices appointees of the manager. It also conferred authority on the county board to eliminate the election of the sheriff and constables, a power that was subsequently exercised.

The five county commissioners in office at the time the charter went into effect were continued in those positions under a provision of the charter. Because their four-year terms had just begun in the previous year, they constituted the entire membership of the board until 1958 when other provisions of the charter relating to the governing board became operative. These called for the election of one commissioner at large from each of five districts, one from each of these areas by the district voters only, and one from each city containing an official population of at least 60,000. When these charter sections first became applicable, the board consisted of 11 members, as Miami was then the only municipality to qualify under the 60,000 population rule. After the federal census of 1960, the board's size increased to 13, because both Hialeah and Miami Beach then exceeded 60,000 people. (As noted later, the composition and size of the commission were changed in 1963 by charter amendment.)

The metropolitan government (Metro) in Dade County encountered major opposition during its initial years when it was subjected to continuing harassment by various municipal officials and former county officeholders. Hundreds of lawsuits were filed against it, with some not reaching final settlement for years.[30] Certain of these actions resulted from the hasty and drastic manner in which the board of county commissioners immediately moved ahead on a number of highly sensitive subjects. Others, however, were deliberate efforts to torment the new government. Attempts were also made by opponents to secure adoption of antimetro charter amendments that would have stripped Metro of most of its powers. These opposition efforts, however, proved to be mostly sound and fury, producing little change in the metropolitan government as originally constituted.

Despite the harassment it has undergone, the new government has registered accomplishments in terms of both its organization and processes and its functional activities. Some major actions are summarized here to indicate the range and direction of its efforts:

1. Integration of a formerly haphazard administrative organization and installation of modern management practices.
2. Completion and adoption of a strong comprehensive land use plan for the county.
3. Adoption of stringent regulations to control air and water pollution.
4. Establishment of uniform, countywide traffic laws, with all violators being tried in the metropolitan court.
5. Assumption of the tax assessment and collection functions from all the cities.
6. Enactment of a uniform subdivision ordinance to control land development, both inside and outside the municipalities.
7. Creation of a department of housing and urban development.
8. Purchase of four bus lines and initiation of a rapid transit system.
9. Provision of fire protection for 19 municipalities as well as the unincorporated areas.
10. Launching of a major capital improvement program after voter approval of a $553 million bond issue in 1972.

---

[30]Joseph Metzger, "Metro and Its Judicial History," *University of Miami Law Review* 15 (Spring 1961): 283–293, considers a number of cases.

Problems and Challenges

Finance and leadership continue to be vexing and persistent problems in Dade County. The constitutional amendment authorizing county home rule furnished the means of creating a metropolitan government but failed to confer additional taxing powers on the new unit. In essence, the county government has had to utilize its prereorganization tax structure to finance new and improved areawide services as well as municipal-type functions to the hundreds of thousands of residents in the unincorporated areas. It obtained some financial assistance in 1967 when the state legislature revised its gas tax distribution formula. It has also been aggressive in seeking intergovernmental aid, increasing its share of state funds since 1957 at a greater rate than other urban counties in Florida and faring even better in its fiscal relations with the national government.[31] Nevertheless, these have been only relative gains and not financial solutions.

The fiscal problems in Dade County are further aggravated by the fact that 45 percent of its total population resides in the fast-growing unincorporated areas. Besides having primary responsibility as a metropolitan instrumentality, the county government must also function as a local unit in these areas. As a result, it is compelled to use an important part of its resources and revenues to provide local-type services. This arrangement, in effect, penalizes the municipalities by compelling them to pay a share of the cost of furnishing such services to the unincorporated residents. Official proposals were advanced in the early 1960s and again in 1971 to establish service districts in these sections so that their inhabitants could be charged for urban functions, but these efforts have met with only partial success.

The absence of strong political leadership, both inside and outside the metropolitan government, has been a long-standing complaint in Dade County. Various individuals and groups attribute much of the problem to the manager form of government. This dissatisfaction led to the amendment of the charter in 1963 to provide

[31]Parris N. Glendening, "The Metropolitan Dade County Government: An Examination of Reform." Unpublished Ph.D. dissertation, Florida State University, Tallahassee, 1967. Professor Glendening also demonstrates how claims about probable effects of the Dade County reform on the electoral system, such as increased citizen participation, have generally been erroneous, whereas those about the impact on the governmental system, such as greater efficiency, have usually proved valid. See also the same author's "Metropolitan Dade County: A Test of the Local Government Reform Model." Paper presented at the 1968 meeting of the American Political Science Association.

for a county-governing commission of nine members, eight elected countywide with district residence requirements (on the premise that at-large elections would bring a greater areawide perspective to this body), and one elected as mayor to serve as permanent board chairperson. Supporters of the amendment believed that at least part of the needed political leadership would be produced by independently electing an official who would be designated as mayor. Such, however, has not been the case. The mayor remains merely the first among equals, a commissioner who serves as the ceremonial head of Metropolitan Dade County.

Other advocates of more effective leadership have sought to supplant the county manager operation with a strong mayor–commission system. Such a proposition was placed on the ballot in 1972 as part of a package measure. It called for an elected mayor with broad appointive authority and for an appointed general administrator to handle the day-to-day operations of the government. It also provided for a 14-member commission (the mayor would possess veto power over its actions), 11 chosen from districts and 3 elected at large. Although the Hispanics and blacks supported the district election feature (no Hispanic or black has as yet been elected to the governing body), the measure was roundly defeated by a vote of more than two to one. Opponents either did not want to give the mayor extensive power or felt that the county manager arrangement is essential to the efficient operation of the system.[32] Many people acknowledge that a leadership gap exists but attribute it to the fragmentation and diffusion of community relations rather than to the metropolitan governmental structure.[33]

Important as the shortcomings of finance and leadership may be, the overriding uncertainty about the two-level system in Dade County centers on the municipalities. According to most observers, effective working relationships between the county and the cities have been slow in developing. This failure was pointed out in 1962 by the county manager and reemphasized four years later when the Dade County state legislative delegation warned that the problem of city–county relationships was crucial to Metro's success. The slow progress that has been made in correcting this situation is reflected in the conclusion reached in 1971 by a study group organized by the county commission: "Much of the local history of

---

[32]Edward Sofen, *The Miami Metropolitan Experiment*, rev. ed. (Garden City, N.Y.: Anchor Books, 1966), pp. 253–255. See also by the same author, "Quest for Leadership," *National Civic Review* 57 (July 1968): 346–351, and Aileen R. Lotz, "Strong Mayor Plan Defeated in Dade," *National Civic Review* 61 (June 1972): 303–304.
[33]John M. DeGrove, "Southern Regionalism" in Kent Mathewson (ed.), *The Regionalist Papers*, 2d ed., (Southfield, Mich.: Metropolitan Fund, 1978), p. 114.

Dade County after the adoption of the Metropolitan Home Rule Charter in 1957 can be written in terms of the unstable relationships and continuing struggle between the two levels of government—county and municipality—for the allegiance and control of the citizens to whom they are both responsible and over whom they both operate."[34]

The Dade County metropolitan government now has a budget of over $1 billion and a work force of 18,000 employees to serve the 1.5 million residents within its jurisdiction. It has won general public approval and serious moves to abolish it or curtail its powers are no longer evident. Community leaders, as noted recently by a *Miami Herald* reporter who has covered Metro since its inception, continue to disagree as to its original purpose and final destiny.[35] One group, the consolidationists, look on it as a step toward complete merger and the elimination of the municipalities. The other, the federationists, maintain that the major goal—to create a government capable of handling areawide needs—has been achieved by the two-tier system, and the task that remains is to improve it.

To most Dade countians the question of governmental structure is of little interest at the present time. Their attention is concentrated on more pressing community concerns related principally to the ethnic and racial composition of the area and high crime rates. Approximately 15 percent of the county's population is black and well over one-third of Hispanic origin, predominantly Cuban. The Miami SMSA is rapidly developing into a commercial and financial center of trade with Latin America (and also a center of illegal drug activity). The latest wave of Cuban refugees (over 100,000 within a two-month period in 1980) has strained the locality's resources and aggravated ethnic and racial tensions. The riot that erupted in May 1980 in a black section of Miami—the worst outbreak of racial violence in an American city since the mid 1960s—underscored the growing magnitude of the problem.

Although the riot was sparked by the acquittal of four white police officers of the Dade County (Metro) force who were charged with bludgeoning to death a black businessman, the event reflected the depth of disaffection among the area's black residents. This disaffection is attributable in part to poverty, high unemployment, and grievances against the criminal justice system, but it is also fueled

---

[34]Irving G. McNayr, "Recommendations for Unified Government in Dade County" (A Report of the County Manager to the Board of County Commissioners, Miami, September 25, 1962), p. 7. *Report of the Dade County Metropolitan Study Commission,* p. 43.

[35]Juanita Greene, "Dade Metro: Turbulent History, Uncertain Future," *Planning* 45 (February 1979): 14–16.

by what many blacks perceive as favored or preferential treatment of the Cuban population by governmental agencies (and by the private business sector as well). White Anglos are also evidencing signs of resentment at the continued influx of Cubans (and now Haitian) refugees and the growing political and economic power of the Hispanic-origin residents.

FEDERATION: METROPOLITAN TORONTO

Federation, the second variation of the comprehensive two-level approach, involves the creation of a new government of intercounty territorial scope. It is almost identical with the comprehensive county approach except for its involvement of more than one county and its non-retention of the county government as the metropolitan agency.[36] It may differ, however, in one additional respect, that pertaining to representation. Federation plans usually provide that the metropolitan governing board be composed of representatives of the municipalities, but it is doubtful that this method would now meet the constitutional test of "one person-one vote." Similar to the comprehensive urban county approach, federation places areawide powers in the upper tier of the system and leaves the municipalities intact (sometimes after being territorially enlarged) to carry out local functions.

Interest in federation plans in the United States had virtually disappeared by the 1950s at the very time the concept was gaining attention in neighboring Canada. Today four major metropolitan areas in that country operate under federated systems: Toronto, Niagara, Ottawa, and Quebec.[37] Metropolitan Toronto, Canada's second most populous settlement, was the first to experience governmental restructuring. A combination of factors was responsible for the change (which occurred in 1953), principally the existence of

---

[36]A federation plan conceivably could be utilized in a single-county SMSA. Its use would require abolition of the county government and its replacement with a new metropolitan agency. Some of the earlier reform proposals in the United States, including those in the 1930s for Allegheny County (Pittsburgh) and Alameda County (Oakland) called for such action.

[37]A metropolitan government was also established in Montreal but it encompasses only the Island of Montreal and not its substantial urban overspill. For treatments of the Canadian reorganizations see Thomas J. Plunkett, "Structural Reform of Local Government in Canada," *Public Administration Review* 33 (January/February 1973): 40–51; Eric Hardy's chapter on the Toronto and Montreal metropolitan areas in William A. Robson and D. E. Regan, *Great Cities of the World: Their Government, Politics, and Planning*, 3d ed., vol. 2 (London: Allen and Unwin, 1972), pp. 987–1037; and Allan O'Brien, "Metropolitan Forms of Government in Canada," *Municipal Year Book, 1978*, pp. 73–77.

critical financial and service problems in the area, the recommendations of an official board, and the favorable attitude of the Ontario provincial parliament (state legislature).

Following World War II the needs of several Toronto suburbs began to outdistance their financial resources, causing tax rates to rise rapidly and greatly increasing the costs of borrowing money for capital improvements. When the local communities proved incapable of working out adequate solutions to their problems through interlocal agreements, two of the municipalities took their plight to the Ontario Municipal Board, a province-appointed agency with certain quasi-judicial and administrative powers. This body exercises control over various aspects of local government finance and, on application by one or more municipalities, can order boundary adjustments.

After many months of hearings on the requests of the two units, each seeking a different remedy, the board announced its denial of the application but stated that it was assuming "the responsibility of presenting its own proposals for the organization of a suitable form of metropolitan government in the Toronto area . . . [because the petitioning communities] have clearly established the urgent need for some major reform of the existing system."[38] In line with this intention, the board submitted to the provincial premier a recommended plan of federation for the 13 municipalities in the Toronto metropolis. A bill, closely following the proposed changes, was promptly enacted by the Ontario parliament. Passage of the act marked the first large-scale metropolitan governmental restructuring in Canadian history.

The Initial Years

The federation plan as originally adopted embodied several major features. First, it established a strong areawide government, the Municipality of Metropolitan Toronto (soon popularly shortened to Metro), encompassing 13 municipalities within its boundaries (a total of 241 square miles, containing at the federation's inception about 1,200,000 residents). Second, it provided for the continued existence of the city of Toronto and the 12 suburban governments to carry out functions not assigned to the metropolitan level. Third, it gave representation on Metro's governing board to each of the municipalities. And fourth, it created a metropolitan school board

[38]Ontario Municipal Board, *Decisions and Recommendations of the Board* (Toronto, January 20, 1953), p. 42. This publication is also known as the Cumming Report (after the board chairman, Lorne Cumming).

(composed of *ex officio* representatives from the 11 existing local districts) to exercise certain fiscal functions in elementary and secondary education matters.

The legislation endows the metropolitan government with considerable power over a broad range of functions including water supply, sewage disposal, arterial roads, health and welfare services, administration of justice, and regional parks. In the case of some activities Metro shares responsibility with the municipalities. For example, it maintains the water and sewage treatment plants and the trunk lines, and the local governments operate the water distribution facilities and sewage collection systems. The arrangement is similar in the case of the road network, with Metro responsible for constructing and maintaining the arterial highways, whereas the individual units have jurisdiction over the local streets.

The reorganization act gives Metro the power to appoint the members of the Toronto Transit Commission, the area's exclusive supplier of public transportation and the operator of a modern subway system. It also authorizes the areawide government to undertake housing and redevelopment projects and to assess property at a uniform rate throughout the larger community for use in both metropolitan and local tax levies. Finally, it vests another function of great significance—planning—in the upper tier, directing Metro to formulate and adopt a general plan for the physical development of the area. This plan becomes binding on the local units after its approval by the provincial minister of municipal affairs.

Until 1967 the Toronto federation provided for equal representation on the 24-member metropolitan council between the central city and the suburbs, with each of the latter, regardless of population size, having one seat. All members must be elected officials of the constituent municipalities; their terms, originally one year, were increased to two years in 1956. A chairperson, designated as the government's executive officer, is selected from either within or outside the council by its members (the initial appointment was made by the provincial premier). The term of the office is the same as that of the other members.

The 1967 Modifications

The major changes that went into effect in 1967, as the result of provincial legislation, pertain mostly to the local tier in the two-level system and to the size and representational base of the metropolitan council. The 13 municipalities were consolidated into six municipal governments, composed of the city of Toronto and five boroughs. The boundaries of the central city and those of three boroughs were extended through mergers, but the limits of the two others (the most populous suburban towns under the original federation) were left unaltered (Figure 11.4). The 11 local school boards were consolidated into six and their territorial bounds made coterminous with those of the six municipalities.

The revision increased the size of the metropolitan council to 32 (33 if its chairperson is chosen from outside its membership). During the lifetime of the federation, the only persons to occupy the top office have been former local officials selected from outside the council. The new formula gave the enlarged city of Toronto 12 seats, the same number as previously, and allotted between 2 and 6 to each suburban borough, thus appreciably increasing the proportion of representatives from the outlying areas. By 1977 the membership had risen to 37, with the suburbs gaining 4 additional seats. (In 1980 it increased to 39, with 2 more in the suburbs.)

These alterations in the metropolitan governing body emanated from persistent dissatisfaction with the original arrangements. From the start, most criticism centered on the allotment of

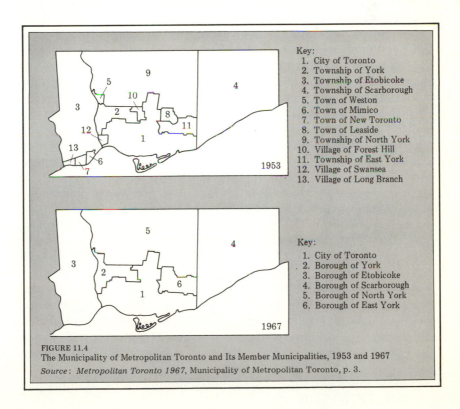

FIGURE 11.4
The Municipality of Metropolitan Toronto and Its Member Municipalities, 1953 and 1967
Source: Metropolitan Toronto 1967, Municipality of Metropolitan Toronto, p. 3.

one seat to each suburban government, irrespective of its population. At the inception of the federation plan, some suburbs had more than ten times the population of others, and these disparities became even greater with the passage of time. Controversy over the equal division of representation between the central city and the outlying municipalities was not present at the outset. Toronto, which then had almost three-fifths of the population, was deliberately underrepresented in the initial stage to avoid the possibility of its dominating the metropolitan government. Opposition to its proportion of the total representation developed as the outlying areas surpassed it in population; when the 1967 reforms went into effect, Toronto had only about 40 percent of the area's residents (now down to one-third).

The new legislation also lengthened the terms of office of the chairperson and other members of the metropolitan council to three years and increased the size of the executive committee from seven to eleven members. This powerful committee—consisting of the chairperson, five representatives from Toronto, and five from the suburban governments—is responsible for preparing the annual budget, awarding contracts, nominating all directors and chief deputies of departments, and proposing policies. A two-thirds vote of the council is necessary to overrule its actions on contract awards and personnel nominations.

The 1967 reforms also brought about several important changes in educational financing. Under the original legislation the metropolitan school board made uniform per pupil payments to the local districts to provide a minimum floor. The individual boards were then permitted to levy a local tax—if they so desired—to provide funds beyond those received from the metropolitan agency and the province. Although this arrangement brought about a measure of equalization, it still enabled the wealthier districts to spend more on education than their less affluent neighbors. Under the new provisions the metropolitan school board, after reviewing the operating budgets of the local districts, provides them with the required funds through a uniform areawide levy. The local boards may tax their people for limited additional money only for special purposes. Financing school construction and other capital needs is now also the responsibility of the metropolitan board. These procedures have eliminated the earlier disparities in school financing and have made it possible to furnish an equivalent standard of education to every student in the metropolis. (The local boards retain the power to engage teachers and administrative staff and to operate the schools.)

Amid these various changes, two prominent aspects of the fed-

eration remained unaltered. The powers of the metropolitan government were left undisturbed and its territorial boundaries were
not expanded despite the argument of some observers that urbanization had spread beyond its original limits. At a minimum, the
total impact of the new provisions represents a strengthening of the
metropolitan tier and a further integration of the system.

Gains and Limitations

The Toronto area federation has made its greatest progress in dealing with highly critical needs of the prereform period, particularly
those relating to education, water supply, and sewage disposal.
Many new school buildings have been completed and the capacities of the water supply and sewage disposal facilities greatly enlarged. Extensive expressway construction has taken place, and
mass transit has progressed through subway and bus line extensions. A regional park system has been developed and public housing and homes for the aged erected. Unified law enforcement has
helped to produce a reduced crime rate and increased clearance of
crimes. The equalization ability of the areawide school unit has improved public education. Investment rating services have given
Metro a triple "A" designation in Canada and a double "A" in New
York City, the highest classification a foreign corporation can receive in the United States. Interest savings of many millions of dollars on bond issues have been gained because of this excellent financial standing.

As political scientist Harold Kaplan has pointed out, the metropolitan federation was a necessary but not sufficient cause of these
achievements. One important contributor to the attainments has
been the powerful role played by the chairpersons of the metropolitan council, all of whom, according to one observer, have proved to
be "just the kind of individuals that Metro Toronto required at the
time of their accession to office." They have worked with the executive committee to secure approval of their policy proposals (com-
mittee-sanctioned propositions have seldom been overturned in
the full council). They have also followed the practice of securing
agreement among department heads on policy matters before placing them on the legislative agenda. In other words, the chairpersons have operated basically as intermediaries between the metropolitan councilors and the bureaucracies. Other factors contributing to Metro's effectiveness have been the weak involvement of interest groups in areawide issues, the absence of major
influence of factions and parties in the council, and the general
willingness of the members to go along with the chairperson. The

last-named factor grows out of the emphasis in Canadian political culture on deference to individuals in positions of authority and to the time-consuming involvement of metropolitan representatives in the affairs of their own municipalities.[39]

The accomplishments of Metro have been far less impressive in what Frank Smallwood, a political scientist, has called "the softer, more socially oriented issue areas where results are usually less tangible and more controversial."[40] This point was reiterated as late as 1972 by Albert Rose, dean of the faculty of social work at the University of Toronto. Although acknowledging the extraordinary physical developments that the metropolitan government had accomplished, he charged it with ignoring or giving scant attention to the social problems of the central city. Toronto, which was a "have" municipality at the inception of the reform, had become a "have not" city as its proportion of the population and wealth of the area declined, and its needs intensified. In Rose's words, the real test of the durability of the two-level system "is not the clear and impartial sharing of areawide resources that occurred between 1954 and 1969, but the transmutation of that process to benefit the City during the 1970s and 1980s."[41]

The most recent study of Metro, conducted over a three-year period (1974–1977) by a royal commission, stressed that local government must now give the planning and delivery of human services the same priority it placed on the provision of schools, roads, sewers, and water supply when the reorganization had gone into effect almost a quarter-century before. The commission, headed by former Ontario premier John Robarts, concluded that the metropolitan system had worked well in meeting the challenge of urban growth and providing a high level of services. It noted, however, that the period of "buoyant revenues" from a rapidly expanding tax base was over, a fact necessitating refinement of the machinery of government "to enable local decisionmakers to adapt to the new circumstances." To achieve this end the commission made 126 rec-

[39]Harold Kaplan, "Metro Toronto: Forming a Policy-Formation Process," in Edward C. Banfield (ed.), *Urban Government: A Reader in Administration and Politics*, rev. ed. (New York: Free Press, 1969), pp. 623–625. Also, see Harold Kaplan, *Urban Political Systems: A Functional Analysis of Metro Toronto* (New York: Columbia University Press, 1967).

[40]Frank Smallwood, *Metro Toronto: A Decade Later* (Toronto: Bureau of Municipal Research, 1963), p. 35.

[41]Albert Rose, *Governing Metropolitan Toronto: A Social and Political Analysis, 1953–1971* (Berkeley and Los Angeles: University of California Press, 1972), pp. 155, 175–179, 183–184.

ommendations pertaining to the structure, organization, and financing of the metropolitan system.

The Robarts report rejected the idea of total amalgamation in favor of continuing the two-tier arrangement. Its most controversial proposal called for the direct election of representatives to the metropolitan council from districts of equal population size throughout the area, a change that would have increased the number of suburban seats. The recommendations as a whole were designed to strengthen the entire local governmental system in the area by reducing provincial supervision and increasing the powers of Metro and its six constituent units. The proposed changes, however, met a cool reception from the Ontario legislature and were quickly dropped.[42]

The metropolitan government concept is firmly established in the Toronto area. No interest is manifest—even among the suburbs that initially opposed the reorganization—in returning to the pre-1954 system. The changes made since Metro came into existence have been in the direction of more comprehensive reform, witness the additional functions assigned to the metropolitan level and the reduction in the number of municipalities by more than half. For a time many observers felt that these modifications (and the growing problems of the central city) pointed to eventual consolidation. Now the view is otherwise. Little public support for amalgamation has materialized and the two-tier model appears to be widely accepted as the permanent solution.

NEIGHBORHOOD DECENTRALIZATION: COUNTERPOISE TO BUREAUCRATIC BIGNESS

The idea of using neighborhoods as centers for public services, citizen–government communication, and public decision making has gained considerable prominence in recent years. Such a concept, which is concerned with decentralizing activities and power in big cities through structural arrangements, is a counterbalance to that of the one-government and two-level metropolitan approaches. Interestingly, some of the leading exponents of centralized control for the metropolis are also advocates of the regeneration of neighbor-

---

[42]Toronto Bureau of Municipal Research, *In Reponse to the Robarts Report* (Toronto: October, 1977). The complete Robarts report is contained in two volumes: Report of the Royal Commission on Metropolitan Toronto, Volume 1: *Metropolitan Toronto: A Framework for the Future* and Volume 2: *Detailed Findings and Recommendations*, both published in June 1977.

hoods as governmental areas in large municipalities. The Committee for Economic Development and the National Commission on Urban Problems are illustrations. The CED has suggested the possibility of forming neighborhood districts in big cities for the purposes of clarifying locality needs and proposing solutions to them. The national commission similarly noted that such cities should have manageable decentralized areas because "the psychological distance from the neighborhood to City Hall has grown from blocks, to miles, to light-years. With decreasing communication and sense of identification by the low-income resident with his government have come first apathy, then disaffection, and now [1968]—insurrection."[43]

The various forms of municipal decentralization fall into two broad categories: administrative and political.[44] The first relates to the internal delegation of power to territorially based subordinates within the municipal bureaucracy; the second involves the transfer of authority to personnel who are responsible to a district electorate or service clientele. When public officials speak of decentralization they usually have in mind the former; when neighborhood advocates employ the term they invariably refer to the latter. The physical or administrative decentralization of various local governmental activities is a well-established practice. Facilities such as police precincts, fire stations, and branch offices of various operating departments have long been common in many large cities. More recently, little ("mini") city halls (mainly for information and referral purposes) and multiservice centers have been set up in some municipalities on a district basis.[45] Proposals have also been made for the use of neighborhood boards in advisory, monitoring, and advocacy capacities. The Los Angeles Charter Commission, to cite one instance, recommended the creation of neighborhood organizations "with an elected board and an appointed neighborman as an institutional mechanism for communicating neighborhood needs and

---

[43]Committee for Economic Development, *Modernizing Local Government* (New York, 1966); and National Commission on Urban Problems, *Final Report,* part IV, (Washington, D.C.: 1968). This latter report has also been published by Praeger as *Building the American City.*

[44]Various decentralization proposals are outlined or discussed in Report of the National Advisory Commission on Civil Disorders (New York: Bantam Books, 1968). For a review of the literature on decentralization see Henry J. Schmandt, "Municipal Decentralization: An Overview," *Public Administration Review* 32 (October 1972): 571–588.

[45]George J. Washnis, *Neighborhood Facilities and Municipal Decentralization,* 2 vols. (Washington, D.C.: Center for Governmental Studies, 1971).

goals, involving citizens in city affairs, and reducing feelings of alienation.[46]

Proposals for political decentralization move beyond these essentially administrative and advisory devices to forms of community control. The Advisory Commission on Intergovernmental Relations took this approach in recommending state legislation to permit the establishment of municipal subunits of government in metropolitan areas.[47] Community or neighborhood development corporations (CDCs) organized in some cities also take on certain features of locality governments. In Oakland, California, and Dayton, Ohio, for example, such corporations were formed as a means of bargaining for resident control over program planning and execution in the model cities areas.[48] A "minigov" bill enacted by the Indiana legislature in 1972 as a follow-up to "Unigov" also moved in this direction. It called for subdividing the entire area of the consolidated city into communities or districts, each with a population of not more than 40,000. Residents of each area could then petition the city–county for a referendum to create an elective neighborhood board. Fearful that such bodies might become focal points of political opposition, Unigov council members urged the legislature to repeal the law. Although the act was left standing, the provisions relating to the powers of the community boards were substantially watered down. Their emasculation eliminated neighborhood support for the idea and it remains inoperative.

The move for community government arose in the late 1960s out of the convergence of several forces: the belief on the part of racial minorities and other disadvantaged groups that they could not receive equitable treatment from the local governmental system as presently constituted; the mounting aversion to large-scale and impersonal bureaucratic power; and the impetus given to citizen or client participation by various federal programs. Advocates of this form of decentralization argue that it is a way of making local government more sensitive and responsive to the needs and preferences of the diverse groups it serves. Critics contend that it would promote racial separatism, intensify social friction, weaken the capacity of local government for effective action, and result in oligarchical patterns of rule by neighborhood cliques and interest groups.

[46]*City Government for the Future* (Los Angeles: City Charter Commission, 1969).
[47]*ACIR State Legislative Program: New Proposals for 1969* (Washington, D.C., 1968).
[48]Corporations of this type are discussed in Geoffrey Faux, *CDCs: New Hope for the Inner City* (New York: Twentieth Century Fund, 1971).

New York City has made the most use of submunicipal decentralization devices.[49] Sixty-two community boards, appointed by the borough presidents, were created in 1963 to provide citizen input into the planning process. Twelve years later amendments to the city charter provided for the establishment of administrative service areas (police, street cleaning, refuse collection, social services, and parks) to be coterminous with the community districts. The locality boards have the responsibility for preparing neighborhood improvement plans and reviewing all applications pertaining to land use within their area by public agencies and private developers. Each community board is authorized to appoint a district manager to assist in monitoring the delivery of services by municipal departments. The city also has inaugurated a measure of political decentralization in its school system. Under a 1969 state law, 31 community school districts have been set up, each with its own elected board. However, a central school board continues to exercise control over the most critical aspects of the educational process: budget, personnel, and programs.

Some proponents of neighborhood government recognize the need for a political structure that embodies the merits of centralization as well as decentralization.[50] To be workable, as they point out, political control at the submunicipal level must be complemented by a governmental unit with certain powers over the urban area as a whole. Such an agency is essential to handle the major maintenance functions of the metropolitan system; assure the openness of the opportunity structure for all segments of the population as to place of residence, housing, and education; and see to it that the area's public resources are allocated on an equitable basis and according to the needs of its various sections. In the absence of such an overall mechanism, neighborhood government would work to the serious disadvantage of the poorer sections of the community by leaving them to their own inadequate resources.

Despite all that has been written about municipal decentralization since the mid-1960s, only its lesser forms have achieved a measure of limited acceptance. Although neighborhood organizations

---

[49]New York City in the early 1970s set up an experimental program to provide for the decentralized delivery of services in five districts. A manager was assigned to each of these areas to coordinate the activities of the departments involved. Studies of the program show that little decentralization of authority to the districts actually took place. See Allen H. Barton and others, *Decentralizing City Government: An Evaluation of the New York District Manager Experiment* (Lexington, Mass.: Heath, 1977).

[50]See in this respect Howard W. Hallman, *Small and Large Together: Governing the Metropolis* (Beverly Hills, Calif.: Sage, 1977).

have grown in number and strength during the past decade, most of them prefer to act as special interest groups (rather than mini-governments) pressuring municipal authorities for service upgrading and capital improvements. Viewing the neighborhood itself as a political unit is not, of course, a revolutionary or radical concept. Suburban municipalities, the analogue of large city neighborhoods, have long enjoyed a substantial degree of autonomy over the local service delivery system and its regulatory mechanisms.

COMPREHENSIVE REFORM: ITS PROSPECTS

Despite declining birthrates and shifting migration patterns, metropolitan expansion is certain to continue (although at a slower pace) for at least another generation. The problem of accommodating growth—especially in the sunbelt SMSAs—will become even more complex than at present as energy and environmental considerations intensify and public resistance to taxes persists. These factors are likely to generate pressure for more efficient government in urban areas but are unlikely to lead to comprehensive structural reorganization except in rare cases. Along with the traditional impediments to metropolitan reform, new political obstacles to such action have arisen as a by-product of federal court decisions relating to racial discrimination in voting, education, and housing.

Although such was not their intention or purpose, recent cases have adversely affected the prospects of both annexation and city–county consolidation. In 1971 the Supreme Court held that annexation comes within the purview of the Voting Rights Act of 1965.[51] Under this ruling the Justice Department must preclear proposed annexations in those states subject to the restrictions of the act to determine that such territorial expansion does not discriminate against racial minorities. Petersburg, Virginia, for example, was denied the right to absorb a large area outside its boundaries because the extension would have substantially increased its percentage of white residents, thereby diluting the voting strength of the city's black population. The Supreme Court subsequently softened this position in a suit instituted by the city of Richmond, Virginia, challenging the Attorney General's action in withholding approval of a contemplated annexation. The high tribunal ruled that the city by substituting single-member districts for its formerly at-large elections to the council afforded "fair" representation to blacks.[52] The

---

[51]*Perkins* v. *Matthews*, 400 U.S. 379 (1971).
[52]*City of Richmond* v. *United States*, 422 U.S. 358 (1975). This ruling was recently affirmed in *City of Rome* (Alabama) v. *United States*, 48 Law Week, 4463 (1980).

necessity of going through the preclearance process and risking judicial mandates to change their electoral systems has been a factor in discouraging cities (where race is relevant but other conditions favorable) from engaging in large-scale annexation activities.

Decisions in the school (and housing) desegregation cases pose similar difficulties for city–county consolidation. The Supreme Court (as pointed out in Chapter 9) has held that metropolitanwide remedies to achieve integrated schools can be ordered only when there is evidence of discriminatory action by the suburban districts as well as by the central city. As one veteran analyst of metropolitan reorganization observed, this ruling has dealt a virtual deathblow to city–county consolidation in areas where race is a decisive issue.[53] To merge the two major political units but leave the school districts untouched (as most amalgamation plans of the past have proposed) would open the door to court-ordered desegregation remedies of metropolitan or countywide scope. This issue, in fact, has been pivotal in the Indianapolis desegregation case where it is charged that the creation of Unigov (which excluded the school districts) constituted an act of deliberate discrimination against blacks in violation of the Fourteenth Amendment.[54]

The comprehensive one-government approach to metropolitan restructuring is now more a matter of history than a subject of current action. A few fairly large annexations and isolated instances of city-county consolidation will continue, particularly in the South and West, but little more can be anticipated. The comprehensive two-level concept will retain its theoretical appeal for the larger SMSAs because of its potential for balancing areawide management needs with grass roots autonomy, but it will receive little application. Governmental reorganization will remain an issue on the metropolitan agenda, to be dealt with mostly by incremental adjustments to the existing system and by increased federal and state intervention.

---

[53]Joseph F. Zimmerman, "Recent Trends in Local Governance in the United States." Paper presented at the International Conference on the Future of Public Administration, Quebec, Canada, May 30, 1979, p. 33. Also see his article "The Federal Voting Rights Act: Its Impact on Annexation," *National Civic Review* 66 (June 1977): 278–283.

[54]See also in this connection Vincent L. Marando, "City-County Consolidation: Reform, Regionalism, Referenda, and Requiem," *Western Political Quarterly* 32 (December 1979): 409–421.

Chapter 12
Governmental Reorganization: Incremental Approaches

Because of the repeated failures to achieve comprehensive restructuring of the governmental pattern in SMSAs, interest has turned in recent years to incremental approaches of more modest dimensions. The Advisory Commission on Intergovernmental Relations expressed the prevalent sentiment among urban analysts when it counseled those interested in metropolitan reform to "accept the facts of life about annexation and metropolitan government and consolidation, and find a mechanism which will achieve important results without intolerable political breakage."[1]

The decentralized governmental pattern of SMSAs has demonstrated considerable capacity to adapt to changing circumstances and needs (although at what cost is problematic). Despite severe criticism from many quarters, the fragmented structure has managed to survive in all but a few metropolitan areas. The argument that an integrated system would have brought about more rational urban development and raised the quality of life in the large population centers continues to fall largely on deaf ears. Political decentralization obviously does not disturb the majority of metropolitan dwellers and may even be compatible with their desires. To some social scientists the history of reorganization failures suggests that more attention should be given to determining the manner in which the present structure evolved, how it is maintained when confronted by changing demands, what values it satisfies, and what factors tend to stimulate or inhibit organizational changes.[2]

The decentralized pattern of government in metropolitan areas has been likened for theoretical purposes to both a market place and a system of nation states. Under the first conception (advanced by those known as "public choice" theorists) the various munici-

[1]Advisory Commission on Intergovernmental Relations, *Regionalism Revisited: Recent Areawide and Local Responses* (Washington, D. C., June 1977), p. 1.
[2]See Robert O. Warren, *Government in Metropolitan Regions: A Reappraisal of Fractionated Political Organization* (Davis: University of California Institute of Government Affairs, 1966).

palities are regarded as competing producers or suppliers of public goods.[3] By providing different bundles or levels of services, they present citizen consumers with a range of choices that would not be possible under a monolithic governmental structure. If, for example, families want high-grade education for their children they can live in a city or village that operates a first-rate school system. Or if they are less concerned about quality education, they can choose a community where less money is spent on the schools. Implicit in this model is the assumption that both the producers (the governmental units) and the consumers (the residents) will act to maximize their self-interests. The public agencies will behave so as to protect their competitive position and retain or extend their power. The citizens in turn will select the supplier that appears to satisfy their preferences best, at the lowest cost.[4]

Under the second model the SMSA pattern is likened to an international system of sovereign states.[5] Most metropolitan areas are administered by a host of local units, each with jurisdiction over a territorial segment of the whole, each enjoying legal autonomy, and each protective of its turf. Their actions resemble in many ways those of nation states. They compete with one another for scarce resources (taxes, industry); they bargain for needed supplies and

[3]The public choice or municipal market model is based largely on the work of Charles M. Tiebout, "A Pure Theory of Local Expenditures," *Journal of Political Economy* 64 (October 1956): 416–424. See also Vincent Ostrom, Charles Tiebout, and Robert Warren, "The Organization of Government in Metropolitan Areas: A Theoretical Inquiry," *American Political Science Review* 55 (December 1961): 831–842; Robert Warren, "A Municipal Services Market Model of Metropolitan Organization," *Journal of the American Institute of Planners* 30 (August 1964): 193–204; and Robert Bish and Robert Kirk, *Economic Principles and Urban Problems* (Englewood Cliffs, N.J.: Prentice-Hall, 1974).

[4]Critiques of the market model are found in Joseph Friedman, *Housing Location and the Supply of Local Public Services* (Santa Monica, Calif.: Rand Corporation, 1975) and Max Neiman, "From Plato's Philosopher King to Bish's Tough Purchasing Agent: The Premature Public Choice Paradigm," *Journal of the American Institute of Planners* 41 (March 1975): 66–82.

[5]Victor Jones first called attention to the analogy between metropolitan and international political organization in "The Organization of a Metropolitan Region," *University of Pennsylvania Law Review* 105 (February 1957): 539. The concept was developed more fully by Matthew Holden, "The Governance of the Metropolis as a Problem in Diplomacy," *Journal of Politics* 26 (August 1964): 627–647. See also David Scott, "The International Relations Metropolitan Analogy: An Evaluation." (Unpublished paper, Northern Illinois University, De Kalb, 1973), and Paul Friesema, "Cities, Suburbs, and Short-lived Models of Metropolitan Politics," in Louis H. Masotti and Jeffrey K. Hadden (eds.), *The Urbanization of the Suburbs* (Beverly Hills, Calif.: Sage, 1973), pp. 243–249.

facilities (water, sewers); they seek to expand their sphere of control (annexation); they form coalitions for defensive purposes (suburban leagues of municipalities); and they create "mini-United Nations" to provide a forum for dealing with the problems that grow out of their coexistence (councils of governments). If either model—municipal market or international relations—is a reasonable analogue of reality (which many observers question), it would serve to explain the unacceptability of comprehensive reorganization plans and the appropriateness of devices of more moderate scope to keep the system operational.

The incremental approaches examined here—interlocal agreements, transfer of functional responsibilities, metropolitan districts, and COGs—have been widely used as means of sustaining the multinucleated metropolitan pattern. Favored by the polycentrists and optionists and accepted by the pragmatists, these approaches rest on (1) retention of the decentralized political structure; (2) cooperation among local communities in dealing with common problems; (3) the transfer of single functions to the county or state when their administration becomes impractical or too burdensome financially; and (4) the creation of special districts to handle specific needs that are beyond the capacity of the existing units.

INTERLOCAL AGREEMENTS

The simplest form of governmental adjustment to change in urban areas is the interlocal agreement or contract. To a limited extent this approach provides a convenient and ready means of dealing with needs and problems without infringing on grass-roots determination and control. Many local officials look on it as at least a partial response to demands for the creation of strong metropolitan governments that would substantially reduce the authority of existing units if not eliminate them altogether. Most officeholders, however, regard the contract device as more than a defense mechanism; they see it as a positive means of providing certain services more economically and efficiently. Local jurisdictions, for example, can resort to this approach when they want to avoid hiring personnel and making capital investments to produce services for which they are legally responsible.

Although not a recent innovation, intergovernmental contracts have experienced a marked upsurge since World War II, mainly in the well-populated areas where the problem of political structure is more pressing. A survey in 1972 revealed that almost two-thirds of the responding cities and towns with more than 2500 residents were receiving services from other governments or private firms under contract.[6] This type of interlocal cooperation takes many forms. At one extreme are informal verbal understandings between administrators involving matters such as the exchange of information about street construction plans or proposed zoning changes in adjacent areas of the two jurisdictions. At the other are formal written agreements among a sizable number of local units relative to the joint ownership and operation of a major facility, such as a sewage treatment plant or a water supply system.

The cooperative method, as used in SMSAs, embraces a broad sweep of activities and facilities and involves every type of local government. Among the functions covered by interlocal agreements are fire protection, law enforcement, planning, building inspection, road maintenance, sewage disposal and treatment, and water supply. Also included are agreements concerning such capital operations as government office buildings, airports, hospitals, sports arenas, and jails. Especially numerous are arrangements relating to libraries, personnel examinations, public health, purchasing, and tax assessment and collection.[7]

Municipalities are by far the most frequent participants in cooperative arrangements, with the large communities exhibiting the highest use of this approach.[8] The majority of the agreements by cities and towns are with other municipalities, but a growing number are with counties and to a lesser extent with other types of local entities. The quantity of intergovernmental contracts entered into by counties is steadily rising as this element of the metropolitan political structure increasingly becomes a provider of urban services.[9] School districts are also turning to this device with greater frequency. Agreements on recreational and library services are

[6]Joseph F. Zimmerman, "Intergovernmental Service Agreements and Transfers of Functions," in Advisory Commission on Intergovernmental Relations, *Substate Regionalism in the Federal System,* vol. 3 (Washington, D.C., 1974), pp. 29–52, 176–184.

[7]A detailed treatment of the cooperative movement up to the early 1960s is presented in W. Brooke Graves, *American Intergovernmental Relations: Their Origins, Historical Developments, and Current Status* (New York: Scribner, 1964).

[8]A survey by Joseph Zimmerman indicates a positive relationship between the population size of a city and the number of intermunicipal contracts: The larger the community, the more cooperative agreements it is likely to have. *Intergovernmental Service Agreements for Smaller Municipalities* (Washington, D.C.: International City Management Association, Urban Data Service, 1973).

[9]Research by John E. Stoner disclosed a high degree of association between the metropolitanism of Indiana counties (here defined as location in a metropolitan area) and their incidence of interlocal cooperation. U.S. Department of Agriculture, Economic Research Service, *Interlocal Governmental Cooperation: A Study of Five States* (Washington, D.C., 1967), pp. 21, 26.

common between them and municipalities. Townships and non-school special districts engage in cooperative enterprises the least, principally because their narrow scope of functions makes them less likely prospects for such activity.

Cooperative Features

Formal interlocal agreements are of three types: (1) a single government performs a service for one or more other local jurisdictions, (2) two or more units administer a function or operate a facility on a joint basis, and (3) two or more local governments assist or supply mutual aid to one another in emergency situations. Most of the agreements fall into the first category and concern a single activity. A number of municipalities in an SMSA, for example, may contract with the county government for police protection. A separate agreement for this one activity is negotiated between each individual city and the county, often resulting in numerous pacts. The limited nature of most of these contracts should be remembered before becoming awed by the seeming magnitude of interunit arrangements.

The cooperative approach has a predominantly service orientation. (Joint ventures for the construction and operation of capital facilities are undertaken from time to time but they are relatively few in quantity.) Many of the agreements, moreover, are of a standby nature. They are operative only when certain conditions arise and they continue only so long as these circumstances are present. Known as mutual aid pacts, such commitments are activated when fires, civil disturbances, or other local emergencies are too large to be handled by the personnel and equipment of one of the contracting parties. The extent of the aid furnished is determined by the supplying government, which may at any time withdraw the assistance.

Although mutual aid contracts commonly specify that each party is to maintain adequate protective services within its own boundaries, some participants fail to comply with this requirement. The key element is reciprocity, but it is not always present. Small communities having mutual aid agreements with an adjacent large and well-equipped city know that they are assured of help if a major fire or other serious emergency occurs. As a consequence, those that do not maintain adequate protective services tend to rely on mutual aid to compensate for the deficiency. This improper use of the device contributes to the continuance of inadequate fire and police departments in various metropolitan areas.

Agreements between local units are usually for set periods of time. Some of them provide for automatic renewal unless either party gives notice of withdrawal. Others specify that the contract terminates after a fixed date unless renegotiated. In practice, most interlocal arrangements have a long life, as shown by political scientist Paul Friesema's study of the Quad-City (Illinois-Iowa) SMSA.[10] Longevity is particularly true in cases where capital facilities are involved and the withdrawing party would have to invest in construction or acquisition of a replacement.

Local governments must be authorized by the state to enter into contracts with each other. The customary practice in the past was to enact laws allowing such agreements to be made in a particular functional field. This approach required new enabling legislation each time local units wanted to cooperate in the handling of a service not covered by previous authorization. The trend now is for the states to adopt permissive laws of broader scope. One form lists the services and facilities that can be the subject of cooperative arrangements; the other grants general power (without specific enumeration of functions) to the locality governments to contract with each other.

Cooperation in Large SMSAs

Studies of interlocal agreements in two major SMSAs, Philadelphia and Detroit, provide insight into the use and impact of this approach. In the Philadelphia area cooperative activity, as revealed by three research projects conducted at different time intervals, is characterized by the large number of participating governments and the frequency of cooperation among suburbs (rather than between the central city and outlying jurisdictions). The first survey, which covered eight counties, identified 756 agreements involving 427 local units. More than three-fifths of the cities, boroughs, and townships and only a slightly smaller proportion of the school districts were participants.[11] A similar study, made seven years later but limited to five counties, disclosed a continuation of the high level of cooperative activity. It found that the greatest amount of participation was occurring in the densely populated suburbs and

[10]H. Paul Friesema, *Metropolitan Political Structure: Intergovernmental Relations and Political Integration in the Quad-Cities* (Iowa City: University of Iowa Press, 1971).

[11]Jephtha J. Carrell, "Learning to Work Together," *National Municipal Review* 44 (November 1954): 526–533.

was highly concentrated in law enforcement, fire protection, education, and sewage disposal.[12]

The third and most recent investigation, also concerned with five counties, focused on determining the impact of community differentiation (in socioeconomic terms) on the willingness or tendency of local units to cooperate. The study was particularly interested in ascertaining if some types of suburbs enter into intergovernmental arrangements more than others. It hypothesized that (1) high social rank municipalities are more prone to cooperate than those of lower status, and (2) for functions affecting life-styles, such as education and planning, communities will seek relations with other units of similar social characteristics as opposed to those of different status. To test these hypotheses, attention was given to three kinds of agreements—school, sewage disposal, and police radio; the first of these services directly affects the life-styles of communities, the second has less to do with them, and the third has no such impact at all. The municipalities examined were characterized in terms of social rank (based on the population attributes of education and occupation) and wealth.

The findings of the study are revealing. School cooperation tends to develop between governments of similar social rank and financial resources. Sewage agreements also occur more frequently between units of comparable social status and, where a range of choice exists, this factor appears more important than the taxable resources of the respective municipalities. Although, as the authors of the study point out, school and sewerage systems have far different social and cultural connotations, both involve expensive capital facilities and lengthy negotiations among local authorities. Apparently, officials prefer to deal with their counterparts who are socially similar to themselves. In the case of police-radio agreements, on the other hand, socioeconomic distance between municipalities appears to have no apparent effect on contractual patterns. Such cooperation does not relate to life-styles; it involves only modest sums of money, and it is of concern primarily to technicians. The researchers sum up their findings in these words:

> Social and economic distance between municipalities [including school districts] influences cooperative activities involving life-styles and large capital investments. However, differences in social rank appear to be more significant than inequalities of resources. . . . Generally, given a choice as to the selection of partners to an agreement,

[12]George S. Blair, *Interjurisdictional Agreements in Southeastern Pennsylvania* (Philadelphia: University of Pennsylvania Institute of Local and State Government, 1960).

cooperation occurs among municipalities with similar social rank and tax resources, in that order. Where agreements are necessary for the performance of a particular function, and little choice with respect to social rank is available, the resources of prospective partners become the prime consideration. This scale of values is not operative for some minor cooperative activities [police-radio agreements, for instance] with but slight social and financial impact.[13]

The study of interlocal cooperation in the Detroit area generally supports the Philadelphia findings. Its analysis of formal contracts among 58 municipalities confirmed the assumption that social rank of a community is importantly related to the frequency of joint arrangements affecting life-styles but not of those having little social implication. The study found, in fact, that contracts concerning functions most closely related to the social characteristics of a community (planning, zoning, housing, and urban renewal) were nonexistent and other services of potential life-style effect only minimally used.[14]

The research also revealed an association between type of government structure and cooperative activity. Council–manager municipalities, regardless of social rank, participated in joint arrangements to a markedly greater degree than mayor–council governments. As the evidence suggests, city managers and their department heads communicate and share ideas about mutual problems with their counterparts in other local units more often than do mayors and their administrative personnel. These professional contacts tend to provide a basis for establishing cooperation on more formal terms. Both the Philadelphia and Detroit studies serve to emphasize that useful as cooperative arrangements are in aiding local governments to provide services more efficiently, they have certain limitations when considered in a metropolitan context. Most important, they do nothing to lessen the social and economic disparities that exist among local units in the same urban area. Municipalities cooperate only when they benefit by the arrangement, and they choose partners to suit their own interests. It is indeed a

---

[13]Oliver P. Williams, Harold Herman, Charles S. Liebman, and Thomas R. Dye, *Suburban Differences and Metropolitan Policies: A Philadelphia Story* (Philadelphia: University of Pennsylvania Press, 1965), p. 264. A later analysis by Williams distinguishes between life-style services and system-maintenance services, such as water and sewer functions, indicating that attempts to centralize administration of the latter generate less resistance than in the case of the former. See "Life Style Values and Political Decentralization in Metropolitan Areas," *Southwestern Social Science Quarterly* 48 (December 1967): 299–310.

[14]Vincent L. Marando, "Inter-Local Cooperation in a Metropolitan Area," *Urban Affairs Quarterly* 4 (December 1968): 185–200.

rare case in which a wealthy community will voluntarily assist a poorer unit in meeting its needs.

The Lakewood Plan

The most extreme use of the contract device is represented by the once highly publicized Lakewood plan (formally known as the contract services plan). In 1954 residents of the unincorporated area of Lakewood, California, fearing annexation by the adjacent city of Long Beach, took the necessary legal steps to form a municipality. The new city, its population then 60,000, immediately contracted with Los Angeles County to provide it with a broad range of services. The plan was the product of a combination of factors: the enactment of a uniform retail sales and use tax law that made it financially attractive for areas to incorporate; the continued rapid growth of the county's population in the unincorporated sections; the existence of quality county departments already staffed and equipped to furnish municipal services; and the willingness of county officials to act as service entrepreneurs.

Almost all communities incorporated in Los Angeles County since 1954 have followed the Lakewood lead and entered into agreements with the county government to supply many of their municipal services directly and through special taxing areas (county-administered districts set up to supply fire protection, street lighting, and sewer maintenance, among other items). The cities now using the plan range in size from less than 1,000 to more than 100,000 population. No pre-Lakewood municipality has adopted this device, indicating that once a local unit has established its own service delivery system it is little inclined to favor any large turnover of functions to another government. However, contracts for individual services between the "old line" cities and the county have increased substantially in recent years, particularly in specialized fields such as subdivision engineering and street construction and maintenance.

Although the service package idea is central to the Lakewood plan, cities operating under it do not all purchase the same bundle. The common practice has been for the newly incorporated municipalities initially to buy all or most of the urban services they need. Over time a number of them have terminated contracts for specific items or withdrawn from particular county-administered districts. Such action is usually taken when a community determines that it can perform a service at a lower figure than the county charges or when its residents indicate a preference for local administration of a function. The contract rates are set at the county's full costs (based on the number of units of each service provided and a share of general administrative or overhead expenses) and are subject to revision annually.

Political scientist John Kirlin's study of law enforcement contracts in Los Angeles County concludes that Lakewood plan cities have traded greater control over the quantity of services for lesser influence over the manner in which they are carried out. Discretion in law enforcement execution rests with the sheriff's department which performs the function as it deems appropriate. As a result, variations in styles of police activity that normally occur among communities with different socioeconomic and racial characteristics have been materially reduced. In the three municipalities that have terminated contracts with the sheriff's office, this lack of variation was an important factor and one that is a potential source of contention in suburbs with substantial numbers of minority group residents. Kirlin feels, however, that the Lakewood plan has opened the sheriff's department to influence by the contracting cities, because they may establish their own police forces if they become dissatisfied with the county's services.[15]

The Lakewood plan is of broad import, for it offers a means of separating the provision of public goods from their production. This separation not only eliminates the need for municipalities to make large investments in capital facilities and equipment but also enables them to benefit from any economies of scale that result from a centralized delivery system. It leaves their policy-making powers intact (including control over land use and development) and permits them to determine what services they want and in what quantities and at what levels. When the plan was inaugurated, some observers hailed it as the answer to metropolitan restructuring, whereas others condemned it as contributing to further governmental fragmentation (some even called it a travesty on the concept of a city). Despite the national attention it received during the initial years of operation, its use remains confined almost wholly to the Los Angeles area. It nevertheless has acted as a catalyst, stimulating wide interest and some action in the use of metropolitan county governments as large-scale providers of urban services.

[15] John J. Kirlin, "The Impact of Contract Services Arrangements upon the Los Angeles Sheriff's Department and Law Enforcement Services in Los Angeles County," *Public Policy* 21 (Fall 1973): 553–584. For an analysis of the Lakewood plan in general, see Sidney Sonenblum, John J. Kirlin, and John C. Ries, *How Cities Provide Services* (Cambridge, Mass.: Ballinger, 1977).

The Urban County

Mainly because of the Lakewood plan, Los Angeles County ranks as the most extensive user of cooperative agreements in the United States. It is also the most prominent example of what is referred to as the "urban county" approach to metropolitan reorganization (not to be confused with the "comprehensive urban county plan" discussed in Chapter 11, which involves the simultaneous reallocation of a broad array of urban functions from the municipalities to the county government, as in the case of metropolitan Miami). This approach has several major characteristics: (1) county provision of many municipal-type services to the unincorporated areas; (2) extensive use of cooperative agreements under which the county furnishes urban services to the cities and towns; and (3) the piecemeal transfer of various functions from the municipalities to the county.[16]

The Los Angeles county government supplies a wide range of urban services to the approximately one million people who live in the unincorporated sections. This activity has intermittently brought vigorous protests from city officials who charge that the system is inequitable. They point out that the residents of incorporated places pay both a municipal and a county tax and are in effect being forced to subsidize urban services extended by the county (and financed from general county tax funds) to the built-up unincorporated areas. This complaint is common in SMSAs where a significant proportion of the population lives outside municipal boundaries. The subsidy situation can be corrected, as it is to some extent in most urban counties including Los Angeles, by the creation of taxing districts in the unincorporated sections to finance municipal-type services furnished by county departments.

Los Angeles County's most notable feature as an urban county is the provision of services to municipalities under cooperative arrangements. Including the Lakewood plan participation (which accounts for two-thirds of the total), it is a party to over 1200 such agreements, involving all 81 incorporated places within its borders. The number of services furnished ranges from six in three cities to thirty-five in another. The county handles election administration for all municipalities, tax assessment and collection for all but two, and health services for all except three. Various other functions are performed for at least one-half of the incorporated entities: emergency ambulance, prosecution of ordinance violations, subdivision

[16]The urban county development in Los Angeles County is discussed in Winston W. Crouch and Beatrice Dinerman, *Southern California Metropolis* (Berkeley and Los Angeles: University of California Press, 1963), chap. 7, and pp. 222–225.

final map check, and library. Many others—including engineering, industrial waste regulation, building inspection, and fire protection—are supplied to about one-third of the cities (Figure 12.1). In total, about 50 types of services are available and the number continues to grow. In recent years radar equipment maintenance, tree planting, and helicopter patrol for crime prevention and detection have been added.

FUNCTIONAL TRANSFERS

The transfer of responsibility for a function or service from a local unit to one of larger territorial jurisdiction offers another incremental approach to metropolitan restructuring. This device may involve a transfer from a municipality to the county government, the most common practice, or to a metropolitan district, council of governments, or the state (assumption of local functions by the state is

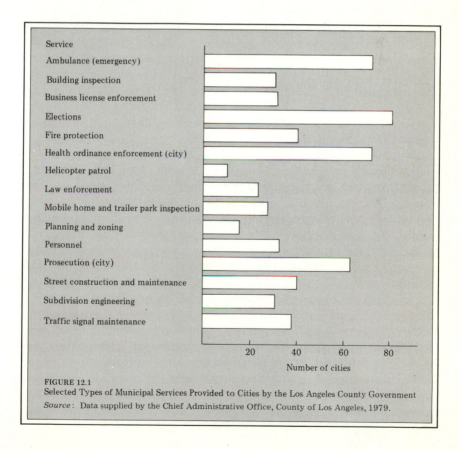

FIGURE 12.1
Selected Types of Municipal Services Provided to Cities by the Los Angeles County Government
Source: Data supplied by the Chief Administrative Office, County of Los Angeles, 1979.

discussed in Chapter 6). It may take place by voluntary action or be mandated by state law, and may include one or more local units. If the transfer is made by the central city or by all or most of the municipalities in the county or SMSA, it is referred to as functional consolidation.

Functional transfers differ from interlocal agreements or contracts in that the acquiring government assumes full and permanent responsibility for the activity, including policymaking, financing, and administration. (The distinction, however, is blurred in some states where a transfer can be revoked or reimbursement is required for providing the function.) Although most transfers are accomplished on a voluntary basis, the states have mandated such action in some cases. Florida, for example, shifted property tax assessment from the municipal to the county level; Mississippi requires that health services be automatically transferred from the cities to county health departments where they have been established; and Minnesota has moved welfare administration from the municipalities to the counties.

A survey of cities conducted in 1975 revealed that almost one-third of the respondents had turned over responsibility to another government for at least one function during the previous ten years. The large cities were by far the most frequent participants, 79 percent of those over 500,000 population indicating that they had transferred functions as compared to only 25 percent of those under 5,000. Central cities showed a pronounced higher rate of activity in this respect than suburban communities. The most common service involved was solid waste collection and disposal; others were public health, law enforcement, sewage collection and treatment, property assessment, and social services. Most of the transfers were made to the county but about one-fifth went to special districts (principally utility-type operations) and one-seventh to the states (mainly social services). The major reasons given by municipal authorities for shifting the responsibilities were achievement of economies of scale, elimination of duplication, and lack of facilities and equipment.[17]

Local governments traditionally have shown little receptivity to the divestment of any of their functions. However, the fiscal difficulties of recent years have made the approach more attractive, particularly to officials in the older municipalities. During the last decade, to cite one of the more prominent examples, the city of Cleveland turned over to the county government responsibility for

[17]Joseph Zimmerman, "Transfer of Functional Responsibilities," *County Year Book, 1976*, pp. 59–68.

sewers, mass transit, ports, jails, and health and welfare services. This action was in decided contrast to the vigorous opposition of Cleveland officials in 1959 to a comprehensive urban county reorganization plan that would have transferred a number of similar functions to the county government.

The Advisory Commission on Intergovernmental Relations has lauded the use of functional transfers as a basic way of reallocating service responsibilities to meet the changing demands on metropolitan governmental systems.[18] Many obstacles, however, stand in the way of their extensive employment. Less than one-fourth of the states presently authorize such transfers, and some of these require voter approval, usually by concurrent majorities in the jurisdictions involved. A second impediment is that the transfers, unless mandated by state law, are dependent on the willingness of the county government or other unit to assume responsibility for what may be a costly service. A classic case is Milwaukee where attempts to turn over the city-owned museum to the county have been repeatedly rebuffed. Another drawback is that county governments in many SMSAs remain ill-equipped organizationally to perform urban-type services on a large scale. This situation, however, has improved as a growing number of metropolitan counties have shown a willingness to strengthen their administrative capabilities and take on new assignments beyond their traditional role as outreach agents of the state.

METROPOLITAN DISTRICTS

Metropolitan district governments represent a third approach of moderate scope to the organizational problem of SMSAs. These are special districts that encompass an entire metropolitan area or a major portion of it (some even extend beyond the boundaries of individual SMSAs). Established to administer a single function (or in a few cases more than one), they now number about 250. They are found in more than one-half of the SMSAs and are most numerous in California, Ohio, and Texas.[19] Collectively, they perform a wide range of service activities, from insect control to the operation of

---

[18]Advisory Commission on Intergovernmental Relations, *Government Structure, Organization, and Planning in Metropolitan Areas* (Washington, D.C., July 1961), p. 30.

[19]Many district governments other than those of metropolitan scope exist in SMSAs, such as school and fire districts. Metropolitan districts are governments and should not be confused with units that are adjuncts of state and local governments, such as some public housing authorities.

mass transit systems. The list is long and includes sewage disposal, water supply, public housing, hospitals, libraries, ports, pollution control, airports, and parks.[20]

The performance record of metropolitan district governments is impressive despite their functional restrictiveness. They have done much to satisfy or alleviate some of the most pressing areawide needs of the SMSAs they serve. A sampling of their activities, often unrecognized as district operations by the citizens, is enlightening. The Port Authority of New York and New Jersey runs airports, bridges, and a host of other transportation facilities (Figure 12.2). The Bi-State Development Agency (St. Louis area) operates a mass transit system; the Cleveland Metropolitan Park District and

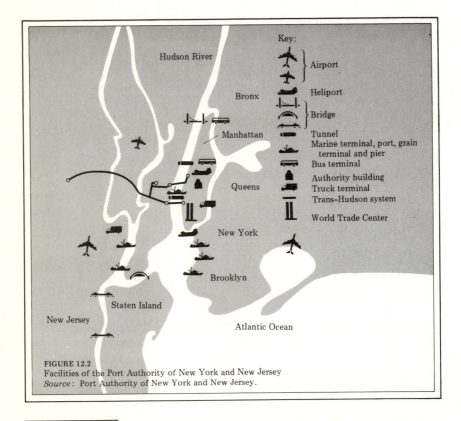

FIGURE 12.2
Facilities of the Port Authority of New York and New Jersey
Source: Port Authority of New York and New Jersey.

---

[20]Comprehensive analyses of metropolitan districts are found in John C. Bollens, *Special District Governments in the United States* (Berkeley and Los Angeles: University of California Press, 1957) and Max A. Pock, *Independent Special Districts: A Solution to the Metropolitan Area Problem* (Ann Arbor: University of Michigan Law School Legislative Research Center, 1962).

the East Bay Regional Park District (San Francisco Bay area) provide regional parks; and the Metropolitan Sanitary District of Greater Chicago, the Metropolitan St. Louis Sewer District, and the Municipality of Metropolitan Seattle (a district government) handle sewage disposal. The Metropolitan Water District of Southern California is the wholesale supplier of water (after transporting it hundreds of miles from the Colorado River) to a large number of cities and other water agencies in six southern California counties (Figure 12.3). And the Bay Area Rapid Transit District (San Francisco area) operates an extensive rapid transit system.

Two features in particular have contributed to the attractiveness of metropolitan districts as a means of handling areawide needs. First, they are usually self-supporting, their operating costs derived mainly from service charges and tolls and their capital needs from revenue bonds. Second, they can be created with relative ease because most states have liberal enabling legislation authorizing their formation. Only a single areawide vote is necessary in some cases, and in others popular ratification is not required. The air pollution control district in the San Francisco Bay area, for example, was established by special act of the state legislature and the Port Authority of New York and New Jersey by interstate compact.

Composition of Governing Bodies

The governing boards of metropolitan districts are constituted in various ways, some quite complex. In the case of the metropolitan sewer district in the St. Louis area, the central city mayor with the concurrence of the circuit court judges designates three of the six members, and the elected executive of St. Louis County selects the other three with the endorsement of the local judges. The composition of the Metropolitan Water District of Southern California is even more mixed, with 52 members distributed among local water districts, municipalities, and irrigation districts (Figure 12.4). In both instances the governing body is at least one step removed from the citizens, and the divided method of appointment leaves the members without direct responsibility to any one public official or elected unit.[21]

Dissatisfaction over the remoteness of many metropolitan districts from the control of the residents they serve has generated in-

---

[21]The size of some of these districts underscores the need for a better system of public accountability. For instance, the Port Authority of New York and New Jersey has more long-term outstanding indebtedness than some state governments.

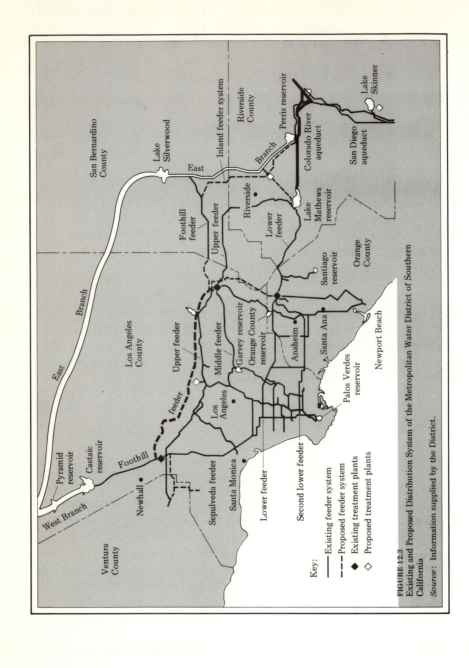

FIGURE 12.3
Existing and Proposed Distribution System of the Metropolitan Water District of Southern California

Source: Information supplied by the District.

Key:

——— Existing feeder system

– – – Proposed feeder system

◆ Existing treatment plants

◇ Proposed treatment plants

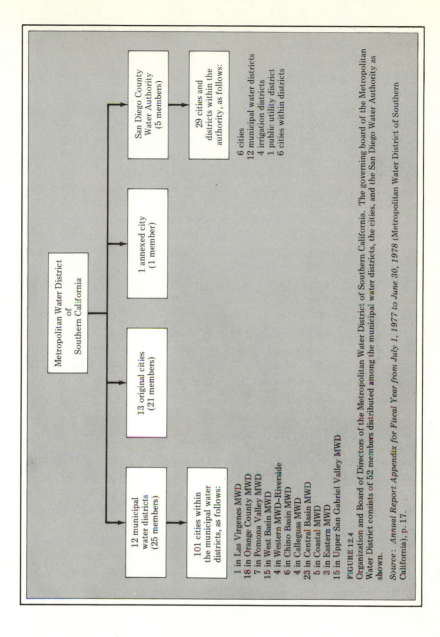

Metropolitan Water District
of
Southern California

12 municipal
water districts
(25 members)

13 original cities
(21 members)

1 annexed city
(1 member)

San Diego County
Water Authority
(5 members)

101 cities within
the municipal water
districts, as follows:

1 in Las Virgenes MWD
18 in Orange County MWD
7 in Pomona Valley MWD
15 in West Basin MWD
4 in Western MWD–Riverside
6 in Chino Basin MWD
4 in Calleguas MWD
23 in Central Basin MWD
5 in Coastal MWD
3 in Eastern MWD
15 in Upper San Gabriel Valley MWD

29 cities and
districts within the
authority, as follows:

6 cities
12 municipal water districts
4 irrigation districts
1 public utility district
6 cities within districts

FIGURE 12.4

Organization and Board of Directors of the Metropolitan Water District of Southern California. The governing board of the Metropolitan Water District consists of 52 members distributed among the municipal water districts, the cities, and the San Diego Water Authority as shown.

Source: Annual Report Appendix for Fiscal Year from July 1, 1977 to June 30, 1978 (Metropolitan Water District of Southern California), p. 17.

terest in more rational ways of selecting members. The proposals that have won most acceptance, particularly among local officials, are based on the constituent-unit principle of representation. This principle calls for the appointment of board members by (and if desired from among) the elected officials of the municipalities and counties within the district.[22] The process offers a means of linking the districts more closely to the local units they overlie. The San Francisco Bay Area Rapid Transit District is one of an increasing number of metropolitan agencies that employ this method of selection. Its 12-member board consists of four representatives from each of the three participating counties, chosen by the mayors and county supervisors from among residents of the district.[23]

Although constituent-unit representation offers a more logical process of selecting board members than other methods of appointment, it provides only indirect and circuitous channels of accountability to metropolitan residents through their municipal or county officials. Yet so long as districts perform only a single function, as the overwhelming majority do, the problem of representation will persist. Popular election is the most direct means of citizen control, but with the proliferation of metropolitan agencies this method would expand the already long list of elective local offices and thereby discourage citizen oversight. If such districts, however, should become multifunctional, popular election would be feasible and desirable.

The Multipurpose District Concept

A major criticism of metropolitan districts is that they contribute to the political fragmentation of urban areas. Because such agencies normally provide only one service or activity, it has been common practice in many SMSAs to create additional districts when the need arises in other functional fields. Proponents of metropolitan reorganization object to this piecemeal approach, contending that it results in an ineffective and uncoordinated attack on areawide problems. This criticism has led to proposals to expand the service

---

[22]For a discussion of the constituent-unit idea see Arthur W. Bromage, *Political Representation in Metropolitan Agencies* (Ann Arbor: University of Michigan Institute of Public Administration, 1962) and Stanley Scott and Willis Culver, *Metropolitan Agencies and Concurrent Office-Holding: A Survey of Selected Districts and Authorities* (Berkeley: University of California Bureau of Public Administration, 1961), pp. 12–13.

[23]The constituent-unit method has been confined to newly created districts; it has not been employed to change the membership composition of any existing agency.

responsibilities of these bodies. Scattered advocacy of the multi-purpose district concept can be found as far back as the early 1920s, but major support for it has come only in the last 25 years through the recommendations of the Advisory Commission on Intergovernmental Relations and the Council of State Governments.

The multipurpose concept can be realized by endowing existing districts with additional functions, consolidating those presently operating in the same SMSA, or creating new metropolitan agencies with broad service responsibilities. The likelihood of any of these actions occurring at this time is remote. Few of the present districts have shown any inclination to take on more activities. Most of them have been (and continue to be) content to perform their one service even when local residents have urged them to seek broader functional authority.[24] Consolidation of existing districts is equally unpromising. The built-in positions of influence enjoyed by the commissions and administrative officials who run these units militate against such mergers. Most reformist interest has been shown in the establishment of new multipurpose bodies; but prospects for the enactment of enabling legislation that would facilitate their creation are also dim.

State lawmakers have been reluctant to authorize the establishment of multipurpose districts without severely circumscribing the process by which such agencies can assume functions. The Metropolitan Municipal Corporations bill enacted by the Washington legislature in 1957 is an example. Although the law authorized the creation of multipurpose districts to handle major services such as public transportation, water supply, waste disposal, and parks, it provided that proposals to set up such agencies must name the specific functions to be undertaken and receive concurrent majorities in the central city and the rest of the metropolitan area. The experience of Seattle with this law demonstrates its weakness as an avenue for broadscale change. In 1958 a proposal to create a district to handle sewage disposal, public transportation, and comprehensive planning received an overwhelming majority vote in the area as a whole but was defeated outside the central city. In September of the same year a proposition to establish a district limited to sewage disposal carried, receiving the more decisive majority in the sub-

---

[24]The East Bay Municipal Utility District (San Francisco Bay area), for example, which was organized in 1923 served only as a water supplier until the late 1940s when it added the sewage function. Its governmental board has shown no interest in undertaking any of the many other activities included in its grant of power despite periodic public advocacy.

urbs where the waste problem was acute. In 1962 and again six years later, the agency unsuccessfully tried to add public transportation as its second function. Finally, in 1972 voters authorized the district to operate a transit system and approved a sales tax increase to support it.

Efforts to implement the metropolitan district concept by constitutional authorization have also proved ineffective. A provision written into the Missouri constitution of 1945, and applicable to the St. Louis City–St. Louis County area, permits a locally appointed charter commission to draft a plan for the creation of such an agency and to specify its functional powers. The first use of the procedure in 1954 resulted in the acceptance by dual majorities in the city and county of a single-purpose district for sewage disposal. (Although the charter empowers the agency to assume other activities with the consent of the electorate, it has made no attempt to do so.) A second utilization of the constitutional provision in 1955 produced a proposal for another single-purpose district to operate a transit system, but the measure was soundly defeated both within and outside the city. Four years later a third plan—the formation of a multipurpose agency to handle a wide range of areawide functions—was voted down by a two-to-one count in the city and a three-to-one margin in the county.

Portland: A Breakthrough?

The promising developments of the 1960s when three large-scale city–county consolidations—Nashville, Jacksonville, and Indianapolis—were recorded gave way to a period of relative quiescence in metropolitan structural reform during the 1970s. The only significant reorganizational accomplishment in any large SMSA during the last decade occurred in 1978 when Portland (Oregon) area voters by an eleven-to-nine majority approved the merger of the Columbia Region Association of Governments (CRAG) with the Metropolitan Service District (MSD). CRAG was the metropolitan planning agency with A-95 review powers; the MSD was a metropolitan district that handled the areawide aspects of waste disposal and administered the Portland zoo.

The new agency (the title Metropolitan Service District is retained) has territorial jurisdiction over the urbanized portion of the three-county Portland SMSA, with a population of nearly 900,000. The state enabling legislation under which the reconstituted MSD was set up authorizes it to run Tri-Met, the Portland regional transportation agency, and to assume responsibility for a broad array of functions, including water supply, parks and recreation, human services, libraries, jails, and cultural facilities. No such activity, however, may be taken over unless area voters approve both its transfer and the method of financing it.[25]

Although of limited scope, the Portland reorganization is important in two respects: It places the areawide planning and review responsibilities in a metropolitan unit with functional powers, a situation that exists in only a few other SMSAs, and it provides for direct popular election of the agency's governing board, a practice that is not followed by most other regional bodies in the United States. MSD's 12 commissioners are selected in single-member districts and its full-time executive officer is chosen at large, all on nonpartisan ballots. The organizational change in metropolitan Portland is representative of the incremental or moderate approach to a more viable political system for SMSAs. The potential exists, however, for MSD to provide a comprehensive solution by evolving into a multipurpose government with broad areawide powers. Whether the agency will move in this direction should become clear during the next several years.

COUNCILS OF GOVERNMENTS

The metropolitan or regional council of governments (COG) is the latest form of institutionalized cooperation in SMSAs. Employed for the first time in the 1950s in only a few areas, its use spread rapidly after the mid-1960s. Called a "fourth component or layer" in the American system of federalism by one observer, a metropolitan council is a voluntary association of governments designed to provide an areawide mechanism for key officials to study, discuss, and determine how best to deal with common problems. This mechanism is not a government in the usual sense of the term, as it has no mandatory financing and enforcement authority. Instead, it is a continuing agency to furnish research, plans, advice, recommendations, and coordination. The legal basis for its organization is either a specific state enabling law, a general state interlocal agreement act, or nonprofit corporation legislation.

The use of the COG idea originated in 1954 with the establishment of the Supervisors Inter-County Committee in the Detroit area; its inception thus trailed by many years the inauguration of other metropolitan approaches of a more drastic nature. Even after

[25]For a brief description of the new agency see Sylvia Lewis, "Portland Tries Something New in Regional Government," *Planning* 45 (June 1979): 13.

its introduction the concept did not promptly catch hold on an extensive basis despite its simplicity and moderateness and the widespread praise and support given to it, especially by national organizations of local officials. New councils—in such widely separated urban complexes as Washington, Atlanta, San Francisco, and Seattle—were subsequently created, but by 1965 only nine were in operation in SMSAs. These pioneering bodies all came into being primarily for two reasons: a belief that collaborative governmental decisions were necessary to deal with areawide problems; and a fear that local units were about to lose power to proposed metropolitan governments. The early organizations of this type were few in number and trouble-laden; according to one analysis, "all of them suffered from uncertainties, inexperience in metropolitan cooperation, and lack of adequate financial resources."[26]

A marked transformation has taken place in the COG development since 1965. The number of these agencies has multiplied until at present close to 600 are in existence, serving approximately 250 SMSAs and 350 nonmetropolitan areas.[27] (Some regional planning commissions of pre-1965 vintage have been converted into COGs.) Two federal stimulants mentioned earlier (Chapter 7) have been largely responsible for this growth: congressional action making such councils eligible to receive federal grants for planning purposes and administrative costs; and the legislative requirement that applications for many types of federal grants and loans be submitted to an areawide agency for review (the A-95 process described earlier).

Another important development supportive of COGs occurred in 1967 when the National Association of Regional Councils (NARC) obtained its own staff and offices and greatly enlarged its program. A government interest group, the organization had been formed five years earlier by the National League of Cities and the National Association of Counties to encourage the formation of councils and strengthen their operations. NARC serves as a clearinghouse for information on COG activities and relevant federal and state programs. It acts as a lobbyist for the interests of its members before Congress and federal administrative departments and agencies. The association is composed of both COGs and other types of regional units such as metropolitan planning bodies.

[26]Royce Hanson, *Metropolitan Councils of Governments* (Washington, D.C.: Advisory Commission on Intergovernmental Relations, 1966), p. iv.
[27]This total includes all types of voluntary associations of local governments, not all of which have planning and review authority.

Membership and Activities

The membership of most COGs is made up of cities and counties, although in some cases other local units, the state government, and even civic organizations are included. The governing board representatives are usually elected officials whose first loyalty is to their home community. The council's structure in the case of many of the large COGs consists of a general assembly (comprising all the members) and an executive committee (typically composed of officials from the major city and each county with representation from the smaller municipalities). The executive committee convenes at least monthly; it handles most of the business and its actions are seldom reversed by the full membership (the assembly meets only once or twice a year). Appointed administrators in the area governments, although normally not eligible to serve on the general assembly or executive committee, are frequently members of technical study groups.

The commonly employed procedure of permitting each member government, irrespective of size, to have one vote on the governing board has come under attack by minority groups and central city officials as discriminatory and unrepresentative. A number of councils have moved to revise their membership composition to reflect population size, but in the case of most the constituent unit principle of representation and voting continues to prevail. The Supreme Court decisions mandating the "one-person-one-vote" rule for local general governments has caused some concern among COGs. Although such councils do not fall within the purview of present holdings, it is readily conceivable that the standard might be applied in the future, particularly if their importance as metropolitan political instrumentalities should grow. More than prompting changes in the membership pattern, this possibility has acted as a deterrent to expanding COG powers.

Representation by unit was utilized initially to overcome the reluctance of small and medium-sized governments to joining areawide councils, but the formula has not allayed their fears of central city dominance. Because of this continuing distrust among many suburban members, COGs generally have been unable to relate well to the problems of the central city; in fact, many of their executive directors are explicitly opposed to making such problems the focal point of their organizational activities.[28] As a study of the

---

[28]*Regional COGs and the Central City* (Detroit: Metropolitan Fund, 1970), pp. 4, 25.

Cleveland area COG disclosed, two years of pleading by central city board representatives and federal officials for the organization to give more attention to major needs of the core municipality only stiffened suburban resistance to doing so.[29]

Membership in metropolitan councils is technically voluntary; governments join of their own volition and withdraw as they wish. The degree of voluntarism has shrunk, however, in the case of those COGs responsible for reviewing various types of federal grant applications. Although the review requirement extends to nonmembers as well as to members, the former are without a voice in either their own or other applications that may concern them so long as they remain outside the council. Membership therefore is not strictly one of free choice.

The chief activities of COGs center on regional planning and attempts to formulate areawide policies. Only a few metropolitan councils, most notably the Association of (San Francisco) Bay Area Governments, have sought to gain operating service responsibilities. The overwhelming majority have spent much of their time making studies of specific areawide needs, most often pertaining to physical facilities. Some have prepared plans for land use, regional parks and open space, transportation, sewer and water facilities, and conservation of natural resources. Some also have sponsored training programs in law enforcement, drug abuse, housing development, and health services and worked out joint purchasing arrangements for their members. So far, only a small number have given serious attention to social problems and issues, although they are being increasingly pressured to do so by federal agencies, member governments of low socioeconomic status, and minority groups. Plans developed by regional councils frequently have been criticized for their failure to consider the needs of minority people and the poor, such as low-income housing and mass transit. Mostly, this neglect is due to the preference of COGs to deal with noncontroversial matters on which consensus can be reached.[30]

In performing their role as the review agency to comment on federal grant requests, COGs tend to approve most such applica-

[29]Frances Frisken, "Metropolis and Central City," *Urban Affairs Quarterly* 8 (June 1973): 395–422.

[30]Nelson Wikstrom, *Councils of Governments: A Study of Political Incrementalism*, (Chicago: Nelson Hall, 1977), pp. 106–108. For case studies of individual COGs see Citizens Research Council of Michigan, "Southeast Michigan Regionalism," pp. 83–95, and Victor Jones, "San Francisco Bay Area Regionalism," in Kent Mathewson (ed.), *The Regionalist Papers*, 2d ed. (Southfield, Mich.: Metropolitan Fund, 1978), pp. 133–159.

tions without criticism. This low rate of disapproval is due principally to three factors: the ability of the agencies to secure modifications of applications through informal consultations before their official submission; the frequent absence of areawide plans to use as a guide in judging the soundness and compatibility of proposed projects; and the fear of political retaliation (such as withdrawal of membership by units whose applications are commented on adversely). The review authority, in short, places an instrumentality of potential power in the hands of the COGs but it is a resource that remains largely untapped.

The plans and recommendations of metropolitan councils are advisory only. Their implementation is wholly dependent on the action of the member governments, and in some cases state and national authorities. The likelihood of voluntary compliance is not great, particularly in instances where execution would be disadvantageous or costly to individual local units. Since almost every proposed action of significance will entail at least short-term sacrifices on the part of some members, only intervention by higher levels of government (such as a threat to withhold capital improvement grants) can further implementation. Seldom, however, have federal or state authorities been willing to take measures of this nature.

One drawback to the independence of the councils is their lack of power to levy taxes. They must rely for their revenue on dues from member governments (usually calculated on the basis of population, assessed valuation of property, or a flat rate); state aid; and federal grants. On the average almost two-thirds of their funding comes from federal agencies, about 10 percent from the states, and the remainder from the local units. Another handicap to COGs in many of the smaller areas is the lack of a professional staff. Because of budget limitations they often must operate with only an executive director and office personnel. At the other extreme, the councils in most of the large SMSAs have sizable staffs composed of planners, engineers, draftsmen, computer technicians, and specialists in various fields such as transportation, housing, conservation, and recreation. A survey by NARC in 1976 found that the average staff size was 17 and the typical annual budget about three-quarters of a million dollars.

Evaluation of COGs

A nationwide survey conducted jointly by the International City Management Association and the national Advisory Commission on Intergovernmental Relations provides a comprehensive picture of how municipal and county officials view metropolitan councils and appraise their performance.[31] The results of the survey reflect wide differences in local attitudes toward such bodies. Respondents who support the COG concept cite the need for an areawide instrumentality to obtain federal and state funds, the possible contributions such an agency can make to the solution of metropolitan problems, and the role it can serve as a forum for discussing regional differences. Those who express negative feelings maintain that COGs produce a loss of local autonomy, are dominated by the large cities or counties, provide planning and other services inferior to those supplied by local units, and delay federal or state funding of local programs.

In terms of performance, city and county officials judge the councils to be most effective in the review and coordination of federal and state grant applications, facilitating communications among local officials, and development of functional plans. They look upon them as least effective in communicating with citizens, performing social planning, securing implementation of general and functional plans, and educating the public on metropolitan and regional affairs.

Despite the general sentiment of support for regional councils among municipal and county officials, dissatisfaction stemming from many concerns is also evident. Some regard such bodies as too weak, whereas others lament what they consider their growing powers. And although there is general consensus that COGs should continue to exist, officials are sharply divided over the future direction they should take. More than two-thirds of the respondents in the survey believe that the councils should be designated as the official regional planning organization for federal and state programs and should also serve as a limited umbrella agency to review and coordinate functional plans prepared by single-purpose metropolitan districts. Surprisingly, a substantial minority—approximately 45 percent—believe they should act as a general coordinating body with veto power (and not simply advisory review) over local government plans and projects that do not conform to areawide plans. Less than a fourth of the respondents want them to take on operating services, such as sewerage, water supply, and transportation. As the various views of COGs indicate, the obstacles to their successful development "have their roots in the wide disparities in goals, attitudes, and social characteristics which prevail throughout metropolitan areas."[32]

[31]Douglas Harmon and Mary Ann Allard, *Local Evaluation of Regional Councils* (Washington, D.C.: International City Management Association, Urban Data Service, 1973), pp. 1–14.
[32]Frisken, "Metropolis and Central City," p. 418.

Political scientist Nelson Wikstrom in a recent study gives COGs a highly positive assessment. He states that they provide an "ideal, responsible, democratic mechanism" for program coordination, policy direction, and management in metropolitan areas. As he views their record, they have stimulated greater horizontal cooperation (among units at the local level) and vertical cooperation (among local, state, and national agencies), mediated central city-suburban conflict, furthered the concept of regionalism, and served as vehicles of incremental change. He believes that in some instances COGs will evolve into limited areawide governments with various functional responsibilities, but the changes will be moderate because of the strong anti-metropolitan government tradition in the American polity.[33]

Not all observers would agree with this favorable appraisal. A National Academy of Sciences committee concluded in 1975 that COGs had solved no major metropolitan problem or given any indication of taking on an areawide government role.[34] Joseph Zimmerman in like vein states that they have concentrated on the solution of relatively minor problems and will most likely continue to do so. As he describes COGs, they suffer all the disadvantages of the United Nations, including the inability to rise above narrow self interests.[35] Even their strongest supporters would hardly maintain that these bodies provide the ultimate answer to what one scholar almost four decades ago called the "great unsolved problem of modern politics"—the adequate governmental organization of metropolitan areas.

Beyond COGs: The Twin Cities Model

The Metropolitan Council of the Twin Cities (Minneapolis–St. Paul area) is in many respects an umbrella-type agency similar to that envisaged by respondents in the ICMA–ACIR survey. Some observers regard it as a prototype for the future evolution of COGs.[36] Basically an areawide planning and coordinating agency,

---

[33]Wikstrom, *Councils of Governments*, pp. 130–131.
[34]*Toward an Understanding of Metropolitan America* (San Francisco: Canfield Press, 1975), p. 120.
[35]"Recent Trends in Local Government in the United States," Paper presented at International Conference on the Future of Public Administration, Quebec, Canada, May 30, 1979, p. 47.
[36]Also see recommendations by an International City Management Association Committee in support of UMJO, an umbrella, multi-jurisdictional organization, in *Public Management* 55 (September 1973): 24–29 and Stanley Scott and John C. Bollens, *Governing a Metropolitan Region: The San Francisco Bay Area* (Berkeley: University of California Institute of Governmental Studies, 1968), pp. 36–37, 76–79.

the Twin Cities council possesses greater power than the conventional COG with respect to its review and recommendatory authority. Replacing a regional planning commission, the council was formed in 1967 by state legislative action prompted by metropolitan area initiative. Its membership is appointed by the governor from state senatorial districts, combined by twos for this purpose, thus assuring a representative body based on population (the chairperson is appointed at large).

The council's ability to act as a coordinating and directing agency for metropolitan development rests on two kinds of power that it enjoys. The first includes the authority to approve or suspend plans or projects of independent special districts and boards whose jurisdiction is multicommunity (such suspension or veto may be appealed to the state legislature); review and place on a 60-day hold, while attempting to mediate differences, plans and projects of municipalities and counties that have metropolitan implications; and review local applications for federal assistance. The second set of powers relates to the fiscal and appointive controls that the council exercises over certain areawide operating agencies. It approves the capital budget of the Metropolitan Transit Commission, and appoints the membership and reviews the capital and operating budgets of the Metropolitan Sewer Board. With the evolution of the Twin Cities council a basic distinction pertinent to the question of metropolitan organization and functional allocation has emerged: between areawide programs or functions that need to be operated as a system, such as mass transit and airports, and those that need only to be planned as a system, such as parks and solid waste disposal.[37] This is a distinction that is supplementary to the criteria listed in Chapter 10 for determining the proper placement of functional responsibilities.

An in-depth analysis of the Twin Cities council by political scientists John Harrigan and William Johnson suggests that the agency's impact has been strongest when (1) it serves as a link between the general goals of national and state policies and their local implementation; (2) it is able to organize a function on a regional level that the local governments could not perform adequately for themselves; (3) its plans reflect the interests of the individual units that are to execute them and exact little or no costs in return; and (4) it is able to correlate various functional plans and resolve conflicts among them as they affect the member units. The analysis also

[37]Ted Kolderie, "Regionalism in the Twin Cities of Minnesota," in Kent Mathewson (ed.), *The Regionalist Papers*, 2d ed. (Southfield, Mich.: Metropolitan Fund, 1978), pp. 26–47.

points up the failure of the council in two important respects: the low priority given to social policies and the tendency to avoid the problems of the central cities. These deficiencies, as we have already noted, are common to COGs generally.[38]

INCREMENTAL APPROACHES: THEIR PROSPECTS

What is surprising about the incremental approaches, particularly service agreements and metropolitan councils, is not the large increase in their use in recent years but the fact that this expansion did not come much earlier. One would surmise that the moderate methods of handling service problems—methods that pose no threat to the autonomy of existing governments—would have been widely employed when difficulties were initially developing in the early decades of the twentieth century. But such was not the case. Equally astonishing, interlocal service agreements are still not in common use in many SMSAs.

The expanded use of intergovernmental contracts has brought about some economies and ameliorated many minor difficulties but has had little impact on the solution of critical areawide problems. Even in Los Angeles County where the greatest number of contracts involving a single unit of government are in operation, cooperative arrangements have been of restricted scope and limited largely to noncontroversial activities. Most important, service contracts are not distributive devices for promoting congruency between needs and resources in a politically fragmented metropolis. The poorer communities that desire services from their more affluent neighbors or the county government must reimburse the suppliers.

Despite their drawbacks, interlocal agreements contribute to the day-to-day functioning of the multinucleated SMSA. They will continue to increase in number—although at a modest pace—if for no other reason than the pressure to keep taxes down through more effective operations. Similarly, efforts to effect functional transfers are likely to become more common as financially distressed central cities (and some of the older suburbs as well) seek to relieve themselves of certain costly services. The fiscal restraints on the county and state governments, however, will deter any rapid assumption of activities on their part.

Metropolitan districts limited to a single function have been

[38] John J. Harrigan and William C. Johnson, *Governing the Twin Cities Region: The Metropolitan Council in Comparative Perspective* (Minneapolis: University of Minnesota Press, 1978), pp. 116–118, 126.

the most popular means of handling service problems of an areawide nature. The use of this incremental approach will also continue but probably at a much slower pace than in the past. In the Proposition 13 era the creation of any new governmental agency—even a single-purpose unit—will be subject to close scrutiny. Public approval is unlikely unless the need for such a district and its advantages to the taxpayers can be clearly demonstrated. The prospects for establishing multipurpose districts are extremely remote at this time. The traditional inability of this device to attract popular support is now compounded by public skepticism of big government in general.

Councils of governments will remain in existence and continue to function in much the same way as at present. Few of them will take on any significant operating activities or assume new roles. Little likelihood exists that they will evolve into metropolitan governments or become important policy-making bodies for areawide issues. Well over a decade has passed since the Twin Cities council was reconstituted with several key powers—many observers at the time hailed the action as a breakthrough for metropolitan restructuring—but no other SMSA (with the exception of Portland) has taken steps to follow the Minnesota model.

The usefulness of the incremental approaches should not be ignored. They have made it possible for metropolitan political systems to function without serious breakdown and to meet the basic service needs of a swiftly expanding urban population. They have kept down the scale of government in SMSAs, enabled smaller units to survive, and contributed in various ways to enhancing the quality of life (through cultural and recreational districts, for example). What they have failed to do is provide an effective mechanism for intrametropolitan conflict resolution and areawide policymaking. This failure is reflected in the inability of SMSAs to resolve central city–suburban differences, deal with the problem of service inequities arising from the variances in fiscal capacity among local units, and promote more orderly growth in the interest of conserving natural resources (including land) and protecting the environment. As a result, a political vacuum exists at the metropolitan level that is gradually being filled by the national and state governments.[39]

---

[39]An example of this occurred recently in the St. Louis SMSA when the existing incremental mechanisms, including the area's COG, proved incapable of reaching agreement on the location of a new regional airport. The decision was consequently made by federal authorities.

Chapter 13
The Politics of Reform

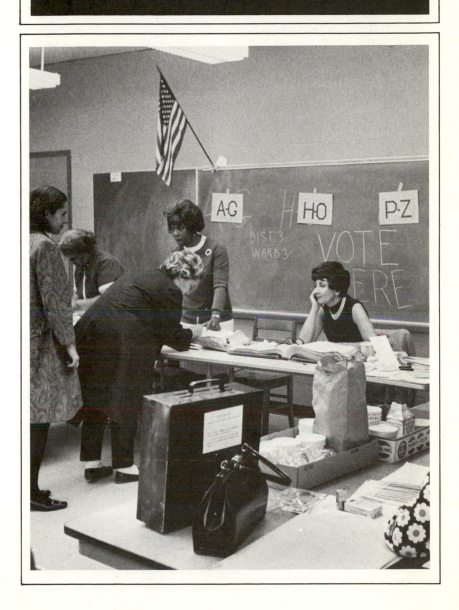

The post-World War II period witnessed a rash of attempts in the United States (and in other countries as well) to adapt the political structure of metropolitan areas to contemporary needs. These efforts ranged from simple tinkerings with internal administrative mechanisms to the creation of unified areawide governments. The reorganization movement peaked during the 1950s when well over 100 metropolitan surveys were conducted, many under the auspices of officially appointed commissions. Despite the huge commitment of time and resources represented by these endeavors, the record of reform accomplishment has not been impressive. Of the 63 comprehensive proposals (those involving a substantial degree of structural integration) submitted to the electorate between 1947 and 1978, only 18 won acceptance. Most of the victories were confined to smaller areas where the bulk of the population was concentrated in the central city and the governmental machinery was relatively uncomplicated.[1] This record of formally presented proposals, moreover, does not tell the whole story, because numerous other attempts failed even to reach the referendum stage.

Reformist dogma from the beginning has reflected a simplistic view of the metropolis and its maladies. Until recent years most reorganization supporters concurred in the belief that the nub of "the metropolitan problem" was the multiplicity of local governments. Their perception, however, has shifted over time. Originally they conceived the reform objective to be the elimination of overlapping jurisdictions and service duplications. Efficiency and economy were the guiding norms within this frame of reference. Later as the problems of sewage disposal, pollution, transportation, and

[1] Joseph F. Zimmerman, "The Metropolitan Governance Maze in the United States." Paper presented at Governmental Research Association conference, August 1978. The adoption rate should be viewed with caution because seven mergers occurred under the special annexation circumstances prevailing in Virginia and five others took place in nonmetropolitan areas. For an earlier summary of developments in this field see Joseph F. Zimmerman, "Metropolitan Reform in the U.S.: An Overview," *Public Administration Review* 30 (September/October 1970): 531–543.

urban sprawl mounted, their preoccupation with administrative management principles gave way to a concern for the formulation and implementation of regional policies. Here the determining norm was effectiveness or the ability of the governmental structure to achieve areawide goals. More recently, they have stressed the importance of reorganization for raising the quality of urban life.[2]

The long obsession with structural change led reformers to de-emphasize the metropolis as a social and political system and to regard it merely as a service provider. It was only gradually that they came to view governmental reorganization as a highly charged political question rather than an exercise in management efficiency. As the lessons of defeat showed them, every proposal for redesigning the governmental pattern of an urban area—whether in minimal fashion through cooperative devices or in more fundamental ways such as consolidation or the comprehensive urban county plan—must at some point meet the test of political acceptability, a test provided in some cases by popular referendum, in others by the governing bodies of the units involved, and in rare instances by the state legislature. The very fact that the question is political requires it to be approached in a political manner and not as a civic crusade for a new convention center or sports arena. Changes in the governmental structure involve alterations in the division of power, rewards, and labors. These changes may, and often do, jeopardize the positions of local officials and employees, threaten the protective controls exercised by suburban units, affect the representation of different constituencies, and modify the impact of taxes and services on various groups. It is naive to expect a reorganization proposal to have such overwhelming logic from the standpoint of efficiency or equity that it can avoid attacks from those who perceive it as a threat to their interests.

BARRIERS TO CHANGE

Sociologist Scott Greer in his analysis of metropolitan civic life lists three groups of interrelated impediments to governmental reorganization: (1) the underlying cultural norms of Americans concerning local government; (2) the legal-constitutional structure; and (3) the political-governmental system.[3] These obstacles relate to the ideology and theory on which the urban polity is based and to the attitudinal and value patterns of its citizenry.

---

[2]John H. Rehfuss, "Metropolitan Government: Four Views," *Urban Affairs Quarterly* 4 (June 1969): 91–111.
[3]Scott Greer, *Governing the Metropolis* (New York: Wiley, 1962), pp. 124–125.

The norms that have helped shape the American system of local government are derivatives of Jeffersonian and Jacksonian ideologies. From Jefferson we inherited the "grass-roots" concept of government and the distrust of those who exercise the powers of office. His ideas on local rule were always couched in terms of the small community of educated yeomen rather than the large city with its teeming populace. To him, the New England town with its meetings of all the citizenry was "the wisest invention ever devised by the wit of man for the perfect exercise of self-government and for its preservation." Jacksonians too stressed the "sacred right" of local self-rule, but unlike their aristocratic predecessors they welcomed the urban masses to share in the function of government. Public office was opened to all on the premise that any citizen of normal intelligence could satisfactorily manage the affairs of the city or county. Rotation in office, popular election of numerous officials, and the spoils system became standard features of the local political system during the second half of the nineteenth century.

The municipal reform movement at the turn of this century was a repudiation of Jacksonian practices but not of its grass-roots ideology. To combat the corruption of city politics, the reformers offered the short ballot, professional management, nonpartisan elections, and the initiative, referendum, and recall, which exposed the governmental system to the direct action or veto of the voter. The inherent right of the community to govern itself free from undue interference by the state legislature, a right implicit in both Jeffersonian and Jacksonian theory, was also institutionalized during this period by state constitutional and legislative provisions relating to municipal "home rule." These enactments supplemented the earlier guarantees of local self-determination, such as the generous incorporation laws, difficult annexation requirements, and legal provisions that made it virtually impossible to consolidate or eliminate existing units.

The governmental pattern that has evolved at the local level has managed to maintain itself without submitting to major surgery. Few incumbent officeholders or others who benefit from existing arrangements are willing to gamble on possible gains that a reordered structure might bring them. Similarly those who aspire to the rewards of local public office are usually willing to play the game within the present system and according to its rules. Defenders of the *status quo* also hold a strategic weapon. Unlike the reformers who have no ready-made machine for mobilizing support, they have access to political cadres and mass-based organizations that serve as important reference points for voters. This advantage is generally the controlling factor in the absence of serious community problems that call into question the responsive capability of the existing structure.

It would be wholly erroneous to assume that metropolitan reorganization represents a battle between the enlightened and unselfish on one side and the ignorant and self-seeking on the other. The tendency of many reformers, and even some academic writers, to conceptualize the issue in these simple and moralistic terms has handicapped the movement by divorcing it from reality. It has also impeded understanding of the forces and factors that are brought into play when governmental changes are sought. Reorganization involves not only jobs and rewards but, more important, value differences among residents and subcommunities in the metropolitan complex. It changes the relative access of groups to official policy-making bodies and raises legitimate issues of governmental philosophy and political power.[4] In this light, the notion that voter rejection of seemingly rational proposals for metropolitan restructuring is due to ignorance or misunderstanding requires considerable qualification.

THE ACTORS

Much of the impetus for metropolitan reorganization has come from the top business and civic leadership of the area acting through either the chamber of commerce or more exclusive organizations. The prime movers in the Dade County restructuring, for example, were the *Miami Herald* and the central city business interests who were unhappy with rising taxes. In Cleveland the economic notables provided the initiative for the urban county plan presented to the voters in 1959; in Nashville the chamber of commerce was instrumental in securing the enabling legislation to permit the drafting of a city–county consolidation charter; in Jacksonville, Florida, it was also the chamber of commerce, disturbed by inefficient government and the slow rate of the area's growth, that spearheaded the amalgamation drive. In the successful consolidation of the city of Lexington and Fayette County, Kentucky in 1972, the initiative came from the League of Women Voters and a good government coalition group; and in Salt Lake City the unsuccessful effort to merge the city and county governments in 1978 was spearheaded by the League of Women Voters.

Variations from the common pattern do take place, as in the

[4]See in this connection Robert Warren, "Federal-Local Development Planning: Scale Effects in Representation and Policy Making," *Public Administration Review* 30 (November/December 1970): 584–595.

1959 metropolitan district effort in St. Louis where the original impetus came from a young and politically ambitious central city alderman (later mayor), A. J. Cervantes, who was looking for a "live" issue to promote his candidacy for president of the city council. An analogous example is the Indianapolis–Marion County reorganization, where the central city mayor, Richard Lugar, was the principal architect. Aside from the organizational and administrative advantages to be derived from the change, Lugar saw political gain both for himself and his party in the merger of the city and county. He later became the first chief executive of the consolidated government and in 1976 was elected United States senator. These are not typical cases, however, and their rarity serves only to emphasize that the reform initiative or push has come predominantly from the nonpolitical sectors of the community and groups without mass-based support.

Civic and Business Organizations

The civic groups that evidence concern over the governmental structure and processes of the metropolis are, in a sense, heirs of the municipal reform spirit and philosophy of the early 1900s. They began to turn their attention to the larger community as central cities became better governed and the critical urban problems outgrew individual corporate boundaries. Their interests were channeled into the metropolitan reform field largely by the professionals who staff the key civic organizations, by concerned political scientists, and by the promptings of the National Municipal League, the patriarch of the good government groups. The role played by the economic and social influentials is usually not one of personal involvement; more often it consists of legitimizing the issue as worthy of community support. The actual task of carrying the campaign forward is generally left to the professional staffs and younger aspirants in the group, to public relations hirelings, and to the workhorse civic organizations such as the League of Women Voters and local municipal research bureaus such as the Citizens League of Minneapolis–St. Paul and the Municipal League of Seattle and King County.

One element of the business community, the downtown interests, has a more personal stake in metropolitan reorganization. Concerned with the economic position of the central business district, many merchants and building owners tend to feel that areawide governmental integration can aid the CBD by giving it greater prominence in a reconstituted polity. In the Miami case the chamber of commerce pushed vigorously for metropolitan government, seeing it as a means of relieving the tax pressure on property in the core city by spreading the base over a larger area. But aside from any direct economic stakes, business groups are ideologically disposed to regard reorganization with favor. The booster spirit that is characteristic of them commonly finds expression in the gospel of "a bigger and better community." Typical was the plea in the Dade County charter campaign: "Give Miami a chance to be a big city." This same theme, "One Great City," was also employed recently by the Young Men's Business Club of Birmingham, Alabama, in its unsuccessful drive to consolidate the city and the surrounding urbanized area. Suburban chambers of commerce and the local merchants they represent seldom share this view of metropolitan aggrandizement through governmental integration. To them, such a change means a loss or diminution of their influence over the public affairs of the communities in which they operate.

The Press

The daily newspapers in the central city are usually staunch advocates of metropolitan reform, although on a few occasions, as in the Jacksonville–Duval County consolidation, their close relationship to the local political machine may lead them to take an opposing position. Their role has been primarily one of lending editorial and news support to reform efforts or of prodding the civic elite into action.[5] As organs with an areawide audience and outlook, they are attracted to metropolitan reorganization as an appropriate cause for their crusading zeal. And by championing the vision of the larger community, they can fulfill their role expectations as "integrative" symbols of the metropolis.

In contrast to the large dailies, the suburban community press is almost always opposed to major change in the existing system. Long characterized by bias against the central city and an equally strong antimetropolitan press attitude, the suburban papers find areawide reorganization measures useful targets. By picturing such proposals as the products of central city politicians or of "undesirable" elements seeking to invade suburbia, they can pose as protec-

---

[5]Occasionally, as in the Dade County charter campaign in 1957, the newspapers play a more direct role. There the associate editor of the *Miami Herald* was a key strategist and major participant in the movement. Because the mass-based organizations, such as political parties and labor unions, are relatively weak in that area, Miami newspapers enjoy considerable influence as a referent for voters on local public issues. On this point see Thomas J. Wood, "Dade County: Unbossed, Erratically Led," *Annals of the American Academy of Political and Social Science* 353 (May 1964): 64–71.

tors of small community virtues. Metropolitan reorganization gives them an opportunity to launch a "safe" crusade of the type they can rarely afford on local issues for fear of alienating some of their readership. As locally based and locally oriented instrumentalities dependent on the business advertising of the village merchants, publication of legal notices of the suburban governments, and the subscriptions of residents in their limited area, they feel a personal stake in keeping the existing governmental system intact.

Local Officialdom

Wherever a "going system" of local government exists, it reacts against radical transformation. If it did not, it could hardly be called a system. Incumbent officeholders are usually found in the camp of the opposition, although there are many exceptions, some of them significant. The city manager of Miami, the county engineer of Cuyahoga County, the president of the St. Louis Board of Aldermen, the mayors of Nashville, Memphis, and Indianapolis all supported metropolitan reorganization efforts in their areas. In each instance, however, the incumbents saw in the proposed reform an opportunity to extend their sphere of control or obtain other rewards. The Nashville mayor, for example, supported the first consolidation effort in 1959 when he was regarded as the most likely choice for the proposed office of metropolitan chief executive, but he strongly opposed the successful 1962 movement at a time when he had become the target of intense local opposition because of the city's vigorous annexation policy.[6]

Central city officials generally supported total merger in the past, viewing such action as an enlargement of the municipality's boundaries and hence an enhancement of its political powers. Conversely, they usually reacted in negative fashion when lesser remedies were proposed, such as federation or multipurpose metropolitan districts, that would reduce the powers of the core municipality. The Cleveland mayor's action in opposing the 1959 charter referendum on a comprehensive urban county plan was typical; he took this position because several important facilities such as the water-

[6]The Nashville experience is analyzed in David A. Booth, *Metropolitics: The Nashville Consolidation* (East Lansing: Michigan State University Institute for Community Development and Service, 1963); Daniel R. Grant, "Metropolitics and Professional Political Leadership: The Case of Nashville," *Annals of the American Academy of Political and Social Science* 353 (May 1964): 72–83; and Brett W. Hawkins, *Nashville Metro: The Politics of City-County Consolidation* (Nashville: Vanderbilt University Press, 1966).

works and airport would be removed from city control.[7] His two department heads who had the most to lose in the way of functions and powers were the most effective campaigners among the opposition.[8]

Generalization about the position of central city officials is presently more difficult. Those in the smaller SMSAs tend to support reorganization, although the stand they take is heavily influenced by the specific provisions of the proposed change. The chief executive of Columbus, Georgia, for example, endorsed the charter that merged the city with Muscogee County in 1970; conversely, the Tampa mayor shortly thereafter led the opposition to the proposed (but defeated) city–county consolidation in that area. In the first instance the plan provided for a mayor-council form of government; in the second it called for the appointment of a professional manager as the chief executive, an arrangement not palatable to many political officials. On the whole the big city mayors now regard merger with less favor than they once did because of the risk that political control may shift to the periphery where the suburban population of many areas already exceeds that of the core. The 1962 merger attempt in St. Louis elicited such a response, with the Democratic city committee going on record against the proposal by a vote of 53 to 1 and the board of aldermen by 21 to 3. The likelihood of this kind of reaction is greatest in areas where the politics of the central city is predominantly Democratic and that of the suburbs Republican. No comprehensive reorganization proposal except the state-imposed Indianapolis consolidation has, in fact, been adopted in areas split by strong partisan antagonisms.

Officialdom in the urban fringe stands almost solidly against any major restructuring of the existing system. This position was documented in a 1970 survey of officeholders in six SMSAs of varying size. Those in the central city were in general agreement that governmental consolidation is desirable, whereas those in suburbia were virtually unanimous in their condemnation of such action. Al-

[7]The background of the Cleveland charter attempt is described in James A. Norton, *The Metro Experience* (Cleveland: The Press of Western Reserve University, 1963). Also, see Matthew Holden, Jr., "Decision-Making on a Metropolitan Governmental Proposal," in Scott Greer, Dennis McElrath, David Minar, and Peter Orleans (eds.), *The New Urbanization* (New York: St. Martin's Press, 1968), pp. 315–338.
[8]Cleveland's piecemeal transfer of certain functions to the county in recent years for fiscal reasons has not lessened the hostility of its officials to the county government. As the president of the city council, a black leader, bitterly remarked, "All we are going to end up with is police and firemen ... services the county doesn't want anyway." *New York Times*, November 9, 1979, p. 1A.

though both sets of officials recognized the need to improve the quality of government, fringe area officeholders would limit changes to modifications or adjustments in the system as it is presently organized.[9] Suburban officials have long expressed a willingness to have "true" metropolitan functions handled on a unified basis. Such a function, as they conceive it, is one they badly need but cannot perform for themselves because of costs or the nature of the operation. Water supply, sewage disposal, and pollution control are common examples. In such cases officials of the affected communities will usually acquiesce in the assumption of the service by the county government or a single-purpose metropolitan district. This kind of areawide administration involves little loss of power for the local units and wards off the possible danger of more drastic changes by taking care of the most immediate and troublesome deficiencies.

Other Actors

Political parties are at times found among the reorganization participants, but their involvement is usually nominal. Rarely do they take official positions on proposals to restructure the local government pattern. A notable exception was the partisan activity in the Indianapolis merger. There the Republican party, having captured the key government posts at the city, county, and state levels, seized the opportunity to enhance its prospects for retaining political control over the capital city. Party regulars in the wards and townships and in various public posts have on occasions utilized the organizational machinery to mobilize support or opposition to reform proposals. One such instance was the action of the county board chairman in Allegheny County (Pittsburgh), a well-known Democrat, who brought the weight of his party against a proposed restructuring of the county government in the early 1970s.[10] Activity of this type is not common. Individual party leaders seldom use their political muscle to influence the outcome of reorganization efforts although they may take public stands on them. Neither metropolitan reform nor the potential rewards of an altered system appear to provide sufficient motivation for this kind of commitment.

Like the political parties, organized labor's involvement in reorganization movements has ranged from token endorsement or op-

[9]Amos H. Hawley and Basil G. Zimmer, *The Metropolitan Community: Its People and Government* (Beverly Hills, Calif.: Sage, 1970).

[10]David K. Hamilton, "Political Officials and Areawide Government," *Urbanism Past and Present* No. 8 (Summer 1979): 43.

position to moderate activity. Seldom has its stake in the outcome been considered sufficient to warrant substantial expenditures of resources. Its position and the extent of its activity in each case are dictated largely by the possible effects of the proposed restructuring on existing political arrangements and coalitions. If the influence of those officials or political groups with whom it has established working relationships will be expanded by the change, labor is likely to favor the movement; if these interests are threatened by the proposed action, it will probably join the opposition. In neither case is it likely to make large-scale commitments of energy and money.

Blacks constitute another important group in reorganization issues because of their growing numbers in the central cities. Their attitudes toward metropolitan government are mixed. Most black politicians at the local level look with disfavor on efforts to reorder the system. They tend to regard areawide government as an attempt to thwart the hard-won and long-in-coming political influence of blacks by joining the predominantly white electorate of suburbia to that of the core municipality.[11] Richard Hatcher, the black mayor of Gary, Indiana, expressed this view when he charged that the move to develop metropolitan government seeks "to mute black votes" by including more territory. Other minority leaders, however, believe that if blacks forego a role in areawide decision making until they dominate the politics of the central city, the delay may be costly.[12] Blacks in Jacksonville, Florida, for example, supported the consolidation effort, opting for representation now rather than "waiting to get the whole city." (The charter assured them of no less than one-fifth the seats on the council by providing that 14 of the 19 members were to be chosen by districts in contrast to the old system of elections at large.)[13] As one of their leaders explained: "I

---

[11]A statistical study of the vote on metropolitan reform issues in Cleveland over a period of years revealed that the attitude of blacks toward areawide reorganization became more negative as their political strength increased in the central city. See Richard A. Watson and John H. Romani, "Metropolitan Government for Metropolitan Cleveland: An Analysis of the Voting Record," *Midwest Journal of Political Science* 5 (November 1961): 365–390.

[12]For a discussion of this question see Willis D. Hawley, *Blacks and Metropolitan Governance: The Stakes of Reform* (Berkeley: Institute of Governmental Studies, University of California, Berkeley, 1972).

[13]Blacks, on the other hand, voted solidly (almost 9 to 1) against an attempt to merge Tampa and Hillsborough County, Florida. In this case the plan provided that all seats on the consolidated governing body were to be filled by countywide elections. See P. N. Glendening and J. W. White, "Local Government Reorganization Referenda in Florida: An Acceptance and a Rejection," *Florida State University Governmental Research Bulletin* 5 (March 1968).

might have been the black mayor, but I would have been only a referee in bankruptcy." The prevalent sentiment among central city blacks at the present time appears to be one of opposition to metropolitan restructuring. This fact has further deflated what little interest local Democratic leaders might have in governmental reorganization.

THE REORGANIZATION ODYSSEY

Political scientists Walter Rosenbaum and Thomas Henderson have suggested a model of revolutionary change as the basis for a theory about comprehensive governmental reorganization struggles.[14] According to their formulation, campaigns for structural reform are precipitated by changes within the urban environment that cause serious community problems and widespread concern about them. Demands are then made on the governmental system to take measures to alleviate the trouble, but the response is too inept or inadequate to alter the situation materially. As a result "power deflation," or a growing lack of public confidence in the existing governmental structure and its personnel, follows. For the reorganization movement to succeed, an "accelerator" or catalyst is normally required at this stage. This is an event, in the form of a sudden emergency or major scandal, that stimulates public attention and provides an emotional impetus for the campaign (see Figure 13.1). The model provides a framework for looking at reform efforts, as do other theoretical constructs that endeavor to link referendum results to socioeconomic and political system variables.

The Setting

It would be reasonable to assume that metropolitan reorganization attempts have been initiated because of dissatisfaction with the present system. That this dissatisfaction exists to any great degree, however, is questionable. Reform efforts, as we have seen, commonly originate with certain elite groups in the community; seldom, if ever, do they emanate from the rank and file of the citizenry. There is little evidence, moreover, that the claims of the sponsoring

---

[14]Walter Rosenbaum and Thomas Henderson, "Explaining Comprehensive Governmental Consolidation: Toward a Preliminary Theory," *Journal of Politics* 34 (May 1972): 428–457. Another theoretical formulation is contained in Willis D. Hawley, "On Understanding Metropolitan Political Integration," in Willis D. Hawley et al., *Theoretical Perspectives on Urban Politics* (Englewood Cliffs, N.J.: Prentice-Hall, 1976), pp. 100–145.

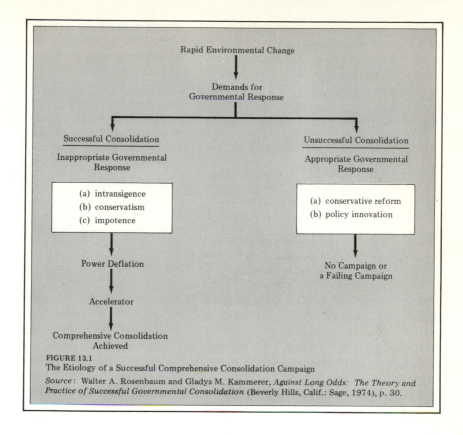

FIGURE 13.1
The Etiology of a Successful Comprehensive Consolidation Campaign

Source: Walter A. Rosenbaum and Gladys M. Kammerer, *Against Long Odds: The Theory and Practice of Successful Governmental Consolidation* (Beverly Hills, Calif.: Sage, 1974), p. 30.

groups are representative of "grass-roots" feelings. Numerous surveys, in fact, indicate that most metropolitan dwellers are at least moderately satisfied with their local governments and the services they are performing. In SMSAs such as St. Louis, Cleveland, and Dayton, where extensive reorganization efforts were made, most residents had no strong criticism of any of their governments and few complaints about services.[15]

More recent surveys continue to confirm these earlier findings. Sociologists Amos H. Hawley and Basil G. Zimmer found in interviewing some 3000 households in six SMSAs that a large majority of the respondents (in most cases over 80 percent) both within and

[15]John C. Bollens (ed.), *Exploring the Metropolitan Community* (Berkeley and Los Angeles: University of California Press, 1961), pp. 188–190; *Metropolitan Challenge* (Dayton: Metropolitan Community Studies, 1959), pp. 241–251 and Norton, *The Metro Experience*. Similar findings were made in a study of suburban governments in the Philadelphia area. See Charles E. Gilbert, *Governing the Suburbs* (Bloomington: Indiana University Press, 1967), pp. 272–275.

outside the central cities expressed satisfaction with the public services they were receiving.[16] The interviews gave no indication of any widespread dissatisfaction with the responsiveness of local government to community needs and demands. Suburban officials, in particular, were regarded as competent, approachable, and interested in the well-being of their constituents. The Urban Observatory's survey of citizen attitudes in ten large central cities in 1970 produced similar findings, although the proportion of satisfaction was somewhat lower.[17] When asked what services in their neighborhoods they would like to see improved, about 40 percent of the respondents in most of the cities could name no specific item. These findings give little indication of a sense of crisis on the part of the public or a state of "power deflation" (lack of confidence in the existing system of local government to cope with problems).

It is against this background that reorganization movements have proceeded. Proponents of change have invariably rested their case on grounds of efficiency, economy, and improvement of the economic base. Aiming their fire at overlapping jurisdictions, governmental fragmentation, confusion of responsibility, outmoded administrative structures, and uncoordinated growth, they have consistently emphasized the theme that problems of metropolitan scope and impact demand handling by an agency with areawide authority. In their campaigns they have stressed the general advantages to be gained from reorganization: improved services, more efficient administration, coordinated planning, more equitable distribution of costs and benefits, and better representation. Supporters of the St. Louis district plan in 1959, for example, pointed to the inability of individual local governments to cope with areawide problems, such as traffic and transportation, the stifling effects of the existing system on the economic progress of the area, and the need for overall guidance and direction in planning the total community.[18]

[16]Hawley and Zimmer, *The Metropolitan Community: Its People and Government.*
[17]A summary of the Observatory's findings is contained in *Nation's Cities* 9 (August 1971). See also Walter A. Rosenbaum and Thomas Henderson, "Explaining Attitudes of Community Influentials Toward Government Consolidation," *Urban Affairs Quarterly* 9 (December 1973): 251–275. The disaffection with government now shown by many citizens is directed at the political system generally rather than at any particular structural or organizational feature of it.
[18]The St. Louis effort is examined in Henry J. Schmandt, Paul G. Steinbicker, and George D. Wendel, *Metropolitan Reform in St. Louis* (New York: Holt, Rinehart and Winston, 1961) and Greer, *Metropolitics: A Study of Political Culture* (New York: Wiley, 1963).

Opponents of metropolitan restructuring have similarly capitalized on common themes. Two of their most effective arguments have been the destruction of grassroots government and higher taxes. Adversaries of consolidation in Nashville, Memphis, Tampa, and elsewhere contended that the proposals would result in big government, loss of individual rights, and tax increases. Opponents have also pictured the existing system as adequate or have maintained that reformist objectives can be achieved by less drastic changes.[19]

Those pressing for reorganization are at a disadvantage in answering the arguments of the opposition. Neither the problems of metropolitan areas nor the solutions to them can be articulated in simple and readily understandable terms. To the plea "keep government close to the people" advocates of change can speak only of the more desirable environment and brighter future the proposed plan will promote. To the challenge "show the people why they should discard a system that has served them for so long," proponents can reply only with generalized statements about efficiency, orderly growth, and future dangers, or with arguments so complex that their significance often escapes the average citizen.[20] To the charge of higher taxes the reformers can only respond that reorganization will result in better services. In the present antitax mood, public support might quicken if supporters could guarantee that reorganization would lower taxes. But no such promise can legitimately be made because of the greater responsibilities usually taken on by the reconstituted government in meeting long-neglected service needs and upgrading public facilities suffering from deferred maintenance.

The "Accelerator"

The municipal reformers of the early 1900s had simplified the issue of governmental reorganization for the voters by attacking corruption and machine politics and effectively utilizing the battle cry of "throw the rascals out." Charges of this nature are less relevant to-

[19]See Richard L. Cole and David A. Caputo, "Leadership Opposition to Consolidation," *Urban Affairs Quarterly* 8 (December 1972): 253–258. A different type of opposition comes from right-wing groups that attempt to link reorganization efforts to "one-world government" advocates, left-wingers, and a network of professional government associations purportedly seeking a federal takeover of local government.

[20]These difficulties are discussed in Greer, *Metropolitics: A Study of Political Culture.*

day with the demise of machine politics in most cities, the professionalization of the local civil service, and the use of competitive
bidding for contracts. Yet it is interesting to note that in each of the
three major reorganization successes since 1950 that involved popular referendum—Miami–Dade County, Nashville–Davidson
County, and Jacksonville–Duval County—the issue of corruption
or machine politics played a part. The situation reflected in these
charges provided what Rosenbaum and Henderson (and later Rosenbaum and Kammerer) refer to as the "accelerator" or the event
that dramatizes the need for major governmental reform.[21]

Miami city politics, at the time of the 1957 charter movement,
had been marked by considerable infighting among council members and by recurring charges of corruption. The police department
in particular had been under fire for its alleged failure to enforce
the laws against gambling and other forms of vice. In contrast, the
county government was generally well regarded and free from any
taint of corruption. These circumstances enabled proponents to jux-
tapose the "good" county against the "evil" city government.[22]

In Nashville several events, fortuitous to the 1962 consolidation proposal, occurred after the defeat of the earlier effort. Following the initial rejection of the merger charter, the city of Nashville
took two steps that were deeply resented by suburban residents.
First, it adopted a ten dollar "green sticker" tax on automobiles to
be paid by residents and all other persons whose automobiles used
its streets during more than 30 days a year. Second, taking advantage of the strong annexation powers granted by the Tennessee legislature in 1955, the city moved quickly to more than triple its territorial size.[23] Without the necessity of a vote in the affected sections,
it annexed 7 square miles of prime industrial land only two days
after the consolidation referendum, and 42 square miles of residential area with over 82,000 residents 18 months later. Among other
effects, the two annexations drastically reduced the road tax reve-

---

[21]Rosenbaum and Henderson, "Explaining Comprehensive Governmental Consolidation," 428–457.

[22]The Miami reorganization movement is documented in Edward Sofen, *The Miami
Metropolitan Experiment,* rev. ed. (Garden City, N.Y.: Anchor Books, 1966) and
John DeGrove et al., "Southern Regionalism," in Kent Mathewson (ed.), *The Re-
gionalist Papers,* 2d ed. (Southfield, Mich.: Metropolitan Fund, 1978), pp. 108–115.

[23]A similar situation aided the Columbus-Muscogee County, Georgia, merger in
1970. Following an unsuccessful consolidation attempt in 1962, Columbus em-
barked on an aggressive annexation program that brought more than 90 percent of
the county's population within its borders. Because separate majorities were required only inside the central city and in the county as a whole, the plan passed. Had
a separate majority outside the city been necessary, the proposal would have been
defeated.

nue of the county government and created serious financial difficulties for the schools that remained outside the central municipality.

These actions by the city revived the consolidation movement and led to the creation of a new charter commission. The proposal presented to the voters in 1962 was essentially the same as the one that had been rejected four years earlier. The Nashville mayor, Ben West, in contrast to his vigorous support of the first merger efforts, led the opposition. Knowing that a victory for the charter forces would be a serious blow to his political career, he brought the full weight of his organization into the fray. City employees were mobilized for the fight and police and firemen, as well as schoolteachers, were used to distribute anticonsolidation literature. These activities enabled the *Tennessean*, one of the two metropolitan dailies in the area, to hit hard at the "city machine" theme and, in the process, reiterate earlier charges of "police corruption" and poor law enforcement.

The Jacksonville–Duval merger in 1967 took place at a time when the local political machine was seriously discredited by exposures of corruption among city and county officeholders. News telecasts of irregularities in purchasing practices and other governmental activities had led to a grand jury investigation and the indictment of 11 officials on various charges, including bribery. Many observers believe that the indictments provided the multiplier factor that put the consolidation referendum over the top.[24] The situation was different in Tampa-Hillsborough where voters emphatically rejected a consolidation proposal less than two months before the Jacksonville victory. In that area none of the three elements suggested by the Rosenbaum-Henderson model was present. There was no widespread public recognition that grave problems confronted the community and were not being coped with adequately (crisis climate), no growing disenchantment with local governmental structures and processes (power diffusion), and no triggering event (an accelerator).

Unlike the other successful reorganization efforts, the Indianapolis Unigov was preceded by no crisis situation or dissatisfaction with local government, or by any scandal. (Certainly the model of revolutionary change cannot explain its adoption.) The city, in fact,

---

[24]Richard A. Martin, *Consolidation: Jacksonville–Duval County* (Jacksonville: Crawford Publishing Company, 1968). A crisis was also a major accelerating factor in each of four Virginia city–county consolidations. David G. Temple, *Merger Politics: Local Government Consolidation in Tidewater, Virginia* (Charlottesville: University Press of Virginia, 1972).

was experiencing an unprecedented building boom, and the general property tax had only recently been lowered.[25] Whether the attempt would have been successful had a popular referendum been required is doubtful. Whatever the case, Unigov and the other comprehensive reform efforts underscore the political nature of metropolitan restructuring and the need, as two Nashville consolidation leaders emphasized, to wage a "political" rather than a "community project" campaign in order to win.[26]

VOTER RESPONSE

With few exceptions, reorganization plans are required by law to be submitted to the local electorate for approval. This is the critical stage in the reform process, a stage that only a modicum of proposals have managed to survive. Many reasons have been advanced to explain the unfavorable voter response, among them apathy, low electoral turnouts, ignorance of the issues, fear of change, and satisfaction with the status quo. The evidence to sustain the relevance and import of these various factors is mixed.

Voter apathy, as manifested by low turnouts, has been common to reorganization elections. Based on a survey of 18 major plans submitted to popular referendum between 1950 and 1961, the Advisory Commission on Intergovernmental Relations summed up the situation in a few words: "Proposals for governmental reorganization in metropolitan areas have faced a largely apathetic public."[27] The commission found that in 14 of the elections less than 30 percent of the voting-age population bothered to cast their ballot on the issue. These 18 attempts and later reoganization efforts offer no evidence, however, that increased activity at the polls augurs well (or poorly) for the adoption of a proposal. The Augusta–Richmond County (Georgia) merger in 1974 and the multipurpose district plan in the Portland, Oregon, area in 1978 obtained favorable majorities with limited turnouts; others, such as the 1971 merger attempt in the Augusta area, lost in spite of a relatively high percentage of

---

[25]The Indianapolis consolidation is analyzed in York Willbern, "Unigov: Local Government Reorganization in Indianapolis," in Kent Mathewson (ed.), *The Regionalist Papers*, 2d ed. (Southfield, Mich.: Metropolitan Fund, 1978), pp. 48–72.

[26]Hawkins, *Nashville Metro: The Politics of City-County Consolidation*, p. 80. One observer, in contrasting the two Nashville efforts, noted that in the second campaign: "It was as if the professionals and the politicians had taken over from the amateurs and do-gooders." Booth, *Metropolitics: The Nashville Consolidation*, p. 85.

[27]Advisory Commission on Intergovernmental Relations, *Factors Affecting Voter Reaction to Governmental Reorganization in Metropolitan Areas* (Washington, D.C., May 1962), p. 24.

participation.[28] Too much significance, moreover, should not be placed on voter apathy in metropolitan reform matters because similar indifference is commonly exhibited toward other local referenda questions and toward municipal and school district elections in general.

Studies indicate that the better educated citizenry tend to be less hostile to metropolitan restructuring and more sympathetic to the efficiency and effectiveness arguments. In the Miami SMSA the precincts highest on the socioeconomic scale favored the charter most strongly, whereas those at the bottom gave it the least support. The Nashville and St. Louis findings were similar: the higher the level of their education and income, the more likely were voters to favor the proposed changes. Normally also, we would expect higher participation rates among those better off socioeconomically. This association, however, has not proved strong according to available evidence. The Miami survey, for example, discovered no important difference between the high- and low-status precincts in voter turnout on the charter issue. The St. Louis study also revealed that the proportion of those voting on the district plan did not differ significantly among the various social ranks. One explanation for this deviation from the general pattern of voting behavior lies in the more intensive organizational activity usually displayed by opponents at the grass-roots level. This activity often leads to a more-than-normal turnout of lower status voters in reorganization elections.[29] Another explanation is that many individuals in the higher socioeconomic categories feel that comprehensive restructuring proposals have little chance of passing, and therefore do not bother to vote.

Voter Knowledge

A factor frequently pointed to as an obstacle to areawide restructuring is citizen unfamiliarity with metropolitan issues. This lack of knowledge is well documented. A sampling of residents in Cuyahoga County several weeks before the charter election in 1959 re-

[28]An examination of 28 city–county consolidation attempts between 1945 and 1971 likewise found no evidence to imply that high voter turnout increases the chance for approval. See Vincent L. Marando and Carl R. Whitley, "City-County Consolidation: An Overview of Voter Response," *Urban Affairs Quarterly* 8 (December 1972): 181–204. Analyses of participation in 470 local referenda elections covering a wide spectrum of issues also found no relationship between voter turnout levels and passage or defeat of the measure. W. Bruce Shepard, "Participation in Local Policy Making: The Case of Referenda," *Social Science Quarterly* 56 (June 1975): 55–70.
[29]As these results further illustrate, political environment and the political activity surrounding reorganization campaigns cannot be overlooked in seeking to link referenda results to socioeconomic and demographic variables.

vealed that one of every three persons did not remember reading or hearing anything about the proposed new document despite the extensive publicity that had been given to it. More than three-fourths of the respondents could not name a single reason advanced for or against the charter.[30] Similarly a survey in the St. Louis area after the 1959 metropolitan district referendum showed in convincing terms that the voters knew little about the issue and those who were involved in the campaign. In 40 percent of the cases, leaders mentioned by the interviewees as supporters of the plan were publicly on record as opposed to it.[31]

It is not clear whether this unfamiliarity is related to voter opposition to metropolitan reform. A study in the Flint (Michigan) SMSA concluded that resistance to governmental unification rests largely on ignorance of local government and what to expect from it.[32] However, a survey of Nashville area voters after the successful charter election found only partial support for the assumption that lack of knowledge is an impediment to structural reorganization. As the author speculated, ignorance is manipulable and can go either way.[33]

Transmitting to the electorate the complex issues associated with governmental reorganization is a difficult, if not impossible, task. Change of this type does not ordinarily give rise to the use of effective and attention-capturing symbols. Instead, voters are caught in a crossfire of conflicting and abstract arguments that often have little meaning for them. Mayor Lugar rationalized his opposition to a popular referendum on the Indianapolis merger by pointing to the complexity of the plan and the unfamiliarity of the electorate with the intricacies of the local governmental pattern and its processes. In his words, "To throw an issue which has tested the wisdom of the best constitutional lawyers in the state to persons

[30]Greer, *Metropolitics: A Study of Political Culture*, p. 189.
[31]Ibid., p. 101. A survey of voters in the unsuccessful merger attempt in Charlotte–Mecklenberg County, North Carolina, (1971) revealed that only 13 percent were able to answer more than three of five simple questions about basic features of the charter. Schley Lyons, *Citizens Attitudes and Metropolitan Government* (Charlotte: University of North Carolina, 1972).
[32]Amos H. Hawley and Basil G. Zimmer, "Resistance to Unification in a Metropolitan Community," in Morris Janowitz (ed.), *Community Political Systems* (New York: Free Press, 1961), pp. 173–174. One observer attributes this unfamiliarity to lack of funding to inform the electorate as well as to the complexity of reform plans. D. Michael Stewart, "Local Government Modernization, Reflections on Salt Lake City-County," *National Civic Review* 67 (June 1977): 291–299.
[33]Hawkins, *Nashville Metro: The Politics of City-County Consolidation*, p. 217.

who have not the slightest idea of what government was before or after is not wise."[34] But reorganization is more than a technical or an administrative question; it involves the reallocation of power as well as functions. As such, it is a matter for public consideration and public action and not one to be left solely to the experts.

Because of the intricate nature of governmental reorganization issues, even those pertaining to municipal or county charter reform, the stand of public officials is important as a referent point for the individual citizen. One observer hypothesizes that the single most important cause of the success or failure of restructuring proposals is the ability of elected officeholders to influence voters.[35] This assumption may be overdrawn but there is little doubt that such officials play an important role in the outcome of reform efforts. A study of attempts to effect organizational changes in 67 local governments in Pennsylvania during a recent three–year period showed that the influence of the elected functionaries was significant. In those cases where they supported the proposed reform, 82 percent received voter approval, and where they opposed, only 44 percent passed.[36]

Related Factors

Two additional factors—service dissatisfaction and difference in life-styles—are assumed to influence popular attitudes toward metropolitan reform. The first finds support in several studies in which favorable attitudes toward governmental reorganization were found to be linked to negative views toward public services.[37] The strength of this relationship, however, is uncertain. Other research, although acknowledging that discontent with the status quo helps create an environmental setting conducive to reform impetus, suggests that the influence of this factor must be weighed against other values held by metropolitan residents. Suburbanites in general are reluctant to sacrifice the autonomy of their community for a more

[34]"City-County Consolidations, Separations, and Federations," *American County* 35 (November 1969): 17.
[35]Hamilton, "Political Officials and Areawide Government," p. 42.
[36]Larry Gamm, *Community Dynamics of Local Government Change* (State College, Pa.: Pennsylvania Policy Analysis Services, Pennsylvania State University, 1976). Another study showed that the more elective offices the reorganization plan retains, the better the chances of adoption. Vincent L. Marando, "Voting on City-County Consolidation Referenda," *Western Political Quarterly* 26 (March 1973): 90–96.
[37]See, for example, John H. Kunkel, "The Role of Services in Annexation of Metropolitan Fringe Areas," *Land Economics* 36 (May 1960): 208–212.

economical or efficient governmental system. Fringe area dwellers in the Grand Rapids (Michigan) SMSA who recognized the existence of service problems were only slightly more inclined to favor political integration than those who saw no cause for complaint.[38]

Similar findings emerged in an attitudinal survey of residents in a small suburb outside Iowa City. Here also, dissatisfaction with local services was not enough to overcome the "communal" or "grass-roots" ideology of the respondents. For them, the existing governmental structure had become the embodiment of certain values (desire for privacy, small-town atmosphere, friendly neighbors) so that proposals to change it in any substantial fashion were perceived less in terms of greater efficiency than as threats to these values.[39] As Charles Press has aptly observed, the desire to maintain local control apparently persuades many suburbanites to tolerate more inefficiency in the metropolitan system than civic reformers deem appropriate.[40]

The second factor—differences in life-styles—assumes that a family-oriented way of life (more characteristic of suburbia) is associated with opposition to integrative proposals, and nonfamilism (more typical of central cities with their large proportion of single-person households and childless couples) with voter support. The underlying rationale is that suburbanites are unwilling to subject the protection of their life-style to a consolidated or areawide government which must also respond to core-city residents with different social characteristics (lower status, less familistic, more ethnic and racial). If this assumption is correct, it follows that the greater the diversity of life-style between city and fringe, the more likely will the latter resist political integration.

Although logic would seem to support the life-style thesis, the empirical findings are far from conclusive. Earlier studies tended to confirm the diversity hypothesis,[41] but a more recent statistical analysis of 42 metropolitan referenda indicates that as life-style distance (in terms of higher social status and a greater degree of familism) increasingly favors the fringe, the stronger is the tendency for

[38]Charles Press, "Efficiency and Economy Arguments for Metropolitan Reorganization, *Public Opinion Quarterly* 28 (Winter 1963): 584–594.
[39]Marian Roth and G. R. Boynton, "Communal Ideology and Political Support," *Journal of Politics* 31 (February 1969): 167–185.
[40]Press, "Efficiency and Economy Arguments for Metropolitan Reorganization," p. 593.
[41]See, for example, Walter C. Kaufman and Scott Greer, "Voting in a Metropolitan Community: An Application of Social Area Analysis," *Social Forces* 38 (March 1960): 196–204.

suburban voters to support some type of governmental reorganiza-tion.[42] Studies in the Lexington (Kentucky) SMSA and the Augusta (Georgia) area, however, give little support to either of these find-ings. Both indicate that variations in living patterns among fringe dwellers have little impact on individual attitudes toward the polit-ical integration of urban governments.[43] As these varying results demonstrate, more than life-style differences or citizen perceptions of public services are involved in shaping voter views toward gov-ernmental restructuring. Political, economic, historical, and situa-tional factors are also relevant in explaining popular attitudes to-ward reorganization.[44]

THE POLITICS OF COOPERATION

The discussion up to this point has touched on the politics associ-ated with comprehensive reorganization proposals; it has not dealt with those involved in the use of cooperative devices. These latter ventures are also suffused with politics, although they may not be so visible or intense. As we saw in Chapter 12, social distance among communities is a factor influencing the choice of partners in joint enterprises. Although municipalities in metropolitan areas do not necessarily restrict their cooperation to units with like socioeco-nomic characteristics, they do tend to contract selectively on agree-ments that have social implications, choosing in such cases partners of similar status. Cooperation among local governments, moreover, rarely occurs with respect to functions that could affect the life-styles of their residents, nor does it take place in instances where the distribution of benefits and costs would favor one of the par-

---

[42]Brett W. Hawkins, "Fringe-City Life-Style Distance and Fringe Support of Politi-cal Integration," *American Journal of Sociology* 74 (November 1968): 248–255. See also Vincent L. Marando, "Life Style Distances and Suburban Support for Urban Political Integration: A Replication," *Social Science Quarterly* 53 (June 1972): 155–160.

[43]W. E. Lyons and Richard L. Engstrom, "Life Style and Fringe Attitudes: Toward the Political Integration of Urban Governments," *Midwest Journal of Political Sci-ence* 15 (August 1971): 475–494 and "Life Style and Fringe Attitudes Toward the Political Integration of Urban Governments: A Comparison of Survey Findings," *American Journal of Political Science* 17 (February 1973): 182–188.

[44]For a consideration of a number of variables that at times affect referenda decisions on metropolitan reform, see Parris N. Glendening and Patricia S. Atkins, "The Poli-tics of City-County Consolidation," *County Year Book: 1977*, pp. 62–69 and Parris N. Glendening and Mavis Mann Reeves, *Pragmatic Federalism* (Pacific Palisades, Calif.: Palisades Publishers, 1977), pp. 301–304. Another general summary is con-tained in Vincent L. Marando, "The Politics of City-County Consolidation," *Na-tional Civic Review* 64 (February 1975): 77–81.

ties.[45] This pattern of intergovernmental cooperation is congruent with the attitudes of local public officials, but the extent to which it reflects the views of the residents generally has not been empirically tested.[46]

The initiative for interlocal action comes mainly from four sources: civic groups, business interests including developers and realtors, federal and state agencies, and local officials and administrators—most often the last. The move may be prompted by dissatisfaction with a particular service; the fiscal or jurisdictional inability of a unit to provide unilaterally a needed function or to build a necessary facility; the intent of local authorities to head off pressures for governmental reorganization (a series of gradual changes in the Sacramento area, for example, acted as a safety valve and reduced the appeal of major reform);[47] or by the desire of elected officials and professional administrators to achieve more efficient operation of specific activities.

County departments that provide urban-type services to large unincorporated areas may actively promote the cooperative approach, fearing a loss of service clientele unless they work out agreements with newly incorporated municipalities. Occasionally a local official will see political or career opportunities in championing cooperation. A Detroit city councilman was the moving force behind the creation of the Supervisors Inter-County Committee, the nation's first COG; the city manager of Salem, Oregon, was instrumental in establishing the widely publicized Mid-Willamette Valley Council of Governments; and the mayor of Los Angeles has served as president of the Southern California Association of Governments.

Unlike reorganization movements, which generate conflict among the affected groups and interests, interlocal cooperation is normally the result of careful negotiation and a meeting of the minds on the part of all concerned. This process can best be conceptualized in terms of a bargaining model in which each of the parties seeks to advance its interests at the least cost to itself. The

[45]Vincent L. Marando, "Inter-Local Cooperation in a Metropolitan Area," *Urban Affairs Quarterly* 4 (December 1968): 185–200.

[46]A survey in the Oklahoma City SMSA showed that local officials there were less negative toward the areawide performance of systems maintenance functions (such as sewage disposal, water supply, and transportation) than of services with life-style import. See Samuel A. Kirkpatrick and David R. Morgan, "Policy Support and Orientations Toward Metropolitan Political Integration Among Urban Officials," *Social Science Quarterly* 52 (December 1971): 656–671.

[47]For a study of Sacramento's sixth unsuccessful effort at governmental reorganization see Glen W. Sparrow, *Sacramento's Attempt at City-County Consolidation* (Davis: University of California, Institute of Governmental Affairs, 1977).

politics involved are largely of a consensual nature and the strategies employed are similar to those utilized in economic transactions. Also unlike major metropolitan reform efforts, cooperative arrangements relate predominantly to only one field of concern and involve no relinquishment of power. This focus on a single substantive area limits the actors who take part in the endeavor. Aside from the "good government" groups that traditionally support all efficiency and economy movements, a cooperative effort will activate only those elites and others who happen to be interested or have a stake in the specific subject of negotiation. Thus if the proposal is for the establishment of a common data-processing center, the only concerned parties will likely be the department heads and officials of the individual governmental units; or if the plan relates to the joint operation of a hospital facility, the major participants, other than local officials, will be the medical society and interested physicians. By narrowing the field of actors in this way, trade-offs of benefits and costs are more easily negotiated and settlement reached.[48]

In proportion to the countless opportunities for meaningful joint undertakings among local governments, the number in effect is remarkably small. This situation is partially attributable to political factors. Suburban units are reluctant to enter into contracts with the central city, even when it is to their advantage to do so, for fear of establishing a dependency relationship that might jeopardize their autonomous status. Central cities, in turn, are often unwilling to extend services, such as water, to the outlying communities so as not to strengthen the latter's ability to compete for industry. Even among themselves, suburban governments are more inclined to develop their own bureaucratic establishments for reasons of power and prestige than they are to become committed to joint control devices. Local department heads and employees, particularly in units where the degree of professionalization is not high, tend to perceive such arrangements as threats to their position and status, and hence they provide little initiative or support for extensive cooperation.

THE REFORM PERSPECTIVE

Ratification of the comprehensive urban county charter by the voters of the Miami, Florida, area in May 1957 was widely heralded as a major breakthrough for the cause of metropolitan reform. The victory bolstered the hopes of reorganization proponents through-

---

[48]In recent years the spectrum of participants has tended to expand with the proliferation of public interest groups and the rise of public employee unions.

out the United States, leading many to believe that American urban areas were standing on the threshold of significant governmental change. These hopes, however, proved to be short-lived. Out of the numerous reform efforts that developed after the Miami success, only three of major significance—Nashville, Jacksonville, and Indianapolis—bore fruit. Considerable interest in city–county consolidation was manifested during the first half of the 1970s, particularly in the South where metropolitan areas are generally less fragmented than in other regions.[49] Since then, however, the movement has waned and now evidences little activity.

Redesigning the metropolitan political structure almost always involves incompatible values and needs. The objectives commonly advanced for altering the system include operational efficiency and economy, effectiveness, equity, responsiveness, representativeness, and citizen access to the policymakers and administrators. Those who argue for change usually contend that their proposals will advance all of these goals. Efficient government, they say, is more responsive to popular will, and representativeness results in a more equitable distribution of costs and benefits and permits greater access. The relationships, however, are not that clear. Suggested reforms may, and frequently do, promote one value at the expense of another. The same dilemma exists with respect to needs. The kind and size of organization that may be best for areawide administration may be dysfunctional for the management of conflict or the protection of valid neighborhood concerns.

The competing interests and values characteristic of SMSAs have prompted some social scientists to view metropolitan reform in terms of game theory. The ideal approach in this conceptualization is to design a reorganization plan that involves a nonzero-sum game (one in which the gains for one contestant do not mean a loss for the others). Such a situation, according to two observers, existed in the Jacksonville consolidation. As they described it:

> A non-zero sum game was perceived in Duval County. The central city voters gained the expanded tax base and the modernized government needed for an expansion of desired services. The white suburbs gained an assurance of political control over the city in which they must work and play. The Negroes gained a degree of political influence and representation. No major group perceived an important loss for itself.[50]

[49]The less complex governmental pattern in the South is discussed in Robert H. Connery and Richard H. Leach, "Southern Metropolis: Challenge to Government," *Journal of Politics* 26 (February 1964): 60–81. Also, see John DeGrove and others, "Southern Regionalism."

[50]Glendening and White, "Local Government Reorganization Referenda in Florida: An Acceptance and a Rejection," p. 4.

The circumstances in few of the large SMSAs present the opportunity to engage in such a game. When one party, the suburbs, holds most of the strategic cards, there is little incentive for it to engage in trade-offs.

The assumption that the growing political strength of blacks in the central city will bring the suburbs to the metropolitan bargaining table to support consolidation (in order to prevent a black political takeover of the core municipality) is open to serious question.[51] What appears more likely is that fringe area dwellers will retreat farther behind their protective walls as the minority population increases. Representatives from both the outlying communities and the black neighborhoods of the central city opposed amalgamation of Atlanta and Fulton County when the measure was before the Georgia legislature in 1969. Similarly, interviews with suburban whites following the Augusta-Richmond merger attempt in 1971 indicated that the threat of a black-controlled central city (blacks constituted a slight numerical majority in Augusta) played an insignificant role in generating support for the proposal.[52] But regardless of whether race is an influential factor in determining attitudes toward metropolitan reorganization, an increasing number of SMSAs will be faced with the problem of working out satisfactory political arrangements between central cities with black (or Hispanic) majorities and the predominantly white-Anglo suburbs.

Many urban analysts believe that the future of metropolitan reform rests with the national and state governments and their willingness to promote action either through persuasion and incentives or penalties and mandatory requirements. Neither level, however, has shown much inclination to interfere with local political systems; in fact, both have tended to play negative roles. Grant programs—federal revenue sharing is an illustration—have often worked to shore up the weak financial condition of small units that otherwise would be more amenable to structural changes. The states also stacked the deck against reorganization by the dual majority referendum, easy incorporation provisions, and difficult annexation and consolidation laws. In recent years a number have made the rules of the game somewhat more reasonable by tightening the requirements for incorporation and creating municipal boundary commissions. Several have also taken more direct steps. Minnesota established the Twin Cities Metropolitan Council; the

---

[51]There were racial overtones in several of the consolidation movements, including Indianapolis and Jacksonville, but other factors were far more influential in determining the outcomes.

[52]Richard L. Engstrom and W. E. Lyons, "Black Control or Consolidation: The Fringe Response," *Social Science Quarterly* 53 (June 1972): 161–167.

Alabama assembly failed by only a single vote to merge a part of Jefferson County with the city of Birmingham; and the Nevada legislature in 1976 consolidated the governments of Las Vegas and Clark County (later voided by the Nevada supreme court). Actions of this nature remain the exception, with most states continuing to do relatively little to improve the structural pattern of their metropolitan areas.

Montana is one of the few states that has taken direct measures to promote local government reform. A constitutional amendment adopted in 1972 mandates all counties and municipalities to weigh the merits of alternative structures at least every ten years. To implement this requirement the legislature has ordered the creation of local government study commissions in each unit to draft proposals for submission to the voters. The recommendations that have emerged from these bodies vary from comprehensive reorganization to minor adjustments in the existing system. In the first round of proposals presented to the electorate, city–county merger plans were approved in two small nonmetropolitan areas and defeated in a third that is approaching SMSA status. An analysis of the early experience with the review process shows that the cast of major actors and the campaign activities closely resemble those commonly found in reorganization attempts elsewhere in the United States.[53] The Montana approach is unique and has the merit of compelling local residents to examine their governmental system periodically and consider available options. Beyond that it faces all the impediments to change that have been associated with metropolitan reform movements in the United States.

Metropolitan reorganization activity has waxed and waned over the years. Currently it is in a state of relative dormancy, with little interest being manifested in the issue. Concern over inflation, energy, and the economy occupy the attention of the traditional sources of reformist initiative, and federal aid programs help prevent crises at the local level. The basic problem of structure nevertheless remains. Other priorities may obscure its presence, but they will not cause it to vanish.

[53]See Lauren S. McKinsey and James L. Lopach, "Montana Local Government Review: In the Home Stretch," *National Civic Review* 65 (September 1976): 384–389.

Chapter 14
The Future

The future has always been a subject of fascination. Throughout history men and women have turned to astrologers, seers, and prophets to divine what is in store for them in the years ahead. In more recent times projections of the future have taken on professional and practical aspects as businesses and governments seek to anticipate the state of things to come in formulating their long-range plans. Today the study of futures has become, as one analyst describes it, "a nascent profession." Courses on alternative futures are taught in the universities, and research units in the private sector are busily engaged in speculative forecasting of technological changes and their social impact. Scientists are developing scenarios of various facets of the world, such as food supply and the availability of energy, as they will be found in the year 2000 and beyond. Public administrators have evidenced a growing interest in this field as reflected in the recent appointment of a Committee on Future Horizons by the International City Management Association to examine predictions of probable futures as they relate to local government.[1]

One of the critical questions occupying the attention of those engaged in the study of futures is that of growth. Some experts such as Herman Kahn (head of Hudson Institute, a futurist research center) hold that technological advances will assure sufficient resources to sustain rapid economic expansion for at least another 200 years.[2] This technological optimism is sharply attacked by other researchers, such as economist E. F. Schumacher (*Small Is Beautiful*), and challenged by results of computer modeling done by Donella and Dennis Meadows at the Massachusetts Institute of Technology. Another dispute is over the extent to which citizens can help shape the future of society. Some writers believe that the

[1]The popularity of studies concerning futures is reflected in the appearance of such journals as *The Futurist* and *Futures,* and in the formation of the World Future Society in 1966.
[2]Herman Kahn, *World Economic Development: 1979 and Beyond* (Boulder, Colo.: Westview Press, 1979).

future is largely predetermined and the overall pattern of our lives fixed. Others contend that people can have control over their destiny (the future is what we make it) and can design a better world. It is this more optimistic view that has dominated American social and political thought since colonial times.

Explorations of the future are no longer equated with fortune-telling or Cassandra's gift of prophecy, yet modern methods of social forecasting have enjoyed only limited success. Social analysts did not foresee the domestic violence of the 1960s, and few anticipated the national issues—energy, environment, and the economy—that were to dominate the 1970s. Even the shortrun projections of economists have frequently missed the mark.[3] Predicting the future is at best an uncertain enterprise. Unexpected dislocations (wars, depressions, natural disasters), the human factor (people do not always behave in predictable fashion), and the unanticipated consequences of public policies and programs (the damaging effect of the interstate highway system on central cities), all contribute to the difficulty of social forecasting. As David Beam, an ACIR analyst, has said, the future is neither fixed nor singular; a variety of outcomes is always possible.[4]

METROPOLITAN SCENARIOS

This concluding chapter attempts to draw together the major forces and factors that are discussed at various points in the book and to speculate as to how the future of urban areas may be affected by them. The three brief scenarios presented here are representative of three alternate paths that metropolitan communities could conceivably take during the remainder of this century. The first is based primarily on current trends and continuities (links with the past); the second on a combination of continuities and discontinuities (breaks with the past); and the third largely on discontinuities.

The Continuity Scenario

This scenario depicts no radical change during the rest of the 1900s in the physical shape, social ecology, or government structure of American metropolises or in the major problems they face. Present

[3]Failures of social science forecasting are discussed by Seymour M. Lipset, "Predicting the Future of Post-Industrial Society: Can We Do It?," in Seymour M. Lipset (ed.), *The Third Century: Post-Industrial Society* (Chicago: University of Chicago Press, 1979), pp. 1–35.
[4]"Forecasting the Future of Federalism," *Intergovernmental Perspective* 6 (Summer 1980): 6–9.

development trends will continue, long-standing social issues will remain basically unresolved, and further deterioration will occur in the central cities and older suburbs. Fiscal difficulties will become more severe, with many municipalities cutting services, some defaulting on their bonds, and a number being taken into receivership by the state. Downtowns will decline in importance, some of them being reduced to entertainment and convention centers and others limited to officebuilding activities.

Physically, the metropolis of the year 2000 will look little different from today, only somewhat shabbier. New residential, commercial, and industrial development will continue to take place in the outlying areas. Some cosmetic face-lifting will be undertaken in sections of the central city but will not be of sufficient scope and magnitude to halt the spread of blight. The physical infrastructure of the older cities—sewers, water systems, streets, public buildings—will increasingly experience breakdowns and face the need for replacement because of their age and long-deferred maintenance. The automobile will remain the predominant mode of transportation, with public transit continuing to play only a relatively minor role. Restrictions of modest scope will be placed on outward growth or sprawl to curtail the conversion of prime agricultural land to urban uses (now taking place at the rate of 1 million acres annually).

The movement of the middle class to suburbia will continue but many of those departing will be black. Spillover of low-income minority families into the older suburbs on the immediate fringe of the expanding ghettos will also intensify as the housing stock of the core city further deteriorates. Crime will remain a serious problem although some diminution will take place because of the smaller proportion of teenagers (the highest offender group) in the population. Only slight improvement in race relations will be achieved, efforts to integrate the schools through court action will be abandoned, and housing for low-income families with children will remain in short supply. Unrest among the poor will grow as inflation and spiraling energy costs cut heavily into their meager resources while the amounts expended by government for social programs and income transfers are curtailed.

Governmentally, no significant change will occur in the existing metropolitan pattern, with the incremental approaches being employed almost exclusively. Public decision making in matters of areawide concern will remain highly decentralized. Federal and state intervention in metropolitan affairs will increase but will not displace the fragmented process of policy formulation or substitute for local action. Coordination among national, state, and local agencies in urban programmatic efforts will become even less effective than at present as municipal and other units scramble to survive in a period of austerity and declining revenues. By the year 2000 the situation will have reached such a chaotic state that metropolitan America will be ready for a drastic overhaul of its governmental machinery.

The Middle-Course Scenario

The second scenario accepts certain trends as irreversible and sees others as undergoing major change. The continuing trends include the leveling off of population in the larger SMSAs, a slowdown in economic growth, smaller family size, lower birthrates, an increasing proportion of women in the work force, the shift from a manufacturing to a service economy, and the decline of CBDs as retailing centers. Those that will break sharply with past developments and practices relate to land use, intra-area settlement patterns, local transportation, and governmental structure.

Major steps will be taken by government to curb sprawl and rejuvenate central city neighborhoods. Land development outside the urbanized perimeter will be strongly discouraged by stringent environmental regulations, agricultural zoning, and more extensive requirements that developers provide the social infrastructure—schools, roads, sewers, water supply, transportation facilities—necessary to serve the subdivisions they build. On the positive side, incentives will be given to stimulate redevelopment in the central city. Businesses and industries that relocate there will receive priority in public contracts, be given certain tax privileges, assured of site improvements needed for their operation, and provided with ready access to the interstate highway system.

Similar incentives and encouragement will be given developers and individual citizens to join with government agencies in reconstructing selected inner-city neighborhoods and converting them into "urban villages." These largely self-contained subcommunities will have a variety of housing (new and rehabilitated), shops and other commercial enterprises, and small businesses that will offer employment opportunities for village residents. Each subcommunity will provide its fair share of housing for the area's low- and moderate-income families. Funding will come from such sources as the federal windfall profits tax on oil companies and large corporate investments induced by tax advantages and government guarantees. These efforts, along with energy shortages and

rising transportation costs, will reverse the city-to-suburbs movement that has dominated metropolitan migration patterns for almost
a half century.

The automobile—limited to small cars that meet strict pollution standards and high mileage capability—will retain its hold as
the primary mode of local transportation but its use will decline
substantially. Gasoline rationing, mandatory car-pooling, and the
availability of a vastly improved mass transit system (funded partially by gasoline taxes and the shift of money from road and highway
construction) will contribute to this reduction. Battery-driven cars
and buses will make their appearance in increasing numbers and
by the end of the century will be well on their way toward displac-
ing gasoline-fueled vehicles.

The political structure of the larger SMSAs will be reorganized
into a three-tier system. The upper level will be a general-purpose
government with a broad range of areawide functions and powers,
including a veto over municipal planning and zoning, the coordination of urban revitalization activities, and the administration of
housing assistance programs for poor families. (In single-county
SMSAs, a reconstituted county government will serve as the
areawide authority; in other instances the existing county governments will be abolished.) The middle layer will consist of the
former municipalities and unincorporated areas consolidated into
units of approximately 150,000 population. The third tier will comprise elected neighborhood councils with limited authority over locality matters.

The public school system will remain independent but will be
reorganized along the lines of the Toronto plan. An elected metropolitan school board will exercise general supervision and control
over district school boards. This action will permit school desegregation to be accomplished on an areawide basis. To assure fiscal
equality among the districts, the state will take over the responsibility for funding public education in its entirety. For similar reasons the national government will assume full financial responsibility for all public welfare programs.

The Discontinuity Scenario

The metropolis described by this scenario represents a radical departure from the existing system. The physical face of the city will
undergo major surgery, and individual SMSAs will become integral
parts of a network of urban settlements. As such they will be
obliged to conform to national plans that are designed to conserve

resources, coordinate social and economic development, capitalize on the country's strengths, and shore up its weaknesses. The centralization of industrial planning and the imposition of controls over metropolitan area activity will be precipitated by continuing international threats, both economic and military, to the vital interests of the American people.

The SMSA of the year 2000 will incorporate the latest technological advances available. Although the process will still be in its initial stages at that time, metropolitan functioning and development will be dominated by the philosophy and methods of space-age technology. Solar energy will be tapped, solid waste recycled, housing construction revolutionized, and new means of sewage disposal inaugurated that will eliminate the need for sewerage mains and treatment plants. Geodesic domes for climate control, moving sidewalks in congested areas, and voting from home or office by telecommunication are other innovations that will be seen. Robberies will decline as the use of cash is almost totally eliminated, with all transactions—from riding a bus and eating in a fast food restaurant to attending a theater and purchasing goods—electronically recorded.

The central business district, limited primarily to office complexes, civic buildings, and specialized service facilities (medical, banking, legal), will become the managerial and governmental headquarters of the metropolis. It will be linked by telecommunications to a series of secondary employment concentrations located at strategic sites throughout the SMSA. Housing appropriate to the needs and income levels of the workers will be developed around each of these industrial subcenters to reduce commuting time and energy costs. That portion of the central city adjacent to the CBD and extending out for several miles will be devoted entirely to high rise condominiums and rental apartments and the supporting services. Automobile travel will be banned within the urbanized area and permitted only for interregional transportation. Residents will be served by a modernized transit system combining rail, battery-driven buses and jitneys, people movers, and special vehicles for the handicapped.

Life-styles will undergo material changes. There will be less traveling to distant recreational areas, nighttime sports events will be barred, and the marriage with the automobile dissolved. The single-household detached dwelling will become a relic of the past, and the traditional family will be replaced by alternate forms of relationships. Scarcity of natural resources will grow more acute and standards of living will decline slightly. People will be compelled, as Robert Theobold has observed, to move away from their preoccupation with the creation of "more" to an understanding of the idea of "enough."[5]

Politically, SMSAs will in effect become administrative arms of the national and state governments. Authority will be centralized in an elected metropolitan council and chief executive who will govern the area within the policy framework and guidelines established at the two higher levels of the political system. The municipalities, school districts, counties, and other local entities now in existence will be abolished. Urban services, including public education, will be provided through administrative district units established by the metropolitan government and accountable to it. All general plans for urban development and revitalization will be subject to federal and state approval. Such plans will be carried out by teams of professionals organized by the areawide agency and containing, in addition to its own personnel, members from the private sector and from federal and state agencies. The structure will not be designed to promote citizen participation but to assure the furtherance of national goals by local areas, efficient resource utilization, and unified direction and control over the development of urban concentrations.

STATUS QUO OR CHANGE?

There is no single future for the nation's metropolises, as one analyst puts it, just as there is no single present.[6] Certain features and problems are common to all SMSAs, but each also has its distinctive characteristics and potentialities. Some will undoubtedly show considerable vitality in the immediate decades ahead, whereas others will struggle to maintain the quality of urban life at a reasonable level for their residents. The future for most is likely to fall somewhere between the continuity and middle-course scenarios, with metropolitan America of the year 2000 looking more like than different from the metropolitan America of today. The huge economic investments and personal stakes in the existing structures and facilities of urban communities and their institutions—both

[5]Robert Theobold, "Managing the Quality of Life," in Kenneth E. Wilson (ed.), *Prospects for Growth: Changing Expectations for the Future* (New York: Praeger, 1978), p. 79. The President's Commission for a National Agenda for the Eighties reported in a similar vein that "Personal fulfillment will need to come increasingly from family and community activity and relatively less from personal consumption and professional advancement."

[6]Joseph F. Coates, "The Physical Nature of the American City in the Year 2000," *Municipal Year Book, 1979*, p. 15.

public and private—serve as deterrents to the radical reconstruction of their social, political, and physical systems.

All social change of any importance, moreover, involves a reallocation of values and resources. No matter what the proposed reformation may be or how it is to be applied, some individuals and groups will be affected differently from others. Some will gain while others lose in terms of power, wealth, or prestige. A program that redistributes income to poor people, for example, takes something away from other segments of the society. Large numbers of Americans, as events show, are hostile toward major social reform precisely because of fear that its consequences would be deleterious to them. The majority, including many in the lower middle-class, perceive the various movements and proposals to alter the existing system as threatening to their interests, if not disruptive of the established order. These underlying attitudes weaken the pressures for institutional reform and impede efforts at ameliorating social problems. At the same time technological change goes on virtually unchecked, thus widening the lag between scientific advances and the capability of the social system to respond and adapt to them.

Metropolitan areas develop and take their particular form as the result of myriad decisions by both public and private agencies. These decisions are controlled by various factors, including market forces, professional standards, and community attitudes and values.[7] Governmental and private policies at the municipal or metropolitan level can influence the shape of such development, but only in a limited fashion. A resolution by local leaders to encourage industrial growth, for example, can have real meaning only if national economic factors are favorable to such expansion. Or a decision to undertake a major program of public works to enhance the quality of life in the area can be realistic only if financial assistance is forthcoming from higher echelons of public authority and the major industrial and business establishments (many of which are controlled by national corporations) are supportive of such a program.

When communities act, moreover, they must do so within an environmental framework shaped by the cumulative past policies and actions of public agencies and private establishments. Earlier investment decisions relative to buildings, transportation arteries, and public utilities often leave them little choice but to promote additional outlays to protect what already exists. Similarly, past pol-

---

[7] William L. C. Wheaton, "Public and Private Agencies of Change in Urban Expansion," in Melvin M. Webber and others (eds.), *Explorations in Urban Structures* (Philadelphia: University of Pennsylvania Press, 1964), pp. 154–196.

icies of their planning commissions and legislative bodies establish land use patterns that circumscribe the extent to which changes in the physical design of the area can be accomplished. These investments and patterns cannot be ignored in assessing the future not only because of the monetary considerations they represent but also because of the community values they reflect.

CENTRAL CITY: REVIVAL OR DECAY?

A principal subject of debate over the urban future is the fate of the core city. One group of social scientists and planners maintains that the rising price of energy will increase the relative cost of suburban living to the point where central localities will become attractive alternatives for both residential and industrial use. Those who take this position point to the "back-to-the-city" movement that has received considerable publicity from the national press in recent years.[8] Another group, however, believes it most unlikely that either families or business will return to the major municipality in any significant numbers. Acknowledging a modest resurgence of middle-class residents in some central cities, they see no ground swell in this direction developing. In their view the net loss of householders and economic activities to suburbia and nonmetropolitan areas will continue despite energy shortages, increasing transportation costs, and inflation.[9]

For several decades the national government has demonstrated an ambivalence toward the central city–suburban question. On the one hand, it has adopted policies that have encouraged and made possible the outward flow of residents (FHA mortgage guarantees, grants for sewer and water facilities in fringe areas, construction of urban freeways). On the other, it has initiated projects aimed at curtailing flight and repopulating the inner city (urban renewal, model cities, neighborhood redevelopment). This ambivalence was well illustrated during the 1960s when a new towns program was inaugurated simultaneously with the adoption of measures to revitalize central cities. President Johnson expressed strong support for the program, lauding new towns as the communities of the future, "an

---

[8]See, for instance, Wolf Von Eckardt, "New Mood Downtown," *Society* 16 (September/October 1979): 4–7.

[9]Representative of the view of those who see no significant revival of the central city is Leon N. Moses and Alex Anas, "The Great Metropolis: Its Past and Future," Paper presented to Symposium on Challenges and Opportunities in the Mature Metropolis, St. Louis, Mo., June 6–8, 1977. Also see Ira S. Lowry, "The Dismal Future of Central Cities," in Arthur P. Solomon (ed.), *The Prospective City* (Cambridge, Mass.: MIT–Harvard Joint Center for Urban Studies, 1980), pp. 161–203.

urban blueprint for the ills of the inner-city." Starting from scratch on vacant lands, he said, such settlements "would meet the housing needs of millions of Americans, rich and poor, black and white."

The new towns program provided mortgage guarantees together with loans for sewer, water and other facilities to developers who would construct urban communities on the periphery of large SMSAs. Thirteen such undertakings were sponsored by HUD, including Jonathan in the Minneapolis-St. Paul area, Newfields near Dayton, Ohio, Flower Mound outside Dallas, and Park Forest South in the Chicago SMSA. The program proved a colossal failure, with nine of the projects terminating in bankruptcy. Rising inflation, the recession of 1974, and most of all the enormous front-end or start-up outlays required to construct the physical infrastructure of a completely new city (before any financial return can be realized) proved too much for the developers even with federal assistance.[10]

Although central city revitalization has shown somewhat greater promise than the new towns approach, the verdict is not yet in on its potentiality. It is still an unanswered question whether gentrification, urban homesteading, and other forms of neighborhood rehabilitation are harbingers of an extensive movement to resettle the core cities. Factors favorable to such a movement include:

1. Rapidly rising costs of private transportation.
2. Escalating prices of suburban housing (in most cases the cost of new construction in suburbia far exceeds that of rehabilitated units in the central municipality).
3. Growing number of households without children under 18 years of age, a category that increased by almost 3 million from 1970 to 1976 (childless couples and singles are less concerned about the quality of public schools, a major weakness of most large cities).
4. Heightened demand in the housing market from members of the baby boom generation (over 40 million individuals will reach the age of 30 during the 1980s, many of whom will be more receptive to central city living than their parents).
5. Increase in the number of elderly both in absolute numbers and as a percentage of the national population (the conveniences and amenities of the central city are attractive to them and they are not directly affected by the scarcity of

[10]See Hugh Evans and Lloyd Rodwin, "The New Towns Program and Why It Failed," *The Public Interest*, No. 56 (Summer 1979): 90–107.

employment opportunities and the condition of the school system).

6. Occupational shifts to professional, technical, and managerial positions (individuals holding these types of jobs tend to be more attracted to city living than those in other occupational groups).

7. Modification of social and demographic trends that have been contributing factors to central city decline (for example, the period of large-scale immigration of low-income blacks from the South and poor whites from Appalachia and other rural areas has come to an end).

8. Increase in number and influence of locality organizations dedicated to the preservation of core municipality neighborhoods.

9. Current emphasis on inner-city neighborhoods in federal redevelopment programs.

Among the factors that run counter to a more favorable prognosis of future core city resettlement are:

1. Low quality of much of the housing stock in the older central municipalities.

2. Poor condition of the physical infrastructure of many cities.

3. Unattractiveness of core municipalities for families with young children because of the quality and racial composition of the schools and the lack of adequate and safe play space for youngsters.

4. High crime rates and the fear for personal safety.

5. Large increase in multifamily construction in suburbia that serves to accommodate singles, young couples, and "empty-nesters" (middle-aged couples whose children have left home) who might otherwise move to the city.

6. Continuing anticity bias of many Americans and their strong preference for suburban life-styles.

On balance, the odds favor the occurrence of at least modest resettlement in many of the large central cities before the end of the century.[11] The degree will not be of such magnitude as to reverse the socioeconomic pattern—lower income groups and racial minorities will still predominate in numbers—but the composition will be less disproportionate. With the conviction growing that the nation must make the fullest use of its existing resources, efforts to

[11]Predictions as to the future of central cities are discussed in Lowell W. Culver, "America's Troubled Cities: Better Times Ahead?," *Futurist* 13 (August 1979): 275–286.

"recycle" the cities will gain increasing support. As former HUD secretary Carla Hills told a group of mayors, "just as we must stop wasting our air, water, and energy resources, we must also stop wasting our cities." And as economist Gary Gappert wrote about the future of public administration, the managers of self-renewal of the 1980s will replace the managers of growth of the 1950s and 1960s and the managers of decline of the 1970s.[12]

THE METROPOLITAN SYSTEM

The Advisory Commission on Intergovernmental Relations has described the metropolis in these terms:

> In a physical sense, vast *metropolitan economies* have emerged in recent years, but most of these are not *metropolitan polities* in the sense of communities with common social and economic institutions, a common governmental system, a citizenry having a sense of community that embraces the area as a whole; instead these metropolitan entities are fragmented jurisdictionally, fiscally, socially, and economically, and most of their citizens are moving at a very slow pace toward recognizing the problems and opportunities they share with fellow citizens in the area.[13]

The commission depicts the challenges raised by this system as of such magnitude that "no one of the traditional levels of government has the talent, the time, the funds, and the power" to cope successfully with them. Nothing less than the coordinated efforts of all levels of public authority, the active involvement of citizen groups, and the participation of the private sector will be sufficient.

Predictions as to how this system will fare and what changes it will undergo between now and the year 2000 must take into account two recent developments (in addition to the socioeconomic and environmental factors already noted). First, the era of spiraling public expenditures has come to an end, and along with it the rapid growth of state and local government characteristic of the last half-century. (The economy of many of the older central cities will be affected most by this change because the public sector has been the source of virtually all their new jobs in recent years.)[14] Second, the national government is becoming increasingly preoccupied with

[12]Gary Gappert, "The Political Future of the City in the Year 2000," *Municipal Year Book, 1979*, p. 15.
[13]*Improving Urban America: A Challenge to Federalism* (Washington, D.C., September 1976), p. 223.
[14]George Patterson, "Finance," in William Gorham and Nathan Glazer (eds.), *The Urban Predicament* (Washington, D.C.: Urban Institute, 1976), p. 112.

the tense international scene and with a domestic economy that appears immune to conventional analysis and remedies. As a result, metropolitan areas and their problems are likely to receive less attention from the nation's policymakers. Even though this development will compel the localities and states to rely more on their own initiatives and resources, federal action and assistance will remain the key to urban well-being.

Looking to the immediate future, the presence of a conservative administration at the national level augurs changes in urban-related policies and programs, although not to the extent that some observers predict (or some extremists on the right demand). Talk of slashing urban aid, scuttling the Environmental Protection Agency, deregulating business "from top to bottom," and abolishing product and occupational safety standards runs counter to social imperatives and political realities. The nation will witness an easing of environmental restrictions and business regulations, greater deference to the private sector, less emphasis on civil rights and affirmative action, and a curtailment of further growth in federal assistance to the cities and the poor. However, drastic changes in governmental policy are to be anticipated in few areas of social or urban concern.

The Reagan Administration's approach to urban assistance will emphasize the consolidation of grant programs and the decentralization of control over them to the states and localities. General revenue sharing and the community development block grant (CDBG), both adopted under prior Republican presidents, should fare relatively well under the new administration. The urban development action grant (UDAG), although a product of the Carter years, should also receive support because of its stress on leveraging private investment. A number of other aid programs face a more uncertain fate. Some, such as comprehensive employment training (CETA), may be abolished; others, such as mass transit subsidies, are prime targets for cutbacks; and still others, such as the various housing assistance measures, may be merged into block grants. As to aid for the badly distressed communities, administration officials favor the concept of providing tax incentives and other concessions to induce the location of job-creating businesses in inner areas of these cities. (The 1980 Republican platform endorsed the establishment of special or "urban-enterprise" zones in declining municipalities for this purpose.) Even if viable—which many urban specialists doubt—such an approach is not likely to be utilized on any significant scale given the weakened political power of the older urban centers.

THE GOOD CITY

The good city, in philosopher Lawrence Haworth's description, is the place where one finds the kinds of institutional opportunities that permit people to develop their potentialities to the fullest degree.[15] The city, in these terms, is unjust to the extent that it systematically denies to some of its members an equal chance of enjoying the means essential to personal growth and self-realization. Most of the legally discriminatory bars to such opportunities have been removed in the United States but the incapacitating conditions that effectively disqualify certain individuals and groups from participating fully in the society remain. Efforts to remove these obstacles and to secure greater equity in the allocation of the nation's resources and rewards will continue but the struggle will take place in a setting marked by scarcity and slow economic growth rather than by abundance and a rapidly rising standard of living. This radical shift from the country's historical pattern of development carries with it the potential for future instability and social conflict because the impact of a nonexpanding resource base will fall disproportionately on the poor, minorities, and other disadvantaged groups.

To some analysts interpreting present trends and events, the urban future holds few promising prospects. They see a long period ahead in which local communities (and society as a whole) will be dominated by a mood of restraint and control and by opposition to new social programs. They fear that popular attitudes and the reduced growth of real resources will seriously diminish the capacity of local government (and other levels as well) to promote such traditional civic values as equity and responsiveness to human needs. To the more pessimistic the plight of New York City is a harbinger of things to come. As the head of the Municipal Assistance Corporation (set up by New York State to oversee the finances of the nation's largest municipality after its near bankruptcy in 1975) recently said, "If you ask me what can be done and still keep the city a place where people will want to work and live in, I don't know. I don't know if it's do-able."[16] Few communities face such a serious threat but all, regardless of size or geographical location, will be

---

[15]"Deprivation and the Good City," in Warner Bloomberg and Henry J. Schmandt (eds.), *Power, Poverty, and Urban Policy* (Beverly Hills, Calif.: Sage, 1968), pp. 27–47.

[16]Richard Nathan, one of the nation's leading urban analysts, expressed a similar pessimistic view in a recent (November 1980) interview, saying that many of the older cities are clearly in trouble and the country is little inclined to do anything to help them.

subjected to varying degrees of stress as they seek to cope with the challenges of the late 1900s.

Hard choices on energy, inflation, economic growth, and environmental protection will increasingly confront the United States (and other industrial nations) in the years ahead.[17] As the Council on Environmental Quality warned in a 1980 report to the President, within the next 20 years—given the continuance of present trends—the earth will be badly overpopulated, polluted, and depleted of key natural resources. These are realities that Americans generally have been reluctant to face up to, many remaining convinced that everything can be resolved without any great sacrifices on their part or any basic changes in their mode of living. A large number, for example, believe that taxes can be cut sharply with little effect on services simply by eliminating governmental waste and corruption; that energy needs can be met at greatly reduced costs by putting an end to the manipulations of greedy oil companies and conniving politicians; and that unlimited growth can be achieved without seriously damaging the environment.

Philosophically, the basic goal of urban communities is to provide a milieu or setting that is conducive to personal growth and development. This objective is usually lost sight of in the welter of activities and experiences that mark the daily life of metropolitan dwellers. So immersed are we in our personal pursuits and difficulties that the potentialities and promises of the cities escape attention. The problems of urban America are not to be discounted, but neither are its strengths and hopes. Although the good city is far from reality, most observers would say well beyond achievement, raising the quality of urban life (while paying due regard to economic and environmental limitations) is within the capabilities of a determined people. Robert Kennedy once said (quoting George Bernard Shaw), "Some individuals see what is and ask why. I dream of things that never were and ask why not!" Those who are concerned with cities—whether as students, researchers, public officials, or residents—would also do well to ask "why not!"

[17]See in this connection Daniel Yankelovich and Bernard Lefkowitz, "National Growth: The Question of the 80s,"*Public Opinion* 3 (December/January 1980): 44–57.

A Bibliographical Overview

This bibliography is intended to supplement and not duplicate the extensive footnotes to the text. To keep the list within manageable proportions (the urban-related literature is voluminous), we have generally included only books published since 1960 and have, with several exceptions, excluded periodical articles. The material is organized under categories that relate to the topics covered in the text.

BASIC SOURCES

Publications of the U.S. Bureau of the Census provide the most important primary data sources for urban research. Those particularly relevant are the decennial *Census of Population and Housing* (Congress recently authorized mid-decennial population censuses, but budgetary considerations make the first of such scheduled counts in 1985 unlikely), the *Census of Governments*, and the various industrial and commercial censuses (manufacturers, retail trade, wholesale trade, selected services) which appear at five-year intervals. *The County and City Data Book*, also published every five years, is a useful compilation of information assembled from the various censuses. The bureau also issues numerous intercensal reports and special studies on the demographic and socioeconomic characteristics of the population in its *Current Population Reports*. A handbook on the census for students is Charles Kaplan and Thomas Van Valey, *Census '80: Continuing the Factfinder Tradition* (Washington, D.C.: U.S. Bureau of the Census, 1980). Federal journals, such as the *Monthly Labor Review*, and annual reports compiled by the various departments, such as HUD's *Statistical Year Book*, are also important sources of data.

Guidance in locating federally published material is given in the Census Bureau's *Directory of Federal Statistics: A Guide to Sources* (1976) and its *Reference Manual on Population and Housing Statistics* by Paul Zeisset (1977). Of similar use is Joseph K. Lu,

*U.S. Government Publications in the Social Sciences: An Anno-
tated Guide* (Beverly Hills, Calif.: Sage, 1975). The American Political Science Association has also published *U.S. Census Data for
Political and Social Research: A Resource Guide* (along with a manual for students) by Phyllis G. Carter (1977). Information about new
federal programs is contained in *Urban Affairs Reporter* (looseleaf
volumes), a service of Commerce Clearing House. Two late works
listing sources for local government data are Peter Hernon et al.
(eds.), *Municipal Government Reference Sources: Publications
and Collections* (New York: Bowker, 1978) and Thomas P. Murphy
(ed.), *Urban Politics: A Guide to Information Sources* (Detroit:
Gale Research, 1978). The *Index to Current Urban Documents*,
published periodically by Greenwood Press of Westport, Connecticut, contains descriptions of official documents and reports issued
by the large cities and counties.

Other sources of urban-related information include *Urban Affairs Abstracts* (issued weekly by the National League of Cities,
Washington, D.C.), which summarize articles selected from over
800 periodicals; *Newsbank: Urban Affairs Library Index*, covering
reports on urban problems appearing in major newspapers throughout the country (the index references are to clippings organized in
an accompanying microfiche file); the news sections of the *National Civic Review;* the *Municipal Year Book*, issued by the International City Management Association; and the *County Year Book*
published by the National Association of Counties. Also helpful are
the official periodicals of the government interest groups, such as
Nation's Cities (National League of Cities); *Public Management*
(International City Management Association); *County News* (National Association of Counties); and *State Government* (Council of
State Governments).

A number of urban bibliographies have appeared in recent
years. One is the *Dictionary Catalogue of the U.S. Department of
Housing and Urban Development*, a 19-volume listing of all books,
studies, and other material in the agency's Washington library. Also
available is HUD USER, a computer-based information service
covering research sponsored by the department. Bibliographies on
numerous topics and fields of urban concern are published on a
continuing basis by Vance Bibliographies of Monticello, Illinois.
Several compilations of references to the governmental aspects of
metropolitan areas have been made. The first to appear was Government Affairs Foundation, *Metropolitan Communities; A Bibliography* (Chicago: Public Administration Service, 1956). Three
supplements to this work have been published, the last prepared

by Barbara Hudson and Ronald McDonald, *Metropolitan Communities: A Bibliography, Supplement: 1968–1970.*

Recent listings limited to governmental restructuring are Anthony G. White, *Reforming Metropolitan Governments: A Bibliography* (New York: Garland, 1975) and Paula Baker, Elinor Ostrom, and Robert Goehlert, *Metropolitan Reform: An Annotated Bibliography* (Bloomington: Indiana University, Workshop in Political Theory and Policy Analysis, 1979). Another compilation prepared by the Indiana group covers community organization and neighborhood government. A bibliography relating to urban policy analysis, now a popular area of research, is T. R. Carr and Stephanie Colston, *State and Urban Policy Analysis: An Annotated Bibliography* (Norman: University of Oklahoma Bureau of Government Research, 1975). A list of council–manager items is contained in David A. Booth, *Council–Manager Government 1940–1964: An Annotated Bibliography* (Chicago: International City Management Association, 1965). Other compilations of a more general nature are Bernard H. Ross, *Urban Affairs Bibliography: An Annotated Guide to the Literature in the Field,* 3d ed. (Washington, D.C.: CPA Publications, 1974) and Charles R. Bryfogle, *City in Print: An Urban Studies Bibliography* (Agincourt, Ontario: GIC, 1974).

The many studies and reports of the national Advisory Commission on Intergovernmental Relations constitute a prolific source of information and analyses relating to all aspects of local and metropolitan government. Professional periodicals concentrating on urban affairs include *Journal of Urban History, Journal of Urban Economics, Regional Science and Urban Economics, Urban Affairs Quarterly, Urbanism: Past and Present, The Urban Interest, The Urban Review* (dealing with public education), and *Urban Studies.* Journals of the academic associations, such as the *American Political Science Review, American Sociological Review,* and *Social Science Quarterly,* frequently contain urban-related articles.

A good source of analytical treatises is the Urban Affairs Annual Reviews issued by Sage Publications since 1967. Each volume contains a series of essays devoted to a particular aspect of the urban world. The 1980 volume, for example, edited by Gary A. Tobin, is entitled *The Changing Structure of the City: What Happened to the Urban Crisis?* An excellent glossary that includes many terms relevant to urban communities is Jack C. Plano and Milton Greenberg, *The American Political Dictionary,* 5th ed. (New York: Holt, Rinehart and Winston, 1979). A useful compilation of data from a wide variety of Census Bureau publications relating to national, state, and local governments is Richard P. Nathan and

Mary M. Nathan (compilers), *America's Governments* (New York: Wiley, 1979).

GENERAL WORKS

Books dealing with the nature and problems of urban communities published in the 1960s but still widely cited include Jane Jacobs, *The Death and Life of Great American Cities* (New York: Random House, 1961); Scott Greer, *The Emerging City: Myth and Reality* (New York: Free Press, 1962); Edward C. Banfield and James Q. Wilson, *City Politics* (New York: Vintage, 1963); and Banfield's *Big City Politics* (New York: Random House, 1966).

More recent analyses are Willis Hawley and Michael Lipsky (eds.), *Theoretical Perspectives on Urban Politics* (Englewood Cliffs, N.J.: Prentice-Hall, 1976); Kenneth J. Arrow et al., *Urban Processes* (Washington, D.C.: Urban Institute, 1970); Melvin R. Levin, *The Urban Prospect* (Belmont, Calif.: Wadsworth, 1977); Peter R. Gluck and Richard J. Meister, *Cities in Transition: Social Change and Institutional Responses in Urban Development* (New York: New Viewpoints, 1979); and Peter Saunders, *Urban Politics: A Sociological Interpretation* (London: Hutchinson, 1979). A recent critique in the style of Mitchell Gordon's *Sick Cities* is Richard Morris, *Bum Rap in America's Cities: The Real Causes of Urban Decay* (Englewood Cliffs, N.J.: Prentice-Hall, 1980). A Marxist perspective of the city is Manuel Castells, *The Urban Question: A Marxist Approach,* rev. ed. (Cambridge: MIT Press, 1979).

Urban policies are treated in Stephen David and Paul Peterson, *Urban Politics and Public Policy: The City in Crisis,* 2d ed. (New York: Praeger, 1976); David A. Caputo, *Urban America: The Policy Alternatives* (San Francisco: Freeman, 1976); and Marian Lief Palley and Howard Palley, *Urban America and Public Policies* (Lexington, Mass.: Heath, 1977). Recent research findings relating to urban policy are presented in Dale R. Marshall (ed.), *Urban Policy-Making* (Beverly Hills, Calif.: Sage, 1979).

The state of knowledge about urban problems is summarized in Amos Hawley and Vincent Rock (eds.), *Metropolitan America in Contemporary Perspective* (New York: Halstead Press, 1975). John S. Adams (ed.), *Contemporary Metropolitan America,* 4 vols. (Cambridge, Mass.: Ballinger, 1976) contains analyses of the 20 largest SMSAs in the United States from a geographical perspective. Other relevant works by geographers are L. J. King and R. G. Golledge, *Cities, Space, and Behavior: The Elements of Urban Geography*

(Englewood Cliffs, N.J.: Prentice-Hall, 1979); and David T. Herbert and D. M. Smith, *Social Problems and the City: Geographical Perspectives* (London: Oxford University Press, 1979).

Philosophically-oriented works on the city are Harvey Cox, *The Secular City* (New York: Macmillan, 1966); Lawrence Haworth, *The Good City* (Bloomington: Indiana University Press, 1963); David Harvey, *Social Justice and the City* (Baltimore: Johns Hopkins Press, 1973); and Raghaven N. Iyer, *Parapolitics: Toward the City of Man* (Princeton, N.J.: Princeton University Press, 1980). The anti-city bias in American culture is discussed in Morton White and Lucia White, *The Intellectual Versus the City* (Cambridge: Harvard University Press, 1962).

General urban works of international comparative scope include Annmarie H. Walsh, *The Urban Challenge to Government: An International Comparison of 13 Cities* (New York: Praeger, 1969); Samuel Humes and Eileen Martin, *The Structure of Local Government: A Comparative Survey of 81 Countries* (The Hague: International Union of Local Authorities, 1969); and Robert C. Fried and Francine F. Rabinovitz, *Comparative Urban Politics: A Performance Approach* (Englewood Cliffs, N.J.: Prentice-Hall, 1980).

HISTORICAL BACKGROUND

A rich store of historical writings on American cities and urbanization has developed over the last several decades. Particularly helpful for placing the contemporary metropolis in perspective are Gideon Sjoberg, *The Preindustrial City* (New York: Free Press, 1960); Lewis Mumford, *The City in History* (New York: Harcourt Brace Jovanovich, 1961); Mason Hammond, *The City in the Ancient World* (Cambridge, Mass.: Harvard University Press, 1973); and E. A. Gutkind's monumental work, *International History of City Development*, 8 vols., published by Free Press (New York: 1964–1972).

General studies of the early periods of urban growth in the United States are Carl Bridenbaugh's excellent *Cities in the Wilderness: The First Century of Urban Life in America* (New York: Ronald Press, 1938) and his *Cities in Revolt 1743–1776* (New York: Knopf, 1955); Blake McKelvey, *The Emergence of Metropolitan America 1915–1966*, published by Rutgers University Press (1968); Sam Bass Warner, *The Urban Wilderness* (New York: Harper & Row, 1972); Constance M. Green, *The Rise of Urban America* (New

York: Harper & Row, 1965); and Charles R. Adrian and Ernest S. Griffith, *A History of American City Government: The Formation of Traditions 1775–1870* (New York: Praeger, 1976).

Other writings on the American city include Daniel Elazar, *Cities of the Prairies* (New York: Basic Books, 1970); Kenneth Jackson and Stanley Schultz, *Cities in American History* (New York: 1972); Charles N. Glaab and A. Theodore Brown, *A History of Urban America,* 2d ed. (New York: Macmillan, 1976); Blaine Brownell and David Goldfield, *The City in Southern History* (Port Washington, N.Y.: Kennikat, 1977); Paul D. Goins, *From Main Street to State Street,* also published by Kennikat in 1977; and J. Rogers Hollingsworth and Ellen Hollingsworth, *Dimensions in Urban History: Historical and Social Perspectives on Middle-Size American Cities* (Madison: University of Wisconsin Press, 1979). The antiurban origins of American cities are examined in Sylvia D. Fries, *The Urban Idea in Colonial America* (Philadelphia: Temple University Press, 1977). An historical presentation of political and legal theory as applied to local government is found in Anwar Syed, *The Political Theory of American Local Government* (New York: Random House, 1966) and W. Hardy Wickwar, *The Political Theory of Local Government* (Columbia: University of South Carolina Press, 1970).

Scholarly histories of specific cities include Bayrd Still, *Milwaukee: The History of a City* (Madison: State Historical Society of Wisconsin, 1948); Blake McKelvey's three-volume study of Rochester, New York, published by Harvard University Press, 1945–1956; A. Theodore Brown, *The History of Kansas City to 1870* (Columbia: University of Missouri Press, 1964); Sam Bass Warner, *The Private City: Philadelphia in Three Periods of Its Growth* (Philadelphia: University of Pennsylvania Press, 1968); Harold M. Mayer and Richard C. Wade, *Growth of a Metropolis* (Chicago: University of Chicago Press, 1969); Milton M. Klein, *New York City: The Centennial Years, 1676–1976* (Port Washington, N.Y.: Kennikat, 1976); Glenn W. Miller and Jimmy Skaggs (eds.), *Metropolitan Wichita: Past, Present, and Future* (Lawrence: The Regents Press of Kansas, 1978); and Barbara Flanagan, *Minneapolis* (New York: St. Martin's Press, 1973).

The historical development of urban political institutions is covered in John P. East, *Council-Manager Government: The Political Thought of Its Founder, Richard S. Childs* (Chapel Hill: University of North Carolina Press, 1965); Ernest S. Griffith, *A History of American City Government: The Conspicuous Failure 1870–1900* (New York: Praeger, 1974); Melvin G. Holli, *Reform in Detroit* (New York: Oxford University Press, 1969); Jon C. Teaford,

The Municipal Revolution in America: Origins of Modern Urban Government 1650–1825 (Chicago: University of Chicago Press, 1975); and his *City and Suburb: The Political Fragmentation of Metropolitan American 1850–1970* (Johns Hopkins Press, 1979). Related works are Martin Schiesl, *The Politics of Efficiency: Municipal Administration and Reform in America, 1890–1920* (Berkeley and Los Angeles: University of California Press, 1977); Kenneth Fox, *Better City Government: Innovation in American Urban Politics 1850–1937* (Philadelphia: Temple University Press, 1977); Michael Ebner and Eugene Tobin, *The Age of Urban Reform: New Perspectives on the Progressive Era* (Port Washington, N.Y.: Kennikat, 1977); and Bradley R. Rice, *Progressive Cities: The Commission Government Movement in America 1901–1920* (Austin: University of Texas Press, 1977).

A large volume of historical writings on political machines and bosses has appeared during the last two decades. The classic work in this field is Harold F. Gosnell, *Machine Politics: Chicago Model* (University of Chicago Press, 1937), reprinted in 1968 with an introduction by Theodore Lowi. Works dealing with individual bosses are William D. Miller, *Mr. Crump of Memphis* (Baton Rouge: Louisiana State University Press, 1964); Lyle W. Dorsett, *The Pendergast Machine* (New York: Oxford University Press, 1968) and his more general *Franklin D. Roosevelt and the City Bosses* (Port Washington, N.Y.: Kennikat, 1977); William D. Miller, *Boss Cox's Cincinnati* (New York: Oxford University Press, 1968), which describes a political machine under Republican control; and Leo Hirshkowitz, *Tweed's New York: Another Look* (Garden City, N.Y.: Anchor Books, 1977).

Several books on Richard Daley have been published in recent years, the most analytical and balanced being Milton Rakove's *Don't Make No Waves–Don't Back No Losers* (Bloomington: Indiana University Press, 1975). Highly critical of Daley is *Boss* (New York: Dutton, 1970), written by Chicago newspaper columnist Mike Royko. A late treatment of Chicago politics is Thomas M. Guterbock, *Machine Politics in Transition: Party and Community in Chicago* (Chicago: University of Chicago Press, 1980). Other works on political machines are Alfred Steinberg, *The Bosses* (New York: Macmillan, 1972), which outlines the careers of six well-known figures; Fred J. Cook, *American Political Bosses and Machines* (New York: Franklin Watts, 1973); and John M. Allswang, *Bosses, Machines, and Urban Voters* (Port Washington, N.Y.: Kennikat, 1977). The ethnic influence in machine politics is discussed in Raymond E. Wolfinger, *The Politics of Progress* (Englewood Cliffs, N.J.: Prentice-Hall, 1974).

SOCIOECONOMIC DIMENSIONS

The social aspects of urban communities are discussed in a wide variety of books, such as Ceri Peach, *Urban Social Segregation* (New York: Longman, 1976); Constance Perin, *Everything in Its Place: Social Order and Land Use in America* (Princeton, N.J.: Princeton University Press, 1977); Ralph Thomlinson, *Urban Structure: The Social and Spatial Structure of Cities* (New York: Random House, 1969); and David C. Thorns, *The Quest for Community: Social Aspects of Residential Growth* (New York: Halstead, 1976). Network analyses of urban interaction patterns are found in Claude S. Fischer et al., *Networks and Places: Social Relations in the Urban Setting* (New York: Free Press, 1977); and Joseph Galaskiewicz, *Social Networks and Community Politics* (Beverly Hills, Calif.: Sage, 1979). William Michelson, *Environmental Choice, Human Behavior, and Residential Satisfaction* (New York: Oxford University Press, 1977) deals with the social implications of different forms of housing. An overview of community institutions is given in Roland I. Warren, *The Community in America*, 3d ed. (Chicago: Rand McNally, 1978). A more general treatment is J. R. Mellor, *Urban Sociology in an Urbanizing Society* (London: Routledge and Kegan Paul, 1977).

Ethnicity and race in urban settings are the subject of numerous studies, including David Ward, *Cities and Immigrants* (New York: Oxford University Press, 1971); Leo F. Schnore, *Class and Race in Cities and Suburbs* (Chicago: Markham, 1972); Nathan Glazer and Daniel Moynihan, *Beyond the Melting Pot*, rev. ed. (Cambridge, Mass.: MIT Press, 1970); Gerald D. Suttles, *The Social Order of the Slum: Ethnicity and Territory in the Inner City* (Chicago: University of Chicago Press, 1968); Norman M. Bradburn et al., *Side by Side: Integrated Neighborhoods in America* (Chicago: Quadrangle Books, 1971); Lyle and Magdaline Shannon, *Minority Migrants in the Urban Community: Mexican American and Negro Adjustment to Industrial Society* (Beverly Hills, Calif.: Sage, 1973); and Harold M. Rose, *The Black Ghetto: A Spatial Behavioral Perspective* (New York: McGraw-Hill, 1971). Other works on urban ethnicity are Helene Z. Lopata, *Polish Americans: Status Competition in an Ethnic Community* (Englewood Cliffs, N.J.: Prentice-Hall, 1975); Alan L. Sorkin, *The Urban American Indian* (Lexington, Mass.: Heath, 1978); David Colburn and George Pozzetta (eds.), *America and the New Ethnicity* (Port Washington, N.Y.: Kennikat, 1978); Dean Esslinger, *Immigrants and the City*, published by Kennikat in 1975; and Thomas Sowell (ed.), *American Ethnic Groups* (Washington, D.C.: Urban Institute, 1978).

Neighborhoods have been the focal point of renewed interest in recent years. The March 1979 issue (vol. 14) of *Urban Affairs Quarterly* is devoted to this topic. An excellent sociological analysis is Suzanne Keller, *The Urban Neighborhood* (New York: Random House, 1968). Racial sections of the city are treated in Donald I. Warren, *Black Neighborhoods* (Ann Arbor: University of Michigan Press, 1975); ethnic areas in Yona Ginsberg, *Jews in a Changing Neighborhood* (New York: Free Press, 1975); and Andrew Greeley, *Neighborhood* (New York: Seabury Press, 1977).

The social aspects of suburbs have also been a subject of attention in the literature. One of the first scholarly books on the outlying communities was Robert Wood's *Suburbia: Its People and Their Politics* (Boston: Houghton Mifflin, 1959). Later works include John Kramer, *North American Suburbs: Politics, Diversity, and Change* (Berkeley, Calif.: Glendessary Press, 1972); William S. Kornblum, *Blue Collar Community* (Chicago: University of Chicago Press, 1974); Francine Rabinovitz and William Siembieda, *Minorities in Suburbs: The Los Angeles Experience* (Lexington, Mass.: Heath, 1977); David Popenoe, *The Suburban Environment* (Chicago: University of Chicago Press, 1977); and Thomas Clark, *Blacks in Suburbs: A National Perspective* (New Brunswick, N.J.: Rutgers University Press, 1979). The relative economic position of central cities and their outlying areas is the subject of a recent ACIR report entitled *Central City–Suburban Fiscal Disparities and City Distress, 1977* (Washington, D.C., December 1980).

The literature on the new role of women in the public and private sectors is rapidly expanding. Representative books include Jeanne Kirkpatrick, *Political Women* (New York: Basic Books, 1974); Harry Kranz, *The Participatory Bureaucracy: Women and Minorities in a More Representative Public Service* (Lexington, Mass.: Heath, 1976); Ralph E. Smith (ed.), *The Subtle Revolution: Women at Work,* and Lorraine A. Underwood, *Women in Federal Employment Programs,* both published by the Urban Institute (Washington, D.C.) in 1979; Peggy Lamson, *In the Vanguard: Six American Women in Public Life* (Boston: Houghton Mifflin, 1979); Claire K. Fulenwider, *Feminism in American Politics* (New York: Praeger, 1979); Margaret G. Wilson, *The American Woman in Transition: The Urban Influence 1870–1920* (Westport, Conn.: Greenwood, 1979); and Irene Diamond, *Sex Roles in the State House* (New Haven, Conn.: Yale University Press, 1977). Helpful in locating material on the role of women is Hasia Dines (ed.), *Women and Urban Society: A Guide to Information Sources* (Detroit: Gale Research, 1979).

A summation of current knowledge on the economic facets of

metropolitan communities is Peter Mieszkowski and Mahlon Straszheim, *Current Issues in Urban Economics* (Baltimore: Johns Hopkins Press, 1979). Other works include Lowdon Wingo and Allan Evans, *Public Economies and the Quality of Life* (Baltimore: Johns Hopkins Press, 1978); Harry W. Richardson, *The Economics of Urban Size* (Lexington, Mass.: Heath, 1973); and Niles M. Hansen, *The Challenge of Urban Growth: The Basic Economics of City Size and Structure,* also published by Heath in 1977. An analysis of major urban growth theories is Alfred Watkins, *The Practice of Urban Economics* (Beverly Hills, Calif.: Sage, 1980).

Economic models applicable to the study of urban communities (as well as to political behavior in general) are presented in Anthony Downs, *An Economic Theory of Democracy* (New York: Harper and Row, 1957); and James M. Buchanan and Gordon Tullock, *The Calculus of Consent* (Ann Arbor: University of Michigan Press, 1962). A sophisticated attempt to apply formal systems analysis (based on economic assumptions) to the evaluation of urban social programs and policies is Jay W. Forrester, *Urban Dynamics* (Cambridge: MIT Press, 1969). Criticism of the Forrester model is found in Henry Averch and Robert Levine, "Two Models of the Urban Crisis: An Analytical Essay on Banfield and Forrester," (Santa Monica, Calif.: Rand Corporation, 1970). Major works in the public choice literature are discussed in Dennis C. Mueller, *Public Choice* (New York: Cambridge University Press, 1979).

The economy of the central city is discussed in Andrew M. Hamer, *Industrial Exodus from the Central City: Public Policy and the Comparative Costs of Location* (Lexington, Mass.: Heath, 1972); James H. Boykin, *Industrial Potential of the Central City* (Washington, D.C.: Urban Land Institute, 1973); Harry R. Bedford, *Trouble Downtown* (New York: Harcourt Brace Jovanovich, 1978); and Benjamin Chinitz, *Central City Economic Development* (Cambridge, Mass.: Abt Books, 1979). A summary of research on the CBD is contained in Raymond E. Murphy, *The Central Business District* (Chicago: Aldine-Atherton, 1972). A less technical treatment is Jane Jacobs, *The Economy of Cities* (New York: Random House, 1969).

The economic status of inner city ghettos is the subject of Carolyn Shaw, *The Economics of the Ghetto* (New York: Pegasus, 1970); and Frank G. Davis, *The Economics of Black Community Development* (Chicago: Markham, 1972). Submunicipal economies are discussed in David Segal, *The Economics of Neighborhood* (New York: Academic Press, 1979). A series of articles on this topic is contained in Benjamin Goldstein and Ross David (eds.), *Neighborhoods in the Urban Economy* (Lexington, Mass.: Heath, 1977). Related also is Phillip L. Clay, *Neighborhood Renewal* (Lexington, Mass.: Heath, 1979); and Rolf Goetze, *Understanding Neighborhood Change* (Cambridge, Mass.: Ballinger, 1979). The June 1980 issue (vol. 15) of *Urban Affairs Quarterly* is devoted to the revitalization of inner-city neighborhoods. Minority economic development is also discussed in Scott Cummings (ed.), *Self-Help in Urban America* (Port Washington, N.Y.: Kennikat, 1979).

GOVERNMENT ORGANIZATION

The quantity of published material pertaining to the internal structure and management of local government has increased substantially in recent years. A number of theoretically oriented books have emerged from the City Council Research Project of Stanford University's Institute of Political Studies. These include Heinz Eulau and Kenneth Prewitt, *Labyrinths of Democracy: Adaptations, Linkages, Representation, and Policies in Urban Politics* (1973); Robert Eyestone, *The Threads of Public Policy: A Study in Policy Leadership* (1971); and Betty H. Zisk, *Local Interest Politics: A One-Way Street* (1973), all published by Bobbs-Merrill.

City Managers and mayors have also been the subject of attention. Among works dealing with them are Richard J. Stillman, *The Rise of the City Manager* (Albuquerque: University of New Mexico Press, 1974); LeRoy F. Harlow, *Without Fear or Favor: Odyssey of a City Manager* (Provo, Utah: Brigham Young University Press, 1977); Charles H. Levine, *Racial Conflict and the American Mayor* (Lexington, Mass.: Heath, 1974); and John P. Kotter and Paul R. Lawrence, *Mayors in Action: Five Approaches to Urban Governance* (New York: Wiley, 1974).

Individual mayors are treated in such works as Allan Talbot, *The Mayor's Game* (New York: Praeger, 1970) which deals with Richard Lee of New Haven; James Haskins, *A Piece of the Power: Four Black Mayors* (New York: Dial, 1972); John C. Bollens and Grant B. Geyer, *Yorty: Politics of a Constant Candidate* (Pacific Palisades, Calif.: Palisades Publishers, 1973); and Fred Hamilton, *Rizzo* (New York: Viking, 1973). A study of a suburban mayor is Ann L. Greer, *The Mayor's Mandate* (Cambridge, Mass.: Schenkman, 1974).

The administration of local government is treated in Willis Hawley and David Rogers (eds.), *Improving the Quality of Urban Management* (Beverly Hills, Calif.: Sage, 1974); Brian Rapp and Frank Patitucci, *Managing Local Government for Improved Performance* (Boulder, Colo.: Westview Press, 1977); Fremont Lyden and Ernest Miller (eds.), *Planning, Programming, Budgeting* (Chicago: Rand McNally, 1972); John Worthley and William Ludwin (eds.), *Zero-Based Budgeting in State and Local Government* (New York: Praeger, 1979); Scott Greer, Ronald Hedlund, and James Gibson (eds.), *Accountability in Urban Society: Public Agencies Under Fire* (Beverly Hills, Calif.: Sage, 1978); Zane Miller and Paula Dubeck, *Urban Professionals and the Future of the Metropolis* (Port Washington, N.Y.: Kennikat, 1980); and Richard D. Bingham, *The Adoption of Innovation by Local Government* (Lexington, Mass.: Heath, 1976).

Other works dealing with urban administration include Kenneth L. Kraemer and John King, *Computers and Local Government* (New York: Praeger, 1977); David R. Morgan, *Managing Urban America* (North Scituate, Mass.: Duxbury Press, 1979); Jeffrey M. Prottas, *People Processing: The Street Level Bureaucrat in Public Service Bureaucracies* (Lexington, Mass.: Heath, 1979); Selma J. Mushkin and Frank Sandifer, *Personnel Management and Productivity in City Government*, and Robert K. Lin et al. *Changing Urban Bureaucracies*, also published by Heath in 1979. Extensive annotations on county studies are found in John C. Bollens, in association with John Bayes and Kathryn Utter, *American County Government* (Beverly Hills, Calif.: Sage, 1969). An up-to-date treatment of county government is Herbert S. Duncombe, *Modern County Government* (Washington, D.C.: National Association of Counties, 1977). Also of interest is Vincent L. Marando and Robert D. Thomas, *The Forgotten Governments: County Commissioners as Policy Makers* (Gainesville: University Presses of Florida, 1977).

POWER AND PARTICIPATION

Although the number of formal power structure studies of the Dahl and Hunter type has declined considerably since 1970, the literature on community power and decision making continues to grow. Some of the more recent works are Edward C. Hayes, *Power Structure and Urban Policy: Who Rules in Oakland?* (New York: McGraw-Hill, 1972); H. George Frederickson and Lynda O'Leary, *Power, Public Opinion, and Policy in a Metropolitan Community: A Case Study of Syracuse* (New York: Praeger, 1973); Kevin Cox, *Conflict, Power, and Politics in the City* (New York: McGraw-Hill, 1973); Frederick M. Wirt, *Power in the City* (Berkeley and Los Angeles: University of California Press, 1974); Irving Tallman, *Power Action Politics: A Perspective on Social Problems and Social Problem Solving* (San Francisco: Freeman, 1976); and Lynda A. Ewen, *Corporate Power and Urban Crisis in Detroit* (Princeton, N.J.: Princeton University Press, 1978). A general treatment of power at the local level is Dennis Judd and Francis Kopel, *The Politics of American Cities: Private Power and Public Policy* (Boston: Little Brown, 1979).

Increased attention has been focused on power in relation to the public schools. Works relating to this topic are Joseph M. Cronin, *The Control of Urban Schools* (New York: Free Press, 1973); Harmon Zeigler and M. Kent Jennings, *Governing American Schools* (North Scituate, Mass.: Duxbury, 1974); Frederick M. Wirt, *The Polity of the Schools: New Research in Educational Politics* (Lexington, Mass.: Heath, 1975); William J. Grimshaw, *Union Rule in the Schools: Big City Politics in Transformation,* published by Heath in 1979; and Paul E. Peterson, *School Politics, Chicago Style* (Chicago: University of Chicago Press, 1976).

Studies of voting and other forms of political participation at the local level are widely scattered in articles, sample survey reports, and books. An early but still relevant summary of the findings of such studies is Robert E. Lane, *Political Life* (New York: Free Press, 1959). A later bibliography is found in Dale R. Marshall, "Who Participates in What? A Bibliographical Essay on Individual Participation in Urban Areas," *Urban Affairs Quarterly* 4 (December 1968): 201–223. The introductory chapter to John C. Bollens and Dale R. Marshall, *A Guide to Participation* (Englewood Cliffs, N.J.: Prentice-Hall, 1973,) gives an overview of the different types of involvement. Various aspects of the subject are discussed in Stuart Langton (ed.), *Citizen Participation in America* (Lexington, Mass.: Heath, 1978) and Richard L. Cole, *Citizen Participation and the Urban Policy Process,* also published by Heath in 1974. The normative and theoretical dimensions of participation are treated in such interesting works as Carole Pateman, *Participation and Democratic Theory* (New York: Cambridge University Press, 1970); David Ricci, *Community Power and Democratic Theory* (New York: Random House, 1971); Darryl Baskin, *American Pluralist Democracy: A Critique* (New York: Van Nostrand, 1971); and Robert A. Dahl, *Polyarchy: Participation and Opposition* (New Haven, Conn.:Yale University Press, 1971). The ACIR in 1980 published a report entitled *Citizen Participation in the American Federal System.*

The literature on black political power at the local level includes Chuck Stone, *Black Political Power* (Indianapolis: Bobbs-Merrill, 1968); Alex Poinsett, *Black Power: Gary Style* (Chicago: Johnson, 1970); Hanes Walton, Jr., *Black Politics: A Theoretical and Structural Analysis* (Philadelphia: Lippincott, 1972); Edwin R. Lewison, *Black Politics in New York City* (New York: Twayne, 1974); Ernest Patterson, *Black City Politics* (New York: Dodd,

Mead, 1974); Michael Preston, "Limitations of Black Urban Power: The Case of Black Mayors," in Louis H. Masotti and Robert L. Lineberry (eds.), *The New Urban Politics* (Cambridge, Mass.: Ballinger, 1976), pp. 111–132; and William Nelson and Philip Meranto, *Electing Black Mayors: Political Action in the Black Community* (Columbus: Ohio State University Press, 1977). The growing political activism of the elderly is treated in Henry J. Pratt, *The Gray Lobby* (Chicago: University of Chicago Press, 1976).

The more activist and less conventional forms of urban political participation began to receive attention in the literature during the late 1960s, and this interest has continued up to the present. Earlier works on this topic include Ralph M. Kramer, *Participation of the Poor: Comparative Studies in the War on Poverty* (Englewood Cliffs, N.J.: Prentice-Hall, 1969); Dale R. Marshall, *The Politics of Participation in Poverty* (Berkeley and Los Angeles: University of California Press, 1971); and Hans B. C. Spiegel (ed.), *Citizen Participation in Urban Development*, 2 vols. (Washington, D.C.: NTL Institute of Applied Behavioral Science, 1968–1969). The May/June 1972 issue (vol. 32) of *Public Administration Review* contains a symposium on citizen involvement and two special issues of the same publication (September 1972 and October 1972) are devoted to citizen action in the model cities program and in urban neighborhoods generally.

Protest politics are treated in Joan E. Lancourt, *Confront or Concede: The Alinsky Citizen-Action Organizations* (Lexington, Mass.: Heath, 1979) and Francis F. Priven and Richard A. Cloward, *The People's Movements: Why They Succeed, How They Fail* (New York: Pantheon Books, 1977). Studies of specific community action groups are William W. Ellis, *White Ethnics and Black Power: The Emergence of the West Side Organization* (Chicago: Aldine, 1969) and John H. Fisk, *Black Power/White Control: The Struggle of the Woodlawn Organization in Chicago* (Princeton, N.J.: Princeton University Press, 1973). A recent study of low-income organizations is Marilyn Gittell and associates, *Limits to Citizen Participation: The Decline of Community Organizations* (Beverly Hills, Calif.: Sage, 1980).

Power and participation at the neighborhood level are treated in a wide selection of recently published books. These include Karl Hess and David Morris, *Neighborhood Power: The New Localism* (Boston: Beacon Press, 1974); Douglas Yates, *Neighborhood Democracy* (Lexington, Mass.: Heath, 1974); Curt Lamb, *Political Power in Poor Neighborhoods* (New York: Wiley, 1975); David J. O'Brien, *Neighborhood Organization and Interest Group Processes* (Princeton, N.J.: Princeton University Press, 1976); Rita M.

Kelly, *Community Control of Economic Development* (New York: Praeger, 1977); and Jeffrey Davidson, *Political Partnerships: Neighborhood Residents and Their Council Members* (Beverly Hills, Calif.: Sage, 1979). Organizational forms and strategies are the subject of Rachelle B. and Donald I. Warren, *The Neighborhood Organizer's Handbook* (Notre Dame, Ind.: Notre Dame University Press, 1977); and Howard W. Hallman, *The Organization and Operation of Neighborhood Councils: A Practical Guide* (New York: Praeger, 1977).

INTERGOVERNMENTAL RELATIONS

The literature on intergovernmental relations and the growing influence of the national and state governments (particularly the former) on urban affairs is extensive. The general works include Frederic N. Cleaveland (ed.), *Congress and Urban Problems* (Washington, D.C.: The Brookings Institution, 1969); Lee S. Greene, Malcolm Jewell, and Daniel Grant, *The States and the Metropolis,* published by the University of Alabama Press in 1969; Peter A. Lupsha, "New Federalism: Centralization and Local Control in Perspective," in Louis Masotti and Robert Lineberry (eds.), *The New Urban Politics* (Cambridge, Mass.: Ballinger, 1976), pp. 219–233; and Peter Passell and Leonard Ross, *State Policies and Federal Programs* (New York: Praeger, 1978).

Other relevant publications of general interest are Michael Danielson, Alan Hershey, and John Bayne, *One Nation, So Many Governments* (Lexington, Mass.: Heath, 1977); George Berkley and Douglas Fox, *80,000 Governments: The Politics of Subnational America* (Boston: Allyn and Bacon, 1978); and M. Carter McFarland, *Federal Government and Urban Problems* (Boulder, Colo.: Westview Press, 1978). Two useful collections of readings are Richard D. Feld and Carl Grafton (eds.), *The Uneasy Partnership: The Dynamics of Federal, State, and Urban Relations* (Palo Alto, Calif.: Mayfield, 1973) and Douglas Fox (ed.), *The New Urban Politics: Cities and the Federal Government* (Pacific Palisades, Calif.: Goodyear, 1972).

Early federal involvement at the state and local levels is emphasized in Daniel Elazar, *Metropolitan Frontier: A Perspective on Change in American Society* (Morristown, N.J.: General Learning, 1973). Economic aspects of federalism are dealt with in Wallace Oates (ed.), *The Political Economy of Fiscal Federalism;* and Curtis Martin and Robert Leone, *Local Economic Development: The Federal Connection,* both published by Heath in 1977. Analyses of experiences with federal programs in individual cities include Jeffrey

Pressman, *Federal Programs and City Politics* (Berkeley: University of California Press, 1975), which looks at Oakland, California; Donald F. Kettl, *Managing Community Development in the New Federalism* (New York: Praeger, 1980), which examines four Connecticut communities; and Martha Derthick, *New Towns in-Town: Why a Federal Program Failed* (Washington, D.C.: Urban Institute, 1972), a case study of a project in the District of Columbia. Federalism as it related to the poverty and model cities programs is treated in L. Sundquist and David Davis, *Making Federalism Work* (Washington, D.C.: The Brookings Institution, 1969).

The impact of the earlier federal aid programs is the subject of Mark T. Gelfand's *A Nation of Cities: The Federal Government and Urban America 1933–1965* (New York: Oxford University Press, 1975). Charles L. Leven et al., *Neighborhood Changes: Lessons in the Dynamics of Urban Decay* (New York: Praeger, 1976) examines the effect of FHA policies on central city neighborhoods. The role of general revenue sharing is analyzed in Richard P. Nathan and Charles F. Adams, *Revenue Sharing: The Second Round* (Washington, D.C.: The Brookings Institution, 1977). Other impact studies are Bernard J. Frieden and Marshall Kaplan, *The Politics of Neglect: Urban Aid from Model Cities to Revenue Sharing* (Cambridge, Mass.: MIT Press, 1975); Norman J. Glickman (ed.), *The Urban Impacts of Federal Policies* (Baltimore: Johns Hopkins Press, 1979); and Carl Van Horn, *Policy Implementation in the Federal System: National Goals and Local Implementors* (Lexington, Mass.: Heath, 1979). A wide array of articles on intergovernmental relations is found in *Publius,* a journal devoted to studies of the federal system. The evolution of a federal urban program is the topic of an ACIR report by Mavis M. Reeves, *The Federal Role in Fire Protection* (Washington, D.C., 1980).

PLANNING

The planning of urban communities is represented by a voluminous body of literature. Bibliographies in this field are Melville C. Branch, *Comprehensive Urban Planning: A Selective Bibliography* ;(Beverly Hills, Calif.: Sage, 1970); and George C. Bestor and H. R. Jones, *City Planning Bibliography* (New York: American Society of Civil Engineers, 1972). A general reference book in this field is Arnold Whittick (ed.), *Encyclopedia of Urban Planning* (New York: McGraw-Hill, 1974). Planning histories are John W. Reps, *The Making of Urban America* (Princeton, N.J.: Princeton University Press, 1965) and his *Cities of the American West: A History of*

Frontier Urban Planning, also published by Princeton University Press (1979); Mel Scott, *American City Planning Since 1890* (Berkeley and Los Angeles: University of California Press, 1969); and Michael Hugo-Brunt, *The History of City Planning* (Montreal: Haward House, 1972). A list of doctoral dissertations recently published by University Microfilm International, Ann Arbor, Michigan, is found in its *Regional and City Planning: A Dissertation Catalog.*

General works on planning and land use controls include Marion Clawson (ed.), *Modernizing Urban Land Policy* (Baltimore: Johns Hopkins Press, 1973); Marshall Kaplan, *Urban Planning in the 1960s: A Design for Irrelevancy* (New York: Praeger, 1973); Melvin R. Levin, *Community and Regional Planning,* 3d ed. (New York: Praeger, 1977); Bernard H. Siegan, *Land Use Without Zoning* (Lexington, Mass.: Heath, 1972), an analysis of the Houston experience; Robert H. Nelson, *Zoning and Property Rights* (Cambridge, Mass.: MIT Press, 1977); Daniel R. Mandelker and Roger A. Cunningham, *Planning and Control of Land Development* (Indianapolis: Bobbs-Merrill, 1979); Jerold Kayden, *Incentive Zoning* (Lexington, Mass.: Heath, 1980); and Neil Gilbert and Harry Specht, *Dynamics of Community Planning* (Cambridge, Mass.: Ballinger, 1977).

Planning for smaller communities is discussed in Herrington J. Bryce, *Planning Smaller Cities* (Lexington, Mass.: Heath, 1979) and Bert Swanson, Richard Cohen, and Edith Swanson, *Small Towns and Small Towners: A Framework for Survival and Growth* (Beverly Hills, Calif.: Sage, 1979). Planning as related to neighborhoods is examined in Phillip L. Clay, *Neighborhood Renewal,* Eileen Zeitz, *Private Urban Renewal,* and Herrington J. Bryce (ed.), *Revitalizing Cities,* all published by Heath in 1979; and Roger Ahlbrandt and James Cunningham, *A New Public Policy for Neighborhood Preservation* (New York: Praeger, 1979). The role of the state in land use control is the subject of Robert G. Healy and John Rosenberg, *Land Use and the States* (Baltimore: Johns Hopkins Press, 1979). The problems of land use control are analyzed in Robert H. Nelson, *Zoning and Property Rights* (Cambridge, Mass.: MIT Press, 1980).

A collection of the views of planning practitioners is Anthony J. Catanese and W. Paul Farmer (eds.), *Personality, Politics, and Planning* (Beverly Hills, Calif.: Sage, 1978). A profile of urban planners is Michael L. Vasa, *Politics and Planning: A National Study of American Planners* (Chapel Hill, N.C.: University of North Carolina Press, 1979). The new role of planning in an era of economic retrenchment is discussed in Pierre Clavel, John Forester, and William Goldsmith (eds.), *Urban and Regional Planning in an Age of Austerity* (Elmsford, N.Y.: Pergamon, 1980).

Despite the failure of the recent new town movement in the United States, a large number of books on the subject have appeared over the last decade. A bibliography on this topic is Gideon Golany, *New Towns Planning and Development: A World-Wide Bibliography* (Washington, D.C.: Urban Land Institute, 1973). The September 1973 (vol. 39) issue of the *Journal of the American Institute of Planners* is devoted to new towns. The many books in this area include John B. Lansing et al., *Planned Residential Environments* (Ann Arbor: University of Michigan, Institute for Social Research, 1971); Gerald Burke, *Towns in the Making* (New York: St. Martin's Press, 1971); Pierre Merlin, *New Towns: Regional Planning and Development* (New York: Harper & Row, 1973); and Harvey S. Perloff and Neil Sandberg, *New Towns: Why and for Whom?* (New York: Praeger, 1973).

Descriptions of some of the better known planned communities in the United States are contained in Gurney Breckenfeld, *Columbia and the New Cities* (New York: Ives Washburn, 1971). Among the most recent works on new towns are Raymond J. Busby and Shirley Weiss, *New Communities U.S.A.* (Lexington, Mass.: Heath, 1976); Harvey H. Kaiser, *The Building of Cities* (Ithaca: Cornell University Press, 1977); Irving L. Allen (ed.), *New Towns and the Suburban Dream* (Port Washington, N.Y.: Kennikat, 1977); Robert B. Zehner, *Indicators of the Quality of Life in New Communities* (Cambridge, Mass.: Ballinger, 1977); Carol Corden, *Planned Cities: New Towns in Britain and America* (Beverly Hills, Calif.: Sage, 1977); and James M. Rubenstein, *The French New Towns* (Baltimore: Johns Hopkins Press, 1978).

Planning in relation to the environment is covered in Victor Gruen, *Centers for the Urban Environment* (New York: Van Nostrand Reinhold, 1973) and Daniel R. Mandelker (ed.), *Environment and Land Control Legislation* (Indianapolis: Bobbs-Merrill, 1976). The widely publicized book *Defensible Space* (New York: Macmillan, 1972), by Oscar Newman deals with the relationship between physical design and the incidence of crime. A later work on this subject is Richard A. Gardiner, *Design for Safe Neighborhoods* (Washington, D.C.: U.S. Government Printing Office, 1979). The effect of design on behavior is also discussed in Thomas Saarinen, *Environmental Planning: Perception and Behavior* (Boston: Houghton Mifflin, 1976). The issue of urban sprawl is examined in Mark Gottdiener, *Planned Sprawl: Private and Public Interests in Suburbia* (Beverly Hills, Calif.: Sage, 1977).

The politics of planning is treated in Francine F. Rabinovitz, *City Planning and Politics* (New York: Atherton, 1969); Dennis Judd and Robert Mendelson, *The Politics of Urban Planning: The East St. Louis Experience* (Urbana: University of Illinois Press, 1973); Don T. Allensworth, *The Political Realities of Urban Planning* (New York: Praeger, 1975); and R. Robert Linowes and Don T. Allensworth, *The Politics of Land Use Law: Developers versus Citizen Groups in the Courts* (New York: Praeger, 1976).

URBAN FINANCES

Financing government in urban areas has received increasing attention in recent years, particularly since the fiscal difficulties of New York City and other large municipalities became known. General works in this field include Kenneth Greene, William Neenan, and Claudia Scott, *Fiscal Intervention in a Metropolitan Area* (Lexington, Mass.: Heath, 1974); William G. Coleman, *Cities, Suburbs, and States: Governing and Financing Urban America* (New York: Free Press, 1975); Joseph S. Slavet, Katharine Bradbury, and Philip Moss, *Financing State-Local Services: A New Strategy for Greater Equity* (Lexington, Mass.: Heath, 1975); Selma J. Mushkin (ed.), *Public Prices for Public Products* (Washington, D.C.: Urban Institute, 1972); James C. Snyder, *Fiscal Management and Planning in Local Government* (Lexington, Mass.: Heath, 1977); James A. Maxwell and J. R. Aronson, *Financing State and Local Government*, 3d ed. (Washington, D.C.: The Brookings Institution, 1977); George F. Break (ed.), *Metropolitan Financing and Growth Management Policies* (Madison: University of Wisconsin Press, 1978); and Richard Lindholm and Hartojo Wignjowijoto, *Financing and Managing State and Local Government* (Lexington, Mass.: Heath, 1979). Capital financing is treated in Alan W. Steiss, *Local Government Finance: Capital Facilities Planning* (Lexington, Mass.: Heath, 1975).

Among the books and articles dealing with the current "tax rebellion" and its effects are John R. Meyer and John Quigley, *Local Public Finance and the Fiscal Squeeze* (Cambridge, Mass.: Ballinger, 1977); Donald H. Haider, "Fiscal Scarcity: A New Urban Perspective," in Louis Masotti and Robert Lineberry (eds.), *The New Urban Politics* (Cambridge, Mass.: Ballinger, 1976), pp. 171–216; L. Kenneth Hubbell, *Fiscal Crisis in American Cities: The Federal Response* (Cambridge: Ballinger, 1979); two papers issued by the Rand Corporation, Santa Monica, California, in May 1979, the first by Phyllis Ellickson, "The Fiscal Limitation Movement" and the second by Anthony Pascal, "The Effects of Local Fiscal

Contraction on Public Employment and the Advancement of Minorities;" and Charles H. Levine, *Managing Fiscal Stress: The Public Sector in Crisis* (Chatham, N.J.: Chatham House, 1980). Proposition 13 is examined in John J. Kirlin, *The Political Economy of Fiscal Limits* and Jeffrey Chapman, *Proposition 13 and Land Use,* both published by Heath (Lexington Books) in 1980. The New York City fiscal crisis is the subject of Jack Newfield and Paul DeBrul, *The Abuse of Power* (New York: Viking Press, 1977).

The property tax issue is discussed in George E. Petersen et al., *Property Taxes, Housing, and the Cities* (1973) and Steven D. Gold, *Property Tax Relief* (1979), both published by Heath. Educational financing is dealt with in Martin T. Katzman, *The Political Economy of Urban Schools* (Cambridge, Mass.: Harvard University Press, 1971); Seymour Sacks et al., *City Schools/Suburban Schools: A History of Fiscal Conflict* (Syracuse, N.Y.: Syracuse University Press, 1972); and Betsy Levin, *State School Finance Reform: Court Mandate or Legislative Action* (Washington, D.C.: National Conference of State Legislatures, 1977). The political factors related to public financing are examined in Richard Bingham, Brett Hawkins, and F. T. Hebert, *The Politics of Raising State and Local Revenue* (New York: Praeger, 1978).

SOCIAL PROBLEMS

Social problems in general and public policies to cope with them are examined in Anthony Downs, *Urban Problems and Prospects,* 2d ed. (Chicago: Rand McNally, 1976); Richard Cloward and Francis F. Piven, *The Politics of Turmoil: Essays on Poverty, Race, and the Urban Crisis* (New York: Pantheon, 1975); Sharon P. Krefetz, *Welfare Policymaking and City Politics* (New York: Praeger, 1976); Martin Rein, *Social Science and Public Policy* (New York: Penguin, 1976); Irving Howe and Michael Harrington, *The Seventies: Problems and Proposals* (New York: Harper & Row, 1972); Victor B. Ficker and Herbert S. Graves, *Social Science and Urban Crisis,* 2d ed. (New York: Macmillan, 1978). An excellent analysis of the difficulties involved in efforts to achieve social change is Peter Marris and Martin Rein, *Dilemmas of Social Reform: Poverty and Community Action in the United States,* 2d ed. (Chicago: Aldine-Atherton, 1973). Implications of the increase in female–parent families are discussed in Heather Ross and Isabel Sawhill, *Time of Transition* (Washington, D.C.: Urban Institute, 1975).

Among the numerous works relating to housing for low- and moderate-income families are Richard Bingham, *Public Housing and Urban Renewal* (New York: Praeger, 1975); Richard S. Scobie,

Problem Tenants in Public Housing (New York: Praeger, 1975);
Robert E. Mendelson and Michael Quinn (eds.), *Politics of Housing in Older Urban Areas* (New York: Praeger, 1976); Roger Montgomery and Daniel Mandelker, *Housing in America*, 2d ed.
(Charlottesville, Va.: Michie/Bobbs-Merrill, 1979); and Roger
Montgomery and Dale Marshall (eds.), *Housing Policy for the
1980s* (Lexington, Mass.: Heath, 1980). A critique of public housing
is Eugene J. Meehan, *Public Housing Policy: Convention Versus
Reality* (New Brunswick, N.J.: Center for Urban Policy Research,
Rutgers University, 1975). Public housing reform is outlined in
Raymond Struyk, *A New System for Public Housing* (Washington,
D.C.: Urban Institute, 1980). An earlier work highly critical of the
urban renewal program is *The Federal Bulldozer* (Cambridge,
Mass.: MIT Press, 1964) by Martin Anderson, who subsequently
became President Reagan's advisor for domestic affairs.

Exclusionary practices aimed at racial minorities and the poor
are discussed in Richard F. Babcock and Fred P. Bosselman, *Exclusionary Zoning: Land Use Regulation and Housing in the 1970s*
(New York: Praeger, 1973); Donald Hagman, *The White Curtain:
Racially Disadvantaging Local Government Boundary Practices*
(Detroit: University of Detroit School of Law, 1977); Juliet Saltman, *Open Housing: Dynamics of a Social Movement* (New York:
Praeger, 1977); Richard P. Fishman (ed.), *Housing for All Under
Law* (Cambridge, Mass.: Ballinger, 1978); Ann B. Schnare, *The Persistence of Racial Segregation in Housing* (Washington, D.C.: Urban Institute, 1978); and Duane Windsor, *Fiscal Zoning in Suburban Communities* (Lexington, Mass.: Heath, 1979). Other works in
the housing field include Nina and Claude Gruen, *Low and Moderate Income Housing in the Suburbs* (New York: Praeger, 1971);
Stephen Burghart (ed.), *Tenants and the Urban Housing Crisis*
(Dexter, Mich.: New Press, 1972); Michael Stegman, *Housing Investment in the Inner City: The Dynamics of Decline* (Cambridge,
Mass.: MIT Press, 1972); and Donald Reeb and James Kirk, *Housing the Poor* (New York: Praeger, 1973).

School desegregation is treated in Robert Crane et al., *Political
Strategies in Northern Desegregation* (Lexington, Mass.: Heath,
1973); John C. Hogan, *The Schools, the Courts, and the Public Interest* (Lexington, Mass.: Heath, 1974); *Justice Delayed and Denied: HEW and Northern School Desegregation*, issued by the Center for National Policy Review, Washington, D.C., 1974; Everett
Cataldo, Michael Giles, and Douglas Gatlin, *School Desegregation
Policy* (Lexington, Mass.: Heath, 1978); and Emmett Buell and Richard A. Brisbin, *Boston School Desegregation*, also published by
Heath in 1979. A recent comprehensive analysis of the evidence on

the effects of desegregation is contained in a two-part issue of *Law and Contemporary Problems* 48 (Spring and Summer, 1978).

Crime and social disorganization are examined from a wide variety of perspectives. Representative works are Ted Gurr, *Rogues, Rebels, and Reformers: A Political History of Urban Crime and Conflict* (Beverly Hills, Calif.: Sage, 1976); Marshall B. Clinard, *Cities With Little Crime: The Case of Switzerland* (New York: Cambridge University Press, 1978); Joan W. Moore, *Homeboys: Gangs, Drugs, and Prisons in the Barrios of Los Angeles* (Philadelphia: Temple University Press, 1979); Harold M. Rose (ed.) *Lethal Aspects of Urban Violence* (Lexington, Mass.: Heath, 1979); Hugh Graham and Ted Gurr, *Violence in America*, rev. ed. (Beverly Hills, Calif.: Sage, 1979).

SERVICES

Various aspects of the urban service delivery system are covered in J. E. Grollman, *The Decentralization of Neighborhood Services* (Washington, D.C.: International City Management Association, 1971); Frank Levy, Arnold Meltsner, and Aaron Wildavsky, *Urban Outcomes: Schools, Streets, and Libraries* (Berkeley: University of California Press, 1974); Roland J. Liebert, *Disintegration and Political Action: The Changing Functions of City Government in America* (New York: Academic Press, 1976); Sidney Sonenblum, John Kirlin, and John Ries, *How Cities Provide Services: An Evaluation of Alternative Delivery Structures* (Cambridge, Mass.: Ballinger, 1977); Vincent Ostrom and Frances P. Bish (eds.), *Comparing Urban Service Delivery Systems: Structure and Performance* (Beverly Hills, Calif.: Sage, 1977); E. S. Savas (ed.), *Alternatives for Delivering Public Services* (Boulder, Colo.: Westview Press, 1978); and Albert Hyde and Jay Shifritz, *Program Evaluation in the Public Sector* (New York: Praeger, 1979). A study of service agency operations in Detroit is Bryan Jones, with Saadia Greenberg and Joseph Drew, *Service Delivery in the City: Citizen Demand and Bureaucratic Rules* (New York: Longman, 1980).

The question of equality in the distribution of urban services has received attention in Andrew Boots et al., *Inequality in Local Government Services: A Case Study of Neighborhood Roads* (Washington, D.C.: Urban Institute, 1972); Peter Block, *Equality of Distribution of Police Services*, also published by the Urban Institute (1974); Robert Lineberry, *Equality and Urban Policy: The Distribution of Municipal Public Services* (Beverly Hills, Calif.: Sage, 1977); and Paul R. Dimond, *A Dilemma of Local Government:*

Discrimination in the Provision of Public Services (Lexington, Mass.: Heath, 1978). The entire issue of *Urban Affairs Quarterly,* vol. 12 (March 1977), deals with the politics and economics of urban services.

Books dealing with the various service problem fields are continually making their appearance. Transportation has been one of the favorite topics, represented by such works as Alan Lupo et al., *Rites of Way: The Politics of Transportation in Boston and the U.S. City* (Boston: Little, Brown, 1971); David R. Miller (ed.), *Urban Transportation Policy: New Perspectives* (Lexington, Mass.: Heath, 1972); Richard O. Davies, *The Age of Asphalt: The Automobile, the Freeway, and the Condition of Metropolitan America* (Philadelphia: Lippincott, 1975); Delbert Taebel and James Cornehis, *The Political Economy of Urban Transportation* (Port Washington, N.Y.: Kennikat, 1977); and Alan Altshuler, *The Urban Transportation System: Politics and Policy Innovation* (Cambridge, Mass.: MIT Press, 1979). Other works on urban transit are Wilfred Owen, *Transportation for Cities* (Washington, D.C.: The Brookings Institution, 1976); Henry M. Steiner, *Conflict in Urban Transportation: The People Against the Planners* (Lexington, Mass.: Heath, 1978); and two other books published by Heath in 1979—Alan Altshuler (ed.), *Current Issues in Transportation Policy;* and Catherine G. Burke, *Innovation and Public Policy: The Case of Personal Rapid Transit*—and one issued in 1980, Arnim Meyburg and Peter Stopher, *Public Transportation in Urban Areas.* The administration of mass transit is treated in George E. Gray and Lester Hoel (eds.), *Public Transportation: Planning, Operation, and Management* (Englewood Cliffs, N.J.: Prentice-Hall, 1979).

Law enforcement is another service area in which the literature has expanded rapidly. Related books include William A. Westley, *Violence and the Police* (Cambridge, Mass.: MIT Press, 1971); Jack Goldsmith and Sharon S. Goldsmith (eds.), *The Police Community: Dimensions of an Occupational Subculture* (Pacific Palisades, Calif.: Palisades, 1974); James R. Richardson, *The Urban Police in the United States* (Port Washington, N.Y.: Kennikat, 1974); David H. Bayley (ed.), *Police and Society* (Beverly Hills, Calif.: Sage, 1977); Peter K. Manning, *Police Work* (Cambridge, Mass.: MIT Press, 1977); William Ker Muir, *Police: Streetcorner Politicians* (Chicago: University of Chicago Press, 1977); Elinor Ostrom et al., *Patterns of Metropolitan Policing* (Cambridge, Mass.: Ballinger, 1978); Robert Fogelson, *Big City Police* (Cambridge, Mass.: Harvard University Press, 1977); Ralph Baker and Fred Meyer (eds.), *Evaluating Alternative Law Enforcement Policies* (Lexington, Mass.: Heath, 1979); and John L. Cooper, *The Police and the Ghetto* (Port Washington, N.Y.: Kennikat, 1979). The operation of the criminal courts is analyzed in Martin A. Leven, *Urban Politics and the Criminal Courts* (Chicago: University of Chicago Press, 1977).

Environmental issues are the subject of attention in R. L. Meek and John Strayer, *The Politics of Neglect: The Environmental Crisis* (Boston: Houghton Mifflin, 1971); Walter Rosenbaum, *The Politics of Environmental Concern* (New York: Praeger, 1973); Mathew Crenson, *The Un-Politics of Air Pollution* (Baltimore: Johns Hopkins Press, 1970); and Ann Friedlander (ed.), *Approaches to Controlling Air Pollution* (Cambridge, Mass.: MIT Press, 1978). Solid waste disposal is discussed in William E. Small, *Third Pollution: The National Problem of Solid Waste Disposal* (New York: Praeger, 1971); and F. Lee Brown and A. Lebeck, *Cars, Cans, and Drums* (Baltimore: Johns Hopkins Press, 1976). Bernard Frieden, *The Environmental Protection Hustle* (Cambridge, Mass.: MIT Press, 1979) treats the environmental movement as a coverup for elitism. Health services are analyzed in Linda A. Fischer, *The Use of Services in the Urban Scene: The Individual and the Medical Care System* (Chapel Hill, N.C.: University of North Carolina Center for Urban and Regional Studies, 1971); Ruth Roemer, C. Kramer, and J. Frank, *Planning Health Services: From Jungle to System* (New York: Springer, 1975); and Leslie H. Paine, *Health Care in Big Cities* (New York: St. Martin's Press, 1978). The energy problem is examined in Raymond Busby and A. Fleming Bell (eds.), *Energy and the Community* (Cambridge, Mass.: Ballinger, 1978).

GOVERNMENTAL REORGANIZATION

An extensive collection of writings on restructuring the governmental system of metropolitan areas has accumulated over the past two decades. Representative of the earlier works are Robert C. Wood, *1400 Governments*, (Cambridge, Mass.: Harvard University Press, 1961); and John C. Bollens (ed.), *Exploring the Metropolitan Community* (Berkeley and Los Angeles: University of California Press, 1961). Case studies of metropolitan reform efforts are contained in *Regional Governance: Promise and Performance,* issued by the Advisory Commission on Intergovernmental Relations (1973); National Academy of Public Administration, *Four U.S. Reform Efforts: Multi-Tiered Metropolitan Government* (Washington, D.C.: National Academy of Public Administration, 1977); and James F. Horan and G. T. Taylor, *Experiments in Metropolitan*

Government (New York: Praeger, 1977). The successful consolidation of Lexington-Fayette County, Kentucky, is analyzed in W. E. Lyons, *The Politics of City-County Merger* (Lexington: University Press of Kentucky, 1977). A guide to the restructuring of local governments worldwide is Donald Rowat (ed.), *International Handbook on Local Government Reorganization* (Westport, Conn.: Greenwood, 1980).

The economic aspects of reorganization are discussed in Alan K. Campbell and Roy W. Bahl (eds.), *State and Local Government: The Political Economy of Reform* (New York: Free Press, 1976) and Thomas Cowing and A. G. Holtmann, *The Economics of Local Public Service Consolidation* (Lexington, Mass.: Heath, 1976). A theoretical analysis of reorganization efforts is Max Neiman, "Metropology: Toward a More Constructive Research Agenda," (Sage Professional Papers in American Politics, 1975). Criticism of traditional approaches to metropolitan restructuring is found in Robert L. Bish and Vincent Ostrom, *Understanding Urban Government: Metropolitan Reform Reconsidered* (Washington, D.C.: American Enterprise Institute for Public Policy Research, 1973).

The interest in governmental decentralization at the submunicipal level is reflected in such works as Milton Kotler, *Neighborhood Government* (Indianapolis: Bobbs-Merrill, 1969); Alan Altshuler, *Community Control: The Black Demand for Participation in Large American Cities* (New York: Pegasus, 1970); William Farr and others, *Decentralizing City Government: A Practical Study of a Radical Proposal for New York City* (New York: Praeger, 1972); Joseph F. Zimmerman, *The Federated City: Community Control in Large Cities* (New York: St. Martin's Press, 1972); Eric A. Nordlinger, *Decentralizing the City: A Study of Boston's Little City Halls* (Cambridge, Mass.: MIT Press, 1972); George D. Washnis, *Municipal Decentralization and Neighborhood Resources: Case Studies of Twelve Cities* (New York: Praeger, 1973); and Douglas Yates and Robert Lin, *Street Level Government: Assessing Decentralization and Urban Services* (Lexington, Mass.: Heath, 1975).

THE FUTURE

The World Future Society, Washington, D.C., has published a series of books relating to the study of futures. These include a general introduction to the field by Edward Cornish and others, *The Study of the Future* (1977); a bibliography and other information entitled *The Future: A Guide to Information Sources* (1979); and *Student Handbook for the Study of the Future*, edited by Howard

Didsbury (1979). The state of the art of social forecasting is discussed in David Loye, *The Knowable Future* (New York: Wiley, 1978). A special issue (May 1979) of the *Journal of Urban History* focuses on the city and future technological developments. Alternative futures are examined in Robert C. North, *The World That Could Be* (New York: Norton, 1978); Sterling Brubaker, *In Command of Tomorrow* (Baltimore: Johns Hopkins Press, 1975); Willis W. Harman, *An Incomplete Guide to the Future* (New York: Norton, 1979); and Robert Ayres, *Uncertain Futures: Challenges for Decisionmaking* (New York: Wiley, 1979).

The issue of future resources is discussed in Donnella H. Meadows et al., *The Limits to Growth* (New York: Universal Books, 1972); Peter W. House and Edward R. Williams, *Planning and Conservation: The Emergence of the Frugal Society* (New York: Praeger, 1977); and Herman Kahn, William Brown, and Leon Martel, *The Next 200 Years: A Scenario for America and the World* (New York: Morrow, 1976). The emerging nature of society in the United States is the focal point of Seymour M. Lipset (ed.), *The Third Century: America as a Post-Industrial Society* (Stanford, Calif.: Hoover Institution Press, 1979).

Technological developments in various fields are considered in James Martin, *Future Developments in Telecommunications* (Englewood Cliffs, N.J.: Prentice-Hall, 1977); Sam Davis (ed.), *The Form of Housing* (New York: Van Nostrand Reinhold, 1977); Roy Meador, *Future Energy Alternatives* (Ann Arbor, Mich.: Ann Arbor Science, 1978); and Robert Stobaugh and Daniel Yergin (eds.), *Energy Future: Report of the Energy Project at the Harvard Business School* (New York: Ballantine, 1980). A recently published book looking at the political issues of the future is Peter Duignan and Alvin Rabushka (eds.), *The United States in the 1980s* (Stanford, Calif.: Hoover Institution Press, 1981) which contains articles by such well-known conservative economists as Milton Friedman, Murray Weidenbaum, and Alan Greenspan. A related book predicting key changes in national programs and policies is Jack Kemp et al., *The Future Under President Reagan* (Westport, Conn.: Arlington House, 1980).

Index of Names

This is an index of personal names.* The names of places and organizations appear in the Index of Subjects. The letter *n* after a page number indicates that the reference is in a footnote.

* Names in "A Bibliographical Overview" are excluded from this index.

Index of Subjects

Organizations in "A Bibliographical Overview" are excluded from this index. Page references to illustrations are printed in **boldface** type.